Elvis in Vegas

Other books by Paul Lichter

Elvis in Hollywood

Elvis: Portrait of a Legend

The Candid Elvis

Elvis TV Memories

Elvis, The Tour Years: The Fifties

Elvis, The Tour Years: 1969–1971

Elvis, The Tour Years: 1972–1974

Elvis, The Tour Years: 1965–1977

Elvis Today Complete Record & Memorabilia Price Guide Vols. 1–6

Elvis: The Boy Who Dared to Rock

The Definitive Elvis

The Elvis Presley Memorial Book of Days 1978

The Elvis Presley Memorial Book of Days 1980

The Elvis Presley Memorial Book of Days 1981

Elvis: The Legend Lives On

Paul Lichter's Elvis Memories Are Forever

Behind Closed Doors

Elvis Memories: A Love Story

Elvis: A Portrait in Music

Rebel Heart

Magic Moments

Thank You Very Much

All My Best

From the City of Brotherly Love to the Big Apple

E.P. in Concert

Millennium Elvis: As Good As It Gets, The Concerts/Larger Than Life, The Candids

Elvis Immortal

In Person

Elvis in Vegas

Paul Lichter

OVERLOOK DUCKWORTH
New York, NY • London

This edition first published in the United States in 2011 and the United Kingdom in 2012 by Overlook Duckworth, Peter Mayer Publishers, Inc.

NEW YORK
141 Wooster Street
New York, NY 10012
www.overlookpress.com
For bulk and special sales, please contact sales@overlookny.com

LONDON:
Duckworth
90-93 Cowcross Street
London EC1M 6BF
www.ducknet.co.uk
info@duckworth-publishers.co.uk

Cataloguing-in-Publication Data is available from the Library of Congress.
A catalogue record for this book is available from the British Library

Design and typeformatting by Bernard Schleifer
Printed in China
1 3 5 7 9 10 8 6 4 2

ISBN 978-1-59020-187-9 (US)
ISBN 978-0-71564-172-9 (UK)

For my wife, Betty Lichter, and our son, Tristan-Elvis Paul Lichter
Always . . . Today, tomorrow, and forever

And for Elvis and the Colonel
Who were, are, and will always be

Contents

Some people call me a teenage idol. They even say they envy me.
I guess they got no way of knowing just how lonesome I can be.

—Ricky Nelson, "Teenage Idol," Imperial Records, 1962

Preface

When Paul Lichter asked me to write the preface for his new *Elvis in Vegas* book, I could not say no. I've known Paul since 1971, which was the year after he launched the Elvis Unique Record Club. Since that time, now almost forty years ago, we have continued to be friends.

Paul's first book, *Elvis in Hollywood*, came out in 1975, and believe me, there was nothing else like it. This was an era where any book on Elvis was hard to come by, let alone a book put out by a dedicated fan. It was truly exciting to see the rare photos and to read Paul's opinions on each film. I have to say that *Elvis in Hollywood* and Paul's later book, *The Boy Who Dared To Rock*, were very inspirational.

In this book I am astonished by the detailed information. Never before have so many of the Las Vegas set lists been found in one book. I am also knocked out by the layout of the book. The photographs are very exciting and, of course, many of these photos have never been seen before.

Paul Lichter is one of the legends of the Elvis world and this new book will continue to add to that legend.

—Joseph A. Tunzi, March 2010

New Frontier
HOTEL
LAS VEGAS, NEVADA
In Person
ELVIS PRESLEY

CHAPTER 1

The Nation's Only Atomic Powered Singer

April 23, 1956–May 6, 1956

IN 1829 RAFAEL RIVERA, a young man of European ancestry, discovered a beautiful American valley where shimmering grass grew wildly. He gave the valley a name, Las Vegas—in Spanish, "The Meadows." It was found that this part of the desert had natural springs and the water brought pioneers to the area.

In the mid-1800s Mormons built what was known as the Mormon Fort. It served as a place for members of the Mormon Church to stop and rest when they would travel from Salt Lake City to Los Angeles for supplies.

Nevada would become the United States' thirty-sixth state in 1844. In the late 1800s gold and iron were discovered and people flocked to the area full of hope and dreams. Las Vegas continued to grow because of their liberal divorce laws. In 1911 you could obtain a "quickie" divorce after six weeks of residency. These short-term residents stayed at dude ranches that were forerunners of the strip's hotels.

In 1931 the building of the Hoover Dam caused a population boom. That same year gambling was legalized in Nevada. Al Capone thought of building a hotel and gambling casino in the desert in the mid-thirties. At the time the desert town was populated by broken-down cowboys and a few slot machines. This all changed when mob boss Lucky Luciano, along with partner Meyer Lansky, saw potential in Sin City. They enlisted Bugsy Siegel to drum up mob money. Siegel was good at this job and in 1946 the Flamingo Hotel and Casino opened. Vegas boomed and Meyer Lansky basked in its glory while Siegel, the real Vegas architect, was murdered, taking five bullets in a mob hit. It was alleged that Bugsy had been skimming profits from the hotel.

Las Vegas soon became an adult's fantasyland, bringing people from everywhere who wanted to gamble or be serviced by one of the city's many so-called escort services. It had Sammy, Dino, and Frank, all great entertainers, but it didn't have a king until 1969 when Elvis Presley opened at the then-largest and most colossal Vegas hotel, the International. Elvis, the King of Rock and Roll, was now the undisputed king of Las Vegas too. He would never play to an empty seat in seven years. He had filled the town's largest showroom hundreds of times. Even his December 1976 "dead season" booking would, once again, fill the ancient desert town to capacity.

ELVIS PRESLEY FELL IN LOVE with Las Vegas the moment he landed in 1956. He spent time at the local amusement park, shopping for clothes, flirting with fans at the hotel's pool, going to the movies, and catching as many shows as possible. Elvis met and dated Vegas showgirls, but didn't drink and never once gambled, saying it didn't appeal to him. He went to the movies to see a Randolph Scott western and missed an interview with Aline Mosby, a Hollywood columnist who had flown to Las Vegas just to talk to him.

A defining moment in music history occurred when Elvis attended a lounge show at Vegas' Sands Hotel. Freddie Bell and the Bellboys, a group that originated on the East Coast, were performing their brand of rock and roll mixed with comedy. As part of their repertoire they included a song, "Hound Dog," that had been a minor hit for them earlier in the year. Big Mama Thornton originally released "Hound Dog," written by Jerry Leiber and Mike Stoller, as a blues song in 1953. Elvis was familiar with the Big Mama version but was knocked out by Bell's rocking treatment of the song. Freddie and The Bell Boys brought the house down with their show-stopping delivery. Elvis decided he wanted to record it and his version was very similar to the Bell Boys'. In July 1956 RCA shipped "Hound Dog" as the B-side to "Don't Be Cruel." "Don't Be Cruel," written by Otis Blackwell, went to Number One with "Hound Dog" at Number Two on the charts. Six weeks later, "Hound Dog" would replace "Don't Be Cruel" as the number one song in the country. In all, RCA sold 13 million copies in 1956 alone, effectively pushing Elvis' success into the stratosphere.

Colonel Parker, Elvis' manager, has often been criticized for booking Elvis' first Vegas engagement. Many consider Elvis' 1956 appearance at the New Frontier Hotel as the only failure of his career, but the Colonel didn't agree. He said, "It opened my eyes to the potential of reaching a bigger audience and showing Elvis' talent in a different way." Some thirteen years later he would be proven right.

Elvis, for his part, had this to say: "Man, I really like Vegas. I'm going back there the first chance I get."

COLONEL PARKER FIRST BOOKED Elvis into the New Frontier Hotel in Las Vegas for a two-week stand opening on April 23, 1956. The headline act was Freddy Martin and his orchestra.

When Elvis took up residency at the hotel's Venus Room he had his first million-selling record, "Heartbreak Hotel," which was Number One on the charts at that time. His first album, titled *Elvis Presley*, was released by RCA Victor, sold 360,000 copies, and reached the top spot on *Billboard* and *Cash Box* (popular trade magazines).

The Venus Room held one thousand people. The Colonel had arranged for Elvis to be paid the sum of $8,500 a week in cash. He told a reporter, "No check is any good—they're testing an atom bomb out there in the desert. What if someone pressed the wrong button?" Colonel Parker, no doubt, remembered this story when instructing the

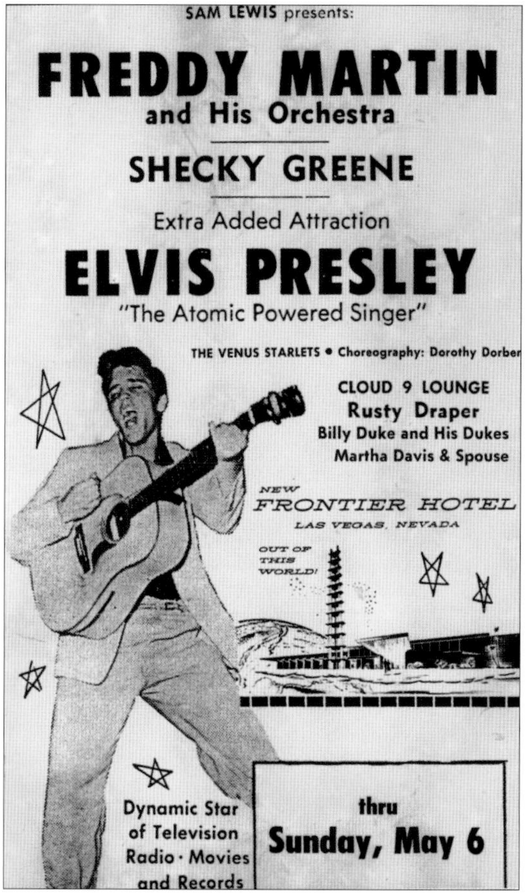

Original advertisement for Elvis' first Las Vegas engagement at the New Frontier Hotel, 1956.

publicity department at RCA to promote Elvis as "America's Only Atomic Powered Singer." He began using the slogan on all posters and handbills for Elvis' personal appearances and chose the photograph used on the cover of Elvis' first album, as well as the many licensed Elvis Presley Enterprises products. He chose an iconic image, originally shot in Tampa, Florida, which captured Elvis at his gyrating best, to welcome those entering the New Frontier Hotel. The Colonel had the image blown up to a two-story-high cutout standee. This action Elvis figure was placed outside the casino entrance. The hotel's marquee read, "Freddy Martin and His Orchestra, Shecky Greene and Extra Added Attraction—Elvis Presley."

The Las Vegas audience consisted of society people, high rollers, and grown-ups on vacation. They were not Elvis' crowd; there was hardly a teenager in sight. Bandleader Freddy Martin had had a steady stream of pop hits. His act featured a floor show, a seventeen-piece orchestra, female and male singing groups, and show-stopping dancers. The Vegas crowd loved Freddy Martin's show and applauded enthusiastically as Freddy and the orchestra played Broadway tunes. At the conclusion of their set they played their version of Bill Haley's "Rock Around The Clock."

Elvis was fresh from his first appearance on *The Milton Berle Show*. "Uncle Miltie" was the king of television to millions of viewers in the fifties, but in 1956 his ratings began to slip. In an attempt to cash in on the daily publicity that Elvis was getting, he signed Elvis for two appearances on his show that aired on Tuesday nights. On April 3, 1956, live from the flight deck of the USS *Hancock*, Elvis appeared along with Esther Williams, Harry James, Buddy Rich, and Arnold Stang. The Berle Show came on at 8 p.m. and was broadcast in color. Elvis' performance on the "Uncle Miltie" show was perhaps the wildest TV performance he ever gave. The critics accused his act of being "lewd and obscene." Forty million people watched the show, and, love it or loathe it, I'm sure they never forgot it.

On that first night at the Venus Room, barely weeks later, the curtain rose showing a very nervous Elvis, Bill Black on bass, Scotty Moore on guitar, and D. J. Fontana on drums. They were met with quiet stares of amazement. To this audience they appeared

New Frontier Hotel, Las Vegas postcard, 1950s.

to be a bunch of hillbillies or some form of alien life. Many couldn't understand Elvis' rambling or music. One high-roller sitting at a ringside table shouted, "God damn it, shit! What is all this yelling and noise?" He got up, as did the rest of his party, and they stalked out of the showroom.

Scotty Moore once commented, "We're the only group who are led by an ass. We just watch Elvis' behind and try to follow his movements." Owing to the high decibel of screams that Elvis' female admirers greeted them with at every concert, they could not hear Elvis' singing or their own playing. Scotty and Bill Black commented that this Vegas engagement was the first time they could hear what they were playing and actually know if their instruments were in tune. Elvis said, "It was strictly an older group of people, they weren't my kind of audience, they didn't applaud, and I couldn't tell if they were dead or alive." With that said, many celebrities came to his Vegas performances either out of professional curiosity or admiration, celebrities such as Phil Silvers (TV's Sergeant Bilko), Liberace and his brother George, Ray Bolger (the Scarecrow in *The Wizard of Oz*), the Four Lads, Hal Wallis (who had just signed Elvis to his first motion picture contract), and burlesque queen Tempest Storm.

Elvis appeared in the Venus Room twice a night, 8 p.m. and midnight, performing twenty-eight twelve-minute shows for fourteen nights. Maury Friedman, the owner of the New Frontier Hotel, met with Elvis and the Colonel and decided that Elvis would perform a special show on Saturday, April 28. This show would be for all the teenagers who were not able to see their idol because of the alcoholic beverages that were served during the evening shows. Elvis' young fans would be able to attend the special afternoon performance for $1.00, which entitled them to a soft drink. All money from the show was donated to the

Las Vegas Youth Baseball Federation. Elvis rocked and rolled for the mostly female audience.They screamed their approval and both Elvis and his fans were drained by the time he left the stage.

It's been reported by some journalists that the mad behavior displayed by Presley fanatics has actually been caused by shills on Parker's payroll hired by him to instigate hysteria. This method has been used before, most notably by Frank Sinatra's agent, George Evans, who paid girls to swoon for the skinny singer. Colonel Parker's reply to these charges: "I never paid anyone a red cent. I don't have to. They just naturally go for Elvis all by themselves."

A reporter working for Elvis' hometown newspaper, *The Memphis Press Scimitar*, described Elvis' appearance for this special teenage show as follows:

> Because the teenagers couldn't see the regular show and were clamoring to be appeased, the management put on a special show.
>
> The carnage was terrific. They pushed and shoved to get into the one- thousand-seat room and several hundred thwarted youngsters buzzed like angry hornets outside.
>
> After the show, bedlam! A laughing, shouting, idolatrous mob swarmed him; he fled to the insufficient sanctuary of his suite. The door wouldn't hold them out. They got his shirt, shredded it. A triumphant girl seized a button, clutched it as though it were a diamond.
>
> A squadron of police had to be called in to clear the area.
>
> A dazed older woman, who had been bowled over in the teenage tidal wave, was discussing it incredulously at the bar over a glass of a medicinal beverage to calm her jangled nerves.
>
> "My gawd, what those kids did to the ladies room! Lipstick all over the walls . . . baskets turned over and the paper strewn around . . . it looked like a wrecking crew just finished."
>
> Elvis laughed about it; "Shucks," he said, "it wasn't near as bad as some of the times. Like when they threw rocks in the bus windows so they could grab at me and try to get autographs."

Elvis spent most of his leisure time with the attractive divorcée Judy Spreckels, who had been married to sugar king Adolph Spreckels. He originally met the beautiful heiress on the West Coast. They had forged a strong friendship and spent a lot of time together in Hollywood at Elvis' various TV appearances and at some of his RCA recording sessions. Judy accompanied Vernon and Gladys Presley when they went to see Elvis off for his military training in the United States Army. The two remained friends for the rest of Elvis' life. In 1974 at one of Elvis' Las Vegas engagements at the Hilton Hotel, he introduced her from the stage and asked that the spotlight be shown on her. During their time together in 1956 at the New Frontier Hotel in Las Vegas, Judy gave Elvis a large black star sapphire ring that Elvis, many years later, gave to Priscilla.

Some interesting examples that follow of the media's coverage of Elvis' first engagement in Vegas give one a clearer picture of Eisenhower's America in 1956. This press release for Elvis' upcoming engagement read:

> **Elvis Presley, New Singing Find, Booked into New Frontier**
>
> Elvis Presley, unanimously acclaimed by critics as the most important singing find since Johnnie Ray, will open in the New Frontier Hotel's Venus Room

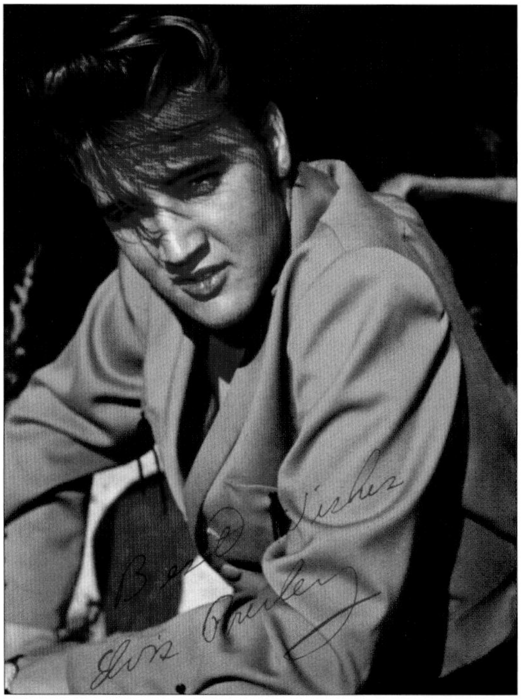

A stunning array of color candid photographs shot outside the New Frontier Hotel, 1956. Top photos were used by Colonel Parker as part of his official Elvis Presley Fan Club package. Below and right photos were lost until now.

Monday, April 23, as a special added attraction to the Freddy Martin show.

The handsome twenty-one-year-old rock and roller's appearance in the latest Sammy Lewis production is considered to be the Las Vegas entertainment scoop of the year.

Presley's sensational rise to fame is largely based on his recent recording of "Heartbreak Hotel," which sold 100,000 the first week it was out and at present is nearing the 1,000,000 mark.

Two years ago the young giant (he stands 6' 2" tall) was driving a truck in Memphis for $45.00 a week. Yet in West Coast appearances last week his unusual singing style attracted turn-away audiences of 5,000 and special police squads were needed to handle the admiring crowds that came to see America's new idol.

Adding to Presley's fame and fortune is a motion picture contract that he signed with Paramount Studios in Hollywood just this week.

The young vocalist will be featured in one of the most lavish productions ever presented in the Venus Room, Lewis stated. Freddy Martin and his band, Shecky Greene, the Venus Starlets and a cast of more than sixty performers will make up the entertainment package.

Bob Lilly, publicity director at the New Frontier Hotel, sent the following release to the *Las Vegas Sun*, who ran it on April 26, 1956:

Just About Everything Under the Sun

Thanks for your note requesting more info on Elvis Presley. You should know nothing makes a publicity man happier than furnishing background on one of his favorite subjects.

These beautiful color candids were shot poolside at the New Frontier Hotel, 1956.

And Elvis certainly is one of my favorite subjects. Here is a nonchalant phenomenon whom, as yet, no one has accurately described. Here is a young man who has an inherent ability to arouse mass hysteria (or should I say ecstasy?) wherever he goes, yet is unassuming and completely untouched by the fabulous success he has achieved almost overnight.

Where Elvis has appeared in the recent weeks since he "hit" he has left behind him tears, screams, wild applause and mangled emotions. Yet it must be a sweet agony he creates because his avid fans already have elevated him to a plane reached only by a few singers of our time.

Far be it for me to analyze this handsome, twenty-one-year-old lad whose rock-and-roll rhythms bring forth squeals and cries not heard since way back when Frank Sinatra first came into his own. It has been suggested to me that Elvis Presley is a combination of Johnnie Ray and Billy Daniels—that he displays the magnetism of Sinatra and Como—that he possesses the tangible attributes of almost any two or three popular male singers you might care to group. I'll go so far as to say I don't agree with this. In my opinion, this boy is one to himself—doing what comes naturally.

The most-used phrase coined by writers across the country to describe Presley's singing is "a peculiar brand of western bop." Yet that "peculiar brand of western bop" alone could inflame followers to mob a theater for just a look at their idol? This is not an unusual incident when Elvis makes a personal appearance. City officials from coast to coast already have learned to place extra police on duty to

Right: Every girl's dream autograph session. New Frontier Hotel, 1956.

control overflow crowds wherever he appears.

Presley is billed as "America's only atomic powered singer." Maybe this explains everything. You and I are witnessing another amazing development in this amazing age of the atom. It makes as much sense as another rationalization of an "irrational situation."

Briefly, he was born in Tupelo, Mississippi, on January 8, 1935. All his training in show business has been through self-instruction. Two years ago he was a truck driver. Last December he was signed to an RCA Victor recording contract and just two weeks ago signed to a seven-year contract with Paramount Pictures in Hollywood. Sammy Lewis, our producer here at the New Frontier Hotel, says he feels this is only the beginning! And there you are.

Bill Willard wrote the following review in the April 28, 1956, edition of the *Las Vegas Sun*:

Review of Elvis' Show

Accent is on pitch and pull for this batch of acts comprising the current Venus Room bill. The powers of the New Frontier are pitching the local premier of Elvis Presley, but the pull will be in Freddy Martin's smooth music-making and word-of-mouth cheering for Shecky Greene's unbridled comedy.

Elvis Presley, arriving here on the wave of tremendous publicity, fails to hit the promised mark in a desert isle surfeited with rock and rollers who play in shifts atop every cocktail lounge on the strip. The brass, loud braying of his rhythm and blues catalog (and mind you, they are big hits everywhere, it seems) which abate, rocketed him to the big time, is overbearing to a captive audience. In a lounge, one can up and go—fast. But in a dining room, the table sitter must stay, look and listen the thing out. Which is perhaps why Presley received applause on his opening show edged with polite inference only. For the teenagers, the long, tall Memphis lad is a wiz; for the average Vegas spender or show-goer, a bore. His musical sound with a combo of three is uncouth, matching to a great extent the lyric content of his nonsensical songs.

On May 1, 1956, a reporter for the *Las Vegas Sun* had this to say:

Vegas Daze and Nights

The Shake and Shiver Kid: Now that I have finally found out what an Elvis Presley really is, I wonder if I will ever be happy again. You see, an Elvis Presley is an intense young singer who opened at the New Frontier a week ago with a very nervous guitar. And though the lad probably has yet to experience his first shave, he and his trio of instrumentalists have already sold a million records of their first recording. Presley sings and I try to recall Burl Ives, Harry Belafonte and Johnnie Ray. Mind you now, I'm not saying he compares with either of the illustrious gentlemen named. However, he doesn't sound too unlike those lads.

So there stands Elvis Presley, who probably has yet to blow out his twenty-first birthday candles, drink his first beer or kiss his first girl, the absolute rage of the juke box business and several million youngsters who compare him to the great in this unique field of hysterical rock-and-roll rhythm. And he stands up there clutching his guitar; he shakes and shivers like he is suffering from itchy underwear

Right: After a wild performance where fans rushed the stage and tore off Elvis's shirt. They only wanted a souvenir. Jacksonville, Florida, 1956.

and hot shoes. There is no doubt, I say to myself, because my wife seems to be pretty much interested in Presley's gymnastics on stage, this is the beginning of another craze. And a cold sweat pops out on my forehead as I full realize that my missus is now on the brink of a shopping spree for Presley records.

Seriously, however, I'd like to see this Presley in a hotel lounge. He would probably be the nearest threat to Louis Prima and his group, the two years that Luigi has dominated Vegas lounge entertainment. However, I don't imagine Presley's board of strategy is listening to the weak chirpings of lounge talent buyers. Especially when millions of youngsters, who buy Presley's records, are forming long lines outside of the music shops of America and Canada. Yes siree, the lad with the sleepy eyes and angry fingers on his electric guitar may crave a steady diet of fried pork chops, but the youngsters still crave a steady diet of Elvis Presley.

And right now the lad is hotter than a cauldron of boiling oil. What is his favorite tune you ask? That is easy. It is the sound of the hard and shiny cash registers which have his name on them.

The *Las Vegas Sun* printed this piece by Ed Jameson on May 12, 1956:

A Cat Talks Back

Mostly about Mr. Elvis Presley, Esq.

I will try to bravely carry on after reading the report of the Sun's police reporter concerning Mr. Elvis Presley now holding forth at the Venus Room of the Hotel New Frontier. I'm not after the teenage vote or to sell Portia's pound of flesh. I come not to bury Caesar, but to praise him. It is a weakness of the mind to preconceive a judgment of your thought before the act is done. And so McDuff, lay on.

Despite the acid hemlock broth stirred by the

Sun's copy boy me thinks Mr. Presley will survive and live to sing some more. Not that for many moons to come his name will be well known about the countryside.

Perhaps this cat should have studied grand opera, the fiddle or just be satisfied herding a truck. I don't join that school of thought. He's happy and he's making lots of other people happy doing just what he is doing naturally. You see, he's a natural. Any dope knows what a natural is.

This cat, Presley, is neat, well gassed and has the heart. His vocal is real and he has yet to go for an open field. He is hep to the motion of sound with a retort that is tremendous. These squares who like to detract their imagined misvalues can only size a note creeping upstairs after dark. This cat can throw 'em downstairs or even out the window. He has it.

Presley has a depth of tone that can sink deeper than a well. He can wilt into a whisper faster than a gossipmonger can throw down a free drink. He is classier than a new sock and a skinner on the strings. He really makes them cry. He's a smooth cast, cool and crazy with new stuff. His sound is dreamy and unique, loaded with mystery.

So settle down Dad. Take your cow straight. Wipe the blood out of your eye. I still got your coat. Music shines in anything that sounds.

Youth is an exuberant stage of life with the top down. Presley's voice is that of American youth looking at the moon and wondering how long it will take to get there. He is not a rock and roller nor is he a cowboy singer. He is something new coming over the horizon all by himself and he deserves his ever-growing audience. Nobody should miss him. Parents would do well to take their children to hear him. It would be a good way to get to know and understand your own kids.

Yep, this boy's sails are set and he's got wind. Good luck boy and the best of everything. I hope they hold you over! After all, ten million cats can't be wrong.

Elvis and Liberace. Las Vegas, 1956.

Bob Johnson wrote in *The Memphis Press Scimitar*, "Elvis, who has played to tough crowds before kept right in there busting guitar strings and shaking his legs and the rafters." The Colonel didn't let any of the reviews faze him. He declared, "Any publicity is good publicity as long as they spell your name right."

This page, and following:
Onstage, Venus Room,
New Frontier Hotel, 1956.

He noted that Elvis' latest RCA Victor release, "I Want You, I Need You, I Love You," had sold 300,000 copies in one week. He went on to claim that Elvis' record sales now accounted for half of RCA Victor's total income from recorded music.

It would take a quarter of a century before the Elvis world would have an opportunity to judge for themselves what all the hoopla that happened in April/May 1956 in Las Vegas was really all about. In 1980 RCA released an eight-album box set titled *Elvis Aron Presley*. Included was a private tape recorded by an audience member in 1956, featuring Elvis' closing-night performance at the Frontier. The record company obtained this recording from a collector who had purchased the original tape from the relative of the original owner.

Elvis and "Uncle Miltie," television's Milton Berle Show. *June 5, 1956.*

THE FOLLOWING IS A TRANSCRIPT of Elvis' May 6, 1956, Vegas performance:

Announcer: Everywhere he went he was breaking records. And speaking of records, he is the number one selling record artist in the country. RCA's pride and joy. And this is his last performance. So I regretfully have to say tonight we hate to see him go. He's a fine young man and a fine talent. Let's welcome, ladies and gentleman, Elvis Presley.

Elvis sings: "Heartbreak Hotel"

Dialogue: Thank you very much, ladies and gentlemen. We'd like to tell you this. It's really been a pleasure being in Las Vegas. This makes our second week here tonight so last night we had a pretty hard time to stay ah we had a pretty good time over here. We've got a few little songs we would like to do for you, we have on record in our style of singing, if you call it singing and ah here's one that I hope you like. And this one really tells a story, friends. It's not only sad, it's plum pitiful. The song is called "Long Tall Sally." It's a new one around here, ain't it? "Long Tall Sally." I want you to listen to this one. It really tells a story.

Elvis sings: "Long Tall Sally"

Dialogue: Thank you music lovers. Thank you very much, friends. Here's one more little song we'd like to do for you and to do this song we'd like to call on Mr. Freddy Martin and his very wonderful orchestra to back us up, back us completely up. Night before last on the stage of this auditorium, of this place here, well, RCA Victor awarded me a gold record for the millionth sale of "Heartburn Motel" that we did earlier out here and ah we're real proud of it because it has made so much money. It's done so well for itself. And here's another one that's coming right up behind that we hope will hit the million mark. This song here, it's called, ah, "Get Out Of The Stables, Grandma, You're Too Old To Be Horsing Around." You know that song Mr. Martin? "Get Out Of The Stables," do you know that? You do? Well you know that one about "take back your golden garter my leg is turning green"? Do you know that one? Let's do "Blue Suede" or something, "Blue Suede" or something. Oh yeah, friends, I'd like to do my whole part of the show and I hope you like something we do up here even if it's wrong. Ah, we have two celebrities that we have in the house. We may have more but these two fellows I ah yeah know are here and I'd like to do this song for them. Mr. Ray Bolger, he's in the audience. Mr. Ray Bolger and also for Mr. Phil Silvers, he's in the audience and to Roy Acuff, he's out there somewhere.

Elvis sings: "Blue Suede Shoes"

Announcer: Elvis, Elvis Presley. How about a great hand for Elvis. You can't let him go with that. Elvis. One more, one for the road.

Dialogue: Thank you friends. I was coming back anyway. In all sincerity, wow! It's about too pooped to pop. I got your tutti-frutti, just wait a minute. Now friends, we got a song here we have on record. This song has really been a big seller for me, it sold forty-three copies, song is called "Money Honey."

Elvis sings: "Money Honey"

Announcer: Elvis! Take another bow. Let's have a great hand, wish him farewell and a nice trip. Elvis!

They Call It a Teenage Crush: Nancy's Story

In 1955 my girlfriend Carla and I went to a Faron Young concert. A new singing sensation, Elvis Presley, was a special added attraction. The show was at the Armory in Albuquerque, New Mexico. I had begged my mother to let me go. Mom finally said OK when she learned that Carla's mother would accompany us. Faron Young was good but the crowd didn't really get excited like they did for Elvis. I soon realized that Carla and I weren't the only girls who were standing up and screaming at the young singer with the guitar and shaky leg.

After the concert the police set up barricades to hold back the barrage of girls trying to enter the alley where Elvis would be exiting. Somehow Carla's mother arranged for us to be in the alley before the barricades were put in place. When Elvis came out Carla pleaded, "Kiss me, kiss me!" Elvis did. I was right behind her with the same request and he responded with a kiss and the most beautiful smile.

I became somewhat of a celebrity at school the next day when the picture of Elvis kissing me appeared on the front page of the *Albuquerque Journal*. My parents were shocked, to say the least, and St. Vincent's Academy, the all girls Catholic school where I was enrolled in the eighth grade, was flabbergasted.

That spring, Mother, Daddy, and I drove to Las Vegas for the Tournament of Champions golf tournament held at the Desert Inn. Daddy was excited because his hero, the legendary comedian Bob Hope, was playing in it. On the drive to Las Vegas we stopped in Gallup, New Mexico for the night. I fell asleep praying that Elvis Presley would be appearing in Las Vegas. When we drove into Vegas I couldn't believe my eyes. I had to pinch myself. There was a two-story-tall cutout of Elvis, the same image as seen on his first album, right in front of the New Frontier Hotel which was directly across the street from where we were staying at the Desert Inn. My dreams and prayers were answered.

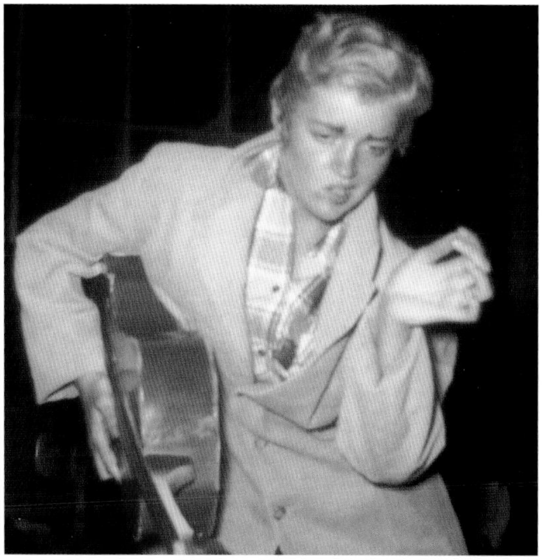

Nancy Kozikowski, 1956.

While checking into our hotel I ran into Bonnie, a friend from Albuquerque, and as soon as we could escape from our parents we ran across the street to the New Frontier to see if we could find Elvis. It was late afternoon, around four or five. We were in luck. Elvis, a few of his buddies and his cousin Gene Smith, who resembled Gene Vincent ("Be-Bop-A-Lula" fame) along with bass player Bill Black were walking through the lobby on their way out of the hotel. Elvis stopped, took the time to talk to us, and smiled that smile again. Outside Bill Black took pictures of Elvis posing with us between the legs of his two-story image.

Colonel Parker had booked Elvis in Las Vegas to expose him to a different kind of audience. This adult crowd came to Vegas to escape their kids, not to sit in the audience with a bunch of screaming teenagers worshipping a singer they could not relate to. I'm pretty sure Elvis was happy to see us as Bonnie and I were the only potential groupies around.

Elvis seemed to have pretty women around him all the time. He often hung out with the very pretty Judy Spreckels, the sugarcane heiress who owned her own plane. He spent a lot of time with Vampira, who was featured as part of *The Liberace Show*. He also dated a bevy of chorus girls but always made time for me, after all I was the perfect fan.

My days consisted of sunbathing and jumping off the high dive at the pool and trying to pass for twenty-one so that I could play the nickel slots. Daddy had given me some change to play so that I could learn the "truth about gambling; that you can't win." I hit the jackpot. I remember talking to some chorus girls who were lounging around the pool. That's where I got some of the Elvis gossip.

I went to watch my daddy at the golf tournament. A guy in an army uniform was helping with crowd control. He found an incredible ring on the course. It was a big gold nugget mounted in a very elegant antique fourteen-carat-gold setting. He gave it to me. It was fun being a thirteen-year-old flirt.

Most days I had lunch in the New Frontier dinning room. On a few occasions I got to visit and spend time with Elvis. He was always nice and flirty. It was really amazing that there was almost no one else around. Months later pictures of me and Elvis appeared in a couple of movie magazines. I was a good prop.

Of course my parents got us good seats to see Elvis perform and I also got to see his show with Bonnie, my friend from Albuquerque, and her parents, Mr. and Mrs. Saunders.

One day I went across the street to the Last Frontier Village, an adjunct like Knott's Berry Farm, to the New Frontier Hotel. I went into the Penny Arcade. It was the middle of the day in the middle of the week and there was no one else there except Elvis. He too was exploring and killing time. (There is a God!) He recognized me and was very nice. We took pictures in the twenty-five-cent picture booth together and alone. We also made a very funny talking record together. We were both very self-conscious and silly. Elvis said, "Hi. Well you aren't going to say my name?" I responded, "Hi Elvis. What are you doing here?" but I don't remember any more of what we said. It was a long time ago. I was embarrassed and I wasn't prepared. The afternoon was very special. It was an occasion for some more kisses. Elvis was very nice, very gentle, a perfect gentleman. His kisses were gifts and mementos, seeds for this remembrance that I am writing many years later.

As the weekend approached the management of the New Frontier thought they needed to do something to promote Elvis. They came up with a great idea to have a matinee on Saturday for the young teenage Las Vegas locales. Elvis had arranged a table next to the stage for me. I noticed that Vampira and Judy Spreckels also had stage front seating. When Elvis sang he looked directly at me. He made me feel so very special. He was very appreciative of having a bona fide fan. Elvis arranged the same seat for me for the rest of the shows that weekend. Thankfully my parents allowed me to go

Nancy Kozikowski and Elvis in the parking lot of the New Frontier Hotel. Note the Desert Inn in the background. Las Vegas, 1956. Below: Elvis solo.

and I got to see Elvis perform up close and personal.

Our family trip to Las Vegas couldn't have been better. Dad met Bob Hope, Mom had a wonderful time, and all of my dreams came true.

When I returned to Albuquerque I was loaded with stories, photos, records, etc. All the girls at school wanted to know about Elvis and couldn't believe that I really knew him. They made me feel almost famous.

The next fall I was in the ninth grade and very religious. I went to 6 a.m. Mass, usually walking in the dark, and after Mass I would stop by a café for coffee and cigarettes. At school, like all of the girls, I had to wear a uniform with a St. Vincent Academy insignia on the front. My mother told me to sew the insignia on but I took a shortcut and pinned it on. It crossed my mind how long it would take for anyone to notice that I had pinned it on upside down. No one did until the day I was pictured on the front page of the Catholic newspaper for selling an outstanding number of Christmas Seals. There were complaints about my insignia and I was in deep trouble. I was interested in school and liked my teachers but my curiosity and intensity made me question everything. This gave my teachers the impression that I was hard to manage, edging on subversive, much like young people would be in the sixties. The sixties had roots in the fifties. I was an artist and I drew pictures in class often of Elvis and James Dean. I daydreamed about Elvis and the time I had spent with him in Las Vegas. I was often misunderstood. The times were changing. There was a purge and I was kicked out of St. Vincent's. I wasn't the only one to go. I ended up at Washington Jr. High.

During my first year at Washington there was a talent show and I decided to enter the competition performing as Elvis. I guess that made me the first Elvis Presley impersonator. I discovered that I could put makeup on to look like him. I thickened my eyebrows, fattened my lips, added some sideburns and combed my hair like him. Completing my transformation I wore my father's jacket, giving me big shoulders, used a cardboard guitar and lip-synced to "Heartbreak Hotel." I thought of Elvis singing to me, imagined him smiling and kissing me.

I walked onstage and became Elvis. I could feel what it was like to be him. I moved, I strutted, I shook and the girls were affected like I was Elvis. Then I did it some more. They screamed and I really wasn't surprised at all. After the performance I was called into the principal's office and told that I couldn't move like that, that is wasn't proper. There was another performance that evening and, of course, I moved just like that.

My boyfriend at the time, Joe, was the original Fonz. Long hair, leather jacket, played the drums and was wild. He was jealous of Elvis. He burned the private record that Elvis and I had made and one of my photographs. I was angry but flattered that he was jealous. Joe was incorrigible and I later found out that he went to prison. I don't know what for. Times were changing.

Private photo of Elvis, taken by Elvis, in a photo booth at the Last Frontier Village, New Frontier Hotel, 1956.

Private photo of Elvis and Priscilla. Wiesbaden, Germany, 1959.

CHAPTER 2

Love Me Love The Life I Live

If Elvis Presley had been a painter, his canvas would have been Las Vegas. He applied the most brilliant and important strokes of his life in the bright-light city. From his first appearance in Las Vegas at the age of twenty-one, his wedding to Priscilla in 1967 at the Aladdin Hotel, and the eventual end of that marriage, Vegas had been witness to the triumphs and tragedies of his life.

In 1959 Priscilla Ann Beaulieu was a fourteen-year-old girl living in Wiesbaden, Germany, as part of a military family. Her mother, Ann, married her high school sweetheart, Jack Wagner, and at the age of eighteen gave birth to their daughter, Priscilla Ann Wagner. Tragically Jack perished in an airplane crash when Priscilla was six months old. Two and a half years later Ann married Joseph "Paul" Beaulieu, a veteran of the Second World War, having served with the United States Marine Corps in Okinawa. The couple would be blessed with four more children and Paul would adopt Priscilla and raise her as his own.

One month after the Beaulieus' arrival in Germany something very unexpected occurred when their young teenage daughter, Priscilla, was invited to meet the world's most famous Private, Elvis Presley. On September 13, 1959, Airman Currie Grant delivered Priscilla, wearing a white and blue sailor-style dress, to Elvis' rented home in Bad Nauheim. Elvis was transfixed by the young girl's beauty. He would later recall that he couldn't take his eyes off of what he described as her perfect porcelain doll-like features. During an impromptu concert with Elvis sitting at the piano located in the living room, he sang "Are You Lonesome Tonight," "At The End Of The Rainbow," "Rags To Riches," and "I Ask The Lord." It was apparent to all present who Elvis was directing these songs to, as his gaze was concentrated totally on Priscilla.

Priscilla returned a week later. This time the

young couple spent most of the evening in Elvis' bedroom listening to music and getting to know each other. They also shared their first good-night kiss. Priscilla returned on a nightly basis and became known at school and on the base as "Elvis' girl."

Captain Beaulieu invited Elvis to his home to better assess Elvis' intentions. He and Mrs. Beaulieu were worried about the frequency of their daughter's visits and late hours with Elvis. Dressed in full uniform, Elvis arrived with his father, Vernon. After exchanging pleasantries, he assured the concerned couple that his intentions were honorable. He displayed his Southern charm and manners on his future in-laws, referring to them as sir and ma'am throughout the entire evening. The captain and Ann were won over. They agreed that their daughter could continue her visits as long as Elvis would bring her home personally. Elvis agreed and kept his word for the most part.

Christmas 1959 found the young lovers together. "Cilla," the nickname Elvis had given Priscilla, gave him a set of bongo drums. Elvis presented her with a pearl and diamond ring along with a gold watch. Elvis told Priscilla that he loved her, and through her tears of happiness they embraced in front of the Christmas tree.

When Elvis' commitment to Uncle Sam ended in 1960, it was Priscilla who accompanied him to the airport. Before his flight back to the United States Elvis asked her to be true to him, assuring Priscilla he would be sending for her soon. The press photographers captured Priscilla tearfully waving good-bye as Elvis departed. *Life* magazine would publish these photos under the headline "The Girl He Left Behind."

Left: Elvis and Priscilla. Wiesbaden, Germany, 1959.

Below: Priscilla accompanies Elvis to the airport as Private Presley's military service ends. Germany, 1960.

Private Elvis Presley.
Wiesbaden, Germany,
1959.

Left: Soldier Boy Elvis, RCA photo shoot. Germany, 1959.

Ann and Paul were hopeful that their lives and their daughter's life would return to normal now that Elvis was gone, but Priscilla's school grades suffered. She missed him terribly, and Elvis didn't make the situation any better by making trans-Atlantic phone calls to distract Priscilla even more.

In the meantime Elvis gave his famous Memphis press conference from his office at Graceland. Seated at a desk behind a nameplate that boldly declared "The Boss," he laughingly declared to reporters that there was no truth to the rumors of "the girl left behind." He was glad to be back in the USA and to be home at Graceland, and didn't have time for a serious relationship, as he would be leaving for Florida to perform on *The Frank Sinatra Show* and then going to Hollywood to begin work on his new movie, *G.I. Blues*.

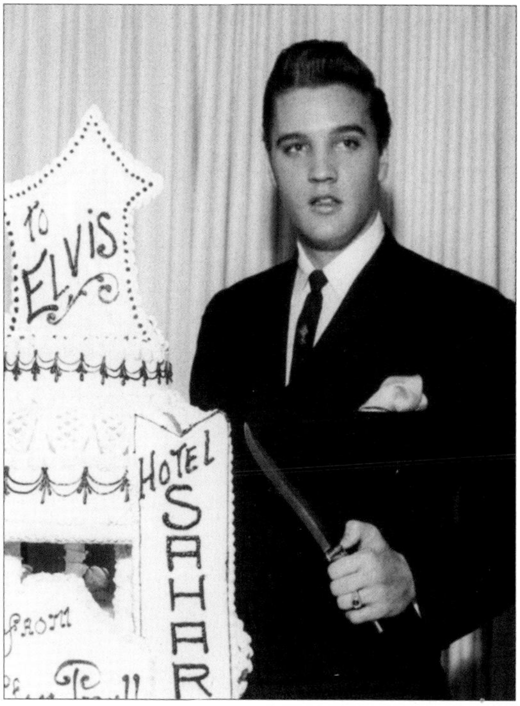

Elvis, Sahara Hotel birthday celebration. Las Vegas, January 8, 1961.

WHILE PRISCILLA CONTINUED moping around the house and going to school, Elvis had reclaimed his stature as a recording artist and movie star. When they weren't burning up the phone lines, they exchanged letters, Priscilla's written on pink stationery, Elvis' on blue.

Priscilla celebrated her seventeenth birthday on May 24, 1962. That June Elvis convinced her parents to allow their daughter to fly to Los Angeles and spend two weeks with him. He promised that Priscilla would be staying with a married couple who were friends of his, George Barris (known as Customizer to the Stars because he designed cars for Hollywood's elite and created Elvis' "Solid Gold" 1960 Cadillac limousine) and his wife, Shirley.

The teenager flew to Los Angeles and was met at the airport by Joe Esposito, a friend from Elvis' military days in Germany. Priscilla and Joe knew each other from the evenings spent at Elvis' home in Bad Nauheim. Joe would eventually become Elvis' righthandman and best man at their wedding. The two drove to Elvis' rented house on Bellagio Road and Priscilla got her first glimpses of Los Angeles as the car passed the Sunset Strip and Metro-Goldwyn-Mayer (MGM) Studios.

The house was crowded when they arrived. Priscilla saw Elvis from across the room, their eyes met, and soon they were embracing. He proudly introduced her to his friends and their wives and girlfriends. He asked Priscilla to go upstairs to his bedroom and told her he would be joining her in a few minutes so it didn't look obvious to the others that they wanted to be alone. In the meantime Priscilla freshened up after her long trip and Elvis joined her shortly thereafter. They were united, but stopped short of consummating the act. "Baby," he whispered, "What we have is special. I want it to be perfect and it will be when the time is right." They told each other about how their lives had been while they were apart. Eventually Pricilla grew tired, and Elvis told her that she would be spending the night at the Barrises as he had promised Captain Beaulieu.

The next afternoon Alan Fortas ("Hog Ears," the nickname bestowed upon him by Elvis) drove to the Barrises to pick up Priscilla. Alan had been a star football player in Memphis who palled around with George Klein (president of Elvis' Humes High School class who would become a celebrity disc jockey and an Elvis insider for life). George had introduced Alan to Elvis in 1957 and shortly thereafter Alan went to work for him. He arrived at the Barrises shortly after 3 p.m. and he and Priscilla drove back to Elvis' home. Elvis greeted Priscilla with, "We're going to Las Vegas to party." She wondered why Elvis had changed his mind about his promise to her father, but didn't question him. Elvis continued, "I'm going to have one of the guys who is staying behind send your parents a postcard every day. We will number them and they will all be postmarked from Los Angeles."

AT MIDNIGHT THEY GATHERED on the front lawn. Elvis, Priscilla, and the guys boarded Elvis' custom bus. They drove all night through the desert and arrived in Las Vegas the next morning. Elvis couldn't contain his excitement. He told "Cilla" that she would love Vegas, that it was his home away from home. He couldn't wait to show her the neon lights along the strip, telling her that seeing them at night would blow her mind. He mentioned that there were no clocks in Sin City.

For the next twelve days Priscilla, Elvis, and the ever-present group of friends rocked and rolled. They gambled, attended shows, partied all night, and slept all day. This was fired by the large bottles of prescription drugs that Elvis took and handed out to Priscilla and the guys. They popped diet pills upon awakening and sleeping pills before going to bed. The young Priscilla was experiencing life with Elvis firsthand. If she had a crystal ball she would have seen her future as Mrs. Elvis Presley: a lifestyle that had Elvis choosing her clothes, telling her how to wear her hair and apply her makeup, and dyeing her hair blue-black to match his. Elvis was creating his dream girl, his perfect woman.

Priscilla's parents received the cards postmarked Los Angeles and never guessed what was really happening. Elvis and Priscilla returned to Los Angeles the day before she was scheduled to return to Germany. The couple spent their final night making love but again stopped short of consummation, as Elvis held back, telling her she was his special angel.

When Priscilla's plane landed in Germany, her parents were understandably shocked by her appearance. They hardly recognized their daughter. Two weeks earlier she had left Germany looking like a sweet teenage girl. Standing in front of them was an overly made-up stranger whose hair was so highly teased that it almost looked comical. Priscilla was home, but her heart was thousands of miles away. Elvis made many calls to her parents, urging them to allow their daughter to move to Memphis. He assured Captain Beaulieu that Priscilla would be living with his father, Vernon, and his wife, Dee Presley (previously Davada, then Dee Stanley, an army wife stationed in Germany when she met Vernon Presley. They had an affair that brought an end to her ten-year marriage to Sergeant Bill Stanley, with whom she had three sons; Dee and Vernon married in Alabama on July 3, 1960, and raised the boys, Billy the oldest, Rick the middle child, and David the youngest).

Although he was pleased to hear that Elvis respected his daughter and that she would not be living at Graceland, Captain Beaulieu flat out said no. He did, however, agree to let his daughter spend Christmas 1962 with him. Priscilla would be coming to Memphis for the first time and would be spending three weeks at Graceland.

AS THE CHRISTMAS SEASON GREW NEAR, Priscilla flew to New York's LaGuardia Airport. She was met by Vernon and Dee and together they flew on to Memphis. Graceland at Christmastime was the most beautiful thing Priscilla had ever seen. This was Elvis' favorite holiday and he went all out decorating the sweeping grounds, long winding driveway, and his stately home so that it resembled a Norman Rockwell Christmas illustration. The inside of the home was a continuation of the surreal Christmas scene, and in the living room was a large white Christmas tree fully decorated and overflowing below with gifts.

The living area was crowded with friends, many of whom Priscilla had met on her last visit. Most of Elvis' relatives were present, including his grandmother, Minnie Mae Presley, lovingly referred to as "Dodger." Priscilla and Dodger had gotten to know and like each other during their time together while Elvis was stationed in Germany. The holiday festivities continued until the early morning hours. An overly exhausted Priscilla, jet-lagged from her long trip, went with Elvis to his second-floor bedroom. Once the couple settled in, Elvis removed two 500-milligram Placidyls, a powerful barbiturate prescribed for sleeping, from a bottle sitting on his nightstand. He told Priscilla that they would help her relax. The young girl washed them down with a glass of water and proceeded to sleep for the next forty-eight hours. Elvis was finally able to wake her by holding her up and walking her around the room. In 1962 doctors in the United States prescribed uppers (speed) and downers (barbiturates) to patients who wanted to lose weight or had trouble sleeping. There was little knowledge and no education concerning both the immediate danger and longtime effects of these powerful drugs. Elvis was especially naïve, convinced that if a doctor prescribed them, they were medicine and not harmful. When Priscilla awoke from her coma-like state she was crushed to learn that she had wasted two days of her holiday.

The rest of their time together flew by. They attended Elvis' all-night movie screenings, roller-skated, rode the Dodgems (Elvis' favorite amusement ride), partied at Graceland, and spent many hours in each other's arms. On New Year's Eve, Elvis arranged a fireworks display on Graceland's lawn. Afterward the couple went to the Manhattan Club, which Elvis had rented for a few hundred of his friends and relatives. Elvis and Priscilla had more than a few screwdrivers (vodka and orange juice) and felt no pain as they ushered in the new year.

As the end of Priscilla's three-week holiday drew near, Elvis called Priscilla's father and attempted to convince him to let her stay longer. The Captain denied them in no uncertain terms and Priscilla returned to Germany with its cold and cloudy climate, her mind stuck in a faraway place, her thoughts only for the one thing in her life that mattered. She didn't tell her parents for fear they would think she was infatuated with Elvis; that her feelings were nothing more than puppy love. Paul and Ann worried about their daughter, who began acting out and rebelling against them, showing no interest in school or her old friends. Elvis kept calling and their conversations sometimes lasted until the morning. Priscilla was often too sleepy to hear the alarm clock ring for school the next day.

Elvis didn't let up. Both of Priscilla's parents felt that their daughter was too young for this grown man. She was only seventeen. Why didn't he find someone his own age? Elvis was ruining their family. They were afraid that if they let her go to him, he would break her heart, and if they didn't let her go she would hate them forever.

Elvis realized that if he wanted Priscilla to move to Memphis, he would have to convince her family how much he needed her, how much he cared for her, and how sincere he was. Drawing on the personality that had charmed the world, Elvis decided to call Captain Beaulieu. He swore to the captain that his intentions were sincere, that Priscilla would be enrolled at a fine Catholic school, Immaculate Conception High. He assured them she would graduate and be chaperoned at all times, she would not be living with him but would reside with his father and stepmother. He said he couldn't live without her and promised to respect Priscilla in every way.

The Beaulieus were persuaded that if Elvis was as sincere as his words, there was a chance that their daughter could find true happiness. They finally gave in. Father and daughter flew to Memphis in March 1963 and Priscilla's life at Graceland, an entrance into the fantasy world of stardom, had finally become reality.

Elvis was in Hollywood completing work on his latest film, *Fun in Acapulco*. As soon as the movie wrapped, he joined Priscilla at Graceland. He kept his word to Captain Beaulieu and Priscilla moved into Vernon Presley's home on Dolan Street; the backyard was adjacent to Graceland. Elvis and Priscilla could be together simply by slipping through the property's adjoining gate.

Vernon drove her to and from school and gave her an allowance. The elder Presley was known for his tight way with a buck and Priscilla barely had enough spending money. She felt uncomfortable living with Dee and Vernon, often feeling out of place in their home. When Elvis suggested she move into Graceland, she already had her bags packed.

Elvis bought her a candy-red Chevy Corvair so she could drive herself back and forth to school. The girls at school were jostling to be her friend; the word had spread that she was Elvis Presley's girlfriend. They needn't have tried so hard, as Elvis had made it perfectly clear that her friends, whom he considered outsiders, were not welcome at Graceland.

Rumors spread as the Memphis newspapers published stories about the new girl in Elvis' life. Elvis quickly squelched them by saying that she was the daughter of a family he had befriended in Germany and the rest of her family would be joining their daughter shortly, that her father was completing his military obligation. Once the rumors were silenced, Elvis breathed a sigh of relief. He didn't want to be branded with the same scandal as Jerry Lee Lewis, who had all but ruined his career by marrying his thirteen-year-old cousin.

Priscilla had to endure long periods of time alone while Elvis was in Los Angeles honoring his film commitments. She was always aware and concerned about the threat to their relationship caused by his Hollywood leading ladies.

When she graduated from Immaculate Conception High School, Elvis remained in the school's

Colonel Parker and Elvis, MGM studios. Culver City, California, 1963.

parking lot, afraid his presence in the school's auditorium would disrupt the graduation ceremony. Elvis continued to pick her wardrobe, makeup, and hairstyle and had her take classes at the Patricia Stevens Finishing School. He was intent on creating the perfect woman as he imagined her to be.

Priscilla joined him in Hollywood during the filming of *Kissin' Cousins*. This worried and concerned Colonel Parker, who was fearful that the news media would pick up on the relationship. One day he told Elvis that he had arranged a flight out of town for Priscilla and that Elvis better make sure she was on it.

Over the next two years, Priscilla traveled to Hollywood frequently and the couple was able to spend more time together. Photographs show Priscilla in tight dresses, high heels, sporting heavy makeup with blue-black hair that matched her boyfriend's. Rumors of Elvis' upcoming marriage to the girl back home appeared in the gossip and movie magazines during the summer of 1966. Elvis, the Colonel, and Vernon Presley quieted them with firm denials.

That Christmas Elvis bought Priscilla a beautiful black horse that she named Domino. He also gave her the most wonderful gift of all, a three-and-a-half-karat diamond ring, the large center stone surrounded by a circle of smaller diamonds. He went down on bended knee and slipped the ring on her finger; the king was making her his queen.

ELVIS AND CILLA CAUGHT horse riding fever early in 1967. After giving her Domino he purchased a magnificent Palomino for himself and named the horse Rising Sun, often riding him at sunrise to avoid the ever-present fans and paparazzi. The original owners of Graceland had kept their horses in stables located at the rear of the property. Elvis had this building remodeled with eighteen stalls and purchased horses for his whole entourage and their wives. Elvis, Priscilla, Vernon, and the gang rode their horses on the grounds as fans gathered to watch the fun, often causing traffic jams.

In February 1967 the newly engaged couple were driving near Horn Lake, Mississippi, when a giant white cross in the distance caught Elvis' attention. This cross was situated on a beautiful 160-acre ranch with rolling hills, lakes, and an adorable little house. Elvis saw this cross as an omen and decided he wanted to purchase the ranch located only twelve miles from Graceland on the Tennessee/Mississippi state line. He bought it for $500,000, paying more for it than it was worth and saying, "You can't put a price on happiness." He borrowed the money from the bank, putting Graceland up as collateral, and christened the ranch the Circle G for Graceland.

Elvis moved the horses from Graceland to the ranch and hired Alan Fortas to be the foreman. He then purchased nine manufactured homes for the ranch and nine pickup trucks, one for each of the guys and their families. Elvis and Priscilla had created their own commune. The times spent at the Circle G Ranch were the happiest times of their relationship; they rode horses, had picnics, and enjoyed the grounds and the lake. Here Elvis could be himself, not "Elvis Presley" or the image that he had been living since his earliest success.

THE DREAM BEGAN TO FADE when the guys and their wives wanted to move back to their homes. Their children missed their friends and their schools. The Memphis Mafia needed money to pay their bills and began selling off the trucks. Elvis himself was having a serious cash-flow problem because of his out-of-control spending. It was time to return to Hollywood and earn another million-dollar payday. Elvis read the script for *Clambake* and hated it, but agreed to acting in it because he needed the money.

When Elvis reported to the set of *Clambake* he had gained thirty pounds and was tipping the scales at 205 pounds. MGM was understandably disturbed by his appearance and ordered him to get in shape fast. Diet pills were the immediate answer.

Colonel Parker was very concerned with Elvis' recent activities. Vernon Presley had confided to the Colonel that Elvis was spending money faster than he could earn it and was very worried that if Elvis weren't careful, they would go bankrupt. There was also concern about Elvis' newfound spiritual quest. The Colonel felt that the metaphysical books that Elvis was reading were messing up his mind. These books were being supplied by Larry Geller, a hairstylist who worked at the Jay Sebring Salon in Hollywood (Sebring, famed hairdresser to the stars, would later become one of the victims of the Charles Manson 1969 massacre at actress Sharon Tate's California home). Geller first cut Elvis' hair at his L.A. home in May 1964. Elvis was impressed by Geller's haircut and deeply moved by their four-hour talk about religion and spiritualism. Larry was hired on the spot and became Elvis' hairstylist and main confidant over the next three years, sharing his books and knowledge with Elvis. Priscilla, as well as members of the entourage, began referring to Geller as "swami" or "the guru." The Colonel told Elvis that he believed Larry Geller had hypnotized him using a mind-control technique, and reluctantly Elvis and Priscilla took all of the books Larry had given him and burned them.

The Colonel asked Elvis to take a good look in the mirror and ask himself what he wanted from his career and upcoming marriage. He told Elvis his records weren't selling as they had in the past and the movies were doing poorly at the box office. It was time to concentrate on his career and get his life back on track.

Elvis had promised Priscilla's father that he would marry his daughter when the time was right; Elvis realized that time was now. His name had been romantically linked with those of every Hollywood leading lady, starlet, and other member of the female species for eleven years. Elvis himself once remarked, "If I slept with every woman they [movie magazines] say I have, I would have been dead a long time ago." America's favorite bachelor would temporarily silence the gossip magazines.

On Sunday, April 30, the Colonel sent telegrams to his friends and associates asking them to come to Las Vegas for an important event. Among them were Abe Lastfogel, president of the William Morris Agency (Elvis' booking agency), the president of RCA, and Stan Brossette, the head of publicity for MGM. Elvis and Priscilla, Vernon and Dee, and the other members of the wedding party flew from Palm Springs to Las Vegas. No one other than the members of this wedding party knew that on May 1, 1967, Elvis and Priscilla would wed. The one hundred invited guests met in the lobby of the Aladdin Hotel and were taken to the private suite of Milton Prell, the hotel's owner. They were told of the wedding and were instructed not to leave the suite until the time of the ceremony; Colonel Parker wasn't taking any chances. Rona Barrett, the famous gossipmonger, had announced on TV that Elvis was getting married in Palm Springs. The media was off and running in the wrong direction. By the time reporters realized they had been sent on a wild-goose chase, the ceremony was about to begin.

The King takes a Queen. Elvis and Priscilla's wedding, Milton Prell's suite, Aladdin Hotel, May 1, 1967.

AT 9:41 A.M. THE BEAUTIFUL double-ring ceremony was performed by Nevada Supreme Court Justice David Zenoff. Elvis wore black tuxedo pants and a black-on-black paisley jacket. Priscilla was stunning in her floor-length gown of white chiffon. The ceremony lasted eight minutes. Joe Esposito was Elvis' best man; Michelle Beaulieu, Priscilla's sister, was the maid of honor. The invited guests and the bridal party were then escorted by guards to the Aladdin Room, where they drank champagne as Elvis and Priscilla danced to the strains of "Love Me Tender." Priscilla would later recall "Love Me Tender" as being the first song of Elvis' that she ever heard. "It has always been my favorite," she claimed. The wedding cake was five feet high and had six tiers; it reportedly cost $3,500. There were eight round tables for the guests and seated at the head table were the bride and groom with their families. The menu included chicken, roast suckling pig, lobster, clams casino, smoked salmon, and oysters Rockefeller.

Following the party a brief press conference was held and the couple answered the reporters' questions. As soon as the Colonel called a halt to the conference, reporters tried to beat one another with their coverage of the "wedding of the decade." At 2:50 p.m. the newlyweds flew to Palm Springs aboard a private jet belonging to Frank Sinatra. Two days later they flew to Hollywood, where Elvis would complete work on *Clambake*.

On May 4, Elvis and Priscilla flew via commercial airline to Memphis. Elvis didn't allow any photos or interviews with the press. Immediately after he and Priscilla were settled at Graceland, Elvis drove to the Circle G Ranch to see the new colt that had been born while he was away. Priscilla gave Elvis a Cadillac Eldorado as a wedding gift. They watched films

Candid of Elvis and Priscilla in the parking lot of the Aladdin Hotel, immediately after their wedding.

Above left: Elvis and Priscilla leaving for their Palm Springs honeymoon. Las Vegas, May 1, 1967.

Right: Elvis and Priscilla at their honeymoon cottage.

like *The Sand Pebbles* and *A Shot in the Dark* and divided their time between Graceland and the Circle G. One evening they bowled from midnight to 4:00 a.m. at the Whitehaven Bowling Lanes. On another occasion they rented the fairgrounds and both Priscilla and Elvis behaved like children as they rode the Pippin, Tilt-A-Whirl, and, of course, the Dodgems.

On May 29 a second wedding reception was held at Graceland. The 125 invited guests included friends and relatives who had not been able to attend the wedding in Vegas. The reception was held on the huge enclosed patio. An attendant parked the guests' cars and as they entered the reception area their wedding gifts were placed on a round oak table. The large bridal arch was covered with red and white carnations. Directly in front of the arch a table covered in white satin held the beautiful four-tier wedding cake. Located in the center of the room were eight tables covered in white satin, each with its own floral arrangement surrounded by lighted candles. The menu included ham, turkey, a variety of cheeses, stuffed lobster, shrimp, meatballs, sausages, hot dogs, potato salad, and coleslaw. There was also plenty of champagne.

At 8:30 p.m. Elvis' grandmother, Minnie, was ushered in and seated at the head table, followed by Vernon, Dee, and Dee's children. Fifteen minutes later Joe Esposito came into the room and signaled accordionist Tony Barasso, to begin playing "Love Me Tender." Elvis and Priscilla entered and stood in front of the bridal arch as their guests applauded. Joe then announced, "In case no one here knows it, that's Mr. and Mrs. Elvis Presley!" Priscilla wore her beautiful

wedding gown with its six-foot train. Elvis was wearing his black brocaded formal suit with vest, formal white shirt, black bow tie, and a white carnation in his lapel. The receiving line formed and the bride and groom were kissed and congratulated by everyone. Elvis and Priscilla mixed with all of their guests and really seemed to be enjoying themselves. Finally he took her in his arms and they danced to the music of "Let Me Call You Sweetheart." After accidentally stepping on her train, he lifted it and wrapped it around her shoulders. The reception ended at midnight and Elvis invited everyone to the Memphian Theater where he put on a Kirk Douglas film.

On June 8 the newlyweds flew to Hollywood where Elvis was scheduled to begin work on his next film, MGM's *Speedway*. A problem soon arose when Priscilla revealed her feelings regarding the Memphis Mafia. She was tired of sharing her man with the boys, many of whom were jealous of her. The Mafia had always used their position with Elvis to get them girls, and Priscilla didn't want this footloose entourage around her. She also felt that Elvis was paying too many salaries. The couple had quarreled over this before and in the end all of the boys, with the exception of Joe Esposito, Richard Davis, and Charlie Hodge, were fired. Joe Esposito was Elvis' bookkeeper and adviser, Richard Davis was his valet, and Charlie Hodge remained a close friend and employee. Elvis had met Charlie when they were on the same army ship, the USS *General George M. Randall*, en route to Germany. Charlie was a Southern boy born in Decatur, Alabama. A natural-born comedian, he provided his boss with friendship and laughs. The friendship lasted until Elvis' death.

The Presleys purchased the Trousdale Estate at 1174 Hillcrest Road in Beverly Hills. The house had a huge pool, four large bedrooms, a circular living room with adjoining recreation room, and six bathrooms, and it was hidden behind an electronically operated gate.

AFTER COMPLETING WORK on *Speedway*, the Presleys, accompanied by Joe Esposito and his wife, Joanie, traveled via commercial airline to Memphis. Once inside the walls of Graceland Elvis announced, "Priscilla is going to . . . uh . . . uh . . . have . . . uh . . . Priscilla is going to have a baby." Everyone congratulated them as he smiled and said, "Yeah, we're going to have another rock 'n' roll singer."

The newspapers across the country gave daily coverage to the event. It's ironic how the boy they once called a threat to the nation's young, an out-and-out sex maniac, was now being praised for his charitable deeds, his humanity, and the shinning example he set for American youth. It had always been Colonel Parker's goal to clean up Elvis' image. He made sure we knew that Elvis loved his mother, his country, God, and his pregnant wife.

On the night before Priscilla gave birth she was asked when the baby was due. She answered, "In a week . . . I'm so excited . . . we're both so nervous; every time I move he's there to catch me." On February 1, 1968, at 8:30 in the morning, Charlie Hodge drove Elvis and Priscilla to the Baptist Memorial Hospital. Joe Esposito followed them in case of an auto emergency. The hospital's entrance was crowded with reporters. Two hospital guards ushered the Presley party inside where Priscilla was admitted immediately and Elvis went to the doctors' lounge to wait for the birth. Joe, Charlie, Vernon, Dee, friend Lamar Fike, and George Klein joined him there. Lisa Marie Presley was born at 5:01 p.m., weighing 6 pounds 15 ounces, nine months to the day after Elvis and Priscilla's wedding.

Private photo of Elvis, Priscilla, and their new baby, Lisa Marie Presley. Graceland, February 1968.

Elvis hired two off-duty policemen to stand guard outside Priscilla's room for the four days she stayed in the hospital. The switchboard there received over ten thousand calls from all over the world. Gifts by the truckload were delivered to Graceland.

FOLLOWING THE GIANT SUCCESS of his 1968 NBC TV special, the Colonel announced Elvis would be performing live for the first time in nine years. He said that Elvis would be appearing for one month at the brand-new International Hotel in Las Vegas.

Elvis' 1969 Summer Festival at the International broke all records. The showroom, the largest in Vegas, held over two thousand people. Elvis filled every seat at every performance. Priscilla had designed the jumpsuits Elvis wore, fashioning them after the karate uniform, or "gi." She sat at a reserved booth along with Vernon, Dee, and, on some occasions, Ricky, David, and Billy, Elvis' stepbrothers.

In January 1970 Elvis opened his second month-long engagement at the International. There was now a "no wives" rule in place. He announced that Priscilla and the wives were welcome for the opening and sometimes for the closing shows. This would play havoc on the entourage's marriages as well as on Elvis'. A pattern was now in place: Elvis would perform twice a year in Las Vegas. He also added Lake Tahoe to his schedule and began crossing the United States performing sold-out one-night stands. He was greeted by audiences who gave him standing ovations just for walking out onstage.

In April 1970 Priscilla and Elvis bought a home in Palm Springs. The Colonel and his wife, Marie, had a home there and lived nearby. At first the couple spent time there together, but later Elvis used the house as a bachelor retreat at the conclusion of a concert tour or a Las Vegas engagement. Elvis would tell Priscilla he and the guys were going to the Palm Springs house to unwind. With the wives once again excluded, Elvis and the entourage were joined there by a steady stream of willing females. Priscilla was naturally upset, but Elvis denied everything.

Priscilla herself began having an affair later that year, with karate champion Mike Stone. Priscilla had become interested in karate at her husband's urging and studied with Ed Parker and Master Kang Rhee. She had first met Stone in 1968 when she and Elvis attended a karate tournament that Ed Parker staged in Hawaii, and became romantically involved with Stone when their paths crossed at Chuck Norris' studio in the summer of

Elvis on his Tennessee Walker.
Graceland, 1968.

Elvis at the Jaycees Ten Outstanding Young Men of America award ceremony. Memphis, January 9, 1971.

1971. When members of the Memphis Mafia told their boss that Priscilla was fooling around, he told them to mind their own goddamn business. Elvis and Priscilla's marriage was crumbling. They spent little time together and, for the most part, they were living separate lives. Elvis was relying more and more on prescription drugs and their relationship was the victim of both his excesses and successes. Elvis continued to tour, often not seeing his wife for several weeks. Priscilla spoke with him on the phone, telling him of Lisa Marie's growth and sending him photos of their daughter.

CHRISTMAS 1972 WASN'T a happy one for the couple, though they spent it together. Elvis' winter engagement at the Las Vegas Hilton was in full swing when Priscilla flew in to join him. After watching her husband's dinner show, she joined him on the twenty-ninth floor in his suite. Priscilla described in her book, *Elvis and Me*, how Elvis threw her on the bed and roughly made love to her. She began to cry and he told her that this is how a man makes love to his woman. She told Elvis the marriage was over, that she was romantically involved with Mike Stone, the karate champion who Elvis had introduced her to. She told him she was leaving him. Elvis, though shattered, still performed his midnight show.

The couple legally separated on July 26, 1972. Their divorce became final on October 9, 1973. Although Elvis never got over the humiliation of

Elvis, Priscilla, and Lisa Marie at Lisa's birthday party at the Hilton Hotel, February 1973.

Priscilla leaving him, they would remain good friends and shared custody of their daughter. Lisa Marie would live with Priscilla and visit Elvis when he was not touring.

Priscilla brought Lisa Marie to Vegas to see her father perform at most of his engagements. Although their marriage had failed, they continued to have feelings for each other. In later years Elvis would have his girlfriends call Priscilla and she would advise them on how to make him happy.

Priscilla and Elvis with Vernon Presley in the background. The couple's divorce is finalized. Los Angeles County Superior Courthouse, October 9, 1973.

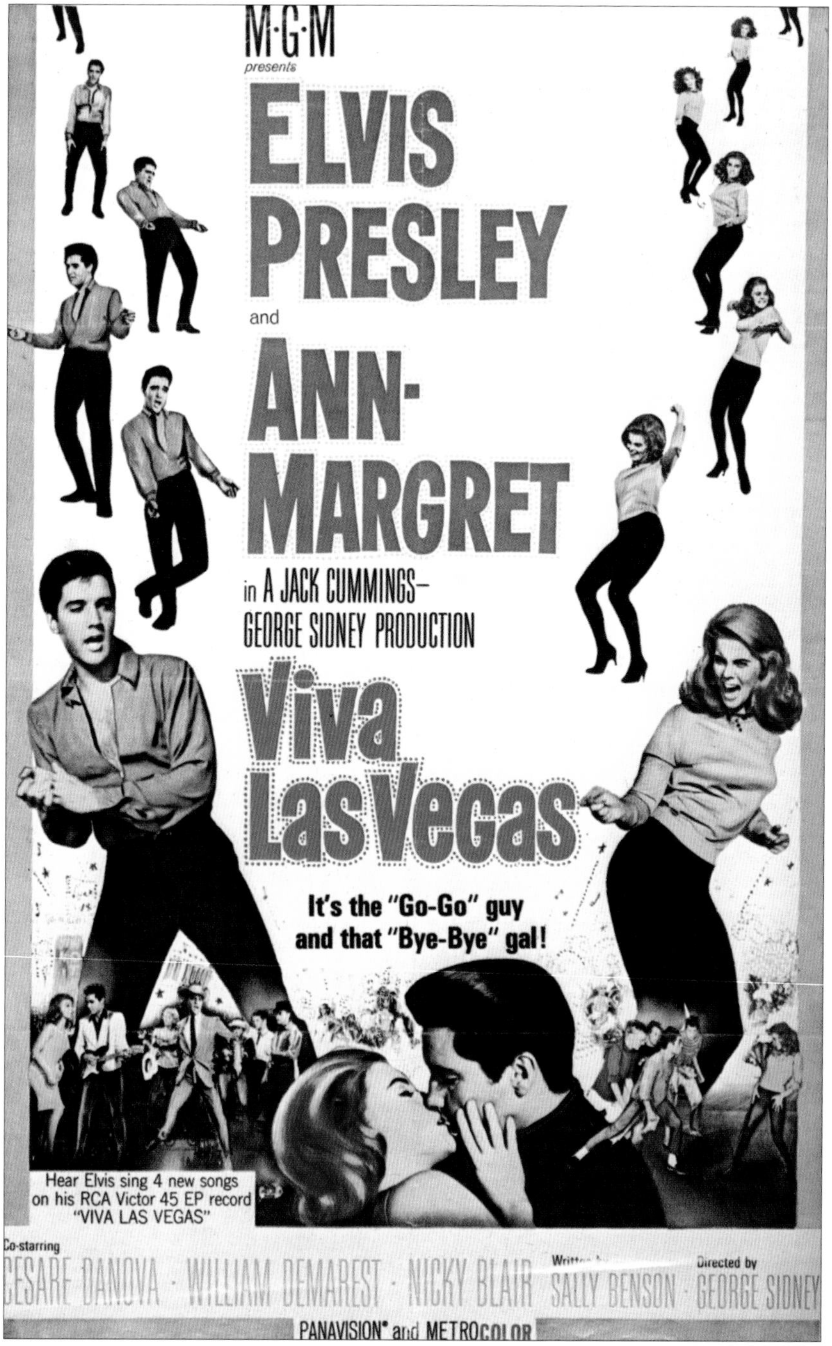

Original MGM one-sheet Viva Las Vegas *movie poster, 1963.*

CHAPTER 3

Viva Las Vegas: A Tender Moment in a Hurricane

July 9, 1963–June 17, 1964

THERE HAVE BEEN MANY STORIES written about the origin of the Elvis Presley/Ann-Margret saga. No matter which version you believe, one thing is certain: Elvis knew what he wanted and he expected to get it.

While his teenage girlfriend, Priscilla, attended high school in Memphis and read movie magazines at Graceland, her boyfriend, Elvis, was telling his buddies that they would all be leaving his Hollywood home on Perugia Way to begin work on his latest film, *Viva Las Vegas*.

George Klein, the famed Memphis disc jockey who was also Elvis' high school friend, flew in from Memphis to spend a couple of weeks with the group. He was present when Elvis said, "I've got a date with Ann-Margret tonight."

George answered, "Great, E! Do you want me to go with you?"

Elvis responded with an emphatic, "No!" and continued with a statement that surprised all present when he declared, "When I get back here with Ann I want you all gone. I don't want to see any of you hanging around." This was extremely unusual, as Elvis never did anything by himself. And so it began—the Elvis Presley/Ann-Margret friendship, a relationship that would last for the rest of Elvis' life.

IN 1963, AS THE NEW YEAR DAWNED, Elvis Presley became the highest-paid actor in the world thanks to the contract that Colonel Parker negotiated with MGM. Elvis would receive $1 million per film plus 50 percent of the net profit. The first film under the new contract would be *Viva Las Vegas*. The movie's costar was a beautiful and sexy young lady, who many in Hollywood had dubbed "The Female Elvis Presley."

Ann-Margret Olsen had starred in *Bye Bye Birdie*, originally titled *Let's Go Steady*, a film loosely based on Elvis being drafted into the United States Army. The film also starred Janet Leigh, Bobby Rydell, Dick Van Dyke, and Ed Sullivan, playing him-

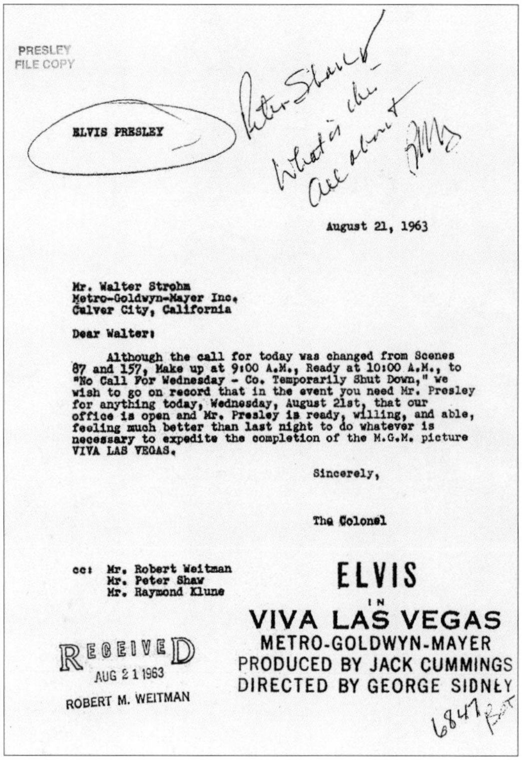

PRESLEY
FILE COPY

ELVIS PRESLEY

August 21, 1963

Mr. Walter Strohm
Metro-Goldwyn-Mayer Inc.
Culver City, California

Dear Walter:

Although the call for today was changed from Scenes 87 and 157, Make up at 9:00 A.M., Ready at 10:00 A.M., to "No Call For Wednesday - Co. Temporarily Shut Down," we wish to go on record that in the event you need Mr. Presley for anything today, Wednesday, August 21st, that our office is open and Mr. Presley is ready, willing, and able, feeling much better than last night to do whatever is necessary to expedite the completion of the M.G.M. picture VIVA LAS VEGAS.

Sincerely,

The Colonel

cc: Mr. Robert Weitman
Mr. Peter Shaw
Mr. Raymond Klune

RECEIVED
AUG 21 1963
ROBERT M. WEITMAN

ELVIS
IN
VIVA LAS VEGAS
METRO-GOLDWYN-MAYER
PRODUCED BY JACK CUMMINGS
DIRECTED BY GEORGE SIDNEY

self. The Elvis character in the movie is named Conrad Birdie, in reference to Conway Twitty who would go on to a legendary career in country music. In 1958 Twitty could have been called the world's first Elvis impersonator; his classic rock ballad, "It's Only Make Believe," sung in the Presley style, had many fans and disc jockeys swearing it was Elvis singing.

Jesse Pearson portrayed Conrad Birdie, sporting a high pompadour, dressed in a gold suit, and performing with a guitar and shaky leg,. A key scene in the film had Conrad being introduced on the *Ed Sullivan Show* by Ed himself. Conrad would then sing his last song to serve two years in the army, leaving millions of brokenhearted teenage girls. Ann-Margret was one of them, and as the winner of a contest she gets to have Conrad sing his last song to her. The movie was a huge hit.

The two stars came from different backgrounds and different countries (Ann-Margret was born in Sweden). They were immediately attracted to each other. Elvis, who captured the hearts of girls all over the world, only had to smile that crooked smile and gaze at Ann with his heavy-lidded smoke-blue eyes to melt her heart. He sensed the electricity immediately.

Far left: Personal document from Colonel Parker to Walter Strohm, August 21, 1963.

Both Elvis and Ann were shy and polite and both shared strong religious beliefs. To Ann, Elvis

Below: Elvis original publicity still, Viva Las Vegas, *1963.*

Elvis and Ann-Margret song sequence rehearsal, Viva Las Vegas, *1963.*

Far left, Elvis original publicity still, Viva Las Vegas, *1963.*

Left, Elvis signing an autograph for an unidentified woman at the Sahara Hotel, 1963.

wasn't a king or a legend but a young man whose talents allowed him to enjoy life to its fullest. In Ann, Elvis saw a sweet girl who could excite him with her smile and thrill him with her presence. They were kids who knew that once the music started, they couldn't stand still.

The first three days of production on *Viva Las Vegas* were spent in Hollywood at Radio Recorders Studio, where between July 9 and July 11 Elvis recorded "The Climb" with his backup group, The Jordanaires. Elvis and Ann recorded three duets. On July 14 the cast and crew arrived in Las Vegas, where they spent the next two weeks filming location shots.

During the day the two stars worked on the film, and afterward they spent their evenings together. They took advantage of Vegas' nightlife and entertainment. Like any young couple in America, they wanted to see their favorite entertainers. Unlike other couples, they were accompanied by Elvis' entourage. The showroom manager at the New Frontier Hotel was a Memphis native whom Elvis had a casual acquaintance with. He arranged for the group to be seated just as Clara Ward began her show. Clara, a legendary singer of gospel and blues, was a favorite of Elvis'. Elvis and Ann loved her performance and everything was perfect until the waitress asked the twenty-three-year-old Ann for her ID before serving her an alcoholic beverage. She obviously didn't recognize the young star. This perceived slight infuriated Elvis. When at the show's conclusion the showroom manager approached Elvis saying he hoped Elvis and his group had enjoyed themselves, Elvis exploded, saying, "If I ever set foot in this goddamn hotel—you tell that fucking waitress not to embarrass anyone I'm with by asking for any goddamn fucking identification." With that off his chest he, Ann, and the guys walked out of the hotel without looking back.

Elvis and Ann-Margret "The Lady Loves Me" song sequence, Viva Las Vegas, *1963.*

Ann-Margret wasn't at all bothered by the guys who constantly surrounded Elvis when they were together. She was used to having company, as her parents accompanied her on dates. Elvis loved Don Rickles and the famed acid-tongued comedian was aware that Elvis was a big fan. One evening the whole gang went to see Rickles, whose nickname was "Mr. Warmth." They snuck in late and were seated at a ringside booth. Don spotted them and quickly began his trademark insults on Elvis and Ann. Both laughed hysterically throughout the comedian's show and later spent time with Rickles in his dressing room.

When the Vegas location shots were completed, the production of *Viva Las Vegas* returned to MGM's Los Angeles studio. All of Hollywood was buzzing about Elvis and Ann's romance. This was great publicity for the movie and would surely help sell tickets. Hedda Hopper, famed Hollywood gossip columnist,

Far left: Elvis and Ann-Margret relaxing between takes, Viva Las Vegas, *1963.*

Left: Elvis original publicity still, Viva Las Vegas, *1963.*

interviewed Ann, asking her, "Have you had dinner at Elvis' house?" Ann responded with the affirmative. "Did he have his Memphis friends there?" Hedda continued. Ann replied, "No comment." This coyness did nothing to derail the rampant rumors spread in the movie magazines concerning the lovers' relationship. Most of the stories were figments of the writers' imaginations. They doctored photos by superimposing Elvis and Ann's heads on other bodies to give the impression that they had obtained exclusive photographs of the couple. These make-believe pictures were even printed on the covers of magazines.

Priscilla would have had to be very naïve to be unaware of the Elvis-and-Ann affair. She spoke to Elvis on the phone about coming to Hollywood to be with him. He offered many rambling excuses for why she couldn't join him—there were problems on the set, the director was in love with Ann-Margret and

Elvis and Ann-Margret publicity still, Viva Las Vegas, *1963.*

Right: Elvis on the set of Viva Las Vegas, *1963.*

Far right: Elvis and Ann-Margret sharing a fun moment on the set of Viva Las Vegas, *1963.*

was giving her all the close-up shots, the production numbers favored Ann. Priscilla stopped him with, "How are you and Ann-Margret getting along?"

Elvis replied matter-of-factly, "She's a typical Hollywood starlet." Priscilla asked him about the stories in the magazines and he replied, "They make these things up. It's all lies. Don't believe a thing they say."

Meanwhile, back on the set the chemistry between the two stars exploded, igniting the music production numbers. The phenomenon of two very talented people sharing the same energy meant that often, no rehearsal was needed. Their facial expressions were sensual, primitive, inviting, and exciting, their body movements explicit, arrogant, and animal-like. The cameras caught all of this, and these images, which would later appear on big screens worldwide, went on to captivate moviegoers.

Between shots they held hands and disappeared into one of their dressing rooms. They ate lunch together and in the evenings Ann visited Elvis' house. On many occasions Elvis spent the evening with Ann and her parents at their apartment. They both shared a love for motorcycles and could often be seen roaring around Los Angeles on giant Harley-Davidsons. On some occasions Elvis would pick up Ann in his new Rolls-Royce and take her out to dinner or to a drive-in. They cruised around late at night listening to music and they confided in each other.

The movie posters for *Viva Las Vegas* would refer to the two costars as "That Go Go Guy" and "That Bye Bye Girl." But all was not well. The Colonel had told Elvis that the film's director, George Sidney, was in fact in love with Ann-Margret. Sidney had directed her in *Bye Bye Birdie* and, thanks to the many close-ups he gave her, she stole the picture. When Colonel

Parker saw the dailies, he flew into a rage. Ann-Margret was getting all the face time while his boy was being relegated to the background. The Colonel was already at war with the studio because the film was over budget owing to the unnecessary time spent on the music production numbers, and the Colonel blamed this on Sidney's infatuation with "that girl." He was infuriated by the studio's planned publicity campaign. This was, after all, an Elvis Presley movie and that's what paid the bills for not only Elvis and himself but for the studio. He reasoned that Sidney's attempts to boost Ann-Margret's career at the expense of his star was taking money out of his pocket. No matter how successful the film became, his and Elvis' share of the profits would suffer as a result of the excessive music production numbers. The Colonel told MGM he would not use his considerable promotional abilities to promote the film. The studio, aware of how good a job the Colonel did promoting their product, began to listen. Colonel Parker had a clause in all of Elvis' movie contracts that prohibited anyone in the cast from singing in an Elvis Presley movie without prior permission from Elvis or himself, and he demanded that the three duets he had earlier agreed to be removed from the movie. In the end the studio gave in and only one duet, "The Lady Loves Me," remained in the film. It was not, however, included in the original RCA extended-play soundtrack. The two duets that were cut from the film, "You're The Boss" and "Today, Tomorrow, and Forever," would not be heard for decades. It is no coincidence that "Today, Tomorrow, and Forever" was featured in the film as an Elvis solo performance. Colonel Parker had, once again, prevailed in protecting his star.

Whatever concerns Elvis may have had, he didn't allow them to interfere with his personal relationship with Ann. Elvis told Ann he thought she needed better management and that Colonel Parker was the best there was. He drove to the Colonel's apartment and once inside he told the Colonel that Ann-Margret was outside in the car, that she was upset with her present management, and Elvis wanted him to manage her. Colonel Parker thought for a moment and then said, "I will be delighted to manage this talented young star. I'll even make her as famous as you, Elvis. This is going to take up a lot of my time. I'll have to talk to the movie studios and the record company and I'll work the phones just as I do for you. Elvis, I would never short-change you, but you have to understand that right now I devote 100 percent of my time to you. I'll have to give the girl 50 percent of my time as that's only fair."

Elvis thought about this for a minute and then

Left, Elvis and Ann-Margret, Viva Las Vegas, *1963.*

told the Colonel, "Maybe it's not such a good idea after all." He returned to the car and told Ann that Colonel Parker would love the opportunity to manage her but he had too much on his plate, and added that handling his own career was a full-time job.

Viva Las Vegas finished filming on September 16, 1963. George Sidney's passion for Ann-Margret didn't do anything to harm Elvis' appeal. In fact, the movie was the best of all the 1960s Elvis musicals. It captured his raw sex appeal, so apparent in his '50s films but so sadly missing in the endless '60s musical travelogues. Ann-Margret would go on to a legendary career but her charisma and sensuality would never again be captured as they were in *Viva Las Vegas*.

As a result of the missing Ann-Margret duets, there would be no RCA long-playing soundtrack album. A four-song extended play was issued instead.

Right: Elvis and Ann-Margret, Viva Las Vegas *wedding, 1963.*

RCA released "Viva Las Vegas" backed with "What'd I Say" as the film's single. The record never reached the Billboard Top Ten and became a modest hit. However, over the course of time Elvis' "Viva Las Vegas" would become the city of Las Vegas' theme song.

The movie was released on June 17, 1964, and ended up being the tenth highest grossing film of the year. The Beatles, who were at the height of their fame at the time, released their first feature film, the classic *A Hard Day's Night*. The movie failed to reach the financial success of Elvis and Ann's *Viva Las Vegas*.

NATIONAL BROADCASTING CO., INC.
NBC COLOR CITY
3000 W. ALAMEDA AVE., BURBANK, CALIF.
STUDIO 4
Saturday
June
29
1968
Show Time
8:00 PM
GUESTS
SHOULD
ARRIVE
7:00 PM
"ELVIS"
starring
ELVIS PRESLEY
IN COLOR
Children Under 12 Will Not Be Admitted

CHAPTER 4

Lonesome in the Desert

July 31, 1969—August 28, 1969

Elvis singing "If I Can Dream" finale, NBC TV Special. Burbank, California, December 3, 1968.

LAS VEGAS HAS CHANGED and grown since the brightest star in the gambling mecca breathed his last.

Elvis reinvented himself and Las Vegas on July 31, 1969, at Kirk Kerkorian's giant International Hotel. He set attendance records that still stand today and proved there was no such thing as a slow season—just announce that the King was coming to town and every hotel in the city was full to capacity. "No Vacancy" meant another Elvis festival at the International, renamed the Las Vegas Hilton after Barron Hilton purchased it in 1971.

TODAY LAS VEGAS HAS BIGGER HOTELS, better marketing, the catchphrase "What happens in Vegas stays in Vegas," and television commercials touting it as a great place for the whole family. The population has grown to overflowing and the traffic rivals rush hour in every major city except, in Vegas, rush hour lasts all night.

The hotels have built lavish showrooms featuring their own house celebrities who appear for months or years at a time; Barry Manilow, Elton John, Celine Dion, Cher, Bette Midler, and Wayne Newton, to name a few. Spectaculars such as David Copperfield, *Jersey Boys*, the many Cirque du Soleil productions, and *Mamma Mia* have become the norm.

Las Vegas also lays claim to being the Elvis impersonator (to be politically correct ETA—Elvis Tribute Artist), capital of the world. ETA's can be found in lounges all over the city; 1950s Elvis, 1968 Elvis, 1970s Elvis, African American, Caucasian, Asian, male, female, young, old, fat, thin, take your choice.

But to any Elvis fan who was there, who witnessed the town in those days and saw Elvis work his magic twice a night for a month, Las Vegas is now a ghost town, a wasteland in the desert.

YOU FLEW INTO LAS VEGAS and rode the pedestrian walkway as Don Rickles' voice welcomed you by calling you a dummy. Once outside the airport you saw the distant mountains and breathed the clean air that surrounded you, marveling at the openness of the desert. You would then get into a cab, which had an Elvis sign on the roof reading "Now Elvis Now." Colonel Parker had turned the strip into an Elvis Presley version of Disneyland. As the cab approached the hotel you could see giant Elvis billboards. The hotel's marquee simply read "Elvis" in three-foot-high lights. The front entrance, partially covered by an overhang, featured canvas banners in red, white, and blue with Elvis' image and "Elvis Now" emblazoned on them.

Many can today remember the excitement and waiting all day, knowing tonight you would be seeing the Elvis Presley Show, standing for hours in a never-ending line hoping to get into the showroom, wondering what your seats would be like, how close to the stage you would be, everyone wanting a stage-front table, and so everyone was your enemy. You finally figure it out. You see the maître d's, Bill and Emilio; a folded one-hundred-dollar bill slips from your palm to theirs. They smile knowingly. You are led to your seat and you realize there is half a showroom in front of you. You make eye contact with the maître d' and without exchanging a word you pass a second one-hundred-dollar bill into his hand and once again the smile and you are led to a stage-front table—mission accomplished. To this day every time I see a crumpled one-hundred-dollar bill, I think of Emilio.

On December 3, 1968, NBC broadcast "Singer Presents Elvis." The sewing machine company sponsored Elvis' first television special and the first time in eight years he would perform live. The special was taped at NBC's studio in Burbank, California, before an audience of two hundred. NBC edited the hours of tape to fifty minutes, and the show made television history. RCA released "If I Can Dream," the message song Elvis closed the show with, and it became his first million-seller in four years. The show's soundtrack reached the Top Ten and was a consistent seller for more than a year.

Fifteen years into his career, the critics were praising him. Elvis Presley had again become everyone's favorite. "There is something magical about watching a man who has lost himself find his way back home," said Jon Landau in *Eye* magazine. "He sang with the kind of power people no longer expect from a rock-and-roll singer. He moved his body with a lack of pretension and effort that must have made Jim Morrison green with envy and while most of the songs

Recording session, American Sound Studio. Memphis, January/February 1969.

Left to right: International Hotel president Alex Shoofey, Elvis, talent booker Bill Miller. Construction site, International Hotel, Las Vegas, March 1969.

were ten or twelve years old he performed them as freshly as though they were written yesterday."

Changes were coming at a fast rate. Tom Diskin (Colonel Parker's right-hand man) told a reporter that Elvis' movie income was dropping rapidly: "For the time that goes into making a film it's more profitable for him to appear in public. It took Elvis fifteen weeks to make a film. If he tours for ten weeks, doing one concert a week at $100,000 each, he can do much better." Elvis said, "I'm planning a lot of changes. You can't go on doing the same thing year after year. It's been a long time since I've done anything professionally except make movies and cut albums. From now on I don't think I'd like to do as many pictures as I've done. Before too long I'm going to make some personal appearance tours. I'll probably start out here in this country and after that play some concerts abroad, probably starting in Europe. I want to see some places I've never seen before. I miss the personal contact with audiences."

Colonel Parker went to work trying to find a suitable venue for his boy's return to live performances. He contacted Bill Miller, the legendary booking agent who came out of retirement to procure acts for the International Hotel. The hotel was still under construction and upon completion would become Las Vegas' largest hotel and tallest building, costing $60 million to build. There were 1,519 guest rooms. It was the first major Vegas hotel not located on the famed strip, and it housed the world's largest casino as well as an eighteen-hole golf course. The giant convention center held five thousand people. Guests had their choice of fine dining in one of the hotel's six restaurants. The Showroom Internationale was more than twice as big as any other showroom in Vegas; it seated over two thousand people and included a balcony.

Colonel Parker and Bill Miller worked out the details. Elvis' original deal with the International had him appearing in Vegas once a year for five years. The hotel would pay Elvis $1 million per engagement with an option for Elvis' future performances. The contract also included some perks. Both Elvis and the Colonel would have suites at the hotel whenever they chose to use them, whether Elvis was performing at the hotel or not. The International would also pay their travel expenses. A photo op was arranged where Elvis signed a contract on the roof of the unfinished hotel. The story of Elvis' return to live performances included a photograph of Elvis signing and holding the contract as the hotel's VIPs, wearing hardhats, looked on.

International Hotel marquee. Las Vegas, July/August 1969.

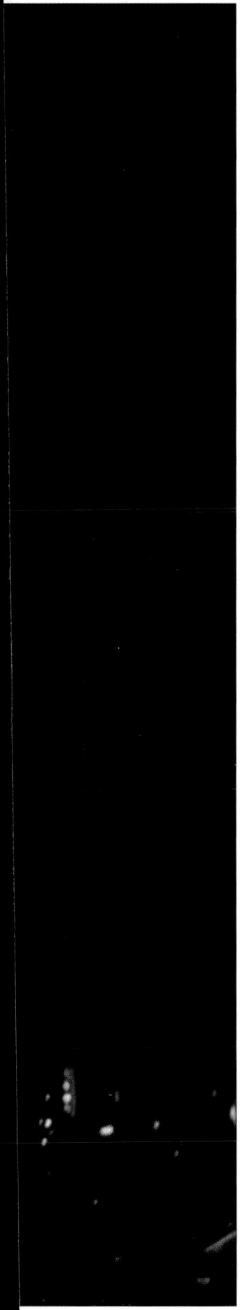

ELVIS TOLD CHARLIE HODGE, "Maybe some of my movies were shit, but my stage show is going to be the best motherfucker anyone has ever seen." He would need a great band to accomplish this. He called guitar legend James Burton, a native of Minden, Louisiana, who first came to fame for his extraordinary guitar work with Ricky Nelson. Elvis originally asked Burton to play on his 1968 TV special, but Burton was unable to because he was working with Frank Sinatra at the time. Now Elvis asked Burton to put together a band for his new gig at the International.

Jerry Scheff, a major studio sessions musician, was invited to audition for Elvis. He had worked on an Elvis recording session in 1966 for the *Double Trouble* movie soundtrack. At the audition Elvis loved Scheff's down and dirty bass playing on some old blues tunes, and he was hired.

John Wilkinson became a member of Elvis' Taking Care of Business (TCB) Band when Elvis called and asked him if he wanted to be his rhythm guitarist. Wilkinson, a major Elvis fan, had met Elvis backstage at the age of eleven in 1956 when Elvis had performed in his hometown of Springfield, Missouri. The kid spoke with Elvis for more than an hour and told him he could play guitar better than him. When the boy was leaving, Elvis told him that he knew one day their paths would cross again.

Larry Muhoberac, who had played on some of Elvis' movie soundtracks, was invited by James Burton to be the TCB Band's piano player. He would leave the band after Elvis' first engagement at the International because of other commitments and be replaced by Glen D. Hardin. Muhoberac's legacy and greatest contribution to Elvis' band can be defined by his recommendation to Elvis of a little-known drummer who had played in a band with Muhoberac. That drummer turned out to be the great Ronnie Tutt.

Tutt was the perfect drummer. He instinctively knew every move Elvis would make. Tutt's style was explosive and Elvis was always slightly out of control onstage. In Tutt, Elvis had found someone that mirrored his performance and personality.

Elvis had assembled a rock-and-roll group made up of the best studio musicians in the world. He added Charlie Hodge to sing backup and play rhythm guitar. Hodge helped Elvis pick songs and rehearse material for his 1969 shows at the International and Elvis gave him the role of stage manager. Onstage Hodge provided Elvis with water and scarves, and he was there to catch Elvis' guitar when Elvis threw it at the conclusion of his opening number.

Nothing was left to chance. Elvis' weight was down to a lean and mean 165 pounds. He was thinner than he had been in years. Elvis wanted something different to wear onstage. He and Priscilla had seen the Tom Jones and Engelbert Humperdinck shows where the two stars appeared in tuxedos. Priscilla, knowing that her husband was always a trendsetter, and that he had an interest in karate, suggested a one-piece jumpsuit fashioned like a karate gi. Elvis loved the idea, reasoning that this type of outfit would allow him the freedom to move around the stage. He got in touch with designer Bill Belew who designed the black leather outfit worn so famously by Elvis on the 1968 TV special and told Bill what he wanted for his Vegas engagement. Bill then created the first of his iconic jumpsuits. He gave the custom designs to I. C. Costume Company, a Los Angeles costume manufacturer who, at the time, were most famous for the costumes they provided for the Ice Capades.

Opposite page: Onstage: Black Karate Suit with red scarf and red kick pleats. Showroom Internationale, July/August 1969.

This page: Onstage: Black Karate Suit with red trim and red/black karate belt. Showroom Internationale, July/August 1969.

Left, above, and facing page: Onstage: White Karate Suit with turquoise scarf. Showroom Internationale, July/August 1969.

Right: Onstage: White Karate Suit with black Apache scarf, Showroom Internationale, July/August 1969.

Right: Onstage: Dark blue Karate Suit with light blue scarf and light blue kick pleats, Showroom Internationale, July/August 1969.

Comedian Sammy Shore was hired by Elvis and the Colonel to open the show. Elvis chose the Imperial Quartet as his backup singers, because they had worked with him on his Grammy Award–winning gospel album *How Great Thou Art*. The Imperials were not his first choice. He had asked the Jordanaires to work with him but they were unable to leave Nashville because of studio work. The Sweet Inspirations were chosen to sing the female backup parts.

Elvis and the TCB Band went to Los Angeles and ran through two hundred songs. They spent two weeks there before leaving for Vegas, where they continued to rehearse for another two weeks. This time Elvis and the band rehearsed with the Sweet Inspirations, The Imperials, and the hotel's orchestra led by Bobby Morris.

The hotel chose to open the showroom with Barbra Streisand, who had just won an Academy Award and was considered the hottest star in the world at that moment. Elvis hadn't been onstage before a live audience in nine years. The hotel thought he would be a draw—he'd be big—but not Streisand big. Barbra Streisand's engagement began on July 2, 1969. She played to empty seats on weekdays and managed to sell out the main showroom on weekends; however, the balcony remained closed for her entire run. The hotel was surprised that the phone lines were ringing off the hook for Elvis' show and reservation requests for the Streisand show were a mere trickle. Barbra Streisand may have been a big star, but Las Vegas would have to add a new word to their vocabulary—superstar—to define Elvis Presley.

Fans flew in from Germany, France, Great Britain, Japan, and every part of America. Many had been too young to attend the Memphis Flash's fifties concerts. For most of the last decade they had watched his larger-than-life image on movie screens

Onstage: Black Karate Suit with red trim and red/black karate belt. Showroom Internationale, International Hotel. Las Vegas, Nevada: July/August 1969.

around the world, and now was their chance to see the greatest entertainer in the world in the flesh.

Kirk Kerkorian and the Colonel invited the media; reporters from the hip underground press to the staid *New York Times* were represented. Kirkorian had them flown in on his private jet. Finally, on July 31, 1969, the lights in the giant showroom dimmed —"Ladies and Gentlemen—Welcome to the International Hotel and the Elvis Presley Show."

The lights are low, the huge gold curtain slowly begins to rise, and the screaming begins. It starts spontaneously and builds into a crescendo as trumpets, electric guitars, and drums blast the rocking opening bars of "Blue Suede Shoes." As he approaches the stage a strobe light flickers and he struts slowly from one end of the platform to the other. They scream! It is July 1969 and Elvis is live onstage for the first time in almost nine years.

He is wearing a black jumpsuit with bright red satin vents on the legs. A red scarf drapes his bare chest and tassels hang from the red belt. His appearance is anything you choose to call it—gaudy, vulgar, magnificent. He looks like a king from another dimension with glaring eyes and sexy mouth. His high cheekbones and bronze face seem to be untouched by the passage of time.

Before he had opened his mouth, the audience was out of their seats screaming and giving him a standing ovation. He smiled and without warning broke into "Blue Suede Shoes," then "I Got A Woman" and "Hound Dog." He had already lifted the audience beyond belief. Exhaling a nervous sigh, he spoke: "Hi! I'm Elvis Presley." There was utter pandemonium throughout the crowd.

FOR OVER AN HOUR he flogged himself to near exhaustion. He was like a wild man! He moved with both grace and animal sexuality, his voice never missing a note as the rest of him did flips and cartwheels.

While he concentrated mostly on his own hits, he also did some other contemporary songs made popular by other artists. By the time he introduced the song that would be his next single, "Suspicious Minds," the audience was in a frenzy. He turned the stage into a karate exhibition: he kicked, crouched, and punched like a man dosed with LSD. The audience had just witnessed a seven-minute resurrection, a rebirth, a reinvention. They rose as one. The applause was deafening. He began to sing the beautiful "Can't Help Falling In Love" and held the final note for what seemed like an eternity as the gold curtain slowly descended. Once again the audience stood, screamed, and shouted "Bravo!" He stood dripping perspiration, his arms outstretched like a modern-day Christ.

Displaying more confidence than would seem possible for any performer, Elvis made believers out of all who ever doubted his talents and abilities. It was a memorable night—a night when Elvis, the founder of modern pop music, proved that he was still King.

THE VEGAS PERFORMANCES were a major triumph. The opening-night audience was there by invitation only; reporters, journalists, movie stars, recording artists, high rollers, their significant others or girlfriends, a mixture of the rich and famous. The poor boy from Tupelo via Memphis had put the red-hot spotlight on Las Vegas. With a single performance he transformed your mother's and father's Sinatra Rat Pack town into a hip and rocking place, home of the King.

The critics were unanimous in their praise. "Elvis Retains Touch In Return" was the headline in *Billboard* magazine. *Rolling Stone* said: "Elvis Is Supernatural." *Variety* called him "Superstar." The

Famed press conference at the International Hotel, July 31, 1969.

Above: unidentified guest with Elvis.

Above: Vernon Presley and Elvis.

Colonel couldn't have written better reviews.

Immediately following the opening show a press conference was held:

Q: Why have you waited so long to perform live again? Did you return to live performing because of the phenomenal successes of Welsh singer Tom Jones and British crooner Engelbert Humperdinck?

A: I think they are great but my decision to return was made in 1965 and it was hard to wait. I don't think I could have waited any longer. We had to finish up the movie commitments we had before I could start on this. I missed the live contact with the audience. It was getting harder and harder to sing to a camera all day.

Q: Can you remember first coming to Vegas?

A: Sure, I was nineteen years old. Nobody knew me. "Where you from, boy?" they would ask.

Q: How do you like being a father?

A: I like it.

Q: Are you and Priscilla planning to add to your family?

A: You'll be the first to know.

Q: What things do you do when you are home at Graceland?

A: I ride horseback, swim and talk with the tourists hanging out at the gates.

Q: How does your wife feel about you being a sex symbol again?

A: I don't know. You would have to ask her.

Q: Do your wife and daughter, Lisa Marie, accompany you?

A: Priscilla is here but my daughter is in LA with her nanny. She could not make it.

Q: How do you manage to stay so young?

A: I don't know. One of these days I'll probably fall apart. I feel I've just been lucky.

Q: Are you tired of your present type of movie? Have you grown tired of the movie plots?

A: Yes, I want to change the type of script I've been doing.

Q: What kind of scripts do you like?

A: Something with meaning. I'm going after more serious material. I couldn't dig always playing "who'd get into a fight, beat the guy up and in the next shot sing to him."

Q: Do you think it was a mistake to do so many movie soundtracks?

A: I think so. When you do ten songs in a movie they can't all be good songs. Anyway I got tired of singing to turtles.

Q: When you met the Beatles no press was allowed. Why was that?

A: I think because we could relax more that way and we could talk candidly.
Q: Do you like to wear leather jackets like the one you wore in your TV special?
A: No, I hate wearing them because they are too hot when you're working.
Q: Where did you get the design for your stage outfits?
A: I got the idea from a karate gi I once had.
Q: What do you think of the Hollywood social scene?
A: I don't go for it. I have nothing against it, but I just don't enjoy it.
Q: How long did you rehearse for these shows?
A: I practiced for three months. Today I went through three complete dress rehearsals. This was the fourth time I did that show today.
Q: How did you choose the songs for the show?
A: I just sang my favorite songs.
Q: Do you want to do more live shows?
A: I want to. I would like to play all over the world. I chose Las Vegas to play first because it is a place people come to from all over.
Q: Are you trying to change your image with songs like "In The Ghetto"?
A: No, "Ghetto" was such a great song I just couldn't pass it up after I heard it. There are a lot of new records out now that have the same sound I started but they're better, I mean, you can't compare a song like "Yesterday" with "Hound Dog," can you?
Q: Why have you led such a secluded life all these years?
A: It's not secluded. I'm just sneaky.
Q: Is it true that you dye your hair?
A: Sure, I've always done it for the movies.
Q: Did you enjoy performing live again?
A: Yes, this has been one of the most exciting nights of my life.
Q: Did you feel nervous during the show?
A: For the first three songs or so. I didn't feel relaxed until after "Love Me Tender," then I loosened up. I thought, "What the heck. Get with it man or you might be out of a job tomorrow."
Q: Do you have a share in the International Hotel?
A: No I don't
Q: Why did you choose a Negro backup group?
A: They help me get a feeling that gets to my soul.
Q: Have you ever met England's Cliff Richard?
A: Yes, I met him in Germany a long time ago.
Q: Mr. Presley, I've been sent here to offer you one million pounds sterling to make two appearances at the Wembley Empire Stadium in England. This price will include a documentary that will be filmed during and after the shows. It will only take twenty-four hours.
A: [Elvis points to Colonel Parker] You'll have to ask him about that. [Colonel Parker]: Just put down the deposit.
Q: Elvis, how much do you get paid for these performances?
A [Colonel Parker]: We are pleased with the deal. I am glad he is here.
Q: Is it true that you get paid in International Hotel stocks?
A [Colonel Parker]: Certainly not. The only thing we get for free are the crickets in the rooms.
Q: Do you still own about ten cars?
A: I have never owned that many. Only four or five at the most.
Q: Elvis, is there any other individual you would rather be?
A: Are you kidding?

Charo and Elvis Dressing Room, International Hotel, July/August 1969.

CHAPTER 5

Everybody Loves Somebody Sometime

January 26, 1970–February 23, 1970

Opposite and right: Onstage: Blue with blue Tapestry Suit. Showroom Internationale, January/February 1970.

In January 1970 Elvis vacationed in Hawaii and worked on his tan in preparation for his upcoming Vegas shows. Colonel Parker booked him for his second monthlong engagement at the International Hotel. He worried it might be too soon to go back. January was a down period in Las Vegas. People were still recovering from the holiday season and still paying for the Christmas gifts bought for friends and family. Elvis, along with all members of the Elvis Presley Show, arrived in Vegas on January 19, 1970, to begin rehearsals.

The hotel instructed their operators that reservations for the Elvis show could only be made by guests staying at the hotel. The hotel realized that Elvis fans were different from any other stars'. They would travel from near and far, check into the hotel, and stay for two weeks, attending two shows a night, every night. Elvis' winter engagement was a complete sell-out. The International announced they would not be taking any more reservations in mid-January.

Opposite, and this page: Onstage: Blue with blue Tapestry Suit. Showroom Internationale, January/February 1970.

Elvis had now replaced original TCB Band pianist Larry Muhoberac with Glen D. Hardin. Hardin played piano and organ and was also a talented song arranger whose arrangements would be heard during this engagement. Drummer Ronnie Tutt, backbone of Elvis' band, was now working with Andy Williams. Bob Lanning replaced Tutt for this engagement.

Monday, January 26, 1970, Elvis opened his second season. He replaced "Blue Suede Shoes" with "All Shook Up" and sang "That's All Right," a song he had recorded sixteen years earlier at Sun Studios in Memphis. He mixed his own hits, both old and new, with songs made popular by other artists. He rocked Creedence Clearwater Revival's "Proud Mary," for example, and Elvis' version would have made John Fogerty jealous. He ran through "Walk A Mile In My Shoes" and Neil Diamond's "Sweet Caroline." By the time he finished, these songs belonged to him. The

This page and opposite:
Onstage: Beaded Suit. Showroom Internationale, January/February 1970.

Bobby Morris thirty-piece orchestra provided wonderful accompaniment to the ballads "Don't Cry Daddy" and "The Wonder Of You."

Elvis wore karate-inspired jumpsuits that differed from the far simpler versions he had worn in 1969. For this engagement his suits came in a variety of colors: black, white, and blue with a tapestry design that accentuated the suits' plunging necklines. The long macramé belt that completed his splendor often slipped and moved during Elvis' showstopping version of "Polk Salad Annie." He would stop and look mis-

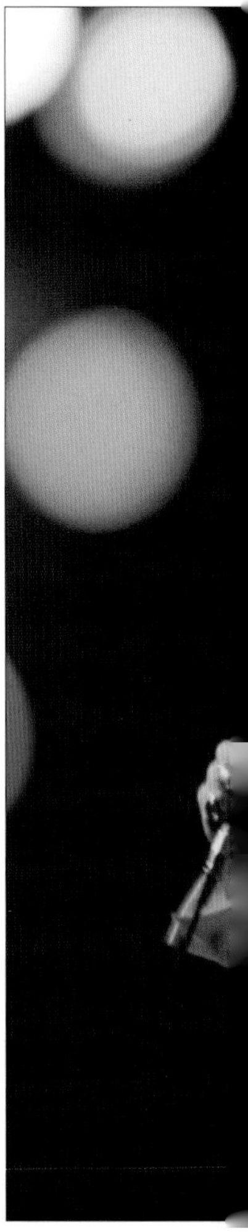

Opposite page, this, and following: Onstage: White with black Tapestry Suit. Showroom Internationale, January/February 1970.

Maître d' Emilio Muscelli and Elvis. Imperial Suite, International Hotel, January/February 1970.

chievously at the women surrounding the stage. He was fully aware that the belts' long ties were hanging between his legs, an open sexual invitation. He grinned, straightening the belt, a bump—a grind—a shoulder—both shoulders—every part of his body pulsating to the bass and drum beat. He growled, threw up an arm as "Polk Salad" came to a climax.

Elvis told the audience, "I'd like to sing my new RCA escape—er—record, 'Kentucky Rain.'" Following "Kentucky Rain" Elvis performed a six-minute version of "Suspicious Minds" that included karate splits and a half dozen kicks, draining both himself and the audience. He thanked them for coming and closed the show with "Can't Help Falling In Love." As the curtain fell, Elvis, down on his knees, sweat dripping, raised his arms in a final salute. At every show women rushed the stage, often throwing themselves at Elvis. They tossed bras, panties, room keys, and notes. The audience were on their feet, their applause and screams threatening to bring the entire showroom down.

RCA was on hand from February 16 through February 19. They recorded Elvis' shows and eight of the songs would be included, along with two additional songs they had previously taped in August 1969, on Elvis' next album, *On Stage February 1970*.

On occasion Elvis would sit at the piano and sing. One evening Fats Domino, who was performing in the International's lounge, came to see Elvis' show. Elvis surprised the rock-and-roll legend when he sat down at the piano and told the audience, "I used to go by the name of Fats Domino but I've lost a lot of weight." Elvis then played "Lawdy Miss Clawdy," segueing into Fats' signature song, "Blueberry Hill." When he finished he said, "Ladies and gentlemen. Allow me to introduce the real Fats Domino." He asked Fats to stand up and take a bow. Elvis continued, saying how important Chuck Berry, Little Richard, and Fats Domino were to the birth of rock and roll. He went on, "You know what? I'm the only white boy in the bunch."

During this engagement Elvis suffered the dreaded "Vegas throat," a condition brought on by the dry desert air. He mentioned this to the audience on occasion but neither his shows nor voice seemed affected by it.

At the dinner show on closing night, Monday, February 23, Elvis performed an extra-long show. He recognized another hero of his in the audience and gave a shout-out to Dean Martin. Smiling, he sang a bit of Dino's, "Everybody Loves Somebody Sometime." When he sang "Love Me Tender," Priscilla approached the stage and as they embraced, the audience applauded. As Priscilla made her way back to her booth, Elvis joked, "Haven't I seen that girl before?"

Private photo of Vernon Presley and Elvis in the hallway of the twenty-ninth-floor Imperial Suite, International Hotel, August/September 1970.

CHAPTER 6

Hot Time In The Summer

August 10, 1970—September 8, 1970

THIS ENGAGEMENT WAS something special—a new challenge for Elvis Presley. In May, the Colonel finalized a new contract with MGM. It was announced that the movie company would be filming Elvis' latest Las Vegas engagement, which Colonel Parker and the International Hotel were now calling "The Elvis Summer Festival."

ELVIS' MONDAY, AUGUST 10 OPENING SHOW was hours away, and Colonel Parker was working hard to transform the huge hotel into Elvis World. Men on ladders decorated the entrance to the hotel with hundreds of red, gold, purple, and green silk triangular pennants reading "Elvis Summer Festival." The signs hung from the ceiling on strings, making the grand entrance even grander.

The fans had come from around the world and were gathering hours early for a chance to stand in the long reservation line, a line that stretched from the office located just outside the showroom through the large casino and out into the parking lot. Once inside the hotel you were greeted with the Elvis souvenir booth, manned by two attractive ladies, a blonde and a brunette, who smiled while they took your money. Elvis tour books were $1.50, Elvis posters were $2.00, or you could purchase the ultimate souvenir, an authentic Elvis scarf, just like the ones he wore onstage, for $5.00.

In the casino the dealers and pit bosses wore old-fashioned straw hats that were made of Styrofoam with a paper band surrounding the top, all proclaiming "Elvis Summer Festival." The Colonel didn't miss an opportunity or space to continue his massive promotion. The bars and restaurants were covered in canvas banners and three-by-twelve-foot Mylar displays showing Elvis in concert and reading "Hear Elvis on RCA Records" were stapled to the walls .

Every room in the hotel was booked for the

entire month. Elvis' show was sold out: two shows a night, seven days a week. Elvis' amazing fans, the most loyal and fanatical, were back; the French Fan Club wearing their "I Love Elvis" buttons greeted fans from England who wore Elvis T-shirts. Fans from Japan mixed with fans from America and the crowd itself became a huge part of the Elvis experience.

This scene was made even more bizarre by the thirty-eight-man camera crew who filmed everyone and everything for a documentary. There were interviews with fans, bellboys, dealers, bartenders, and even someone who was not an Elvis fan but happened

Onstage: White Chain Suit with white macramé belt. Showroom Internationale, August/September 1970.

Above left: Elvis with a fan outside dressing room, International Hotel, August/September 1970.

Right: Cow Palace, San Francisco, California: November 13, 1970. White Ladder Suit with red leather trim.

to be in the lobby of the restaurant, wondering what all the fuss was about.

MGM had filmed Elvis' rehearsals in Los Angeles earlier. While the rehearsals were going on, show business bible *Variety* reported that the International, Las Vegas' biggest hotel, was considering closing half the showroom after Elvis' next appearance at the hotel. The word was that no one but Elvis was able to fill the room. When Elvis saw the article he said, "If they think by cutting the room in half they are going to have me play there four months a year they are mistaken. I never thought the showroom was too big."

Emilio Muscelli was the head maître d' and the most important man in Las Vegas as far as Elvis' fans were concerned. Emilio was born in Italy and worked at New York City's famed Copa Cabana before moving to Las Vegas in 1952. Over the years he was employed by the Sands, Flamingo, and the Dunes hotels. When Kirk Kerkorian built the International he hired Emilio, and it was Emilio who decided where you sat for the Elvis show. It has long been rumored that he made more than $100,000 for every thirty-day Elvis engagement at the hotel. Truth be told, he was kindhearted and often gave fans he knew premier stage-front seats for free. He knew that many Elvis fans scrimped and saved just to get to Vegas. Emilio made sure that presidents of Elvis' fan clubs had extra souvenir Elvis menus from the dinner show to bring home for their members. On occasion he even arranged meetings with Elvis backstage for some of the fans who traveled thousands of miles to see their idol. His kindness makes him a piece of the Elvis legend.

his dressing room, perform, and follow the same route back to his suite, then repeat for the next month.

Colonel Parker now had permanent offices at the hotel that took up a large part of the fourth floor. Upon exiting the elevator you were greeted by the world's largest stuffed teddy bear and hound dog. They sat six feet wide and ten feet tall. The hallway walls that weren't covered by the Colonel's animals were covered with Elvis billboards. Colonel Parker was the ringmaster of this circus, and make no mistake about it, he ran a tight army.

On opening night Elvis was in great spirits. He told the crowd that MGM would be filming his shows

Tour photos. Veterans Memorial Coliseum, Phoenix, Arizona: September 9, 1970. Beaded Fringe Suit with turquoise macramé belt.

This latest Elvis extravaganza had Emilio sitting in his office checking the celebrity reservations. He wondered where to put Dwayne Hickman, Juliet Prowse, Sid Caesar, Xavier Cugat, Charo, Herb Alpert, Trini Lopez, Dale Robertson, Jack Benny, George Hamilton, Sonny Liston, Lana Turner, Sammy Davis Jr., and Cary Grant, among others.

Meanwhile, Elvis was up in his Imperial Suite sleeping. A prisoner of his own celebrity he would take the elevator to the hotel kitchen, walk from there to

Convention Center, Miami, Florida: September 12, 1970. Beaded Fringe Suit with turquoise macramé belt.

and not to let the cameras "throw you and don't you throw the cameras!" The women in the audience were wilder and crazier than had been the case at Elvis' earlier engagements. This time they actually climbed on tables and ran through the steak dinner plates trying to get to him. Elvis sang all the songs that the audience expected to hear and added incredible new performances of Simon and Garfunkel's "Bridge Over Troubled Water" and the Righteous Brothers' "You've Lost That Lovin' Feeling." Opening night was a smash.

Elvis' career was on fire and with that came all of the temptations afforded to a rock-and-roll king. Priscilla was by this time only allowed to come to Vegas for opening and closing nights. She spent the rest of the engagement at home with their daughter and was not oblivious to Elvis' after-hours activities.

Kathy Westmoreland, who replaced Millie Kirkham as a soprano, got to know her boss intimately, as did Barbara Leigh, a beautiful young starlet who was dating the head of MGM, Jim Aubrey. Aubrey was pro-

This page: Onstage: Beaded Fringe Suit with white macramé belt. Showroom Internationale, August/September 1970.

ducing the documentary *Elvis: A Film About Him*, the original title of what would later be called *Elvis: That's the Way It Is*. Joyce Bova, who had met and spent time with Elvis at his August 1969 Vegas engagement, entered the picture again. Like Elvis, Joyce was a twin; she was also a gorgeous brunette. During this 1970 engagement Elvis saw both Barbara and Joyce, often flying one out of Vegas while the other was landing.

Then Patricia Ann Parker filed a paternity suit against Elvis. Parker, a waitress in Los Angeles, claimed to have had sex with Elvis in January 1970 at the International Hotel. She was requesting child support for the child she named Jason Peter Presley. She offered a photograph of her and Elvis outside his dressing room as proof. Later both Elvis and Patricia Parker took blood tests to determine if Elvis was the baby's father, and Elvis dodged the bullet when the test proved that the baby boy was not his.

Top, opposite page: Onstage: Tour Photo Forum of Englewood, California. I Got Lucky Suit with red macramé belt. Showroom Internationale, August/September 1970.

A death threat on Elvis' life was received in an envelope at the front desk of the International. Inside the envelope was a Vegas menu that had a picture of Elvis on the front cover with a drawing of a gun pointed at Elvis' head. The madman was demanding $50,000 or Elvis would be shot at his August 30 show. Colonel Parker met with the FBI and hotel management in his office. They wanted Elvis to cancel the show, but he refused, saying he wouldn't give the "bastard the satisfaction." The evening of the show FBI agents were in the audience. They suspected if an attempt were made it would be from close range. The Memphis Mafia were armed and ready, and Elvis himself had a Derringer in his boot and performed most of the show standing sideways, looking at Glen D. Hardin's piano, hoping to give the shooter a smaller target. When a fan shouted "Elvis!" he froze, but the fan only wanted Elvis to sing his favorite song. Nothing came of the threat but from that night onward Elvis increased security by having the Memphis Mafia licensed to carry guns.

Elvis added a special 3:00 a.m. show on September 8 because the demand for tickets to his September 7 closing show was so great. The season came to an end, though as Colonel Parker said to those who missed the shows, "You can come and see the movie."

Far left: Tour Photo Forum of Englewood, California. I Got Lucky Suit with red macramé belt worn in Showroom Internationale, August/September 1970.

Left: Onstage: Houston Astrodome, February/March 1970.

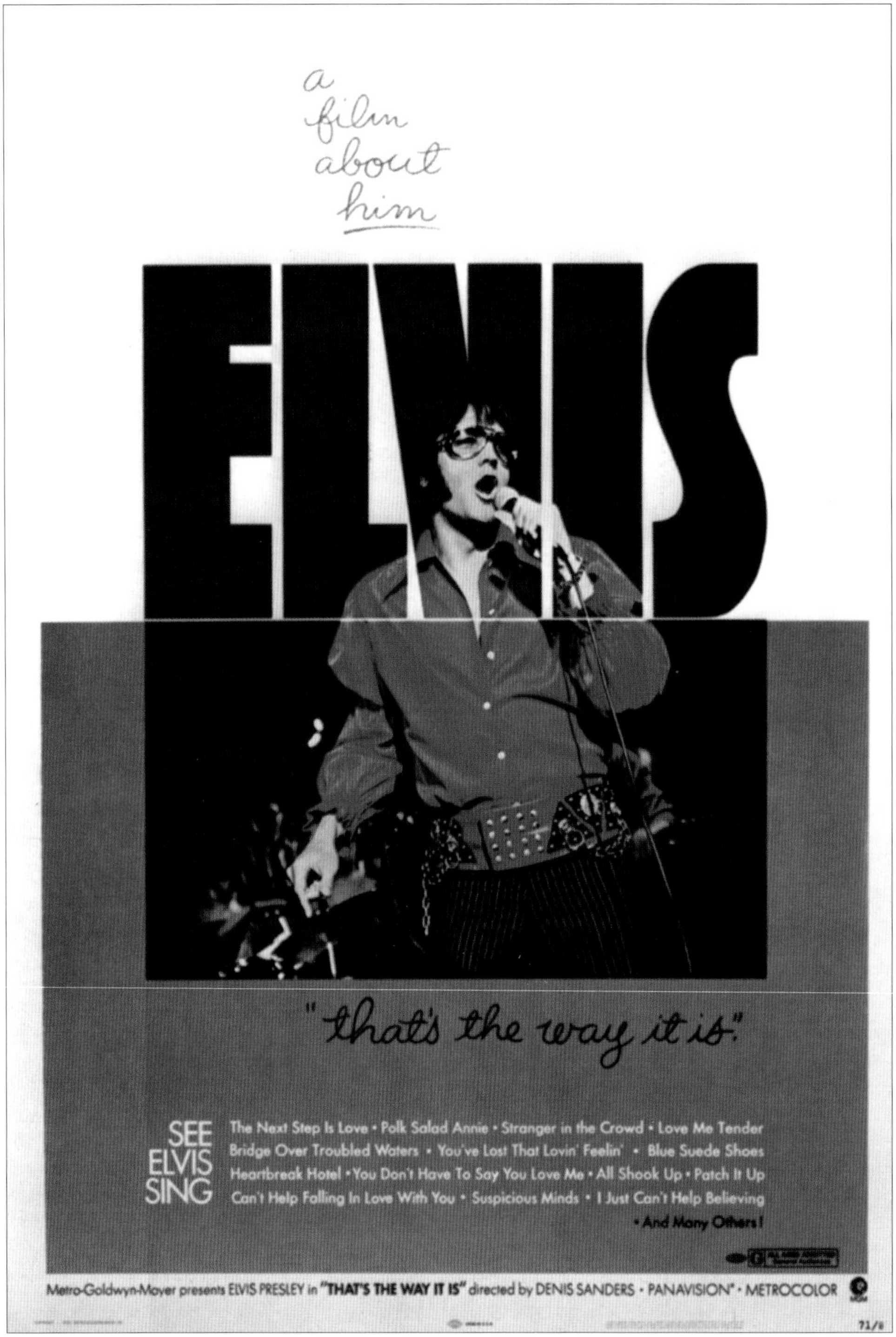

Original MGM one-sheet,
Elvis: That's the Way It Is
movie poster., 1970.

CHAPTER 7

Elvis: That's the Way It Is

July 14, 1970–November 11, 1970

ELVIS' THIRTY-SECOND MOVIE was originally titled *Elvis: A Film About Him*. This was the working title and early promos featured this, while in Paris the title was *The Elvis Show* and MGM Japan called the documentary *Elvis*. *Elvis: That's the Way It Is* had a strange beginning. Its concept was born in early 1970 when Colonel Parker came up with a new money-making idea. Why not present the Elvis Show as a pay-per-view one-night-only closed circuit event? This would be accomplished by broadcasting Elvis live in Las Vegas via satellite throughout movie theaters across America. Elvis would receive $1 million, the largest sum ever paid to a performer for one concert.

Filmways Productions presented Elvis and the Colonel with a nonrefundable check in the amount of $100,000 as a deposit. Days later entertainment reporter Robert Hilburn wrote in the *Los Angeles Times* that Elvis Presley had agreed to a pay-per-view concert that would be broadcast live from Las Vegas in two hundred theaters across America on August 8, 1970. The following week the Colonel called off the deal, telling reporters that the closed-circuit broadcast was canceled because of the leak to the press citing Hilburn's story. The Colonel then pitched the idea to Kirk Kerkorian who, as owner of the International, had worked closely with both Elvis and the Colonel. Kerkorian also happened to be the new owner of MGM. Finally, after all these years, a film showing Elvis, the man behind the image, was conceived. The concert documentary would be filmed in Las Vegas during Elvis' Summer Festival at the International Hotel.

MGM began filming at Elvis' rehearsals for his August 1970 Vegas engagement. The rehearsals were filmed over the next three weeks, first at RCA's studio on Sunset Boulevard and later at MGM's studios in Culver City. Elvis and the band worked on sixty songs. The film crews' cameras were almost always present

as Elvis decided what songs to include in his show. Five of the rehearsals at Culver City were captured by the MGM cameras. Elvis, satisfied with the way the songs were rounding into shape, flew to Palm Springs for five days of rest and relaxation.

He returned to Los Angeles on July 22 and booked another rehearsal at RCA's studio where he and the band worked out from 7:00 p.m. until 1:00 a.m. Once again, the film crew was there. The following evening Elvis requested that no cameras be present so that he and the band could get down to some uninterrupted preparations. At the request of the film's director, two-time Academy Award winner Denis Sanders, Elvis returned to MGM for more filming on July 25. Sanders was able to capture twenty songs on film.

Rehearsal for the MGM motion picture Elvis: That's the Way It Is. *MGM Studios, Culver City, July 1970.*

On August 4, six days before opening night, Elvis, the band, and backup singers moved the rehearsals to the International, where MGM filmed them for insertion in the documentary. Three days

Rehearsal for Elvis: That's the Way It Is. *International Hotel, August 4, 1970.*

later, MGM again started filming, this time in the main showroom with Joe Guercio and his orchestra. This was the first time the two worked together and Joe wasn't impressed with Elvis' rehearsal methods. Later he came to understand and admire Elvis' style. With the full orchestra present this rehearsal was featured prominently in the movie, and every song was performed during this engagement.

Denis Sanders shared the following thoughts about working with Elvis on *Elvis: That's the Way It Is*:

> There is a curiosity about Elvis Presley, just as there is concerning Howard Hughes or the Mafia or any entity who avoids the public eye. Having recently created the MGM motion picture *Elvis: That's the Way It Is* and enjoyed a close working relationship with him, I am repeatedly asked by the press and by my friends what Elvis is all about.
>
> What impressed me most and certainly made my job easier is that Elvis is an absolute professional of the first order. Perhaps blinded by his image and his income people think of him as a legend when what he basically is, and has been for over fifteen years, is a working musician. Inside observers are initially surprised that in putting a show together, Elvis is the captain of the ship. From the songs to be performed through the lighting, sound, and blending of the sections of the orchestra, Elvis makes all of the decisions.
>
> When we had to intrude on his time, he always listened to reason. He knows what makes sense and what doesn't. He seems quite good-natured with a rare sense of humor, but he can get quite uptight when he observes a lack of professionalism or when there is some artistic shortcoming on his part.
>
> Once onstage, before an audience, the thing that he has as a performer is what Brando had at the height of his powers as an actor. That is, you can never anticipate what he's going to do next. Each of his shows is entirely different. Though he is well prepared, it is instinct that guides him onstage. It is difficult to take your eyes off him. I found it difficult to take the cameras off him and focus on some other aspect of the show.
>
> These professional observations don't seem to satisfy those who question me about Elvis. On a personal level, however, I can't be too enlightening. When I began preparing the movie it was quite clear that Elvis' personal life was not to concern me. That was fine. I would not do the real Elvis

Rehearsal for
Elvis: That's the Way It Is.
International Hotel,
July 1970.

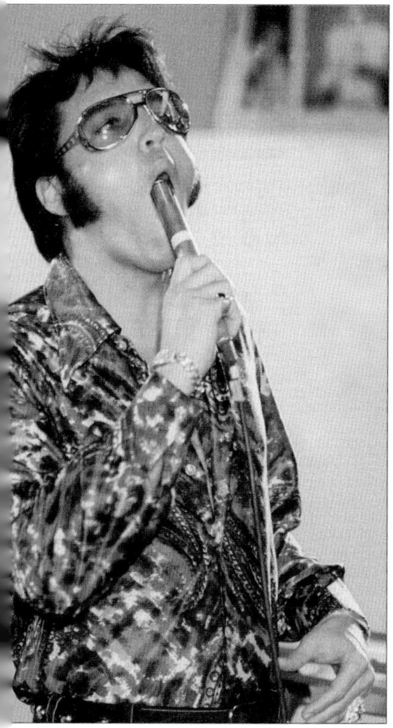
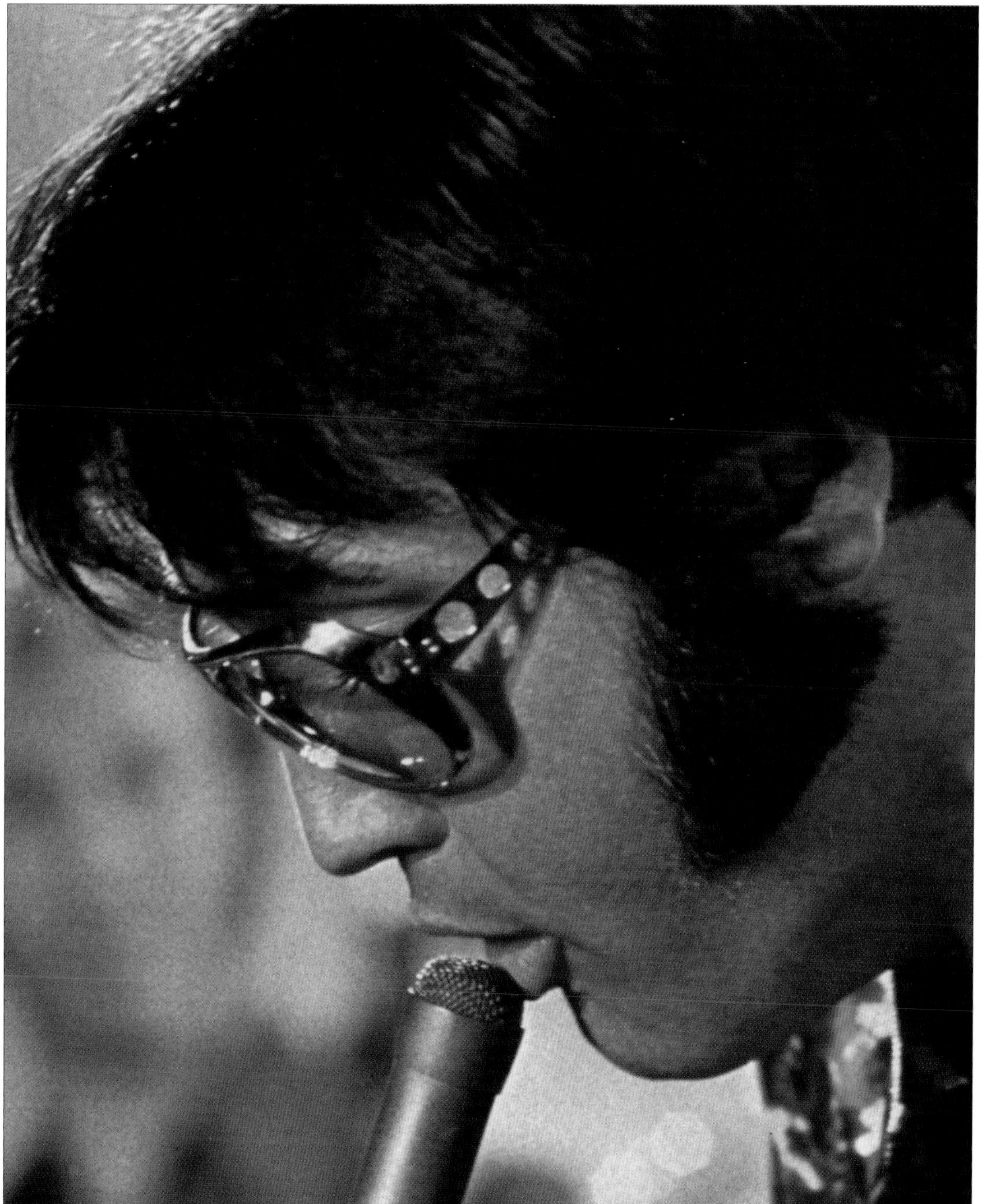

Onstage for Elvis: That's the Way It Is. *White Concho Suit with white macramé concho belt. Dinner show, Showroom Internationale, August 7, 1970*

Top left and left: Onstage rehearsal for Elvis: That's the Way It Is. *Showroom Internationale, August 7, 1970.*

Right: Onstage for Elvis: That's the Way It Is. *White Concho Suit with dark blue macramé belt. Showroom Internationale, August 1970.*

Onstage for Elvis: That's the Way It Is. *White Chain Suit with white macramé belt. Showroom Internationale, midnight show, August 12, 1970.*

Presley personal story unless I had complete control over the film. Otherwise, you're in the same position that William Manchester was when he wrote about the Kennedy family.

Though there is great secrecy concerning Elvis—his family and friends won't talk to outsiders about him—I don't get the feeling there is anything to hide. He seems well adjusted to the necessarily peculiar way of life he leads. He appears happily married to a beautiful woman and

Left:
Onstage for Elvis: That's the Way It Is. *Beaded Fringe Suit with white macramé belt. Showroom Internationale, opening show, August 10, 1970.*

he's a proud father. He enjoys the fruits of his wealth. His relative isolation has allowed his life to remain uncluttered and I guess he prefers it that way.

It was never stated, but I got the impression, that my intrusion into his private life would not be welcome.

We were, however, able to observe and film Elvis and his fans in a variety of atmospheres. We began by capturing his rehearsals and filmed one week of his shows there at the International Hotel. Additionally we took our cameras to Phoenix for the commencement of his first concert tour in thirteen years, plus a fan convention attended by thousands of people in Luxembourg.

The way people respond to this man is an important part of Elvis: *That's the Way It Is*. Did you know he has the largest and most dedicated following in the history of show business? When he appears in Las Vegas the International Hotel must add 30 percent to its staff just to cope with the traffic that comes from around the world.

One fan who we interviewed for possible inclusion in our film explained the phenomenon this way. She said, "Being an Elvis fan is like being in love. You wake up one morning and that's just the way it is. You don't know why you are a fan, just as you can't explain why you're in love."

As I said, in the way of personal gossip I can't tell you any more about Elvis' nonworking hours as I can tell you about Howard Hughes!

I do know, though, that more of the real Elvis Presley will be seen in our film than the public has ever seen before.

Right:
Tour photo. Cow Palace, San Francisco, November 13, 1970. White Ladder Suit with red leather trim worn at Elvis: That's the Way It Is *dinner show at Showroom Internationale, August 13, 1970.*

Far, right:
Private photo of Elvis with Mario, his favorite waiter, at the Imperial Suite, This photo and scene were not included in Elvis: That's the Way It Is. *Las Vegas, August 1970.*

INTERNATIONAL
NOW
LAS VEGAS
HILTON
NOW
INTERNATIONAL
HOTEL
NOW
ELVIS
THRU
FEB.
23
HEAR ELVIS ON RCA RECORDS AND TAPES

CHAPTER 8

Comic Book Hero

January 26, 1971–February 23, 1971

Commuter bench with the Hilton International Hotel in background. Colonel Parker has these Elvis benches strategically placed throughout the city. January/February 1971.

AFTER COMPLETING HIS 1970 Summer Festival, Elvis flew to Phoenix, Arizona, to begin his first concert tour since the 1950s. The Phoenix concert took place on Wednesday, September 9 and parts of it appear during the opening credits for *Elvis: That's the Way It Is*. Elvis gave eight performances in six cities. A new pattern was developing, a pattern that would keep him crisscrossing the United States for the rest of his life. Lake Tahoe became a part of his itinerary and, of course, the Vegas winter and summer festivals continued.

January 1971 began momentously for Elvis. Highway 51, which runs in front of Graceland, became Elvis Presley Boulevard. Elvis was very proud of this and said he considered this achievement the greatest honor of his career.

On January 9 Memphis' newspapers, the *Memphis Press-Scimitar* and the *Commercial Appeal*, reported that Elvis was chosen by the National Jaycees as one of the ten outstanding young men of the year. Elvis was in Los Angeles rehearsing at MGM for his upcoming Vegas engagement when he learned of the honor. He remembered how poor he and his family had been in Tupelo, their financial struggles in Memphis, the public housing at Lauderdale Courts, his mom and dad working incredibly hard. This award showed just how far he had come. Elvis was the living, breathing American Dream.

The Jaycees had been honoring distinguished men since the 1930s. All had one thing in common—they had to be younger than thirty-five. Other honorees include Howard Hughes, John F. Kennedy, Robert Kennedy, Leonard Bernstein, Ralph Nader, Henry Kissinger, Orson Welles, and Nelson Rockefeller.

Memphis' Shelby County Sheriff, Bill Morris, a close friend of Elvis', had suggested that Elvis be considered for the award. Other honorees in that year included Ronald Ziegler (press secretary to President Richard Nixon), Thomas Atkins (Boston's first black councilman), Dr. Mario Capecchi (biochemist), Dr. George Todaro, (cancer researcher), and Rudy Perpich (lieutenant governor of Minnesota).

Former President of the United States Lyndon B. Johnson was on the final selection committee. Vice

Onstage: Cisco Kid Suit, black and green with gold World Champion Attendance belt. Hilton Showroom, January/February 1971.

Onstage:
Elvis Now Suit with white macramé belt and blue turquoise conchos. Hilton Showroom, January/February 1971.

President Spiro Agnew was scheduled to be the keynote speaker. He was unable to attend and was replaced by the then ambassador to the United Nations and future President of the United States, George H. W. Bush.

Elvis and Priscilla flew back to Memphis on January 15 for the award ceremony that would take place on January 16. They missed the dinner that was attended by all of the honorees because their plane arrived late at the Memphis airport. Elvis was both nervous and excited about the acceptance speech that he would deliver. Priscilla recalled in *Elvis and Me*:

> He stayed up in his office next to our bedroom writing on this little scratch pad and he would show me what he had written and ask me what I thought. He was so nervous about making that speech. He was going to be in front of other millionaires and he wanted to be explicit and intelligent to them. So he read it to me and I was amazed. I couldn't believe it came out of him. He shocked me with the eloquence of his speech. I would have thought he took it from something—I wouldn't have put it past him to do that, clever as he was—but I witnessed it. I mean it was just beautiful.

On January 16 Elvis was honored as one of America's Ten Young Men of the Year. The couple attended the prayer breakfast at the Holiday Inn Rivermont. Elvis wore a black fur suit and his thick gold and diamond belt given to him by the International Hotel for breaking every existing Las Vegas attendance record. Priscilla looked every bit his queen with her long flowing hair and white minidress. Elvis' bodyguards did their best to protect Elvis and Priscilla from the overeager press and fans wanting autographs.

The *Memphis Press-Scimitar* reported there was a question-and-answer session and Elvis was asked if he thought today's music had an adverse effect on young people. Elvis' reply was brilliant: "Yes, I don't go along with music advocating drugs and desecration of the flag. I think an entertainer is for entertaining and to make people happy." When the prayer breakfast ended the nominees were asked about their religious beliefs. The majority said they didn't belong to a church and they weren't comfortable with organized religion. Elvis' response was, "Religion is very important, not in the organized sense, but in the sense that I have called on God many times for strength. God is a living presence in all of us."

At the afternoon luncheon Elvis was reportedly impressed by George H. W. Bush's speech. Elvis then invited the other award winners, Jaycee representatives, and their wives back to Graceland for cocktails. He proudly showed his esteemed guests his home and after cocktails took the entire party for a formal dinner at Memphis' five-star Four Flames restaurant.

The award ceremony at Ellis Auditorium was held at 7:30 that evening. Elvis was recognized for philanthropy, his character, and achievements as an entertainer. As Elvis stood and approached the podium, he was living proof that in America, no matter where you came from, no matter who you were, if you have strength and courage there is no limit to what you could achieve. Elvis looked hard at the group of talented and extraordinary men surrounding him and began to address them:

> When I was a child, ladies and gentleman, I was a dreamer. I read comic books and I was the hero of the comic book. I saw movies and I was the hero in the movie. So every dream that I ever dreamed has come true a hundred times. These gentlemen over here, these are the type who care, are dedicated. You realize if it's not possible that they might be building the kingdom, it's not far-

> fetched from reality. I'd like to say that I learned very early in life that without a song the road would never end, without a song a man ain't got a friend, without a song the day would never end, without a song . . . so I keep singing a song. Good night. Thank you.

ELVIS FLEW TO VEGAS on January 24 and rehearsed for two days. There were more death threats, but if Elvis was bothered by them he didn't show it. On Tuesday, January 26 he began his fourth monthlong engagement. Many songs from the previous Vegas seasons remained, but some major changes to the show were apparent and Elvis' stage entrance was grand. He strutted from right to left on the huge stage to the otherworldly strains of "Also Sprach Zarathustra," the Richard Strauss composition written in 1894 that could have been written with Elvis in mind. When the spotlight shone on Elvis, his elaborate jumpsuit reflected the light; his attire had become cutting-edge, and he looked like the man of the future.

Elvis was more guarded and less talkative than during his previous Vegas appearances. The fans again came from everywhere in the world, and the audiences who were never tame grew even wilder.

Elvis added many ballads to his repertoire, the highlight being the gospel song "How Great Thou Art." He hit notes during this performance that many in the audience swore could have opened heaven's gates. Only Elvis could segue from an inspirational "How Great Thou Art" to a rocker "Hound Dog" without missing a beat. He sang Kris Kristofferson's "Help Me Make It Through The Night" with heartfelt urgency, and during this engagement he sometimes closed his show with an incredible version of *The Man of La Mancha*'s "The Impossible Dream."

He had not grown complacent about the repeatedly sold-out shows, and Elvis thought nothing of stopping a song and telling the band to start over if he felt they were playing in the wrong key. On more than one occasion he singled out drummer Ronnie Tutt for playing too fast.

In his dressing room after his performances he would meet and greet celebrities who had attended his show. He would then retire to his lavish Imperial Suite on the thirtieth floor.

Joyce Bova, who bore a striking resemblance to Priscilla, spent quite a bit of time with Elvis during this engagement and found him bored and distracted. To amuse himself he started playing with guns and accidentally shot the chandelier hanging in his suite.

Elvis' use of uppers to wake up and downers to go to sleep were becoming a constant in his life. The years were catching up with him. His practice of turning night into day and day into night was becoming harder to manage. His marriage was hitting the skids, and he no longer felt challenged by his four-week stints at the International. He told the guys that he felt like a prisoner up in his suite and was envious of the people, his fans, who could enjoy Las Vegas for all it had to offer.

Elvis closed his winter season in Vegas with a rousing performance. He was in a playful mood and the audience joined in with laughter and applause. He introduced his father and the Colonel. He told the crowd, "You, ladies and gentlemen, who have come out to see the show, I can't tell you how much I appreciate it. The economy of the country is down and you came anyway. Thank you all very much." Elvis ended the show with an extraordinary rendition of "The Impossible Dream." The audience that had come to expect "Can't Help Falling In Love" were surprised as they stood as one and shouted for more. Elvis posed with his arms outstretched and then he was gone.

Onstage: Cisco Kid Suit, black and blue with studded lion head belt. Hilton Showroom, January/February 1971.

SUMMER FESTIVAL
NOW
LAS VEGAS HILTON
SUMMER FESTIVAL
NOW
IN PERSON
ELVIS
HEAR ELVIS ON RCA RECORDS AND TAPES

CHAPTER 9

Don't Ask Forever

August 9, 1971—September 6, 1971

Left: Hilton Coffee Shop/Restaurant, Hilton Hotel, August/September 1971.

In July 1971 Elvis made his first Lake Tahoe appearance. The room was smaller than the showroom at the International Hotel and Elvis enjoyed the intimate feeling of being closer to his audience. This Tahoe engagement was a complete sell-out.

Elvis had five days off after his Tahoe closing night before opening his fifth Vegas engagement at the Las Vegas Hilton—formerly the International. During this summer festival Elvis received three death threats and began carrying a four-shot Derringer in his boot while performing onstage.

As was the case with Elvis' earlier Vegas engagements, the entire monthlong Summer Festival sold out in less than twenty-four hours. The posters, billboards, and banners were everywhere and the fans, as always, represented all countries and nationalities.

Elvis' show was very short; for the most part, it lasted only forty-five minutes. Elvis was often ill and became lackadaisical onstage. He simply went from

Right: Elvis and Joyce Bova, Imperial Suite, Hilton Hotel, August/September 1971.

Right:
Onstage: Cisco Kid Suit, white and black with gold World Championship Attendance belt. Hilton Showroom, Las Vegas, August/ September 1971.

Middle:
Onstage: Cisco Kid Suit, black and red with gold World Championship Attendance belt. Hilton Showroom, August/September 1971.

Tour photo. Fair Grounds Arena, Oklahoma City, Oklahoma: November 16, 1970. White Tie Suit with beaded white macramé belt.

Below:
On stage: Cisco Kid suit, black and white with studded lion head belt. Hilton Showroom, Hilton Hotel. Las Vegas, Nevada: August/September 1971.

one song to the next with very little dialogue between himself and his audience.

Elvis suffered an allergic reaction to one of the medications he was taking for a throat infection. He had problems hitting the high notes and appeared onstage with a swollen face. While he still moved around, it was noticeable that he was laboring. As usual Elvis performed "Suspicious Minds" with excitement and a great karate display that had the women in the audience spellbound, their husbands and boyfriends standing and shouting "King!"

Although the local press attacked Elvis' show, calling his performances sloppy and mentioning that he had put on a few pounds, the fans saw things differently. Elvis' natural charisma and magnetism overwhelmed them. From the moment he materialized on stage to the last note of "Can't Help Falling In Love" he was theirs and they belonged to him. He broke his own attendance records and received the Bing Crosby Golden Achievement Award from Bing's son, Chris.

Elvis' male backup group, the Imperial Quartet, left the Elvis show after this Vegas stint to tour with country singer and sausage tycoon Jimmy Dean. This Vegas season was notable for the changes that were occurring in Elvis' personal life.

The boys in the band grumbled that the material had grown stale. Others in Elvis' inner circle were concerned about the doctors who were giving Elvis

Personal photo of Elvis in elevator from Imperial Suite to showroom. Cisco Kid Suit, black and green with gold World Championship Attendance belt. Hilton Hotel, August/ September 1971.

his daily shots. Elvis' behavior after his so-called B_{12} injections was growing more bizarre; in addition, Elvis had, once again, began a metaphysical journey that included books, meditation, and self-prescribed medications.

It was at this point that Priscilla revealed that she was involved with Mike Stone. Priscilla was no longer a child, she was now in her mid-twenties, and she was not willing to stay at home playing the little housewife while her husband bedded every groupie and starlet that crossed his path.

On August 16, a date that would later become the blackest day in rock-and-roll history, Joyce Bova, Elvis' sometime girlfriend, arrived in Vegas carrying a gift Elvis had not expected; she was pregnant with their child. Joyce, author of the book *Don't Ask Forever*, had strong religious beliefs and had not considered abortion an option. She never had the opportunity to discuss the situation with Elvis because every time they were together he had the boys around him or was too medicated to talk. She left Vegas without ever sharing news of her pregnancy with Elvis and later aborted their child.

Personal photo of Elvis in hallway, Imperial Suite, Hilton Hotel. Elvis Now Suit with white macramé belt and blue turquoise conchos. August/September 1971.

ELVIS
SOUVENIRS ON SALE HERE!
PHOTO ALBUMS $1.00
LARGE POSTERS $1.50
LARGE HOUND DOGS $5.00
HOUND DOG PUPPIES $3.00
RCA ALBUMS $5.00
ELVIS MADISON SQUARE GARDEN ALBUM $5.00
RCA CAMDEN ALBUMS $2.00
RCA GOLD ALBUMS $15.00
RCA STEREO 8
Jumbo HOUND DOG $35.00
ELVIS
IN PERSON
IN PERSON
HEAR ELVIS ON RCA RECORDS AND TAPES
NOW
LAS VEGAS HILTON
NOW

CHAPTER 10

Maybe I'm Amazed

January 26, 1972—February 23, 1972

Elvis souvenir stand in the lobby of the Hilton Hotel. As was Elvis and the Colonel's custom, all proceeds were donated to various Las Vegas charities. January/February 1972.

AS ELVIS' JANUARY 1972 winter engagement at the Las Vegas Hilton approached, there were changes both on- and offstage.

Christmas at Graceland was different. The decorations were up and all the relatives, friends, and friends of friends were there, but all could sense coldness between Elvis and Priscilla.

Elvis, for his part, displayed his sense of humor when he distributed Christmas envelopes containing a gift certificate to the fast-food chain McDonald's. The holidays continued in their normal fashion, though the atmosphere had changed; Elvis and Priscilla still rented the movie theater and took everyone with them to see the all-night film shows.

Priscilla flew to California the night before New Year's Eve. On New Year's Day, Elvis told all who gathered that Priscilla no longer loved him and was leaving him. He had Joyce fly in and spent his birthday, January 8, with her.

Professionally Elvis had replaced the Imperials with J. D. Sumner and the Stamps Quartet, and comedian Jackie Kahane would now open the show.

Elvis' entrance to the theme from *2001: A Space Odyssey* was godlike and, in case anyone in the audience didn't get the message, he now wore gold and diamond rings on all fingers but his thumbs. He often added a giant diamond cross to his bare chest and started and ended his show wearing a dramatic cape. He would stand on the Hilton's giant stage as the showroom's gold curtain descended, glaring and demanding the audience's attention, his arms outstretched holding, his spread cape and giving the crowd the lasting impression that they had not just seen a show, they had somehow been a part of a larger event

Elvis sang some new ballads that were both dramatic and gave a clear look into his soul. "Until It's Time For You To Go" was not the mellow Buffy Sainte-Marie version; Elvis' rendition was a mournful

Private photo of Elvis modeling Blue Owl suit with silver-lined cape. Imperial Suite, Hilton Hotel, January/February 1972.

Onstage: Blue Owl Suit with silver-lined cape. Hilton Showroom, January/February 1972.

Private photos of Elvis modeling Black Diamond Suit with gold-lined cape. Imperial Suite, Hilton Hotel, January/February 1972.

Private photos of Elvis modeling Blue Nail Suit with white-lined cape. Imperial Suite, Hilton Hotel, January/February 1972.

Private photo of Elvis with two Hilton Showroom photographers in a dressing room hallway at the Hilton Hotel. Blue Nail Suit with white-lined cape. Las Vegas, Nevada: January/February 1972.

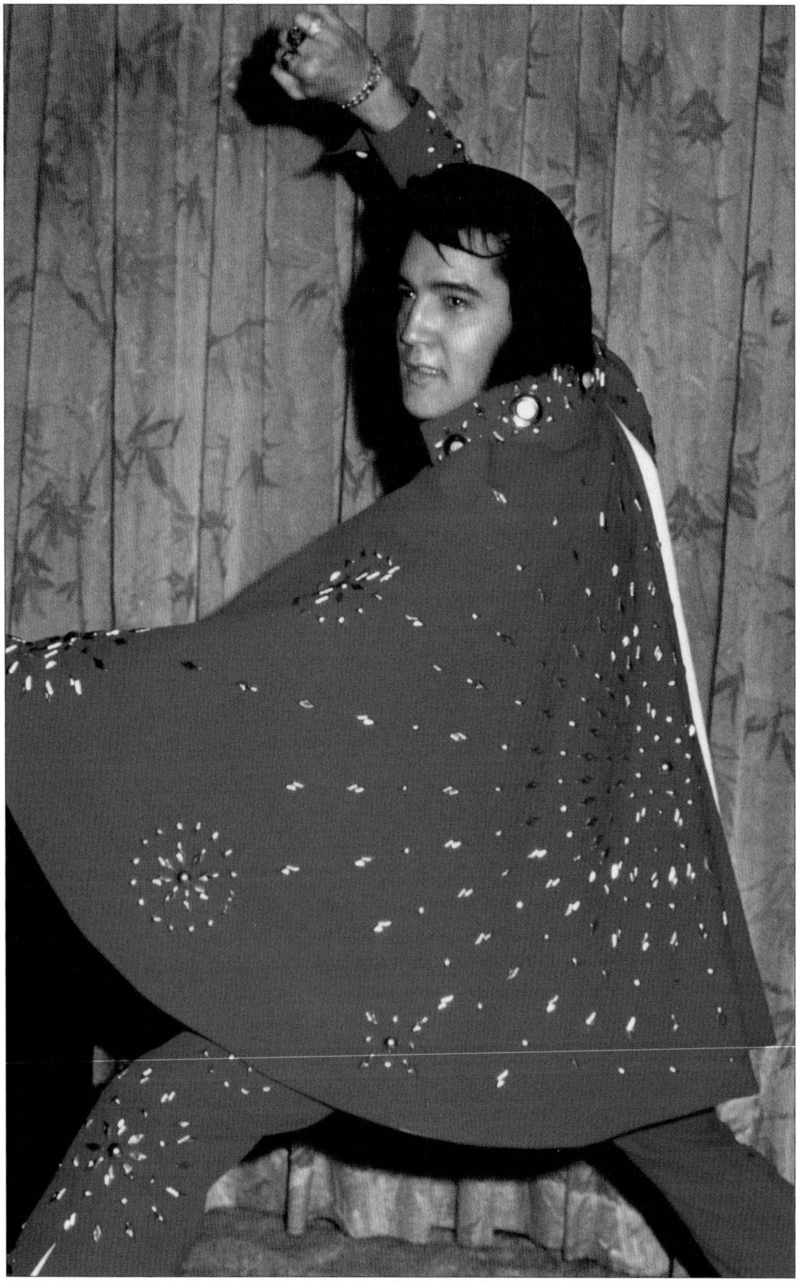

Right page: Onstage: White Star Suit with blue-lined cape. This jumpsuit was the first worn with a cape. Hilton Showroom, January/February 1972.

Private photos of Elvis modeling Burning Love Suit with white-lined cape. Imperial Suite, Hilton Hotel, January/February 1972.

Tour photo. University of Dayton Arena, Dayton, Ohio: April 7, 1972. White Star Suit with blue-lined cape.

Tour photo. Spectrum, Philadelphia, November 8, 1971. White Spectrum Suit with black-lined cape worn.

Tour photo. Boston Gardens, Boston, November 10, 1971. Black Spectrum Suit with red-lined cape.

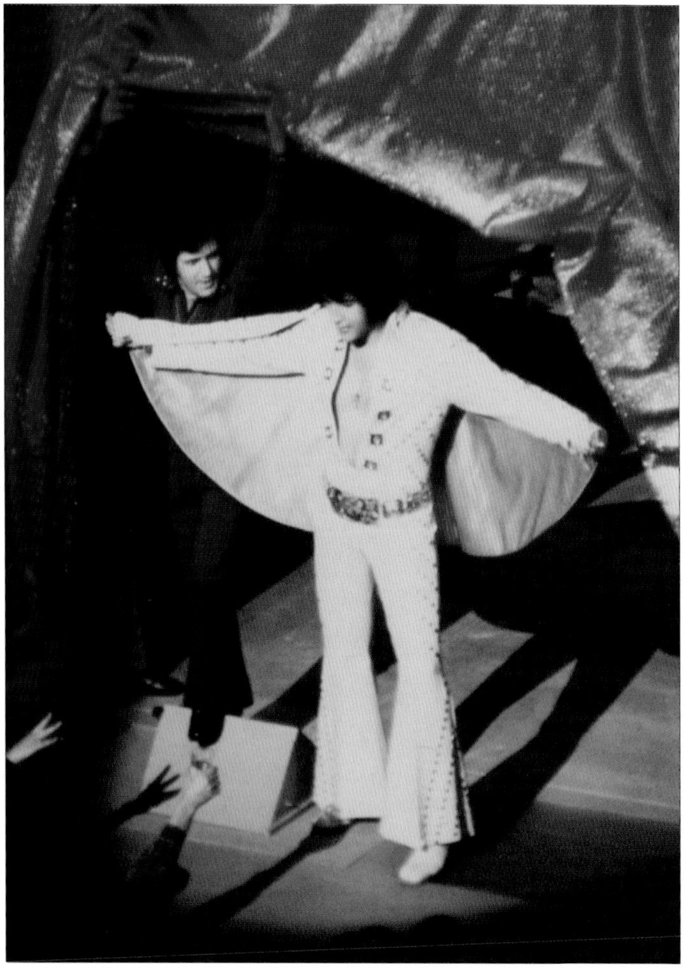

Onstage: White Diamond Suit with yellow-lined cape. Hilton Showroom, January/February 1972.

memory of youth and first love. It was sung as a plea for what once was.

"American Trilogy" was this season's showstopper. The song was written by Mickey Newbury, whose arrangement mixed "All My Trials Lord," an old spiritual, "The Battle Hymn Of The Republic," and the song of Elvis' Southern roots, "Dixie." Elvis' powerful performance had the Vegas crowd standing with their hands on their hearts. The feeling of patriotism was bursting throughout the huge showroom. When Elvis sang Marty Robbins' "You Gave Me A Mountain" it was clear you weren't watching a man singing about pain, you were witnessing a man who was living it.

RCA was present to record some of the shows

Tour photos. Municipal Auditorium, Kansas City, Missouri: November 15, 1971. White Lion Head Suit with red-lined cape.

for a proposed live album, *Standing Room Only* (which was never released). They even advertised it as coming soon on the picture sleeve for Elvis' "American Trilogy" single.

Priscilla attended the opening and then left town. She returned at the end of the engagement and confronted Elvis in his suite, telling him openly that their marriage was over. Elvis responded with rage, according to *Elvis and Me*. She recalled, "He grabbed me and forcefully made love to me. It was uncomfortable and unlike any other time he made love to me before." Elvis would neither believe nor ever fully accept that Priscilla was leaving him for another man. After all, he was Elvis Presley and he did the leaving.

THRU
LABOR
DAY
I'M THE WORLD'S LARGEST STUFFED HOUND DOG
WITH THE WORLD'S LARGEST DOG BONE...

CHAPTER 11

Lost In The Moment Forever

August 4, 1972–September 4, 1972

IN APRIL 1972 ELVIS BEGAN a fifteen-city tour. It had become apparent to the perceptive Colonel Parker that his boy was capable of attracting millions of people, each willing to pay $10 to see him perform. The Colonel didn't need a calculator to figure how much Elvis was earning for his hour onstage. This, coupled with the thought of what the concessionaires were making at every stop, made Parker feel as if it were 1956 all over again. Meanwhile MGM was filming most of the shows to be used in what would later be the Golden Globe Award–winning documentary, *Elvis on Tour*.

In June 1972 Elvis began another eight-city tour. The demand for tickets was so great that extra shows had to be added in several cities. Having had New York hold its red carpet for seventeen years, Elvis Presley finally came to the Big Apple. He would perform four standing-room-only concerts at the city's fabled Madison Square Garden. He drew more than eighty thousand during his stay there, and there were no complimentary tickets, no special guests, and no tickets for the mayor. Both John Lennon and Bob Dylan sat in the rear of the giant arena, and George Harrison sat high in the balcony. From the stage you could hear Big Al Dvorin, the emcee, barking, "Get your super-special Elvis souvenirs; the Elvis poster, the souvenir program, and the eleven-by-fourteen photos especially designed for this tour only."

At the first show, comedian Jackie Kahane ran into an extremely rude New York audience. They hissed and shouted "We want the King!" Jackie bravely continued, but the crowd became even more disrespectful. With the words, "There are twenty thousand of you and only one of me," he surrendered. The Sweet Inspirations followed and were greeted by the predominately white audience with polite yawns. Next, intermission, and another chance to buy one's Elvis goodies.

The World's Largest Stuffed Hound Dog with the World's Largest Dog Bone display. Fourth floor outside Colonel Parker's office and suite of rooms at the Hilton Hotel. Las Vegas, August/September 1972.

ELVIS
RIAA

Above, private photo. Left to right: Joe Esposito's girlfriend, Elvis, and Priscilla. Imperial Suite at the Hilton Hotel, August/September 1972.

Private photo of Elvis receiving a gold record award from RCA executive George Parkhill for 1 million sales of the RCA album Elvis as Recorded at Madison Square Garden. *Inside dressing room at the Hilton Hotel, August/September 1972.*

The lights dimmed, the orchestra and choir broke into the opening bars of "Also Sprach Zarathustra," and Elvis materialized in a white suit of lights sparkling with gold studs. Around his shoulders was a gold-lined cape and his $10,000 gold- and diamond-encrusted belt graced his waist. He started working the mike, his right hand extended, his left leg moving in a corkscrew motion. Time stopped; he dominated the mortals who filled the Garden. He used the stage and played to the people. He strutted, shook, and the girls moaned and stood on their seats. One young lady took a giant leap from the balcony and barely missed the stage. Friday, June 9, 1972, Elvis demonstrated his sexual power as he stood, arms spread, with the great gold-lined cape appearing to give him wings, a sex symbol for the ages. He repeated this amazing spectacle three more times. The gross for Elvis' Madison Square Garden appearances was $730,000.

Elvis returned to the ever-faithful Las Vegas Hilton for the monthlong Summer Festival in his honor. Elvis' opening night show Friday, August 4, 1972, lasted for fifty-two minutes. The opening-night audience boasted stars like Paul Anka, Telly Savalas, Richard Harris, and Sammy Davis Jr. Elvis wore a variety of beautiful two-piece outfits during this engagement. I visited him in his dressing room and found myself dazzled by the collection of various belts, jackets, and multicolored shirts that were lining the wall that Elvis referred to as his wardrobe wall.

Every hotel in Vegas was sold out, filled with the usual worldwide Elvis fans who flocked to the city by plane, motor home, automobile, and, in some instances, using their thumbs to hitch rides.

Elvis was in great voice once more, and he belted out all the songs the fans had come to hear. He introduced Frank Sinatra's "My Way" as the story of his life. His version of "What Now My Love" was both a plea for help and a definitive show of strength.

On August 18 the Colonel met with Elvis in his dressing room and told Elvis that his lawyer, Ed Hookstratten, had filed for divorce—the reason stated was the infamous irreconcilable differences. Priscilla was granted custody of their daughter, Lisa Marie, and Elvis was to have full visitation rights.

Elvis didn't let the news stop him in his search for female companionship. He flew one girl from Memphis to Vegas and after spending three nights with her had her flown home. When she arrived back in Memphis there was a white Mark IV parked in her driveway, a gift from Elvis.

He spent time in his suite with Sandra Zancan, a dancer from Los Angeles, to whom he gave a sports car and ruby ring. George Klein had introduced Linda Thompson to Elvis, who at that time was the reigning Miss Tennessee. She would become Elvis' girlfriend. She

Onstage: Blue Tiffany Suit with silver-lined cape. Hilton Showroom, August/September 1972.

Above: Onstage: White Dude Suit with paisley-lined cape. Hilton Showroom, August/September 1972.

Left: Onstage: White Dude Suit with white-lined cape. Hilton Showroom, August/September 1972.

Left: Onstage: Light-blue Dude Suit with silver-lined cape. Hilton Showroom, August/ September 1972.

Left: Onstage: Light-blue Dude Suit with white lined cape. Hilton Showroom, August/ September 1972.

Top, left and right: Onstage: White Dude Suit with white-lined cape. Hilton Showroom, August/September 1972.

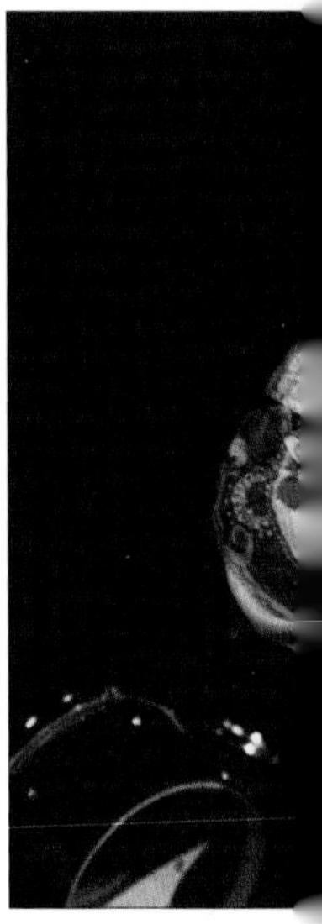

Bottom left: Tour photo. Henry Levitt Arena, Wichita, Kansas: June 19, 1972. White Dude Suit with paisley-lined cape.

Onstage: White Square Lion Head Suit with red-lined cape. Hilton Showroom, August/September 1972.

Below: Tour photo. Henry Levitt Arena, Wichita, Kansas: June 19, 1972. White Dude Suit with paisley-lined cape.

Opposite, bottom right: Onstage: White Dude Suit with paisley-lined cape. Hilton Showroom, August/September 1972.

Onstage: White Square Lion Head Suit with red-lined cape. Hilton Showroom, August/September 1972.

was still a virgin and needed to complete two classes at Memphis State to get her bachelor's degree. Elvis also spent time with actress Cybill Shepherd during this Vegas engagement but in the end he chose the lovely Linda.

Elvis' divorce brought a greater dependence on his Vegas doctors. Where they had provided him with medications before shows and sleeping aids to help him sleep, he was now receiving visits from his doctors six or more times a day.

The Colonel had negotiated a new contract for Elvis with the Hilton and the Colonel was now a technical adviser to his friend, Conrad Hilton. Under the new deal Elvis would be earning $150,000 a week

Tour photo. Honolulu International Center, Honolulu, November 18, 1972, 8:30 p.m. show. Black Way Down Suit with red-lined cape.

while The Colonel would earn $50,000 a year for promoting the hotel.

On Monday, September 4, Elvis gave an outstanding closing-night performance at the dinner show. Between this show and the late closing-night performance, the Colonel arranged a press conference to announce that Elvis would be the first artist in history to have his show broadcast worldwide by satellite. The Colonel had come up with this idea while watching President Richard Nixon's satellite transmission from China. The show was to be called "Aloha from Hawaii Via Satellite," and would eventually be seen by 1.5 billion people, more people than witnessed man's first walk on the moon. Elvis and RCA president Rocco Laginestra were seated in front of a huge wall of Elvis Summer Festival hats, each featuring a band on them with the names of all countries that would be viewing the "Aloha" special. In America NBC would later broadcast it as a ninety-minute television special. The Colonel reckoned if Elvis wasn't going to perform outside the United States, this was a way for Elvis to please all fans worldwide.

Elvis, wearing a custom, two-piece suit, took questions from the reporters:

Q: Are you awake?
A: I'm still on . . . I'm onstage, man.
Q: The Armed Forces network will pick it up. The Armed Forces will show it.
A: This is the first time that I've seen this myself.
Q: Well, it's just astounding.
A: I beg your pardon? Ok. Well now, they shoot me all the way, see, instead of just the waist down. Now I would like to think that I am . . . I have improved as an entertainer and I'd like to get the rapport with an audience 'cause it's a give-and-take thing. If you can do that, it works. If the artist or whoever is performing can get that kind of rapport going with the audience, then it really pays off, it's good.
Q: But do you feel you have more of that rapport now than you did fifteen years ago?
A: I couldn't really answer that. I really couldn't.
A [Rocco Laginestra]: I really should start this conference off by congratulating Elvis because we will have two new firsts. The first first—new first—involves Elvis as the first performer to do a worldwide live concert via satellite, a real spectacular. And the second is that we will have a worldwide album via satellite. All of this has been made possible by the joint efforts of a lot of people, and especially including Colonel Tom Parker. Elvis, again, my congratulations for this spectacular.
A: Thank you sir, thank you. Whew! It's very hard to comprehend it because I . . . in fifteen years, it's hard to comprehend that happening . . . out to all the countries all over the world via satellite, it's

Left: *Onstage: Blue Apollo Suit with blue-lined cape. Hilton Showroom, August/September 1972.*

Above, left and right: Onstage: Blue Tiffany Suit with silver-lined cape. Hilton Showroom, August/September 1972.

very difficult to comprehend. A live concert to me is exciting because of all the electricity that's generated in the crowd and on the stage, but it's my favorite part of the show . . . of the business, is the live concert.

Q: How do you pace yourself?

A: Sir?

Q: So you are up when you need to be up?

A: I just . . . I exercise every day. I vocalize every day, and practice if I'm working or not. So I just try to stay in shape all the time, vocally and mentally.

Q: Which is harder?

A: Well, both is tough. You gotta work at 'em, but I don't mind it, it's worth it.

A [Rocco Laginestra]: I might say this about when we first approached the various countries around the world. Elvis is really the only performer that could do this today. He's well known in every country that

we sought, in fact, in every country in the world. And the acceptance is just fantastic. It wasn't a case of any selling. Because you know he's been in demand for live performances around the world but you just can't do this so this is the way of approaching it. The acceptance has exceeded all of our expectations. Elvis?

A: Thank you very much. That's very nice sir.

This page: Elvis "Aloha From Hawaii" announcement press conference. Hilton Hotel, Las Vegas, August/ September 1972.

ELVIS
LAS VEGAS HILTON

CHAPTER 12

Trouble

January 26, 1973–February 23, 1973

Colonel Parker promoting "his boy": Custom Elvis billboard at the Hilton Hotel entrance. Las Vegas, January/February 1973.

ORIGINALLY THE ALOHA SPECIAL was to be broadcast via satellite on November 18, 1972. This date would conclude Elvis' November tour. Jim Aubrey, the head of MGM, told the Colonel that MGM planned to release *Elvis on Tour* to theaters that week. The Colonel agreed to change the date of the television event. Elvis would still perform the November Hawaiian concerts. He would return in January 1973 to the Big Island to perform a concert so big that it would reach fans the world over.

In author Joe Tunzi's definitive *Aloha Via Satellite* book, Marty Pasetta, producer and director of the "Aloha Satellite" show, recalls how the special came about:

> In 1972, after directing the Academy Awards for NBC, I was called into the office of the vice president of specials at NBC. He proceeded to ask me if I would be interested in producing and directing the first live satellite entertainment show in the world. Silly question! What else would anyone say but *yes*. When I asked him who, what, when and where, he went silent. He said it would be a milestone; needless to say, on that point he couldn't have been more accurate. NBC gave me tickets to a concert on Long Beach. They still wouldn't tell me who was performing other than this was the person that would star in the event. After the concert I went back to NBC and told them I was very impressed seeing Elvis Presley, but what would we do with him for 90 minutes? He didn't move; he stood in one position, didn't show any excitement, performed with five musicians and some singers in front of a blank curtain. What would he do on television . . . Just stand there and sing? That certainly wouldn't keep a worldwide audience watching this event. This landmark satellite show had to be gigantic and

Private photo of Elvis signing an autograph for a fan in the parking lot of the Hilton Hotel, January 1973.

something very special. NBC said that was my problem. I could do anything I wanted to do; they would back me 100 percent. Except before I could start . . . I would have to get Elvis and his manager Colonel Parker's permission for whatever I had in mind. At this point it felt so close, but so far from happening.

Since Elvis didn't move, I felt we had to create movement around him: lots of camera work, moving lights, etc. If we could create excitement without upstaging his performance, this would be a winning combination. I called and asked Ray Klausen, an exceptional art director, to do a drawing showing mirrors, large-scale shapes, lots of neon, all types of lightbulbs, capturing the glitz and glamour of Las Vegas where Elvis performed. Since we're going to telecast around the world, I said, "Let's take advantage of that fact, use all types of fonts and scripts spelling the name ELVIS, and do it in lights." I also said, "Let's put in a ramp getting him close to his audience." At the concert on Long Beach Elvis was standing on a ten-foot-high stage separated by twenty feet of space from the front row of fans. There wasn't any closeness between Elvis and his audience; this would not work well on television.

Ray did a great sketch. I showed it to NBC. They thought it was terrific, but now I had to go to Vegas and get the final approval from Colonel Parker and Elvis. That was easier said than done. I went to Las Vegas, met the Colonel for the first time, showed him the drawing, to which he said, "NOT APPROVED; NO WAY!" Elvis would never work with all those lights; they would upstage him, and the ramp would allow people to get close to him, causing a severe security risk. The Colonel said, ". . . Absolutely NO." After catching my breath, I tried to pick my stomach up from the floor and said, "Since I came all the way from Los Angeles, could I at least present it to Elvis?" He finally said, "OK." I covered the picture and proceeded to the thirtieth floor of the Las Vegas Hilton for my first meeting with Elvis. I was greeted by two large bodyguards who directed me to sit at the end of a coffee table as they sat on my left and right, leaving an empty chair at the other end waiting for Elvis. After about five minutes of silence, which seemed like a lifetime, Elvis arrived wearing a large set of very dark sunglasses, and quietly sat in the empty chair. Nobody said a word . . . .

After already having been rejected by the Colonel I didn't know what to do, so I took a deep breath, and said to myself, "I have to go for

Private photo of Elvis, at the Riviera Hotel to see Engelbert Humperdinck. Las Vegas, 1972.

Above: "Aloha from Hawaii" via satellite. Honolulu International Center, Honolulu, January 14, 1973. American Eagle Suit with blue-lined cape.

Above, left: Private photo of Elvis wearing his custom-made Hilton long fringe jacket. Imperial Suite, Hilton Hotel,January/February 1973.

broke—I have nothing else to lose." I sat up straight, said "Hi, my name is Marty Pasetta. NBC asked me to work with you creating the first LIVE SATELLITE entertainment television show in the world. I went to see your concert on Long Beach . . . I thought you sang great . . . but (gulp) you were boring, you didn't move." His bodyguards sat up straight, put their guns on the table, and were about to get up—"BUT I have some suggestions that will make this the best show ever televised." I whipped out the drawing and showed Elvis the set design, including mirrors, shapes, lights, and, of course, the ramp where we would position girls with flowers for him. If he wanted to distance himself from the girls, we would make the ramp wide enough so all he would have to do is go to the center of the ramp where they'll never be able to touch him. I then told Elvis "This will give you a close, safe relationship with your fans . . . . Also, if you will lose some weight, you'll look great . . . the show will look great . . . and if we work together, the show will be a winner." Elvis jumped up, threw his sunglasses across the room, and started to laugh. He ran over to me, picked me up, and hugged me, saying this is the first time anyone has ever been so truthful with him. Elvis said, "I love it . . . . We'll do it." I told him the Colonel had said no. Elvis said he makes the decisions and "he said yes." From that moment on we worked together on every aspect of the show and became lifelong friends.

The best crew was assembled from New York, Los Angeles, Nashville, Memphis, and all

Left: Onstage: White Jewel of the Nile Suit with blue-lined cape. Hilton Showroom, January/February 1973.

Below, left and right: Onstage: Orange Cosmo Suit with orange-lined cape. Hilton Showroom, January/February 1973.

Onstage: Thunderbird Suit with blue-lined cape. Hilton Showroom, January/February 1973.

Onstage: Elvis Today Suit with yellow-lined cape. Hilton Showroom, January/February 1973.

Onstage: Orange Jewel Suit with orange-lined cape. Hilton Showroom, January/February 1973.

Above:
Tour photo. Richmond Coliseum, Richmond, Virginia, March 12, 1974. Aloha from Hawaii Suit with blue-lined cape.

Top, right: Onstage: Stud Suit with blue-lined cape. Hilton Showroom, January/ February 1973.

Bottom, right: Onstage: Orange Target Suit with orange-lined cape. Hilton Showroom, January/ February 1973.

across the USA. Scenery was built, lighting was packed, trucks were loaded with cameras, and audio equipment was shipped from Los Angeles, via freighter, to Honolulu, Hawaii. We knew this production could be the one that would set the standard for all television concert shows. That certainly turned out to be the case. This show only had six cameras. Now television concerts have upward of twenty cameras.

Elvis lost twenty-five pounds in two months, rehearsed like a schoolchild practicing for a recital, happy that each day brought the date of the live show closer. After the show he ran over and said this was the most exciting night of his life. Later, he wore out many film copies of the show running them all the time, reliving his "most exciting night." We were told that every third person on earth saw this show in 1973. Since then, it has played hundreds of times on network and cable television all across the world, and still does to this day.

After the Aloha show Elvis was exhilarated but emotionally and physically drained. Twelve days later, on January 26, he opened another engagement at the Las Vegas Hilton. It had been reported in *Billboard* magazine that Elvis would be moving his show to the MGM Grand Hotel where he would be the Grand's first headliner that January. The Colonel responded to the story, "It's all a rumor, no fact. Both Elvis and myself would take it as a personal tribute if he could open the MGM Grand, but we are booked up so far in advance here, at the Hilton, we can't unless the Grand wants to wait several years to open."

The Elvis and Colonel business machine was as hot as any jackpot paid out by any one-armed bandit in Vegas. Elvis' tour dates, record sales, films, and TV special were keeping the cash registers clinking. The *Elvis on Tour* documentary opened to great reviews and outstanding box-office receipts. Elvis was cool again. *Rolling Stone* ran a feature story on *Elvis on Tour*, declaring, "At last—the first Elvis Presley movie." "Separate Ways" backed by "Always On My Mind" was Elvis' biggest hit since "Burning Love." The "Aloha From Hawaii" soundtrack album was approaching 2 million sales and the RCA Camden LP, *Burning Love and Hits from His Movies*, was a million-seller.

WHEN ELVIS ARRIVED in Vegas, he was worn out and complained of many physical problems. He was examined and diagnosed by many Vegas physicians including his favorite Dr. Feelgood, Elias Ghanem. The doctors prescribed different drugs for Elvis' various complaints including pain pills and liquid Demerol. Elvis often commented, "These goddamn doctors

Below: Private photo of Paul Lichter and Elvis. Imperial Suite, Hilton Hotel, August/September 1972.

Muhammad Ali wearing the custom-made boxing robe that Elvis presented to him in the Imperial Suite at the Hilton Hotel, January/February 1973.

can't figure out what is wrong with me." Whatever was ailing him caused him to cancel some of his shows. Before performing any show he was given an injection that he thought was vitamin B_{12}. The strain of being Elvis was beginning to take its toll.

Elvis' show was manic. At every performance he gave all he had; always concerned about his audience, never wanting to disappoint them, he worked harder than ever. He would stop in mid-song and instruct the band to keep playing while telling the crowd, "I'm gonna walk around a little bit, just give me a couple of minutes to catch my breath." Those in the audience thought they were sharing an intimate moment with Elvis. They didn't realize how serious what they were witnessing really was.

Lisa Marie's birthday was February 1 and Elvis arranged a birthday party for her. Priscilla brought their daughter to Vegas for a short visit but had to fly back to Los Angeles later that evening so Lisa wouldn't miss any school. Elvis had enjoyed the visit very much but his poor mood continued.

Muhammad Ali, who had visited Elvis in Vegas during his August 1971 engagement at the hotel, was once again back to spend some time with his friend. Elvis had a special boxing robe designed by the I. C. Costume Company (the company that made his extraordinary jumpsuits) that he presented to Ali. It closely resembled his flashy stage attire. Boldly embroidered on its back, it read "The People's Choice." Ali would wear this robe for his March 31, 1974 fight with Ken Norton. Ali recognized the difference in his friend's eyes. They seemed somehow sad and had lost their glow since the last time he had been in Elvis' company. He later recalled, "I felt bad because he wasn't enjoying life. He stayed inside always. I told him he should get out and see people. He said that wasn't possible because they would mob him." Ali told Elvis he had it all wrong. No one wanted to hurt him; all they wanted to do was shake his hand and tell him how much they cared for him.

Elvis didn't have to wait long to find out all of his fears and paranoia were real. The security that had been in place since the assassination threat in 1970 paid off on February 18 at the midnight show. The trouble began during Jackie Kahane's comedy routine that opened the show. A group of Peruvians, who were seated at a table close to the stage, rolled a beer bottle at Jackie's feet. Jackie, looking puzzled, picked the bottle up, pretended to drink from it and finished his routine.

Elvis began his show in the usual manner and immediately had the audience on their feet rocking to his beat. When Elvis began his third song, a woman who was seated with the group from Peru stood up on their table and began walking toward the stage on the row of connecting tables, climbing onto the ramp extending out from the main stage. She approached Elvis and without touching him, used her thumb to remove Elvis' scarf. She didn't try to kiss Elvis or have any interaction with him. She seemed to be in a trance. Both the audience and Elvis were taken aback by her strange behavior; the lady simply turned, walked down the ramp onto her table, and gave the scarf to one of the men there.

When Elvis began his high-energy performance of "Suspicious Minds," the man who had received the scarf from the woman rushed the stage, running toward Elvis. Another man rose and joined the first. The Hilton's stage was very wide and Elvis could not see them from where he was standing. Jerry Shilling, along with Red and Sonny West, sprang into action, hurrying to the center of the stage to protect Elvis. Then a third and fourth Peruvian jumped onstage and joined the melee. All hell broke loose. Red finished off the first assailant. Elvis, who was in a karate stance, landed a solid kick, sending the second man into the stunned audience, while the other two men were beaten down by Jerry Shilling and Sonny West. There was mass confusion. Elvis was furious. Vernon Presley and Tom Diskin were attempting to restrain him—but Elvis couldn't calm down. He shouted, "Come on you motherfuckers—I'll never let any motherfuckers do this on my show." Tom Diskin urged Elvis to consider his audience, saying, "Think of these people who paid to see you."

Elvis apologized to the fans, saying, "If a man wants to shake my hand that's fine, but if he wants to pick a fight I'll whup his ass! I'm sorry, ladies and gentlemen, I'm sorry I didn't break his goddamn neck is what I'm sorry about." While the fight was going on, the band had played the music to Elvis' stage intro, never stopping until the fight was over. This only added to the strangeness. One woman sitting close to the stage had been kicked in the eye. She would later sue the Hilton and eventually accepted a cash settlement from the hotel. She suffered permanent damage to the eye, resulting in blurred vision. Elvis, still angry, performed three more songs, completing the show with no band introductions and little dialogue.

After the show, when Elvis returned to his suite, he still hadn't calmed down. He was convinced Mike Stone was behind it; that the cowardly "motherfucker" wasn't content with stealing his wife and taking his daughter away from him, the "son of a bitch" had hired killers to finish him off right onstage in front of his fans. Elvis repeated, "He took my wife and baby girl—he has to die—he doesn't deserve to live." He screamed at Sonny, "You know I'm right, he did it, he

Private photo of Muhammad Ali and Elvis. Imperial Suite, Hilton Hotel, January/ February 1973.

hurt me man, you know I'm right. I want Mike Stone dead—Sonny, I know I can depend on you."

Red and Sonny were really scared now. They had seen the boss's anger many times but nothing approaching what they were experiencing now. Elvis began to throw things around the room as Linda Thompson, who was becoming more frightened by the minute, began to cry. Elvis continued shouting that Priscilla had told him on February 1 , while they were celebrating Lisa's fifth birthday, that Mike Stone didn't think Vegas was a good environment for their daughter. "Red, don't you see he's trying to take my baby away from me?" Elvis screamed, "Stone and that bitch have my baby sleeping in the same room as them." Elvis grabbed one of his guns and began pointing it menacingly. "Oh god, don't you hear me? Please understand—he destroyed my family—he has to answer—he must die." Elvis raged on until the early morning hours. Linda called a doctor who was summoned to the suite. Elvis was given an injection but it had little effect.

Red finally agreed to contact a friend who knew someone who was a "made man" (who had Mafia connections). Red was told it would cost $10,000 to have Stone eliminated. Red told Elvis about the hit just before the next evening's dinner show. Elvis gave Red an icy stare and said, "The cocksucker doesn't belong in this world." Elvis paused as Red West wondered if this was really the end of everything. Elvis said, "Aw, hell, let's just leave it for now. Maybe it's a bit heavy. Just let's leave it for now."

Elvis' closing-night performance was spectacular. It was as if nothing unusual had happened at the engagement. He was in great spirits, very talkative, and more than happy to perform all of the songs the audience came to hear. He sang with great power and held notes that would have made believers out of the greatest doubters. Ann-Margret was in the audience. Elvis introduced her and had the spotlight put on her. He explained that Ann would be opening at the Hilton the following evening and that he would be there. He said he wouldn't miss it for the world. He told the light man to keep the light on her so that he could stare at her. As the band played "Auld Lang Syne" the gold curtain came down on what had been both a successful and surprising winter engagement.

The following night he and Linda went to Ann's opening. They stayed in Vegas attending many shows, including comedian Marty Allen's performance and Mama Cass Elliot's show. Elvis invited both Cass and Marty back to his suite and Elvis and Cass sang together for the rest of the night.

Onstage: Light blue Flower Suit with blue-lined cape. Hilton Showroom, August/ September 1973.

CHAPTER 13

Caught in a Trap

August 6, 1973–September 3, 1973

IN JULY 1973 ELVIS WENT into Memphis' Stax Recording Studio where he spent many days, or in his case nights, laying vocal tracks for recordings that were owed to RCA as part of his latest contract. Elvis and the Colonel signed the new deal with the record company on March 1, 1973. The agreement called for Elvis to deliver two albums and two singles from these sessions.

Both RCA and the Colonel were desperate for new material but Elvis had shown little interest in recording. They felt that recording in Memphis at Stax Studio would be convenient for him and reasoned that the ten-minute drive from Graceland would motivate the reluctant star. After all, he would be able to return home and sleep in his own bed instead of having to stay at a hotel.

Elvis agreed to record at Stax but on the first night he kept the studio musicians, backup singers and engineers waiting all evening. Elvis never appeared. On the second night he showed up five hours late. Elvis was in a foul mood, and the sessions were a disaster. He hated the studio and complained about the poor acoustics. When he was presented with demos of possible songs he was to record, he refused song after song proclaiming them "pieces of shit." He was late again on the third night and, in all, the recording sessions only produced eight songs—twenty-two less than what was owed to RCA. Most of the songs Elvis was able to record told of lost love and heartbreak. One song in particular was autobiographical. "For Ol' Times' Sake" captured Elvis' feelings and emotional turmoil perfectly.

Elvis was slowly sinking into his own private hell. A world where the love from millions of strangers and all the rights of entitlement he had earned was not enough. He spent the last two weeks of July locked away in his bedroom at Graceland. At the beginning of August he returned to his prison away from home, the Imperial Suite at the Las Vegas Hilton.

This, and opposite page:
Tour photos. Coliseum, Spokane, Washington, April 28, 1973, 3:00 p.m. show. Red Flower Suit with red-lined cape.

This engagement would be notable for many reasons. It would be the last time he would perform a thirty-day engagement at the hotel. In the future his Vegas appearances would be limited to two weeks twice a year. This arrangement was part of a new two-year agreement with the Hilton. Elvis was in a black mood as opening night approached. He no longer considered Vegas a challenge; he thought of it as a trap with no way out.

OPENING NIGHT, AUGUST 6: Elvis wore his Aloha from Hawaii jumpsuit. He entered the stage minus his customary cape. He would don the cape as part of the finale and repeat this for the first two weeks. After that he didn't use a cape and, in fact, never wore a cape in Vegas again. If anything was bothering Elvis, the audience was blind to it. He appeared to be in great humor and the crowd, which had waited in long lines for hours and had tipped generously to be seated closer to their hero, enjoyed what they had traveled miles to see. Elvis sang some new songs including "My Boy," which was met with a standing ovation. "Raised On Rock" was performed without passion, but Elvis sang humorous lyrics to "Memphis Tennessee" that the audience seemed to enjoy.

At one point in the show, as Elvis began "American Trilogy," a large cardboard cutout shaped like the moon was lowered from above the large Hilton stage. It was emblazoned with a portrait of Abraham Lincoln and a bald eagle. Elvis seemed genuinely surprised as he spoke into the mike, "Good God—the moon is falling." Elvis sang all the standards and closed the show with "Can't Help Falling In Love."

ELVIS' SHOWS THIS SEASON were inconsistent. On some evenings he was just plain silly. At one show he came onstage riding big Lamar Fike's back. Attached to Elvis' neck was a stuffed monkey. At another show he had Sonny West roll a bed out onstage. He then performed "What Now My Love" while lying in the bed. Some audience members were confused by these antics, but to longtime fans who had witnessed many of Elvis' live performances, these were the best shows ever.

The "Elvis is on drugs" rumor was all over Las Vegas. The cabdrivers told stories, the waiters repeated them, and, by the time the bellboys told their version the stories had become fact. Elvis, for his part, didn't help matters when he broke a girl's ankle while giving a karate demonstration during one of the late-night parties in his suite.

Elvis constantly changed lyrics to his songs out of pure boredom, and on many nights the lyrics were X-rated. He shocked the crowd when he changed a verse while performing "Lawdy Miss Clawdy." He sang, "Adios, you motherfucker, bye, bye, poppa too—the hell with the Hilton Hotel and screw the showroom too." There were evenings where Elvis seemed distracted. On these nights he said little or nothing between songs, and would speed through the show before saying good night. The after-show parties continued, but on many nights the boss didn't attend. He went straight to his bedroom where he remained until it was time for the next day's dinner show.

Two weeks into this engagement Elvis learned his uncle, Travis Smith, had passed away in Memphis. Travis was Elvis' mother Gladys' older brother. He was married to Aunt Lorene and had two sons, Bobby and Billy. Uncle Travis had been the longtime gatekeeper at Graceland. The family lived in a mobile home on Graceland's grounds. Cousin Billy was very close to Elvis and many considered Billy Elvis' closest

Tour photo:
Kiel Auditorium,
St. Louis, Missouri,
June 28, 1973.
White Nail Suit with
gold-lined cape.

confidant. Elvis had deep feelings for his uncle and the news of his death was devastating. Elvis said, "Now he won't have to suffer anymore. Maybe death ain't so bad—as long as you know you're going to heaven."

IF ELVIS WAS GUILTY OF ONE THING in his life, it was the poor decisions he made when choosing the people he surrounded himself with. Sean Shaver said it best in his *Elvis Book II*:

> It does not matter that this might be the way he wanted it. Friends do not leave friends alone even when asked to. Elvis should have been helped through the rough spots not just yes'd to death. And this, I believe, is exactly what happened. If I had a friend that was mentally in a downward spiral, talking about death and making bad decisions, I would not allow him to be left alone, even if he did want it that way. The one big area of disappointment in Elvis' life was those who surrounded him. Here was a man in his mid-thirties, emotionally upset and talking pleasantly about death. . . . Don't get me wrong, there is nothing wrong with the subject matter, just the timing. When a man's wife leaves him for another guy and the husband says, "Let's kill the sum bitch," we don't try to hire someone to do it, we say, "Look at all the other women in the damn world." We make jokes, we do anything but say "Yes, boss." When we have this same man talking about death we certainly don't agree with, "Yes, heaven is a wonderful place." We tell him that heaven can wait, God has another forty years of life for you right here on earth.

Lisa Marie attended nine of her father's shows. At each show Elvis made sure to introduce his daughter, often telling her to stand up. His little girl was a real ham. She loved the attention and Elvis would have to tell her, "That's enough. Now sit down honey."

There were many highlights during this engagement. Elvis' interpretation of "The First Time Ever I Saw Your Face" was a real crowd pleaser. The beautiful "Softly As I Leave You," which Elvis performed as spoken word, was delivered so dramatically that women in the audience had tears running down their cheeks. Once again Elvis broke all existing attendance

Onstage: Blue Target Suit with blue-lined cape.
Hilton Showroom, August/September 1973.

records including his own. The demand to see Elvis was so great that the hotel added a special 3 a.m. show on September 2.

Closing night, September 3, was anything but ordinary. Elvis changed the words to many old favorites. He inserted Myrna Smith (one of the Sweet Inspirations) and J. D. Sumner into the lyrics of "Fever." He sang "Bridge Over Troubled Water" to the music of "Suspicious Minds." As he was about to begin "Mystery Train/Tiger Man" he told the band to stop playing and said to the audience, "There's a guy here who works in the Italian restaurant. His name is Mario and these people are getting ready to fire him as soon as I leave and I don't want him to go. He needs the job and I think the Hiltons are bigger than that. There's no disrespect, I just want to wake up Conrad and tell him about Mario and his job. That's all." Elvis then went into "Mystery Train" and when he got to the "Tiger Man" part of the medley, he stopped singing and said, "This song is dedicated to the staff and hierarchy of the Hilton Hotel." Elvis finished the show by telling the audience how much he loved to entertain them and "as long as I can do that I'll be a happy son of a bitch."

The Colonel was waiting for Elvis backstage. He was outraged that Elvis had publicly embarrassed the Hiltons. How could Elvis have the nerve to rub the Hilton's private business in their face? Elvis and the Colonel went into Elvis' dressing room. The Colonel slammed the door shut. Out in the hallway shouts of anger could be heard. Minutes later the Colonel, red-faced and agitated, opened the door and stormed off.

Later, up in his suite, Elvis was still furious and had not calmed down. "Who the hell did that old bastard think he was talking to?" No one spoke to Elvis Presley like that. He screamed at Joe Esposito, "Get that motherfucker up here. Tell the son of a bitch I want to see him, now." The Colonel arrived and it was clear that he was still angry and had no intention of kissing his boy's ass. Elvis had gone too far this time. The two men continued to argue loudly. Finally Elvis shouted, "You're fired!"

The Colonel responded, "You can't fire me, because I quit!" Colonel Parker then told Elvis he would have a press conference the next day and tell the world that he quit. He shouted at Elvis, "You're going to have to pay me all the money you owe me!" He turned and left the suite without looking back. Elvis, along with Linda Thompson, retired to the bedroom. The Colonel spent the entire night in his fourth-floor offices crunching the numbers for advances the Colonel had given Elvis. There were commissions still owed him for bookings and royalties from the movies and RCA.

Onstage: White Snowflake Suit with gold-lined cape. Hilton Showroom, August/September 1973.

By the next morning the Colonel had determined that Elvis would have to pay him millions of dollars to leave. When Vernon and Elvis saw the spreadsheets that the Colonel had delivered to the suite, they were beside themselves. Neither man knew what to do. Elvis clearly owed the Colonel a fortune. When the Colonel made no attempt to contact Elvis, Elvis had to relent and contact him. The two men met behind closed doors and in the end

Elvis apologized. The Colonel accepted and, just like that, the war was over.

ELVIS AND LINDA STAYED in Vegas and attended the Tom Jones show at Caesars Palace on two evenings. At one show Tom introduced Elvis, who stood up in the audience as the crowd shouted, "We love you, Elvis!" He walked to the stage where he briefly joined Tom. When Elvis was announced to the crowd at the second show, he stood up and waved. Ed Parker, bodyguard and karate guru, stood alongside him. When the spotlight was directed at them Ed's gun fell from his shoulder holster, embarrassing both Elvis and Ed.

Onstage: Black Spanish Conquistador Suit with blue-lined cape. Hilton Showroom, August/September 1973.

Private photo of Nancy Anderson presenting Elvis with Photoplay Magazine Entertainer of the Year Award. Imperial Suite, Hilton Hotel, January/ February 1974.

CHAPTER 14

Still Loving You

January 26, 1974–February 9, 1974

IN EARLY OCTOBER 1973 Elvis left his Palm Springs home and traveled to Los Angeles. The dreaded divorce was just around the corner. Ed Gregory Hookstratten, Elvis' Beverly Hills attorney, finalized the details with Priscilla's legal representative. The divorce would cost Elvis a cool $2 million. Priscilla would receive $725,000 in cash, $6,000 a month for ten years, and half of the recent sale of the couple's Hillcrest, California, home, which sold for $450,000. She was granted $4,200 a month spousal support for one year plus 5 percent stock in two of Elvis' music publishing companies, Elvis Presley Music and Gladys Music. Elvis also agreed to pay $4,000 a month in child support and share legal custody of Lisa Marie.

On Tuesday, August 9, 1973, the couple met in the Los Angeles County Courthouse. The divorce proceedings were presided over by Judge Laurence J. Rittenband. Twenty minutes later Elvis and Priscilla walked out holding hands, kissed, and went their separate ways. Elvis flew back to Memphis and immediately contacted Linda and asked her to join him at Graceland. Those close to Elvis hoped this would be a new beginning.

Five days later Elvis was rushed by ambulance to Baptist Memorial Hospital in a semi-comatose condition. The King was gravely ill. His labored breathing was a great concern to his doctors. The official statement given to the media was that Elvis had been admitted to the hospital suffering from a persistent case of recurring pneumonia. The doctors' first concern was to get him stabilized. They recognized Elvis' symptoms as a severe drug reaction.

Elvis' personal physician, George C. Nichopoulos, known as Dr. Nick, was questioned as to what prescribed drugs Elvis was taking. It was quickly determined that none of the prescribed medications would have caused the condition that was threatening Elvis' life. Joe Esposito told Dr. Nick in private that Elvis had been receiving shots of Demerol on an almost daily basis. These injections were being administered by one of his California physicians. Elvis, in fact, had flown this doctor to Memphis on many occasions. The doctors at Baptist Memorial consulted with Dr. Nick and it was determined that Elvis would have to be slowly weaned off the drugs, as an addict. He would be given methadone as a substitute—the medication commonly used to help heroin addicts. Elvis' long-term pill abuse had caused him to suffer an enlarged bowel and intestinal blockage.

When Elvis was out of immediate danger he was wheeled out of the emergency room and admitted to the hospital. He had the windows to his hospital room covered with aluminum foil. This was done not only to keep the sunlight out but also to ensure that no photographer using a telephoto lens would be able to snap a picture and sell it to one of the tabloids.

On October 16, 1973, the Baptist Memorial public relations director issued a statement that their famous patient was there for a rest and doing well. Elvis spent two weeks and six days in the hospital with Linda Thompson at his side the entire time. They enjoyed television shows, played board games, and Linda spent hours reading to him. On one occasion a doctor entered the room to find Elvis and Linda in bed together. Taken aback, he remarked, "Make yourself at home."

To which Elvis replied smiling, "I am, and if I couldn't you'd be making a house call at Graceland."

After taking it easy for the next few months, Elvis returned to Stax Recording Studio, where his previous sessions had been disastrous. This time they would be triumphant. He delivered eighteen finished songs to RCA after just one week of recording. The songs included "Good Time Charlie's Got The Blues"; Elvis changed the lyrics by removing the line that referred to messing around with drugs. He rocked "I Got A Thing About You Baby" as well as the Chuck Berry classic, "Promised Land." He performed a soulful version of "Talk About The Good Times" and the Red West composition, "If You Talk In Your Sleep," which would become both a Vegas highlight and a hit single.

Private photo of Elvis receiving an award from the Great Britain Fan Club. Hallway outside dressing room, Hilton Hotel, January/February 1974.

THE CHRISTMAS SEASON was a happy one. Elvis and Linda spent time with her parents. He discovered racquetball and enjoyed the game so much he would later have a full-size racquetball building built behind Graceland.

In January 1974 Elvis returned to Las Vegas where he spent eleven days rehearsing. He hadn't shown this

Onstage: Black Vine Suit. Hilton Showroom, January/February 1974.

kind of excitement about getting back onstage in years. Whether it was the hospital scare, or that he would only be performing for two weeks, one thing was certain, on January 26 when Elvis walked onto the Hilton stage, the King was back. The entire engagement had been sold out for months. Elvis in Vegas was not only good for the Hilton, it was great for the city of Las Vegas. Every hotel in town was filled to capacity. Reservations at restaurants were hard to come by and the town's main showrooms and lounges were filled by the overflow of tourists who were visiting the gambling mecca for only one reason, a chance to see Elvis Presley. The neon city and the brightest star on earth were an unbeatable team.

Elvis' opening-night show was the five hundred and seventeenth time he'd performed on the hotel's stage. Dressed in an ornate jumpsuit, he greeted the audience by saying, "Me and ole blue eyes are back" (referencing Frank Sinatra who had made a Vegas return the night before following his short retirement). Elvis gave the crowd an extra-long show, singing all the songs they had come to hear. He introduced his new vocal group, Voice, which he had discovered in Nashville, and while they sang he left the stage to have his hand bandaged. An overzealous woman had rushed the stage and scratched him earlier. Sherrill Nielsen sang lead; the rest of the group consisted of Tim Baty and J. D. Sumner's nephew Donnie Sumner. Elvis loved Sherrill's high tenor and often invited him to Graceland where Sherrill would sit at the piano and sing for Elvis for hours. The two sang duets onstage including the very beautiful "Softly As I Leave You." Elvis would speak the lyrics while Sherrill would sing them in sweet harmony. The two also performed a killer arrangement of "O' Sole Mio/It's Now Or Never." Elvis' opening show also featured stand-out performances of his latest RCA single, "Help Me," "Spanish Eyes" (Sherrill contributed beautiful harmony), and a recent hit for Olivia Newton-John, "Let Me Be There." He brought back an old favorite, the Righteous Brothers' "You've Lost That Lovin' Feeling." He hadn't included it in his Vegas shows for almost two years. The performance was met with a sponta-

Onstage: Tiger Suit. Hilton Showroom, January/February 1974.

Onstage: King Suit. Hilton Showroom, January/February 1974.

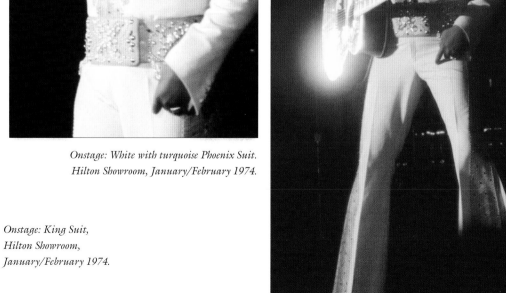

Onstage: White with turquoise Phoenix Suit. Hilton Showroom, January/February 1974.

Onstage: King Suit, Hilton Showroom, January/February 1974.

neous standing ovation. He sang "Can't Help Falling In Love" as the audience began to moan; they knew their evening with the King was coming to an end.

THROUGHOUT THE ENGAGEMENT Elvis addressed the audience, telling them not to believe the crap they read in the movie magazines. He said he knew they had a job to do but when they wrote about him they made it up. "It's all bullshit. Nothing but lies." He continued, "You people hear that stuff but you all still come all the way out here to see me and by God I'm not gonna let you down, I'll sing my ass off." Night after night he gave them all he had. He went all the way back to his days at Sun Records telling the crowd, "I'm going to sing one of my favorite songs, 'Tryin' To Get To You.'" It never failed to bring the house down. He followed it with another of his early Sun recordings, "My Baby Left Me." He poked fun at himself by holding his nose and speaking in a high voice, "I was only a baby when I recorded those two songs. This is how I sounded then."

Perhaps the funniest moment of the season occurred while Elvis was doing his "kissing the girls and tossing them scarves" routine. Marty Allen, the famed comedian who was appearing at another hotel, came to see the Elvis show. While Elvis was on the far right end of the stage kissing a lucky lady, Marty, who was seated at a table stage left, stood up on his chair and yelled in a high female voice, "I wanna a kiss too! Elvis. Elvis! Kiss me too!" Marty, who was wearing a huge Elvis wig, shouted out again, begging Elvis for a kiss. Elvis, who was blinded by the bright stage lights, couldn't see Marty but was becoming annoyed by the loud and persistent plea for a kiss. He walked toward the voice and when he saw Marty in his Elvis hair, standing on the chair, his arms apart and his lips puckered, Elvis couldn't contain himself—he fell to his knees and broke up laughing. Elvis, the audience, and the Colonel laughed so hard they had tears in their eyes.

Onstage: White Stone Eagle Suit. Hilton Showroom, January/February 1974.

Colonel Parker, never one to miss a trick, once told me it was at that moment he got the idea to produce an Elvis talking-album-only. It's title was *Having Fun on Stage with Elvis*. The Colonel would produce a recording that consisted of snippets from Elvis' stage banter from 1969 to 1972 and release it on his own

Boxcar label. RCA would manufacture it and pay Elvis a fifty-cent per album royalty. The album was available for the first time at the Elvis souvenir booth at the Hilton during Elvis' August 1974 engagement and was sold on a limited basis at a few tour stops. In October 1974 RCA would release the album nationwide.

Elvis included some new songs at this engagement. On some nights he told the audience, "I need help, I really do, so here it is." He then performed the Larry Gatlin gospel-flavored "Help Me," which would be released by RCA as an Elvis single backed with "If You Talk In Your Sleep."

There were a few unfortunate incidents that took place during this season. Duke Bardwell had joined the band as Elvis' new bass player. He had been recommended by drummer Ronnie Tutt. Throughout the engagement Elvis was hard on him, and it was embarrassing to both Duke and the audience. Another incident occurred when a girl grabbed and yanked at Elvis' scarf and he shouted into his mike, "Let go, you son of a bitch!" At another show a fan, sitting close to the stage, kept screaming, "Elvis, give me your belt!" Elvis would smile at her and continue singing. When the fan continued to interrupt him, Elvis walked to the edge of the stage, kicked at her, and said, "Shut up, you motherfucker."

Onstage: White Nail Suit. Hilton Showroom, January/February 1974.

But for the most part Elvis enjoyed this engagement and the crowd was more than happy as they left the showroom. They could be heard saying to one another, "God, he was wonderful," "He's beautiful," "He sings better than anybody," "What a show—wow."

Meanwhile, Elvis was back in the Imperial Suite and bored. He decided the opulent suite could use some remodeling. He reached for his gun and shot the television screen. Next he began to shoot out the lightbulbs in the ornate lamps. One bullet ricocheted and hit the wall, penetrating it. On the other side of the wall was the bathroom where Linda Thompson was. The stray bullet buzzed by her head, barely missing her. Linda ran into the room where she found Elvis laughing. As she stared at him he said, "Hey, honey. Just calm down. No need to get excited."

SEEING ELVIS IN VEGAS was magic. Something set him apart from all other performers; that something was his ability to make you believe he was singing just to you. There may have been 2,194 people in the room but Elvis was only there for you. It's hard to explain. Elvis in concert wasn't just a concert, it wasn't just about what you saw and heard, it was what you felt; that connection. Anyone fortunate enough to see Elvis perform recognized an innocence, a beauty, and a love that came from that stage and touched you.

Tour photo. University of Dayton, Dayton, Ohio: October 6, 1974, 2:30 p.m. show. Rainbow Suit.

CHAPTER 15

Anything but Ordinary

August 19, 1974–September 2, 1974

ELVIS' JUNE 1974 TOUR was the third of the year. He had performed twenty-one shows and these concerts grossed $2 million. The sale of Elvis souvenirs brought in another $500,000. The reviews were, for the most part, good. Some mentioned Elvis' weight, many compared his stage attire to Liberace's, all reported that Elvis may be slower but his voice was still outstanding. The audiences were multigenerational; little children, their mothers and fathers, as well as grandmothers and grandfathers. Unlike other rock concerts of that time, the smell of marijuana did not float around the arena.

Elvis' eleventh stand in Las Vegas began on August 19. Now that his Vegas engagements were only two weeks long, many fans were disappointed when they couldn't gain entry to the sold-out showroom. The opening-night performance was an entirely different show. Elvis had changed the repertoire as well as its presentation. For the first time in over two years he didn't enter the stage to the sound of the opening *2001* theme, but instead to Ronnie Tutt's driving drumbeat. He wore his legendary Peacock suit, often referred to as Elvis' favorite, the only stage suit that Elvis had a personal hand in designing. (Years later, Elvis gave this suit to me.) He opened the show with "Big Boss Man" and followed that with "Proud Mary," a song he hadn't performed for a Vegas audience in many seasons. Next up was "Down In The Alley," a blues-rock song that was included as a bonus song on the 1966 soundtrack album *Spinout*. The rest of the show consisted of recent recordings and songs that hadn't been performed live before. Elvis included a few fan favorites but did not perform any hits medleys; "Good Time Charlie's Got The Blues" was followed by "Never Been To Spain" and a heartbreaking "It's Midnight." He performed a karate demonstration as he sang "If You Talk In Your Sleep." The underrated "I'm Leavin'" brought the audience to their feet. "Let Me Be There" and "Softly As I Leave You" followed. Elvis continued with another recent Olivia Newton-John hit, "If You Love Me Let Me

Onstage: Aztec Indian Suit. Hilton Showroom, August/September 1974.

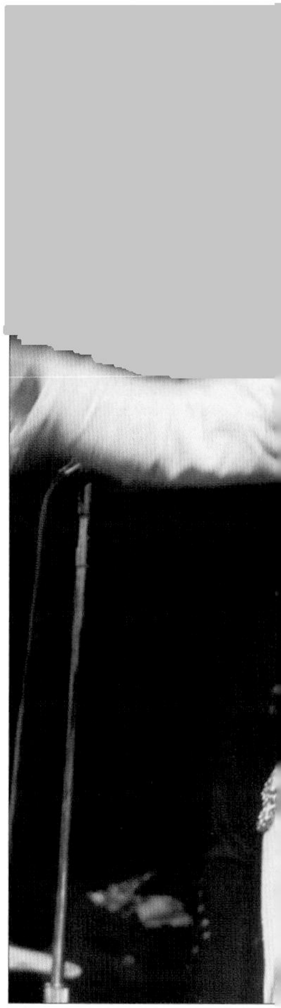

Tour photos. Spectrum, Philadelphia, June 23, 1974, 8:30 p.m. show. Embroidered Eagle Suit.

Know." The performance was fueled by Elvis' high energy. He sang "Love Me Tender" and tore the house down with red-hot rocking versions of "Polk Salad Annie" and "Promised Land." He finished the evening with "My Baby Left Me," "Bridge Over Troubled Water," "Fever," "Hound Dog," and "Can't Help Falling In Love." As the gold curtain came down he pushed his way through its opening and stood center stage dripping sweat, sucking in the mad applause from the electrified crowd.

The following evening's dinner show was entirely different. For reasons only known to Elvis, he abandoned the new routine after his opening-night performance and returned to his familiar and successful material. Elvis' August 1974 engagement is widely regarded as his best Vegas season since August 1970. He was in great spirits, often engaging the audience in candid conversation. He seemed to connect to them in a new and fresh way. The performances were manic and vocally he was at the top of his game.

EVEN THOUGH HIS VEGAS CONFINEMENT was shorter now, Elvis still became bored and restless after a week in the desert. He grew tired of the four walls in his bedroom and the monotony of the showroom. He would stare out at the mountains through the window from his perch on the top floor of the giant hotel. He lamented to anyone that would listen, "I'm stuck in this damn hotel room and, you know, I could buy those mountains if I wanted."

One night after completing the late show, Elvis found a new way to combat his boredom. He told the audience at the dinner show the next evening about one late-night escapade. "You know, I've never liked the way this showroom looked, it's too wide for a performer. I had this ramp made so I could come out a

Left: Tour photo. Spectrum, Philadelphia, June 23, 1974, 3:00 p.m. show. Peacock Suit.

little closer to the audience. I really don't care for those big fat funky angels that are hangin' there on the wall." Elvis told the light man,

Put a spotlight on those angels on the wall. You will notice a slight difference. Those of the Caucasian race, that's what it is, isn't it? Caucasian? It was on my army draft card. I thought it meant circumcised. Anyway, the other night I came down here about 4:40 in the morning with a couple of friends who work for me, Jerry Shilling and Red West. Red is a second-degree black belt in karate. He's got a school in Memphis and I'm very proud of him. . . .Anyway, he climbed the fence where the hotel

Onstage: North Beach Leather Suit. Elvis performing a kata while wearing a karate gi jacket over suit. Hilton Showroom, August/September 1974.

Onstage: North Beach Leather Suit. Hilton Showroom, August/September 1974.

keeps their supplies, the paint and so forth. He climbed the fence, as high as this curtain. He went down and got a little can of black paint, he put it on his belt, came back and climbed over there, and we stacked up two tables. I got up with the paint and the brush and I was Michelangelo, the guy that painted the ceiling in the Vatican, the Sistine Chapel. I painted that statue. It took thirty minutes to do. The hotel hasn't said a word. I just thought I'd share it with you.

To this day it is not known what the Hiltons thought of Elvis' decorating skills, but the black angel remained on the showroom wall for more than a decade. Elvis repeated a variation of the angel story at most shows for the remainder of the engagement.

One evening Elvis included his definition of the word "nigger." "In the dictionary it says that 'nigger' means lazy and helpless. Most of the 'niggers' I've met are white. Just watch *Hee Haw* on TV and you'll see what I mean." The audience would applaud and the Sweet Inspirations would sing "We Shall Overcome." Elvis would break in saying, "That's what the Chinese said, that's why there is so many of them." It took many in the audience a moment to understand the play on words.

During this engagement Elvis' seventeen-year dedication to karate was recognized when he was awarded his eighth-degree black belt in both Pa Sa Ryu (a style of Tae Kwon Do) and Kenpo Karate by Master Kang Rhee and Master Ed Parker, his friend and sometime bodyguard. Elvis was naturally proud of this accomplishment and shared it with his Vegas audiences. He would don a black karate jacket and put his eighth-degree black belt on before performing "If You Talk In Your Sleep." He thrilled the crowds with a complete karate kata, often demonstrating moves on Charlie Hodge and, on occasion, he would call Red West, who wrote the song, to the stage. They would enact a karate fight that was so realistic that the audience would hold their collective breath. Elvis often held long monologues, telling the crowd all they could ever hope to hear about the sport. He often ended with, "Ladies and gentlemen, people do different things to relax. I just break boards and bricks."

Private photo of Ed Parker (bodyguard and karate master), Sergio Mendes (recording artist), and Elvis. Imperial Suite, Hilton Hotel, August/September 1974.

Linda Thompson was, once again, in Vegas with Elvis. She attended the first four shows of the season. Elvis introduced her at each. During his late show on August 22, Elvis noticed Linda was not seated at her reserved booth and he grew angry at this perceived slight. Linda, along with a girlfriend, arrived late and as the performance reached it finale they rushed the stage, throwing a large yellow pair of men's boxer shorts

Onstage: North Beach Leather Suit.
Hilton Showroom, August/September 1974.

at Elvis. He didn't find their joke funny. Elvis banished Linda and had her flown back to Memphis. He wasted little time in finding a replacement, Sheila Ryan. He began to introduce Sheila to his Vegas audiences as his new girlfriend. She was a small-town girl whose life experiences hadn't prepared her for Elvis' bizarre lifestyle. Sheila would later move to Los Angeles, where she would meet and marry film actor James Caan.

The shadow of Priscilla was always present. She was in Vegas to see her ex perform and on one occasion, while singing "It's Midnight," Elvis approached the stage edge and, standing in front of her, sang the song's strongest lyric, "It's midnight and I miss you," directly to her while tears rolled down his cheeks.

Elvis caught the flu and his illness caused the cancellation of some shows. The Hilton had Bill Cosby flown in to replace Elvis on those evenings. But his September 2 closing-night performance is remembered today, not for the songs he sang, but rather for what he said. His sharpest critics refer to it as "the drug story." Priscilla was present and she saw it this way: "I was in shock because Elvis would never let his audience know what his emotions were. Singing was his way of venting his emotions, how he felt about something—he'd get onstage and sing his heart out. And any song, any given song, you know he would beat it to death, with more emotion and more energy—but he never let it out in public. This was out of character for someone who had so much pride; you know—everything he was against, he was displaying. It was like watching a different person." Elvis told the audience:

> I don't pay any attention to rumors, I don't pay any attention to movie magazines. I don't read them because they're all junk. No, I don't mean to put anybody's job down. I'm talking about . . . they have a job to do and they gotta write something, so if they don't know anything they make it up. In my case they make it up. When I hear rumors flying around . . . I got sick in the hospital . . . well I was . . . in this day and time you can't even get sick, you are "STRUNG OUT"! Well, by God, I'll tell you something friend, I have never been STRUNG OUT in my life—except on music.
>
> When I got sick, here in the hotel. I got sick here that one night, had a 102 temperature, they wouldn't let me perform. And from three different sources I heard I was STRUNG OUT on heroin. I swear to God. Hotel employees, jack, bellboys, freaks that carry your luggage up to the room, people working around, you know, talkin' maids, and I was sick, you know, had a doctor,

Top Left: Private photo of Elvis and girlfriend Sheila Ryan. Imperial Suite, Hilton Hotel, August/September 1974.

Right: Private photo of Elvis, singer Freddie Cannon, and wife, Jeanette. Imperial Suite, Hilton Hotel, August 20, 1974.

Far right: Private photo of Elvis, Jackie's wife, Lynette, and Jackie Wilson. Imperial Suite, Hilton Hotel, August 20, 1974.

had the flu, got over it in one day. But all across the town I was STRUNG OUT!

So I told them earlier, and don't you get offended, ladies and gentlemen. I'm talkin' to somebody else. If I find or hear the individual that has said that about me, I'm gonna break your goddamn neck, you son of a bitch!

This is dangerous. That is damaging to myself, to my little daughter, to my father, to my friends, my doctor, to everybody, my relationship with you, my relationship up here on the stage.

I will pull your goddamn tongue out by the roots!

And then, without missing a beat, Elvis told the audience, "Thank you very much." He sang the beautiful "Hawaiian Wedding Song" and then closed his Summer Festival with "Can't Help Falling In Love."

CHAPTER 16

Someone Stop This Train I'm Only Good at Being Young

March 18, 1975–April 1, 1975

IN THE YEAR 1974, ELVIS PERFORMED for 1 million fans in over 150 concerts. Rumors concerning his health were running rampant. An important milestone was approaching; Elvis Presley would be forty on January 8, 1975. Psychologically Elvis was having a hard time dealing with it. After all, he had been the original hero of rock and roll, the boy wonder. He worried that his fans and the public in general wouldn't be able to accept a forty-year-old rock star.

The current issue of *People* magazine featured Elvis on its cover with the headline story reading "Elvis Presley at 40." The tabloids were not as kind, running headlines like "Elvis Fat and 40." Their stories featured unflattering photographs showing Elvis' growing waistline. Radio stations across America announced Elvis' birthday and played his records all day long. Elvis spent the day at Graceland where he had a small dinner party for family and friends.

While resting at home in preparation for his two-week January Vegas shows at the Hilton, he was offered the starring role in a new Hollywood film titled *The Gospel Singer*. The $1.5 million payday would have made him the highest-paid actor in the world. He told the Colonel to turn the offer down.

Days later it was reported in *Variety* that the Hilton had canceled Elvis' January engagement. It was speculated that this was so he could open the newly remodeled six-hundred-room addition at the hotel. In reality, Elvis was sick. On January 29 at 3:30 in the morning he was rushed to Baptist Memorial and admitted in critical condition. Colonel Parker, who had been alarmed by Elvis' state, was beside himself with concern but didn't know what to do. He called Vernon Presley, but Vernon simply said, "I can't control my son." The Colonel considered refusing to book Elvis for any shows but he knew that if he didn't, someone else would. He also reasoned that Elvis, left at home on his own schedule, was more likely to harm himself by overmedicating.

Private photo. Left to right: Mr. & Mrs. Sam Thompson, Lisa Marie Presley, Elvis, Linda Thompson and her parents, Mr. & Mrs. Thompson. Imperial Suite, Hilton Hotel, March/April 1975.

This hospital stay was very much the same as his earlier hospitalization. Once again the windows were covered with aluminum foil and Linda Thompson stayed in his room. Elvis was suffering from a twisted and blocked colon as well as liver damage caused by the barbiturates in the many downers he was taking.

Vernon was sick with worry about his son and on February 5 he suffered a heart attack. He was placed in the intensive care wing at Baptist Memorial. When he was well enough he was moved to a room next to Elvis'. Billy Smith recalls a conversation that father and son had. "Vernon blamed Elvis for his heart attack. 'I can thank you for this.' He also blamed Elvis for Gladys' death, saying, 'You worried your Mama right to her grave.'"

The hospital released a statement to the press confirming that Elvis was a patient and being treated for a liver condition. Baptist Memorial was inundated with get-well cards, teddy bears, and flowers. Elvis' room number was a closely guarded secret but the TV news crews and cameramen had no problem figuring it out. The aluminum foil covering the windows of two rooms on the eighteenth floor was a dead giveaway. On February 13 Elvis was discharged and slipped out a back door in the wee hours. He successfully escaped the reporters and returned home to Graceland.

Vernon was still hospitalized. Elvis was concerned but didn't allow his father's illness to alter his lifestyle. He purchased a bright yellow Pantera sports car that he raced up and down Elvis Presley Boulevard many evenings, and he often would indulge in his latest hobby, racquetball, in the custom court he had built behind Graceland.

Elvis owed RCA some recordings and was due back in the studio. He was not in the mood to record and he told his record company to cancel the planned sessions. Felton Jarvis, his friend and longtime producer, called and told Elvis they needed to deliver new material or he'd be fired by RCA. Elvis agreed to help his friend and told him to set up a recording session. These March 1975 sessions at RCA's Los Angeles studios would be the last time he would ever be in a recording studio. Elvis had his entire band flown into LA, and brought both Lisa Marie and Sheila Ryan. This would be one of the few times he ever

Onstage: White and black two-piece Penguin Suit. Hilton Showroom, March/April 1975.

This page and following: Tour photos. Lakeland Civic Center, Lakeland, Florida: April 27, 1975, 8:30 p.m. show. Black two-piece suit with red, white, and gold-leaf trim.

Onstage: Navy blue two-piece suit with red and gold scalloped trim. Dinner show, Hilton Showroom, March 26, 1975.

recorded in the studio exclusively with his stage band.

The sessions lasted four days and produced ten finished tracks including "T-R-O-U-B-L-E" (a country rocker) and "Green, Green Grass Of Home," which Elvis sang with such sincere emotion that it left everyone present with tears in their eyes. "Fairytale," a song that had been a recent hit for the Pointer Sisters, was given a superb and different approach. Elvis would introduce the song at his upcoming Vegas engagement by telling the audience, "Ladies and gentlemen, this next song, 'Fairytale,' is the story of my life." Billy Swan's "I Can Help" was given the Presley treatment also. Billy was a lifelong Elvis fan and when he learned that his hero had recorded it he wrote the following in the liner notes for his album: "I wish I could get the socks Elvis wore when he recorded my song." During Elvis' March Vegas engagement he learned that Billy was in the audience. After the show Elvis invited Billy back to his dressing room. The two men shook hands and exchanged mutual admiration. When Billy was ready to leave, Elvis stopped him and removed his boots, took off his socks, and gave them to Billy.

ON MARCH 18 ELVIS BEGAN his twelfth season at the Hilton. At his opening-night show, his voice was stronger than ever. He hit notes other singers can only dream about. Elvis was big. There was no other way to describe his weight gain. He wore new costumes that had the look of two-piece business suits that had been modified with brocade designs on the front and back shoulders. This same brocade was present on the outer seam of his pant legs stretching to the exaggerated kick pleats of the flared bell-bottom pants. He wore these suits in white, blue, and black. These Vegas performances were among the most entertaining he ever performed. Elvis frequently told the crowd how much he appreciated them and thanked them for sticking with him for all these years.

On several occasions Lee Majors was in attendance. Elvis would stop the show and say, "All right girls . . . stay in your seats—tonight I have a new bodyguard . . . I would like you to meet him . . . . He's the Six Million Dollar Man. He's working here tonight because he's been out of work in Hollywood." The television star would then run out onstage in slow motion (as he did on the opening of his hit TV series), circle Elvis, take Elvis' scarf, and throw it from the stage. The girls would scream, prompting Elvis to say, "You ladies sure are fickle." He would begin to laugh and continued, pointing at Lee, "He's my friend, he's a very talented actor. Ladies and gentlemen, Mr. Lee Majors. That's it, Lee, get off the stage, this is my show." This routine never failed to entertain the faithful.

During this engagement something very unusual occurred. It was standard fare for two men to try to rush Elvis onstage. They wanted a kiss, a scarf, or to wipe the sweat from his face. One evening, as Elvis was at the end of his show, a man jumped onstage and slowly walked toward Elvis, catching him by surprise. Within seconds Red West rushed to his boss's aid. Elvis' initial reaction was to move to the side but the man just hugged Elvis. Elvis realized the man was mentally challenged but could see the affection in his eyes. As Red grabbed the man Elvis shouted at Red to let him go. He took the scarf from around his neck and placed it gently around the man's neck. Neither Red nor the audience had any idea what was happening. Elvis spoke softly to the gentleman, then put his arm around the man's shoulders and led him to the side of the stage. Once they were behind the stage curtain Elvis talked to the man for a few minutes. He then took the watch he was wearing and put it on the fan's wrist. He left the fellow

Private photo of Elvis and girlfriend Sheila Ryan. Imperial Suite, Hilton Hotel, March/April 1975.

Tour photos. Omni Coliseum, Atlanta, Georgia: April 30, 1975. White two-piece suit with blue trim. March/April 1975.

there and returned to center stage. As the show came to an end Elvis gave a final salute and was gone.

Elvis learned the man had suffered brain damage at birth and that his family had brought him to Vegas to see his hero. They had tipped nicely and were rewarded with a ringside table. The man's mother and father knew how much happiness their son had derived from Elvis' music. They had sat at their table hoping that Elvis would come over and that perhaps the mother would be able to get a scarf to give to her son, but Elvis never came close. As Elvis sang his final song their son stood up and got onstage. Elvis later said, "When I asked why he had grabbed me, he said simply, 'I didn't want you to leave. I love you, Elvis.' After the show was over I spent some time with him and his family. I'm glad he didn't get hurt."

Conrad Hilton attended the early show on the final night and was introduced by his biggest star. Elvis' closing show that same evening was spectacular. He walked out onstage and told the audience he was sorry but the show was canceled. The shocked crowd just stared. Elvis shouted, "April Fool's!" It was, after all, April. He thrilled them by performing an extra-long show. At one point Colonel Parker appeared onstage dressed as Santa Claus. Elvis also had his dog, Get-lo, brought out. While holding the chow's leash he explained, "He's been sick. (Get-lo had a serious kidney problem and passed away a short time later.) I'm having him flown to a Boston hospital right after the show." The crowd applauded and Elvis smiled. The Colonel and his boy showed their mutual respect for each other, and the audience was witnessing the greatest team in show business history.

A woman sitting near the stage handed Elvis a set of Mickey Mouse ears. He put the hat on and led the crowd in singing the theme song for the Mickey Mouse Club. Elvis and the band were armed with water pistols and had a grand old time having an old-fashioned water pistol fight, even shooting the fans sitting at the front of the stage.

When Elvis ended the show there was no doubt those lucky enough to be in Vegas and spend the evening with the King had been a part of something special. Elvis had the usual wrap party in his suite and then flew to Palm Springs to unwind, play, and rest.

ELVIS SOUVENIRS ELVIS
Benefiting
AURALLY HANDICAPPED CHILDREN OF LAS VEGAS
Mini Photo Albums
$1.
Deluxe Photo Albums
$3.
Special
ELVIS FUN ALBUM
$5.
Large Photo Albums
$2.
Hats • Posters
$6.
Scarves
ELVIS
ELVIS NOW
ELVIS

CHAPTER 17

Giving You All That I've Got

August 18, 1975–September 1, 1975

AS ELVIS WAS GETTING READY for his thirteenth season in Vegas, he was offered a starring film role as Rudolph Valentino, whose status as a sex symbol in the 1920s had been unequaled. The part was a natural for Elvis. The producers would have Elvis appear in a Broadway version and later star in the film adaptation. But the offer came at a time in his life when he could no longer muster the ambition or strength for such a project. He again told the Colonel to decline the offer.

Elvis and the gang decided to fly into Vegas a few days early. Red West recalled the flight: "Elvis took some pills and suddenly shouted, 'I can't breathe!' Me and Charlie Hodge tried to give him oxygen and fresh air from a vent in the floor but Elvis shouted, 'I can't do it. Land!' We had an emergency landing in Dallas. We took Elvis to a hotel and stayed there for hours. Eventually Elvis was okay, the effects of the pills had worn off. Those goddamn pills are the reason why Elvis only performed five shows in Vegas before the engagement was canceled by the Hilton and Elvis wound up in a Memphis hospital."

Elvis souvenir stand in the lobby of the Hilton Hotel, August/September 1975.

ELVIS WORE HIS GYPSY SUIT on opening night. He took some requests from the audience, but it was apparent that he was not well. His voice was in good form but he had trouble standing up and often sat down throughout the short, forty-five-minute show. Elvis was so weak that he was unable to make the usual walk from his dressing room to the elevator; he made the trip in a golf cart.

At the next night's dinner show Elvis seemed to be feeling much better. He performed a one-hour concert and even included his classic gospel song "Crying In The Chapel." This would be the first and last time Elvis would perform this song live. Still, he seemed weak and had Charlie Hodge bring a chair onstage.

Elvis' midnight show saw the entertainer give a

Tour photo. Asheville Civic Center, Asheville, North Carolina: July 23, 1975. Gypsy Star Suit.

Far right: Tour photo. State Fair Coliseum, Jackson, Mississippi: June 8, 1975. White with black Phoenix Suit.

Right: Tour photo. Dallas Memorial Auditorium, Dallas, Texas:, June 6, 1975. White with black Phoenix Suit.

Onstage: Gypsy Star Suit. Hilton Showroom, August/September 1975.

brave but flawed performance. He arrived late and after singing, "C.C. Rider" he said, "You'll never guess where I was—I was in the john . . . this is the first time this has happened to me." He continued, "I don't do a thing like that . . . that was what I was told the other day. I went to a football game in Memphis and a lady there says to a friend of mine, 'I hear Elvis is here' and my friend says, 'Yeah, he's sitting in the press box.' The lady asks, 'Can I see him?' and my friend says, 'No you can't because he's in the john.' The lady looked surprised and then got all serious and said, 'I didn't think he did that.'" Elvis smiled and the audience laughed. After fifty minutes the show was over.

On August 20, Elvis' dinner show didn't bring any smiles to the entertainer or any laughter from the crowd. Elvis managed to stay onstage for forty minutes but there was no hiding the truth from the fans; they were watching a brave but very sick man.

That evening at the late show Elvis was a little better. He was onstage for forty-five minutes. He was wearing a watch that he glanced at constantly. As soon as he had performed his contractual time he was gone. One person who was not surprised was comedian Jackie Kahane who had been told to cut his opening act short so Elvis would get onstage and get the show over with. Elvis collapsed on his way to the elevator and had to be carried the rest of the way.

At six in the morning Elvis left the hotel. It has

Onstage: Saber Tooth Tiger Suit. Hilton Showroom, August/September 1975.

been reported that he was carried out on a stretcher, his body covered from head to toe. This is not true. He walked out and flew back to Memphis where he was, once again, admitted to Baptist Memorial Hospital. He was again on the eighteenth floor in the same room when the Vegas crowd woke up and found out he was gone. Elvis' name on the Hilton marquee had been replaced by vocalist Peggy Lee's. Every banner, poster, and mention of Elvis had disappeared. The fans who had driven to Vegas left town, and those who had flown in tried to get reservations on the next plane departing for their destinations.

The hospital released a statement citing internal problems and fatigue as the reason for Elvis' hospitalization. While in the hospital Elvis watched Jerry Lewis' annual Muscular Dystrophy Telethon. He was moved enough to pick up the phone and donate $5,000 for Jerry's kids. The hospital's switchboards were lit up with calls from around the world from fans wanting to wish Elvis a speedy recovery. Before Elvis' sixteen-day stay ended President Gerald R. Ford called to speak to Elvis and had to convince the switchboard operator that he really was the President of the United States. The King and the President had a lengthy conversation. President Ford joked that he could pick up the phone and talk to anyone in the world but when he tried to talk to Elvis he had been given the third degree.

Onstage: White, silver, and blue-studded Tear Drop Suit. Hilton Showroom, December 1975.

CHAPTER 18

Standing Room Only

December 2, 1975–December 15, 1975

Colonel Parker had the Las Vegas Hilton reschedule Elvis' canceled August shows for early December. The hotel was very concerned about the timing, as this was traditionally the slowest time of the year in Vegas. Most folks were home getting ready to enjoy the holidays with family and friends. The few who ventured to Sin City were hardcore gamblers who didn't care what entertainers were performing in town.

When it was announced that Elvis would be having a "Pre-holiday Jubilee," Vegas changed. The telephones began to ring off their hooks. Every room in the giant hotel would be filled because if you wanted to see the Elvis Show, you had to be a guest at the hotel.

Elvis would be traveling to Vegas in style, having purchased his new and most expensive toy yet, a Delta Airlines jet. He had the plane completely redone to his specifications. He had the inside gutted, and once the seats and interior were removed, he had the paint stripped. The main cabin was painted in green and brown, his bedroom was royal blue, the furniture and conference table were made of teak, and gold faucets were installed in his private bathroom. Other perks included an audio and video system. The outside of Elvis' flying palace was painted white and trimmed in red and blue. The plane's tail was inscribed with his TCB (Taking Care of Business) logo. Written boldly across the nose in script was his daughter's name, "Lisa Marie." The number N880EP, which stood for "Elvis Presley's Convair 880," was on the plane's side and wings. The boy who hated flying now owned his own jet.

On November 29 Elvis left Graceland for the Memphis Airport. He wanted time to rehearse once he arrived in Vegas. The Lisa Marie was ready and the plane's pilot, Captain Elwood David, was informed that Elvis was on his way. He turned on the outside lights and the tail section, sporting Elvis' TCB and lightning bolt logo, shone brightly. As Elvis' car pulled onto the runway he saw his logo glowing in the dark Memphis night.

He remembered the long-ago car ride from Tupelo to Memphis, riding with his parents, Vernon and Gladys, with all their belongings strapped to the roof of the car. He recalled the years in the projects, the hunger, the embarrassment of being one of the families that depended on public assistance. As the plane approached its landing at McCarran Airport he realized that things were sure different now. He stepped from his plane surrounded by his paid security and jumped into the waiting limousine that sped toward the Hilton Hotel and the thousands of fans who awaited him.

The Elvis show was again a complete sellout. Many of the showrooms in the city were closed and those that were open were lucky to have a 50 percent crowd, but the Hilton and Elvis set attendance records. The audiences in December 1975 were the largest ever in the town's history. To this day no other performer has come close to what Elvis accomplished during the so-called Vegas dead season.

Elvis wore his Memphis Indian jumpsuit on opening night and appeared happy and healthier. He greeted the audience with, "Ladies and gentlemen, I would like to say that it is a pleasure to be back. We've had a break of around three months. I did a three-week engagement at Baptist Memorial Hospital." This brought a round applause from the audience.

Elvis' shows were at least one hour long and, in some instances, an hour and a half. It seemed as though he didn't want to leave the stage. His old friend Liberace attended the opening-night show and when Elvis introduced him he said, "Lee, you're a great entertainer. You were always my mother's favorite." The season's strongest performance was "America The Beautiful." Some evenings he would speak some of the lines and on other evenings he

Tour photos. Freedom Hall, Johnson City, Tennessee, March 18, 1976. Navy blue with silver Phoenix Suit.

spoke almost the entire song. The audiences would stand up and place their hands on their hearts.

The Christmas spirit abounded in the showroom. The girls who were lucky or rich enough to be seated near the stage all brought Christmas presents to give to Elvis. He would then sing "Blue Christmas." The city of Las Vegas was so happy to have their adopted son back that all of their radio stations played Elvis' Christmas music night and day for the entire time he was in town.

There were changes within Elvis' stage family. Voice had been let go, though Sherrill Nielson remained as Elvis' first tenor. Duke Bardwell, who had grown tired of the way Elvis insulted him onstage, was

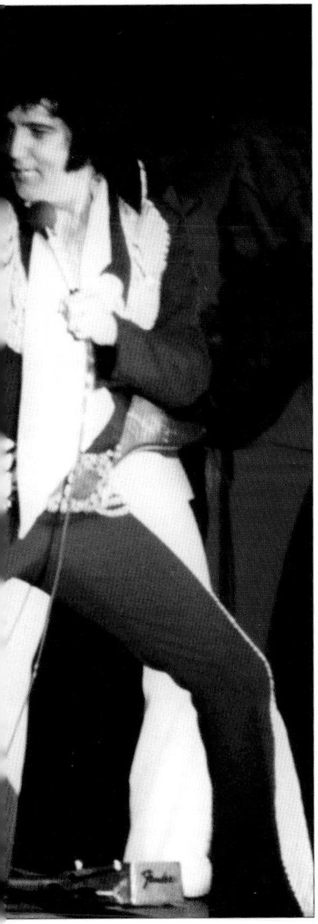

Onstage: Blue with silver Phoenix Suit. Hilton Showroom, December 1975.

gone and Jerry Scheff was back on bass guitar. Glen D. Hardin, arranger and piano player, was growing tired of Elvis' nasty comments and vowed to quit after this Vegas engagement. James Burton, the legendary lead guitarist who had been with Elvis since his return to live performing in 1969, spoke in private of his growing dissatisfaction with the stale material he was forced to play night after night. He, too, was seriously considering leaving with Glen. Ronnie Tutt, who was the beat behind Elvis and a fan favorite, was equally jaded. He said the only time he had any fun was when he sat in during the Sweet Inspirations rehearsals because he got to play new songs.

Onstage Elvis' voice was stronger than ever. The rough and gravelly edge that was so wonderful during his earlier Vegas engagements had been replaced by a more mature, smooth, and powerful instrument capable of reaching notes and holding them for so long that it took your breath away. After many of the shows the showroom crowds spoke of how wonderful Elvis had been. Many considered this engagement to be the best they had ever experienced.

Priscilla brought Lisa to see her daddy and they stayed in town for a few days. They were present at several shows sitting at their reserved booth. After the December 5 show Elvis took Lisa and Priscilla to the airport to see the Lisa Marie. Seven-year-old Lisa was excited to see her name on the plane. Elvis led them on to the plane, the door closing behind them. He went along with them as Captain David flew them back to Memphis and showed them Graceland from the sky. He then instructed the captain to turn around and fly back to Vegas, where they had another show to do.

Once, after completing a very physical version of "Polk Salad Annie," Elvis was out of breath. As he

Left, and far left: Onstage: White with black Phoenix Suit. Hilton Showroom, December 1975.

Below: Tour photo. Auditorium, West Palm Beach, Florida, February 14, 1977. Memphis Indian Suit.

walked around the Hilton stage drinking Mountain Valley Mineral Water and trying to catch his breath. a man seated stage center yelled out, "Hey, Elvis, my wife will be happy to give you mouth-to-mouth resuscitation." Elvis grinned at the guy and said okay. He then laid down on the stage, staring up at the stage lights. The lady walked to where Elvis was lying flat on his back, got down on her hands and knees, and crawled on top of Elvis. In this position she began to kiss Elvis on the lips. After a few seconds Elvis playfully lifted his head and gave the audience a puzzled look. The crowd and Elvis broke up with laughter as Charlie Hodge pulled the woman off of him. Elvis turned toward the husband and said, "That did it all right . . . I'm resuscitated."

Tour photo. Nassau Veterans Memorial Coliseum, Uniondale, New York, July 19, 1975, 2:30 p.m. show. Saber Tooth Tiger Suit.

Onstage: Bicentennial Suit,
Hilton Showroom, December 1975.

This page, and following:
Onstage: V-neck Suit with blue trim.
Hilton Showroom, December 1975.

On closing night Elvis told the audience, "I'm going to be playing to the largest crowd of my career on New Year's Eve. Colonel Parker booked the Silverdome in Pontiac, Michigan. I'm going to be scared to death in that big old place." He continued, "Next year is America's two hundredth birthday and I plan to be in cities all over America. If you want me to come, just ask and I'll be there.

"I would like to say a few words about how good it is to be back to work again. We're going to work a lot next year. Well, maybe we'll come to your hometown wherever you live. I would like to thank our soundman Bill Porter and Felton Jarvis, my friend and producer. I want you to meet my father . . . Dad, get up . . . and to the band and everyone onstage I would like to say with devotion . . . You've done a fantastic job. This has really been a fantastic engagement . . . one of the best we've had. If we don't see each other, have a Merry Christmas and a Happy New Year. God bless you."

Elvis spent Christmas at Graceland with Linda Thompson. The next day he flew to Detroit and on New Year's Eve he welcomed in America's Bicentennial by performing for the biggest crowd of his career, a record-breaking sixty thousand–plus people.

Onstage: Flame Suit.
Hilton Showroom,
December 1976.

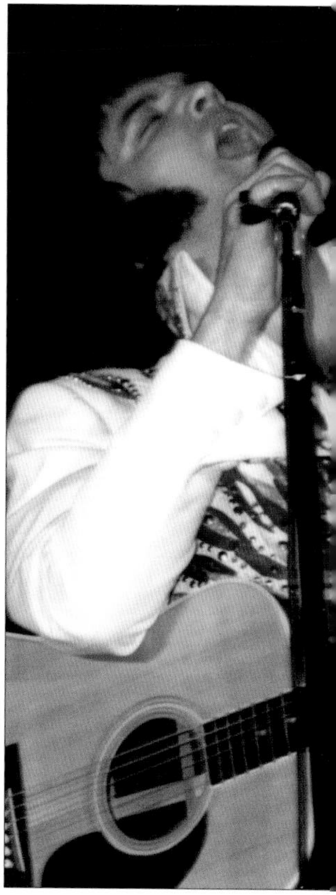

CHAPTER 19

The Last Dance

December 2, 1976–December 12, 1976

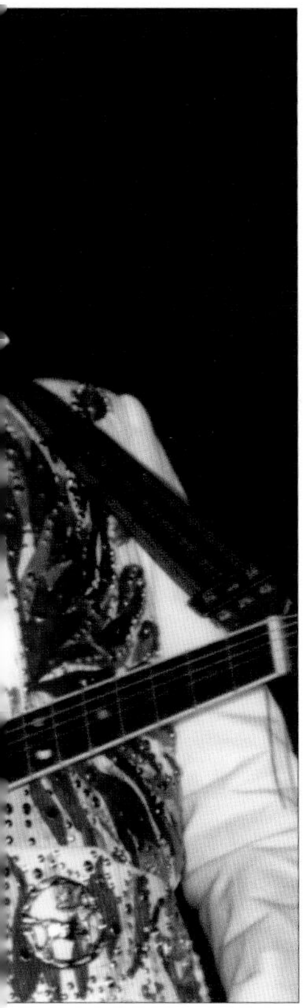

Tour photo. University of Dayton, Dayton, Ohio: October 26, 1976. Flame Suit.

THE UNITED STATES BICENTENNIAL was celebrated on Sunday, July 4, 1976, the two hundredth anniversary of the signing of the Declaration of Independence.

In Tulsa, Oklahoma, fans celebrated America's two hundredth birthday by seeing the King perform. Oral Roberts University's Maybee Center had sold out without a single advertisement. The boy from Tupelo wore his light blue Bicentennial suit and explained to his worshippers that his belt sported the presidential seal. Elvis moved, strutted, and beat himself into a frenzy. The heat of thousands of fireworks couldn't have been more intense than the performance.

On Monday, July 5, fans, friends, and family packed Memphis, Tennessee's Mid-South Coliseum. The big event of their weekend celebration of the Bicentennial Fourth of July was Elvis' homecoming concert. When he strolled onstage the flashbulbs in the audience turned the scene into a pyrotechnic display. "Let me tell you," he told the cheering sold-out arena, "I'll sing all the songs you want. It's the end of our tour and I have as much time as you want tonight." Elvis kept his promise, singing everything they wanted to hear from 10:00 p.m. until forty minutes before midnight. He sang songs from when his career first began. Elvis said, "They say I shouldn't sing 'That's All Right' anymore." Then, picking up his guitar, "By God, watch me!" His swivel hips brought screams. "It never ceases to amaze me," he said, waiting for the waves of sound to die down. When he sang "Help Me," he said, with a twinkle in his eye, "That's from an album that I made two years ago, *Elvis in the Gutter*." The King was serious only once. Obviously irked by past reports on his health, he said, "The last time I was here I was sick a couple of weeks, but I'm over all that and I'm working and I'm happy." After the concert Elvis returned to Graceland, where a giant fireworks display took place.

During the previous year's Vegas engagement Elvis told the fans he would give everybody in America the opportunity to see him in person; he certainly kept his word. I once asked him, "Elvis, why don't you take some time off, play with Lisa, travel, do the things you want to do?"

He responded, "Paul, those people, my audience, they're the other half of me and when I'm onstage we make each other whole. When I feel their love . . . well man, it's the only time I feel alive." Between March 17 and December 31, 1976, he would perform 129 concerts in 97 different cities. This grueling pace would have destroyed a twenty-year-old rocker and Elvis was now forty-one.

On July 6 he and Linda flew to Palm Springs. Six days later Elvis had Vernon fire Red West, Sonny West, and bodyguard/karate expert Dave Hebler with just one week's back pay.

ON AUGUST 27 ELVIS STARTED yet another tour, in San Antonio, followed by a 2:30 p.m. Saturday matinee at the Summit in Houston. Elvis was clearly not himself as he struggled to complete the show. The *Houston Post* music critic Bob Claypool was in attendance and his review of the performance was frightening: "Elvis Presley has been breaking hearts for more than twenty years now and Saturday afternoon in the Summit—in a completely new and unexpected way—he broke mine." He continued, "In short the concert was awful—a depressingly incoherent, amateurish mess served up by a bloated, stumbling and mumbling figure who didn't act like the king of anything, least of all rock and roll."

Dave Hebler and the Wests were writing an exposé book that threatened to blow up Elvis' image as a clean-cut, all-American boy who didn't smoke, drink, use profanity, who loved his mother, served his country, and was always polite. Steve Dunleavy, who worked as a reporter for the weekly tabloid

The National Star, would become the disgruntled ex-employees' ghostwriter. The *Star* ran a story announcing the upcoming book in their October 26 issue.

Elvis had a copy of the book's manuscript and was deeply hurt by its contents. He kept saying, "Why are they doing this?" He was concerned for himself but devastated by what his fans and family would think.

LINDA THOMPSON WAS STILL with him, but after four years of loving and caring for him she realized she had to get away. Linda later recalled, "I loved him with all my heart and he loved me—we were soul mates. I couldn't stand it anymore. He was going to

Onstage: King of Spades Suit. Hilton Showroom, December 1976.

Right: Tour photo.
Cow Palace, San Francisco,
November 28, 1976.
King of Spades Suit.

go ahead and slowly kill himself no matter what I did. I couldn't make him happy and I knew he wasn't going to change—so I left."

On November 19 Elvis was introduced to Ginger Alden, a beautiful twenty-year-old Memphis girl. George Klein had arranged for Elvis to meet Ginger's older sister, Terry, who was the current Miss Tennessee. Terry brought her sisters, Ginger and Rosemary, along for the meeting at Graceland. Elvis was immediately struck by Ginger's dark beauty, later telling George how much she looked like a young Priscilla.

Ginger was with Elvis at his concert in Anaheim on November 30. This show was one of the best concerts Elvis had performed all year. He was inspired by Ginger's presence and told Larry Geller, "This is it"—that he had discovered love on a higher plane. Elvis would say, "Ginger's special. She's the one." This show ended his latest concert tour.

Elvis was due to open in Vegas on December 2. He was happy and in a great mood when he flew to Las Vegas to begin what would become his last Vegas engagement. He would perform one show nightly during the week and two shows on Fridays and Saturdays. There were oversize tickets, costing $29 each, printed for this engagement featuring a photo of Elvis in concert. Colonel Parker instructed the captains to be careful when removing the stubs from those entering the showroom so as not to damage the souvenir that fans were sure to take home with them.

THE DECEMBER 2 OPENING-NIGHT show was attended by fans from as close as Los Angeles and as far away as Japan. Priscilla was in the audience and stayed through the first weekend's shows. Elvis treated the faithful with vitality, pure showmanship, and overwhelming enthusiasm, performing for just under two

Left: Onstage: Saber Tooth Tiger Suit. Hilton Showroom, December 1976.

hours. He wore his King of Spades suit while singing twenty-nine songs in spectacular style. He sang "Hurt" and when the song ended, the audience's applause continued for so long that he performed it again. At one point in the show Charlie Hodge handed Elvis his acoustic guitar. As Elvis put the guitar on he said, "There are a number of people who don't think I can play the guitar . . . they're right!"

Glen Campbell, who was seated close to the stage, shouted, "Elvis—if I had a voice like you I wouldn't worry about playing the guitar."

Elvis smiled and introduced Glen, saying, "Ladies and gentlemen, he's my friend and he's one of the most talented singers and guitar players I know—stand up, Glen. Ladies and gentlemen, Glen Campbell." Elvis sang "Hawaiian Wedding Song" and thanked the audience for coming. He then introduced Priscilla, Lisa, and Ginger Alden before closing the show with the familiar classic from his 1961 film *Blue Hawaii*, "Can't Help Falling in Love."

The next day was Friday and he performed two shows. The first was good but the late show was wild

Onstage: Aztec Indian Suit. Hilton Showroom, December 1976.

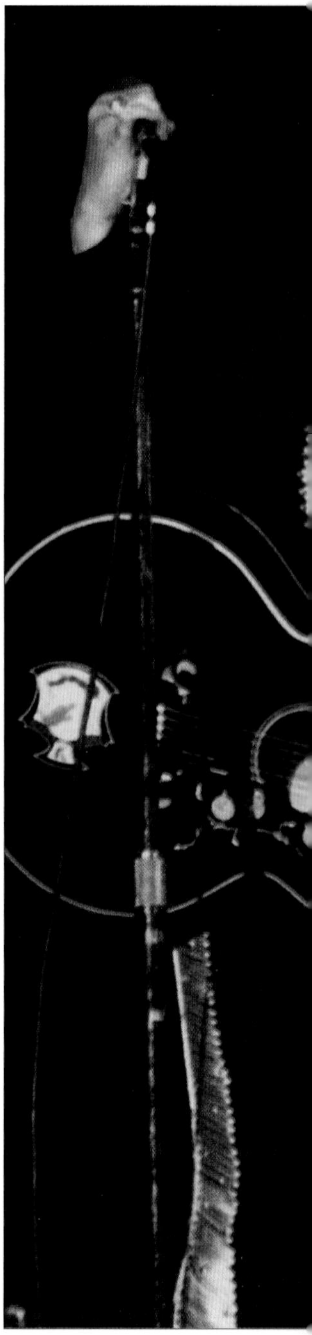

and wonderful. On Saturday both shows were exciting. Roy Orbison and Engelbert Humperdinck were in the audience, as were Priscilla and Lisa.

On Sunday evening Jackie Kahane performed an extra-long show. It lasted so long that the comedian ran out of jokes. He finally said, "Elvis is late because he dropped his wallet, which is very heavy—it has so much cash in it—that when Elvis bent down to pick it up he strained his back." The comedian was rewarded with nice applause when he left the stage.

The stage lights were turned off as Charlie Hodge adjusted the microphone and could be heard telling Bill Porter to turn the sound on. The band blasted the *2001* opening as the audience let out a deafening cheer. Elvis, limping slightly, smiled and grabbed the mike. "Well, I'm here, I am . . . bet you didn't know I used to be Chester on *Gunsmoke*, did you?" Elvis apologized for being late and went to great lengths to make the crowd feel welcome. After each of the first four songs he told funny stories. He also performed the laughing version of "Are You Lonesome Tonight."

The next night's show was a mess. Elvis was in obvious pain and limping badly. The pain pills caused him to either forget the songs' lyrics or mumble them.

Far left: Onstage: Navy blue with silver Phoenix Suit. Hilton Showroom, December 1976.

Left: Tour photo. Freedom Hall, Johnson City, Tennessee, March 18, 1976. Navy blue with silver Phoenix Suit, Hilton Showroom, December 1976.

Above left: Tour photo. Civic Center Arena, Pittsburgh, December 31, 1976. White with black Phoenix Suit.

Above right: Onstage: White with red Phoenix Suit. Hilton Showroom, December 1976.

By the following evening Elvis' sprained ankle seemed to be a thing of the past. The remainder of the week's shows found him in great spirits. He sang everything the audiences had come to hear, performing long one-and-a-half-hour shows. He played around with the audience, kissed more girls, talked more, talked about his life, talked about Tupelo, talked about Graceland, put on funny glasses with fake noses, and wore crazy hats that were given to him by fans in the crowd. In a serious moment he said, "I have always wanted to do a complete show of just gospel songs . . . would you like to hear some?"

Someone in the audience shouted, "Elvis, you're the King!"

Elvis stared in the voice's direction before answering, "No I'm not the King . . . but I'm fixin' to sing about him."

Vernon Presley was in Vegas for the entire

engagement and didn't suffer a heart attack, as was reported in the newspapers. He did spend a few days in the hospital after complaining of chest pains. Elvis mentioned his father's condition to the audience at a few shows and when Vernon was released from the hospital, Elvis happily told the audiences his daddy was feeling better.

Elvis was fantastic at his early show on December 11. Priscilla's parents had flown in, along with their daughter, and were seated at Elvis' reserved booth. Elvis made a point of welcoming them when he told the fans, "There's someone in the room whom I dearly love—you all know perhaps who Priscilla is? Her mother and father are here. He is retired from the air force, this is the first time they've seen me in two years. I will dedicate the next song to him because . . . he's crazy. This song has many words, I have three Indians who come and translate it." Charlie Hodge brings Elvis a sheet of paper with the lyrics to "My Way." Elvis then sang a very heartfelt "My Way" for Priscilla, her mother, Ann, and her father, Paul.

As the sold-out crowd entered the Hilton showroom on December 12 they expected to see Elvis' closing-night show. No one could have guessed that they would be witnessing history; Elvis Presley's last Las Vegas performance.

Elvis opened with "C.C. Rider." Vocally Elvis was at his best as he held the audience in the palm of his hand. He sang of lost love; he rocked and rolled, draining the fans of all their inhibitions. When he sang "Can't Help Falling In Love" they were on their feet cheering for the poor boy from Tupelo who grew up to be a king and never stopped being nice along the way.

Onstage: Memphis Indian suit.
Hilton Showroom, December 1976.

Tour photos. Cow Palace, San Francisco, November 29, 1976. Rainbow Suit.

Onstage: White Bicentennial suit. Hilton Showroom, December 1975.

CHAPTER 20

And Now the End Is Near

December 24, 1976–June 26, 1977

ELVIS SPENT A QUIET CHRISTMAS at Graceland with Lisa Marie. He called a department store at a local mall and arrangements were made for the store to remain open after hours. When Elvis and Lisa arrived at the mall, there were still shoppers hurrying across the parking lot to their cars. Many recognized him and waved and shouted that they loved him. Elvis waved back, wishing them a Merry Christmas. Lisa, looking up at her daddy, asked, "Does everybody love you, Daddy?"

Elvis replied, "I hope so. I don't know why they love me . . . but they always have. Maybe they love me so much because I love them so much."

The Bicentennial year was coming to an end and Elvis performed in Wichita, Kansas, Dallas, Texas, Birmingham, Alabama, and Atlanta, Georgia, as an early New Year's treat for those cities. His New Year's Eve performance in Pittsburgh was one of the finest of his career. From the moment he stepped onstage you could feel the electricity. Elvis thanked everyone for coming to his New Year's Eve party while introducing his father, Vernon; his daughter, Lisa, and the love of his life, Ginger Alden. Someone put a troll doll on the stage that laughed when you pulled its string. Elvis glanced at it and said, "That's the ugliest goddamn thing I have ever seen and I've seen some ugly dolls." After performing everyone's favorite songs Elvis told the crowd, "Father Time shows there are two minutes remaining before the New Year." He wished everyone a Happy New Year and the countdown began, ten . . . nine . . . eight . . . then Elvis asked everyone to join him in singing "Auld Lang Syne." The spotlights swirled as the crowd went wild. Amid all the madness Elvis sat at the piano playing and singing "Rags To Riches" and "Unchained Melody." He then went into his closing number. At its conclusion he strutted from one end of the stage to the other, then knelt on one knee, arms up and head held back. He next went to center stage where he performed a three-minute kata complete with round house, front, side, and spinning back kicks. The King had brought 1977 in with a bang.

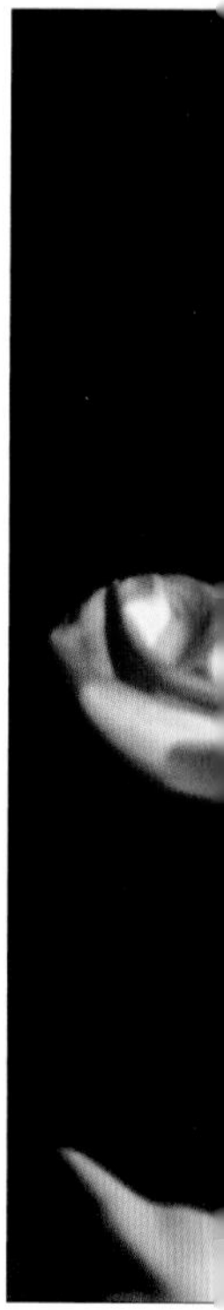

Tour photos. Spectrum, Philadelphia, June 28, 1976. White Bicentennial Suit.

Left, and above: Tour photos. Convention Center, San Antonio, Texas, August 27, 1976. White Bicentennial Suit.

Tour photos. Myriad Convention Center, Oklahoma City, May 29, 1976. Blue Bicentennial Suit.

On January 26, 1977, Elvis gave an eleven-and-a-half-carat engagement ring to Ginger. The two discussed plans for a big Memphis church wedding on Christmas Day of that year. But Elvis had been fighting his inner demons for a long time, and in 1977 it became apparent he was losing the battle. Over a period of six months Elvis would perform fifty-five concerts in fifty cities. I was at every show, and it was obvious that Elvis was struggling. The press was ripping him apart in every town, mentioning his weight, citing his lack of enthusiasm, criticizing him for running through his songs, for not caring. They said he was doing nothing to enhance, let alone assure, his reputation for younger generations. They accused him of taking the money and running. Elvis was having a tough time dealing with his appearance and was embarrassed by what he referred to as "excess baggage." He told the crowds not to pay any attention about the things they were reading about him, that he loved them and would come back and perform for them anytime they wanted him.

Elvis' final tour began on June 17, 1977, in Springfield, Missouri. The tour would be a very exciting one because CBS would be filming Elvis' shows in Omaha, Nebraska, on June 19 and Rapid City, South Dakota, on June 21. The footage would make up a TV special titled *Elvis in Concert*.

The June tour ended on the twenty-sixth at Indianapolis' Market Square Arena. Elvis wore the now-

Tour photo: Notre Dame University, South Bend, Indiana: October 20, 1976. Flame Suit.

Tour photo: S.W. Missouri State University, Springfield, Missouri. June 17, 1977. Sundial Suit.

familiar Mexican Sundial Suit. He sang "Bridge Over Troubled Water" and "Hurt" as though he was living it. He wailed "Release Me." He introduced Ginger, Vernon, and members of both families and sang "Can't Help Falling In Love" with all the vigor of his 1970 Vegas shows. Elvis sang his heart out and said farewell to his last standing ovation. He saluted his audience and ran from the stage. There would be no more concerts. Elvis had left the building forever.

Tour photos: Spectrum, Philadelphia, May 22, 1977. Sundial Suit.

IN CONCERT
MARKET SQUARE
JUNE
26
1977

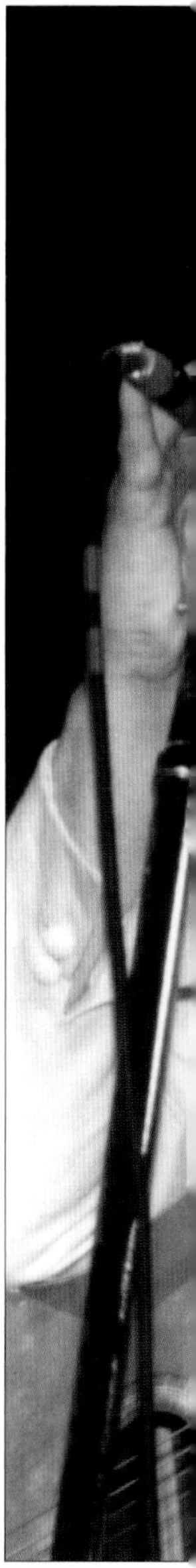

Tour photos: City Auditorium Arena, Omaha, Nebraska: June 19, 1977. Sundial Suit. This show was one of Elvis's final concerts and some footage was filmed by CBS for inclusion in the Elvis in Concert October 3, 1977 television special..

ELVIS PRESLEY 160 Union Ave, Memphis, Tenn.

CHAPTER 21

The Day the Rains Came Down

June 27, 1977–August 16, 1977

Left: Note Sun Records' address on the bottom of the photo. Elvis autographed this photo for Caroline Ballard, his Tupelo neighbor and friend. Caroline accompanied the ten-year-old Elvis to the Tupelo Mississippi–Alabama Fairgrounds, where Elvis won second prize for his rendition of "Old Shep" in the talent show. Elvis shared his prize with Caroline, and they used the tickets he won to go on all of the rides.

ELVIS HAD BEEN IN MEMPHIS six weeks since completing his last tour, rarely leaving his home. Two weeks earlier he had rented Libertyland Amusement Park for Lisa Marie and together, from midnight till dawn, they had a ball. The previous Wednesday he and the boys saw the latest James Bond flick, *The Spy Who Loved Me*, at the UA Southbrook 4. Another evening he and his future bride, Ginger Alden, visited her parents in Southeast Memphis.

MONDAY EVENING, AUGUST 15, 1977, the night before Elvis was to leave on "the tour that never was," Elvis was sitting at the large dinner table at Graceland when Charlie Hodge informed him that he was unable to arrange a private screening of the Gregory Peck movie *MacArthur*. Elvis protested as Charlie explained that the projectionist at the Ridgeway Theater, where the film was playing, would not be available at the late hour Elvis had requested. There, of course, was no way Elvis could attend the theater during public screenings. It had been twenty years since the man who brought joy to tens of millions in countless auditoriums and theaters could enter such a place except by rental and then only under the cover of darkness.

With nothing better to do, Elvis decided to try to get some last-minute dental work done. He called Dr. Lester Hoffman, the Memphis dentist who had treated him since the beginning of his career. Dr. Hoffman answered and Elvis apologized for the late call. He explained that he wanted some work done before leaving on tour and asked if he and Ginger could come by the office. Dr. Hoffman was happy to oblige.

At 10:30 that evening Elvis, along with Ginger, Charlie, and cousin Billy Smith, piled into his custom-made Stutz Blackhawk. They drove down the long driveway to the front gate that was crowded with fans. Elvis waved to them as the car moved out and proceeded down Elvis Presley Boulevard on the way

Louisiana Hayride KW
Be Happy
Go Lucky!
LUCKY STRIKE
CIGARETTES
L.S./M.F.T.

Left page: Tour photo. Left to right: Scotty Moore, James (Sonny) Trammel, Elvis, and Bill Black. Booneville Jr. College Auditorium, Booneville, Mississippi, January 22, 1955.

Right: Tour photo. Mayfair Building, Tyler, Texas: January 25, 1955.

Far right: Tour photo. Gilmer Jr. High School, Gilmer, Texas, September 26, 1955. Elvis appeared as part of the Louisiana Hayride Show sponsored by the Gilmer Lions Club.

Right: Tour photo. North Side Coliseum, Fort Worth, Texas, April 20, 1956.

Far right: Tour photo. Tupelo Mississippi–Alabama Fairgrounds, Tupelo, Mississippi: Saturday afternoon, September 26, 1956.

the dentist's office located at 620 Estate Drive in a wealthy section of East Memphis. Upon their arrival Elvis lovingly introduced his fiancée by her pet name, Gingerbread. Dr. Hoffman smiled as Elvis kiddingly said, "Isn't this an ugly girl?"

Elvis sat in the dentist's chair as Dr. Hoffman cleaned his teeth and put fillings in his upper right bicuspid and upper left molar. Ginger had her teeth X-rayed and made arrangements to return to have her teeth cleaned. Elvis inquired about Dr. Hoffman's wife, Sterling. Dr. Hoffman was a car enthusiast and the two men's conversation turned to automobiles. Elvis told him, "You've got to see my new car. I've got a Ferrari you won't believe."

The dentist asked, "You're not getting rid of the Stutz, are you?"

"No," Elvis said, "but you'll really like the Ferrari. Come on out to Graceland and you'll see it."

As Elvis and his friends were getting ready to leave, Dr. Hoffman asked a favor: "The next time you're going out to California I'd like to come. It would be a nice surprise if I could drop in on my daughter out there."

Elvis replied, "Sure, there's always room on the plane." They said their goodbyes. It was 12:30 Tuesday morning.

Arriving back at Graceland, Elvis called his chief security man, Dick Grob, on the house phone and asked him to meet him upstairs. Elvis planned to add six new songs to his show and wanted Grob to locate the words, music, and chord changes for the stage versions. As Grob was preparing to leave with the song list Elvis said, "I'm going to make this tour the best ever."

Later Elvis and Ginger were alone together upstairs at Graceland. They talked of the upcoming tour

Tour photo. Fort Homer W. Hesterly Armory, Tampa, Florida: August 5, 1956.

Tour photos. Florida Theater, Jacksonville, Florida, August 10, 1956.

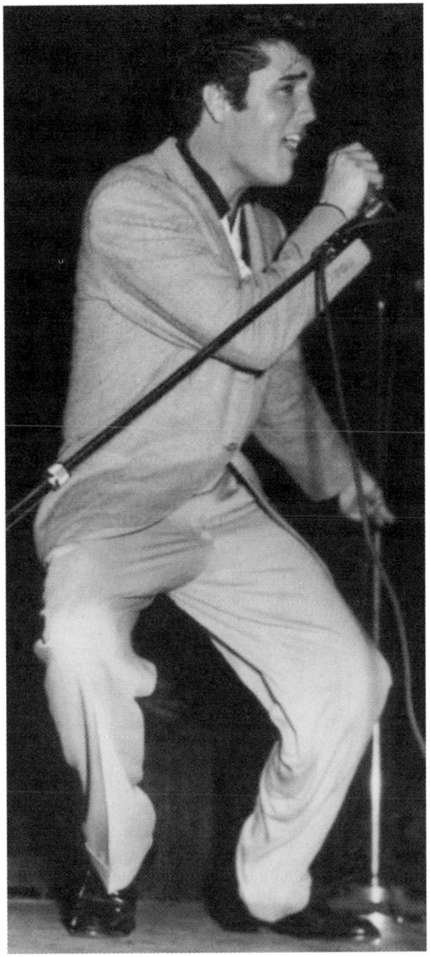

Tour photos. Conroy Bowl, Schofield Barracks, Honolulu, November 11, 1957.

Left page: Tour photo. Unconfirmed location, 1956.

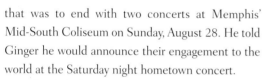

Tour photos. Jefferson County Armory, Louisville, Kentucky, November 25, 1956.

that was to end with two concerts at Memphis' Mid-South Coliseum on Sunday, August 28. He told Ginger he would announce their engagement to the world at the Saturday night hometown concert.

Shortly before dawn Elvis and Ginger decided to play racquetball. He called Billy Smith and invited him and his wife, Jo, to join them. The four of them left for the racquetball building Elvis had built just beyond the main house. He was proud of the giant room that was equipped with saunas, whirlpool baths, and an elaborate sound system. Ginger and Jo played for a little while before the guys got out on the court but Elvis was growing tired and after injuring his shin he decided he'd had enough. The two couples went to the lounge area and gathered around the piano. Elvis sang and played a few songs, ending with "Blue Eyes Crying In The Rain." Ginger was well aware of the chronic insomnia that plagued Elvis and hoped that he would now be able to sleep. They said good night to the Smiths and walked back to Graceland.

Elvis and Ginger went upstairs to the bedroom. They got into bed and Ginger turned on the television. Elvis leaned over and kissed her lightly on the forehead and told her he was going to read in the lounge area of the adjoining bathroom. Ginger fell asleep almost immediately and awoke at 2:00 p.m. and called for Elvis. There was no answer. She got up from the bed, her head still heavy with sleep, and made her way to the bathroom door. She knocked on the door and after no response entered and saw Elvis' figure sprawled on the two-inch-thick carpet. He was lying facedown with the *Shroud of Turin* book beside him and was totally unresponsive. Ginger, sobbing uncontrollably, alerted Al Strada and Joe Esposito who came immediately. Al pushed Ginger out of the room as Joe frantically tried to revive Elvis without success. He then called Vernon, who brought Lisa Marie and others, surrounding the area with growing fear. Eventually Dr. Nichopoulos arrived, at the same time as the ambulance.

Right: NBC Studios, Burbank, California: June 1968. Elvis' 1968 TV special was first broadcast on December 3, 1968.

Tour photo. Madison Square Garden, New York, Saturday afternoon, June 10, 1972.

Elvis was taken to Baptist Memorial with Dr. Nick attempting CPR the entire way, yelling "Breathe, Presley, breathe! Damn you, Presley, breathe!" Elvis Aron Presley was pronounced dead at 3:30 p.m. August 16, 1977. The cause of death: cardiac arrhythmia. The vaguely musical sound of that was somewhat consoling in a way that simple heart failure would not have been. None of us could associate the word "failure" with the heartbeat that for so many years caused a generation to throb to its rhythm.

On the day Elvis Presley died Las Vegas was scorched. It had for months been praying for rain. Because of the near drought, water was served in restaurants only upon request. At the moment of Elvis' death rain began to fall. There was no thunder—no lightning—just constant rain, for hours, drenching the parched earth.

"Aloha from Hawaii" satellite concert. Honolulu International Center, Honolulu, January 14, 1973.

APPENDIX

With a Song in My Heart: Set Lists, Jumpsuits, and Show Members

IN THIS APPENDIX there is no attempt to list a breakdown of songs sung by Elvis from his debut at the New Frontier in Las Vegas in 1956. There is simply no documentation and therefore it is impossible to intelligently discuss here. Any attempt would only be guesswork.

During an eight-year period of almost nonstop Las Vegas engagements, Elvis single-handedly revolutionized and redefined the word "superstar." To those of us who were lucky enough to witness Elvis live onstage in Vegas, there are no words to adequately describe the experience and sadly no way to ever relive the moment. It is really incredible how many people do not realize the importance of Elvis in the 1970s, as I believe it to be one of the landmark highs in his incredible career.

The following is a list of shows broken down by engagement, year, and date. At the conclusion of each engagement you will find a comprehensive alphabetical breakdown of all songs sung at that particular engagement. This information is what I've been able to ascertain with a fair amount of assurance.

After painstakingly researching my private archives and getting as many firsthand accounts as possible, I enlisted the help of Bud Glass, whose collection of Elvis live concert tapes is without a doubt the finest in the world. Elvis scholars and historians Mike Eder and Frode Rorbakk also shared their knowledge and collections with me.

It is important to note that many cassette tapes that were recorded by Elvis' fans during their Elvis Vegas experiences would not get labeled and identified until they returned home. In many cases dinner shows were mistakenly labeled as midnight performances and vice versa. Sometimes cassette tapes also were given the wrong dates. Further confusing the matter. these mistakes are commonly repeated using today's technology by both RCA on their compact disc releases and by fans on their CDRs.

As a rule of thumb I have used a minimum of two sources in reaching the conclusions listed here. Where you see "not available" I was not able to verify the songs in those performances. I believe these listings to be 99 percent accurate. They are not definitive and should be used as they are meant to be: simply a guide.

VEGAS SEASON 1 1969, International Hotel
Thursday, July 31, 1969 through Thursday, August 28, 1969—57 shows—Total attendance 125,400

Jumpsuits Worn During This Engagement—Black Karate Suit with red scarf and red kick pleat, Dark blue Karate Suit with light blue scarf and light blue kick pleat, White Karate Suit with black Apache scarf, White Karate Suit with turquoise scarf, Black Karate Suit with red trim and red/black macramé belt, Black Karate Suit with red trim and red/black karate belt.

Show Members—Musicians: Lead Guitar—James Burton, Rhythm Guitar—John Wilkinson, Acoustic Guitar and Back Up Vocals—Charlie Hodge, Bass—Jerry Scheff, Piano and Organ—Larry Muhoberac, Drums—Ronnie Tutt, Backup Singers: Sweet Inspirations: Cissy Houston, Myrna Smith, Sylvia Shemwell, Estelle Brown, The Imperials: Jake Hess, Jim Murray, Gary McSpadden, Armond Morales, High Voice Singer—Millie Kirkham, Comedian—Sammy Shore, Orchestra—Bobby Morris

July 31, 1969—Opening Night—10:15 P.M.—Complete
Blue Suede Shoes, I Got A Woman, Hound Dog (Hilarious version), Heartbreak Hotel, Love Me Tender, Baby What You Want Me To Do, Runaway, Surrender/Are You Lonesome Tonight (laughing version), Rubberneckin', Memories, When The Snow Is On The Roses, Introductions, Jailhouse Rock/Don't Be Cruel, Inherit The Wind, This Is The Story, Mystery Train/Tiger Man, Funny How Time Slips Away, Loving You/Reconsider Baby, Suspicious Minds,What'd I Say, Can't Help Falling In Love

August 1, 1969—Dinner Show—Complete
Blue Suede Shoes, I Got A Woman, All Shook Up, Love Me Tender, Jailhouse Rock/Don't Be Cruel, Heartbreak Hotel, Hound Dog, Memories, Mystery Train/Tiger Man, Monologue Life Story, Baby What You Want Me To Do, Are You Lonesome Tonight, Yesterday/Hey Jude, Introductions, In The Ghetto, Suspicious Minds, What'd I Say, Can't Help Falling In Love

August 1, 1969—Midnight Show—Complete
Blue Suede Shoes, I Got A Woman, All Shook Up, Love Me Tender, My Babe, Jailhouse Rock/Don't Be Cruel, Heartbreak Hotel, Dialogue, Hound Dog, Memories, Baby What You Want Me To Do, Runaway, Are You Lonesome Tonight, Yesterday/Hey Jude, Introductions, In The Ghetto, Suspicious Minds, Can't Help Falling In Love

August 2, 1969—Dinner Show—Not Available

August 2, 1969—Midnight—Not Available

August 3, 1969—Dinner Show—Complete
Blue Suede Shoes, I Got A Woman, All Shook Up, Love Me Tender, Jailhouse Rock/Don't Be Cruel, Heartbreak Hotel, Hound Dog, Memories, Mystery Train/Tiger Man, Monologue Life Story, Baby What You Want Me To Do, Are You Lonesome Tonight, Yesterday/Hey Jude, Introductions, In The Ghetto, Suspicious Minds, What'd I Say, Can't Help Falling In Love

August 3, 1969—Midnight Show—Complete
Blue Suede Shoes, Baby What You Want Me To Do, I Got A Woman, Are You Lonesome Tonight, All Shook Up, Yesterday, Hey Jude, Love Me Tender, Jailhouse Rock, Don't Be Cruel, Introductions, Heartbreak Hotel, In The Ghetto, Hound Dog, Suspicious Minds, Memories, What'd I Say, Mystery Train/Tiger Man, Can't Help Falling In Love

August 4, 1969—Dinner Show—Incomplete
Blue Suede Shoes, I Got A Woman, Love Me Tender, Heartbreak Hotel, All Shook Up, Don't Be Cruel, Are You Lonesome Tonight, Jailhouse Rock, Hound Dog, In The Ghetto, Tiger Man, What'd I Say, Baby What You Want Me To Do, Yesterday/Hey Jude, Can't Help Falling In Love

August 4, 1969—Midnight Show—Incomplete
Blue Suede Shoes, I Got A Woman, Love Me Tender, Heartbreak Hotel, All Shook Up, Don't Be Cruel, Are You Lonesome Tonight, Jailhouse Rock, Hound Dog, In The Ghetto, Tiger Man, What'd I Say, Baby What You Want Me To Do, Yesterday/Hey Jude, Can't Help Falling In Love

August 5, 1969—Dinner Show—Complete
Blue Suede Shoes, I Got A Woman, All Shook Up, Dialogue, Love Me Tender, Jailhouse Rock/Don't Be Cruel, Heartbreak Hotel, Hound Dog, Memories, Dialogue, Mystery Train/Tiger Man, Monologue Life Story, Baby What You Want Me To Do, Runaway, Are You Lonesome Tonight, Yesterday/Hey Jude, Introductions, In The Ghetto, Suspicious Minds, What'd I Say, Can't Help Falling In Love.

August 5, 1969—Midnight Show—Complete
Blue Suede Shoes, I Got A Woman, All Shook Up, Dialogue, Love Me Tender, Jailhouse Rock/Don't Be Cruel, Heartbreak Hotel, Hound Dog, Memories, Dialogue, Mystery Train/Tiger Man, Monologue Life Story, Further Along (partial), Baby What You Want Me To Do, Runaway, Are You Lonesome Tonight, Yesterday/Hey Jude, Introductions, In The Ghetto, Suspicious Minds, What'd I Say, Can't Help Falling In Love.

August 6, 1969—Dinner Show—Complete
Blue Suede Shoes, I Got A Woman, All Shook Up, Love Me Tender, Jailhouse Rock/Don't Be Cruel, Heartbreak Hotel, Dialogue, Hound Dog, Dialogue, Memories, Dialogue, Mystery Train/Tiger Man, Blue Hawaii (partial), Dialogue, Baby What You Want Me To Do, Runaway, Are You Lonesome Tonight, Yesterday/Hey Jude, Introductions, In The Ghetto, Suspicious Minds, What'd I Say, Can't Help Falling In Love

August 6, 1969—Midnight Show—Complete
Blue Suede Shoes, I Got A Woman, All Shook Up, Love Me Tender, Jailhouse Rock/Don't Be Cruel, Heartbreak Hotel, Hound Dog, Memories, Mystery Train/Tiger Man, Monologue Life Story, Baby What You Want Me To Do, Runaway, Are You Lonesome Tonight, Yesterday/Hey Jude, Introductions, In The Ghetto, Suspicious Minds, What'd I Say, Can't Help Falling In Love

August 7, 1969—Dinner Show—Complete
Blue Suede Shoes, I Got A Woman, All Shook Up, Love Me Tender, Jailhouse Rock/Don't Be Cruel, Heartbreak Hotel, Hound Dog, Memories, Mystery Train/Tiger Man, Baby What You Want Me To Do, Monologue Life Story, Runaway, Are You Lonesome Tonight, Yesterday/Hey Jude, Introductions, In The Ghetto, Suspicious Minds, What'd I Say, Can't Help Falling In Love

August 7, 1969—Midnight Show—Complete
Blue Suede Shoes, I Got A Woman, All Shook Up, Love Me Tender, Jailhouse Rock/Don't Be Cruel, Heartbreak Hotel, Hound Dog, Memories, Mystery Train/Tiger Man, Baby What You Want Me To Do, Monologue Life Story, Runaway, Are You Lonesome Tonight, Yesterday/Hey Jude, Introductions, In The Ghetto, Suspicious Minds, What'd I Say, Can't Help Falling In Love

August 8, 1969—Dinner Show—Complete
Blue Suede Shoes, I Got A Woman, All Shook Up, Love Me Tender, Jailhouse Rock/Don't Be Cruel, Heartbreak Hotel, Dialogue, Hound Dog (extra verse), Dialogue, Memories, Dialogue, Mystery Train/Tiger Man, Baby What You Want Me To Do, Yesterday/Hey Jude, Introductions, In The Ghetto, Suspicious Minds, What'd I Say, Can't Help Falling In Love

August 8, 1969—Midnight Show—Complete
Blue Suede Shoes, I Got A Woman, All Shook Up, Love Me Tender, Jailhouse Rock/Don't Be Cruel, Heartbreak Hotel, Hound Dog, Memories, Mystery Train/Tiger Man, Monologue Life Story, Baby What You Want Me To Do, Runaway, Funny How Times Slips Away, Are You Lonesome Tonight, Yesterday/Hey Jude, Introductions, Celebrity Introductions Darlene Love & Bill Medley, In The Ghetto, Suspicious Minds, What'd I Say, Can't Help Falling In Love

August 9–11, 1969—Not Available

August 12th, 1969—Dinner Show—Complete
Blue Suede Shoes, I Got A Woman, All Shook Up, Dialogue, Love Me Tender, Jailhouse Rock/Don't Be Cruel, Heartbreak Hotel, Hound Dog, Memories, Dialogue, Mystery Train/Tiger Man, Monologue Life Story, Baby What You Want Me To Do, Runaway, Are You Lonesome Tonight, Yesterday/Hey Jude, Introductions, In The Ghetto, Suspicious Minds, What'd I Say, Can't Help Falling In Love

August 12, 1969—Midnight Show—Complete
Blue Suede Shoes, I Got A Woman, All Shook Up, Love Me Tender, Jailhouse Rock/Don't Be Cruel, Heartbreak Hotel, Dialogue, Hound Dog, Memories, Mystery Train/Tiger Man, Monologue Life Story, Baby What You Want Me To Do, Runaway, Are You Lonesome Tonight, Yesterday/Hey Jude, Introductions, In The Ghetto, Suspicious Minds, What'd I Say, Can't Help Falling In Love

August 13, 1969—Dinner Show—Complete
Blue Suede Shoes, I Got A Woman, All Shook Up, Love Me Tender, Jailhouse Rock/Don't Be Cruel, Heartbreak Hotel, Hound Dog, Memories, Mystery Train/Tiger Man, Monologue Life Story, Baby What You Want Me To Do, Runaway, Are You Lonesome Tonight, Yesterday/Hey Jude, Introductions, In The Ghetto, Suspicious Minds, What'd I Say, Can't Help Falling In Love

August 13, 1969—Midnight Show—Complete
Blue Suede Shoes, I Got A Woman, All Shook Up, Love Me Tender, Jailhouse Rock/Don't Be Cruel, Heartbreak Hotel, Dialogue, Hound Dog, Memories, Mystery Train/Tiger Man, Baby What You Want Me To Do, Runaway, Are You Lonesome Tonight, Yesterday/Hey Jude, Introductions, Dialogue, In The Ghetto, Suspicious Minds, What'd I Say, Can't Help Falling In Love

August 14, 1969—Dinner Show—Complete
Blue Suede Shoes, I Got A Woman, All Shook Up, Viva Las Vegas (partial), Love Me Tender, Jailhouse Rock/Don't Be Cruel, Heartbreak Hotel, Hound Dog, Memories, Mystery Train/Tiger Man, Monologue Life Story, Baby What You Want Me To Do, Surrender (partial), Runaway, Are You Lonesome Tonight, Yesterday/Hey Jude, Introductions, In The Ghetto, Suspicious Minds, What'd I Say, Can't Help Falling In Love.

August 14, 1969—Midnight Show—Complete
Blue Suede Shoes, I Got A Woman, All Shook Up, Viva Las Vegas, Love Me Tender, Jailhouse Rock/Don't Be Cruel, Heartbreak Hotel, Hound Dog, Memories, Mystery Train/Tiger Man, Baby What You Want Me To Do, Surrender, Runaway, Are You Lonesome Tonight, Yesterday/Hey Jude, Introductions, In The Ghetto, Suspicious Minds, What'd I Say, Can't Help Falling In Love

August 15, 1969—Dinner Show—Complete
Blue Suede Shoes, I Got A Woman, All Shook Up, Love Me Tender, Jailhouse Rock/Don't Be Cruel, Heartbreak Hotel, Hound Dog, Memories, Mystery Train/Tiger Man, Monologue Life Story, Baby What You Want Me To Do, Are You Lonesome Tonight, Yesterday/Hey Jude, Introductions, Celebrity introduction Jerry Lee Lewis, Whole Lotta Shakin Goin' On (partial), In The Ghetto, Suspicious Minds, What'd I Say, Can't Help Falling In Love

August 15, 1969—Midnight Show—Complete
Blue Suede Shoes, I Got A Woman, All Shook Up, Love Me Tender, Jailhouse Rock/Don't Be Cruel, Heartbreak Hotel, Hound Dog, Memories, Monologue Life Story, Baby What You Want Me To Do, Runaway, Are You Lonesome Tonight, Yesterday/Hey Jude, Introductions, In The Ghetto, Suspicious Minds, What'd I Say, Can't Help Falling In Love

August 16, 1969—Dinner Show—Complete
Blue Suede Shoes, I Got A Woman, All Shook Up, Dialogue, Love Me Tender, Jailhouse Rock/Don't Be Cruel, Heartbreak Hotel, Dialogue, Hound Dog, Memories, Monologue Life Story, Mystery Train/Tiger Man, Baby What You Want Me To Do, Runaway, Are You Lonesome Tonight, Yesterday/Hey Jude, Introductions, In The Ghetto, Suspicious Minds, What'd I Say, Can't Help Falling In Love.

August 16, 1969—Midnight Show—Complete
Blue Suede Shoes, I Got A Woman, All Shook Up, Dialogue, Love Me Tender, My Babe, Such A Night (partial), Jailhouse Rock/Don't Be Cruel, Heartbreak Hotel, Dialogue, Hound Dog, Memories, Monologue Life Story, Mystery Train/Tiger Man, Baby What You Want Me To Do, Runaway, Are You Lonesome Tonight, Yesterday/Hey Jude, Introductions, In The Ghetto, Celebrity introduction Mark James, Suspicious Minds, What'd I Say, Can't Help Falling In Love.

August 17, 1969 Dinner Show—Not Available

August 17, 1969 Midnight Show—Not Available

August 18, 1969—Dinner Show—Complete
Blue Suede Shoes, I Got A Woman, All Shook Up, Dialogue, Love Me Tender, Jailhouse Rock/Don't Be Cruel, Heartbreak Hotel, Dialogue, Hound Dog (extra verse), Memories, Dialogue, Mystery Train/Tiger Man, Monologue Life Story, Runaway, Are You Lonesome Tonight, Yesterday/Hey Jude, Introductions, Dialogue, In The Ghetto, Suspicious Minds, What'd I Say, Can't Help Falling In Love

August 18, 1969—Midnight Show—Complete
Blue Suede Shoes, I Got A Woman, All Shook Up, Dialogue, Love Me Tender, Jailhouse Rock/Don't Be Cruel, Heartbreak Hotel, Hound Dog, Memories, Dialogue, Mystery Train/Tiger Man, Monologue Life Story, Baby What You Want Me To Do, Runaway, Funny How Time Slips Away, Are You Lonesome Tonight, Yesterday/Hey Jude, Introductions, In The Ghetto, Suspicious Minds, What'd I Say, Can't Help Falling In Love

August 19, 1969—Dinner Show—Complete
Blue Suede Shoes, I Got A Woman, All Shook Up, Dialogue, Jailhouse Rock/ Don't Be Cruel, Heartbreak Hotel, Hound Dog, Memories, Mystery Train, Monologue Life Story, Baby What You Want Me To Do, Runaway, Are You Lonesome Tonight, Yesterday/Hey Jude, In The Ghetto, Suspicious Minds, What'd I Say, Can't Help Falling In Love.

August 19, 1969—Midnight Show—Complete
Blue Suede Shoes, I Got A Woman, All Shook Up, Dialogue, Love Me Tender, My Babe, Jailhouse Rock/Don't Be Cruel, Heartbreak Hotel, Hound Dog, Memories, Mystery Train/Tiger Man, Monologue Life Story, Baby What You Want Me To Do, Runaway, Are You Lonesome Tonight, Yesterday/Hey Jude, Introductions, Celebrity introduction Harry James, In The Ghetto, Suspicious Minds, What'd I Say, Can't Help Falling In Love

August 20, 1969—Dinner Show—Complete
Blue Suede Shoes, I Got A Woman, All Shook Up, Love Me Tender, Jailhouse Rock/Don't Be Cruel, Heartbreak Hotel, Hound Dog, Mystery Train/Tiger Man, Monologue Life Story, Baby What You Want Me To Do, Are You Lonesome Tonight, It's Now Or Never (partial), Yesterday/Hey Jude, In The Ghetto, Suspicious Minds, Can't Help Falling In Love

August 20, 1960—Midnight Show—Not Available

August 21, 1969—Dinner Show—Complete
Blue Suede Shoes, I Got A Woman, All Shook Up, Love Me Tender, Jailhouse Rock/Don't Be Cruel, Heartbreak Hotel, Hound Dog, Memories, Mystery Train/Tiger Man, Monologue Life Story, Baby What You Want Me To Do, Runaway, Are You Lonesome Tonight, Words, Yesterday/ Hey Jude, Introductions, In The Ghetto, Suspicious Minds, What'd I Say, Can't Help Falling In Love

August 21, 1969—Midnight Show—Complete
Blue Suede Shoes, I Got A Woman, All Shook Up, Love Me Tender, Jailhouse Rock/Don't Be Cruel, Heartbreak Hotel, Hound Dog, I Can't Stop Loving You, My Babe, Mystery Train/Tiger Man, Baby What You Want Me To Do, Runaway, Surrender/Are You Lonesome Tonight, Words, Monologue Life Story, Yesterday/Hey Jude, Introductions, Happy Birthday to James Burton, In The Ghetto, Suspicious Minds, What'd I Say, Can't Help Falling In Love

August 22, 1969—Dinner Show—Complete
Blue Suede Shoes, I Got A Woman, All Shook Up, Love Me Tender, Jailhouse Rock/Don't Be Cruel, Heartbreak Hotel, Hound Dog, Memories, Mystery Train/Tiger Man, Monologue Life Story, Baby What You Want Me To Do, Runaway, Funny How Time Slips Away, Are You Lonesome Tonight, Yesterday/Hey Jude, Introductions, In The Ghetto, Suspicious Minds, What'd I Say, Can't Help Falling In Love

August 22, 1969—Midnight Show—Complete
Blue Suede Shoes, I Got A Woman, All Shook Up, Love Me Tender, Jailhouse Rock/Don't Be Cruel, Heartbreak Hotel, Hound Dog, My Babe, Mystery Train/Tiger Man, Baby What You Want Me To Do, Runaway, Funny How Time Slips Away, Are You Lonesome Tonight, Yesterday/Hey Jude, Introductions, In The Ghetto, Suspicious Minds, What'd I Say, Can't Help Falling In Love

August 23, 1969—Dinner Show—Complete
Blue Suede Shoes, I Got A Woman, All Shook Up, Dialogue, Love Me Tender, Jailhouse Rock/Don't Be Cruel, Heartbreak Hotel, Dialogue, Hound Dog, I Can't Stop Loving You, My Babe, Monologue Life story, Mystery Train/Tiger Man, Baby What You Want Me To Do, Runaway, Are You Lonesome Tonight, Yesterday/Hey Jude, Introductions, In The Ghetto, Suspicious Minds, What'd I Say, Can't Help Falling In Love.

August 23, 1969—Midnight Show—Complete
Blue Suede Shoes, I Got A Woman, All Shook Up, Dialogue, Love Me Tender, Jailhouse Rock/ Don't Be Cruel, Heartbreak Hotel, Hound Dog, Memories, Mystery Train/Tiger Man, Monologue Life Story, Baby What You Want Me To Do, Runaway, Reconsider Baby, Are You Lonesome Tonight, Yesterday/Hey Jude, Introductions, In The Ghetto, Suspicious Minds, What'd I Say, Loving You/Reconsider Baby, Can't Help Falling In Love

August 24, 1969—Dinner Show—Complete
Blue Suede Shoes, I Got A Woman, All Shook Up, Dialogue, Love Me Tender, Jailhouse Rock/Don't Be Cruel, Heartbreak Hotel, Dialogue, Hound Dog, I Can't Stop Loving You, Johnny B. Goode, Monologue Life story, Baby What You Want Me To Do, Runaway, Are You Lonesome Tonight, Yesterday/Hey Jude, Introductions, In The Ghetto, Suspicious Minds, What'd I Say, Can't Help Falling In Love

August 24, 1969—Midnight Show—Complete
Blue Suede Shoes, I Got A Woman, All Shook Up, Dialogue, Love Me Tender, Jailhouse Rock, Don't Be Cruel, Heartbreak Hotel, Dialogue, Hound Dog, I Can't Stop Loving You, Johnny B. Goode, Dialogue, Baby What You Want Me To Do, Runaway, Are You Lonesome Tonight, Words, Yesterday/Hey Jude, Introductions, In The Ghetto, Suspicious Minds, What'd I Say, Can't Help Falling In Love

August 25, 1969—Dinner Show—Complete
Blue Suede Shoes, I Got A Woman, All Shook Up, Love Me Tender, Jailhouse Rock/Don't Be Cruel, Heartbreak Hotel, Hound Dog, Memories, Mystery Train/Tiger Man, Baby What You Want Me To Do, Runaway, Funny How Time Slips Away, Are You Lonesome Tonight, Yesterday/Hey Jude, Introductions, In The Ghetto, Suspicious Minds, What's I Say, Can't Help Falling In Love

August 25, 1969—Midnight Show—Complete
Blue Suede Shoes, I Got A Woman, All Shook Up, Love Me Tender, Jailhouse Rock/Don't Be Cruel, Heartbreak Hotel, Hound Dog, I Can't Stop Loving You, My Babe, Mystery Train/Tiger Man, Monologue Life story, Baby What You Want Me To Do, Runaway, Are You Lonesome Tonight, Words, Yesterday/Hey Jude, Introductions, Celebrity introductions Nancy Sinatra, Mac Davis, Tom Jones, Buddy Hackett, Shelley Fabares, In The Ghetto, Suspicious Minds, What'd I Say, Can't Help Falling In Love.

August 26, 1969—Dinner Show—Complete
Blue Suede Shoes, I Got A Woman, All Shook Up, Love Me Tender, Jailhouse Rock/Don't Be Cruel, Heartbreak Hotel, Hound Dog, Memories, My Babe, Mystery Train/Tiger Man, Monologue, Baby What You Want Me To Do, Runaway, Inherit The Wind, Yesterday/Hey Jude, Introductions, In The Ghetto, Suspicious Minds, What'd I Say, Can't Help Falling In Love

August 26, 1969—Midnight Show—Complete
Blue Suede Shoes, I Got A Woman, All Shook Up, Love Me Tender, Jailhouse Rock/Don't Be Cruel, Heartbreak Hotel, Hound Dog, I Can't Stop Loving You, Mystery Train/Tiger Man, Monologue Life Story, Baby What You Want Me To Do, Runaway, Are You Lonesome Tonight (laughing version), Rubberneckin', Yesterday/Hey Jude, Introductions, This Is The Story, Suspicious Minds, What'd I Say, Can't Help Falling In Love

August 27, 1969—Dinner Show—Incomplete
It's Now Or Never (partial), Loving You (partial), One Night, Love Me, Baby What You Want Me To Do, Runaway

August 27, 1969—Midnight Show—Complete
Blue Suede Shoes, I Got A Woman, All Shook Up, Love Me Tender, Jailhouse Rock/Don't Be Cruel, Heartbreak Hotel, Dialogue, I Can't Stop Loving You, My Babe, Mystery Train/Tiger Man, Baby What You Want Me To Do, Runaway, Are You Lonesome Tonight, Words, Yesterday/Hey Jude, In Ghetto, Suspicious Minds, What'd I Say, Can't Help Falling In Love

August 28, 1969—Dinner Show—Complete
Blue Suede Shoes, I Got A Woman, All Shook Up, Dialogue, Love Me Tender, Jailhouse Rock/Don't Be Cruel, Heartbreak Hotel, Hound Dog, I Can't Stop Loving You, My Babe, Mystery Train/Tiger Man, Monologue Life Story, Baby What You Want Me To Do, Runaway, Are You Lonesome Tonight, Words, Yesterday/Hey Jude, Introductions, In The Ghetto, Suspicious Minds, What'd I Say, Can't Help Falling In Love

August 28, 1969—Closing Show Midnight—Complete
Blue Suede Shoes, I Got A Woman, All Shook Up, Love Me Tender, Jailhouse Rock/Don't Be Cruel, Heartbreak Hotel, Hound Dog, I Can't Stop Loving You, My Babe, Mystery Train/Tiger Man, Runaway, Are You Lonesome Tonight, Words, Yesterday/Hey Jude, Introductions, In The Ghetto, Suspicious Minds, What'd I Say, Can't Help Falling In Love

Songs Sung by Elvis During This Engagement
All Shook Up, Are You Lonesome Tonight, Are You Lonesome Tonight (laughing version), Baby What You Want Me To Do, Blue Hawaii (partial), Blue Suede Shoes, Can't Help Falling In Love, Don't Be Cruel, Funny How Time Slips Away, Further Along (partial), Happy Birthday to James Burton, Heartbreak Hotel, Hey Jude, Hound Dog, Hound Dog (extra verse), Hound Dog (hilarious version), I Can't Stop Loving You, I Got A Woman, Inherit The Wind, In The Ghetto, It's Now Or Never (partial), Jailhouse Rock, Jailhouse Rock/Don't Be Cruel, Johnny B. Goode, Love Me, Love Me Tender, Loving You (partial), Loving You/Reconsider Baby, Memories, My Babe, Mystery Train, Mystery Train/Tiger Man, One Night, Rubberneckin', Runaway, Such A Night (partial), Surrender (partial), Surrender/Are You Lonesome Tonight, Surrender/Are You Lonesome Tonight (laughing version), Suspicious Minds, This Is The Story, Viva Las Vegas (partial), What'd I Say, When The Snow Is On The Roses, Whole Lotta Shakin' Goin' On (partial), Words, Yesterday, Yesterday/Hey Jude

The following songs are rumored to have been sung at this engagement but are not verifiable.

From A Jack To A King, Love Me, Loving You, Money Honey, One Night, Reconsider Baby, Susie Q (partial), That's All Right

VEGAS SEASON 2 1970, International Hotel
Monday, January 26, 1970 through Monday, February 23, 1970—57 shows—Total attendance 126,300

Jumpsuits Worn During This Engagement—On Stage Suit, White with green Tapestry Suit, White with black Tapestry Suit, Blue with blue Tapestry Suit, Black with gold Tapestry Suit, White with turquoise Conchos Suit, Beaded Fringe Suit

Show Members—Musicians: Lead Guitar—James Burton, Rhythm Guitar—John Wilkinson, Acoustic Guitar and Backup Vocals—Charlie Hodge, Bass—Jerry Scheff, Piano—Glen D. Hardin, Drums—Bob Lanning, Backup Singers: Sweet Inspirations: Cissy Houston, Myrna Smith, Sylvia Shemwell, Estelle Brown, The Imperials: Jake Hess, Jim Murray, Gary Mc Spadden, Armond Morales, High Voice Singer—Millie Kirkham, Comedian—Sammy Shore, Orchestra—Bobby Morris

January 26, 1970—Opening Night—Complete
All Shook Up, That's All Right, Proud Mary, Don't Cry Daddy, Teddy Bear/Don't Be Cruel, Long Tall Sally, Let It Be Me, I Can't Stop Loving You, Walk A Mile In My Shoes/In The Ghetto, True Love Travels On A Gravel Road (false start), Sweet Caroline, Polk Salad Annie, Introductions, Kentucky Rain, Suspicious Minds, Can't Help Falling In Love.

January 27, 1970–January 31, 1970—Not Available

February 1, 1970—Dinner Show—Incomplete
All Shook Up, That's All right, Proud Mary, Don't Cry Daddy, Teddy Bear/Don't Be Cruel, Long Tall Sally, Let It Be Me, I Can't Stop Loving You, Walk A Mile In My Shoes/In The Ghetto

February 1, 1970—Midnight Show—Not Available

February 2, 1970—Not Available

February 3, 1970—Dinner Show—Complete
That's All Right, I Got A Woman, Proud Mary, Don't Cry Daddy, Teddy Bear/Don't Be Cruel, Long Tall Sally, Let It Be Me, Walk A Mile In My Shoes/In The Ghetto, Kentucky Rain, Sweet Caroline, Polk Salad Annie, Introductions, Suspicious Minds, Can't Help Falling In Love

February 3, 1970—Midnight Show—Complete
All Shook Up, I Got A Woman, Proud Mary, Don't Cry Daddy, Teddy Bear/Don't Be Cruel, Long Tall Sally, Let It Be Me, I Can't Stop Loving You, Walk A Mile In My Shoes/In The Ghetto, Kentucky Rain (funny version), Sweet Caroline, Polk Salad Annie, Introductions, Suspicious Minds, Can't Help Falling In Love.

February 4, 1970—Not Available

February 5, 1970—Dinner Show- Complete
All Shook Up, I Got a Woman, Dialogue, Proud Mary, Don't Cry Daddy, Monologue Life Story, Teddy Bear/Don't Be Cruel, Love Me, C.C. Rider, Let It Be Me, I Can't Stop Loving You, Love Me Tender, Dialogue, In the Ghetto, Sweet Caroline, Polk Salad Annie, Introductions, Suspicious Minds, Can't Help Falling In Love

February 5, 1970—Midnight Show—Not Available

February 6, 1970—Dinner Show—Complete
All Shook Up, I Got A Woman/Amen, Long Tall Sally, Don't Cry Daddy, Hound Dog, Love Me Tender, Kentucky Rain, Let It Be Me, I Can't Stop Loving You, C.C. Rider, Sweet Caroline, Polk Salad Annie, Suspicious Minds, Introductions, Can't Help Falling In Love

February 6, 1970—Midnight Show—Complete
All Shook Up, I Got A Woman/Amen, Proud Mary, Don't Cry Daddy, Teddy Bear/Don't Be Cruel, Love Me, C.C. Rider, Let It Be Me, I Can't Stop Loving You, Love Me Tender, In The Ghetto, Sweet Caroline, Suspicious Minds, Introductions, Can't Help Falling In Love

February 7–14, 1970—Not Available

February 15, 1970—Dinner Show—Not Available

February 15, 1970—Midnight Show—Complete
All Shook Up, I Got A Woman, Long Tall Sally, Don't Cry Daddy, Hound Dog, Love Me Tender, Kentucky Rain, Let It Be Me, I Can't Stop Loving You, Walk A Mile In My Shoes, In The Ghetto, Sweet Caroline, Polk Salad Annie, Introductions, Suspicious Minds, Can't Help Falling In Love

February 16, 1970—Dinner Show—Incomplete
All Shook Up, Proud Mary, Kentucky Rain, Sweet Caroline, In The Ghetto, Blueberry Hill, Suspicious Minds

February 16, 1970—Midnight Show—Complete
All Shook Up, I Got A Woman, The Wonder Of You, Proud Mary, Long Tall Sally, Dialogue, Don't Cry Daddy, Teddy Bear/Don't Be Cruel, Dialogue, Hound Dog, Love Me Tender, In The Ghetto, Kentucky Rain, Let It Be Me, I Can't Stop Loving You, C.C. Rider, Sweet Caroline, Polk Salad Annie, Introductions, Release Me, Suspicious Minds, Can't Help Falling In Love

February 17, 1970—Dinner Show—Complete
All Shook Up, I Got A Woman, Long Tall Sally, Don't Cry Daddy, Hound Dog, Love Me Tender, Kentucky Rain, Let It Be Me, I Can't Stop

Loving You, Walk A Mile In My Shoes/In The Ghetto, Sweet Caroline, Polk Salad Annie, Dialogue, Introductions, Celebrity Introductions Steve Allen, Suspicious Minds, Can't Help Falling In Love

February 17, 1970—Midnight Show—Complete
All Shook Up, I Got A Woman, The Wonder Of You, Proud Mary, Long Tall Sally, Dialogue, Don't Cry Daddy, Teddy Bear/Don't Be Cruel, Dialogue, Hound Dog, Love Me Tender, In The Ghetto, Kentucky Rain, Let It Be Me, I Can't Stop Loving You, Walk A Mile In My Shoes, C.C. Rider, Sweet Caroline, Polk Salad Annie, Introductions, Release Me, Suspicious Minds, Can't Help Falling In Love

February 18, 1970—Dinner Show—Complete
All Shook Up, I Got A Woman, The Wonder Of You, Proud Mary, Long Tall Sally, Dialogue, Don't Cry Daddy, Teddy Bear/Don't Be Cruel, Dialogue, Hound Dog, Love Me Tender, In The Ghetto, Kentucky Rain, Let It Be Me, I Can't Stop Loving You, Walk A Mile In My Shoes, C.C. Rider, Sweet Caroline, Polk Salad Annie, Introductions, Release Me, Suspicious Minds, Can't Help Falling In Love

February 18, 1970—Midnight Show—Complete
All Shook Up, I Got A Woman, The Wonder Of You, Proud Mary, Long Tall Sally, Dialogue, Don't Cry Daddy, Teddy Bear/Don't Be Cruel, Dialogue, Hound Dog, Love Me Tender, In The Ghetto, Kentucky Rain, Let It Be Me, I Can't Stop Loving You, Walk A Mile In My Shoes, C.C. Rider, Sweet Caroline, Polk Salad Annie, Introductions, Celebrity introduction Fats Domino, Lawdy Miss Clawdy/Blueberry Hill (partial) Release Me, Suspicious Minds, Can't Help Falling In Love

February 19, 1970—Dinner Show—Complete
All Shook Up, I Got A Woman, The Wonder Of You, Proud Mary, Long Tall Sally, Dialogue, Don't Cry Daddy, Teddy Bear/Don't Be Cruel, Dialogue, Hound Dog, Love Me Tender, In The Ghetto, Kentucky Rain, Let It Be Me, I Can't Stop Loving You, Walk A Mile In My Shoes, C.C. Rider, Sweet Caroline, Polk Salad Annie, Introductions, Release Me, Suspicious Minds, Can't Help Falling In Love

February 19, 1970—Midnight Show—Complete
All Shook Up, I Got A Woman, The Wonder Of You, Proud Mary, Long Tall Sally, Dialogue, Don't Cry Daddy, Teddy Bear/Don't Be Cruel, Dialogue, Hound Dog, Love Me Tender, In The Ghetto, Kentucky Rain, Let It Be Me, I Can't Stop Loving You, Walk A Mile In My Shoes, C.C. Rider, Sweet Caroline, Polk Salad Annie, Introductions, Release Me, Suspicious Minds, Can't Help Falling In Love

February 20, 1970—Dinner Show—Complete
All Shook Up, I Got A Woman, Proud Mary, Don't Cry Daddy, Teddy Bear/Don't Be Cruel, Love Me, C.C. Rider, Let It Be Me, I Can't Stop Loving You, Love Me Tender, In The Ghetto, Sweet Caroline, Introductions, Suspicious Minds, Can't Help Falling In Love

February 20, 1970—Midnight Show– Complete
All Shook Up, I Got A Woman, My Heavenly Father (partial), Long Tall Sally, Don't Cry Daddy, Everybody Loves Somebody Sometime (partial), Hound Dog, Love Me Tender, Kentucky Rain, Let It Be Me, I Can't Stop Loving You, Dialogue, Walk A Mile In My Shoes (false start), C.C. Rider, Sweet Caroline, Polk Salad Annie, Introductions, Suspicious Minds (reprise), Can't Help Falling In Love

February 21, 1970—Dinner Show—Incomplete
All Shook Up, I Got A Woman/Amen, Long Tall Sally, Don't Cry Daddy, Hound Dog, Love Me Tender, Kentucky Rain, Let It Be Me, I Can't Stop Loving You, Introductions, Suspicious Minds, Can't Help Falling In Love

February 21, 1970—Midnight Show—Complete
All Shook Up, I Got A Woman, Long Tall Sally, Don't Cry Daddy, Hound Dog, Love Me Tender, Kentucky Rain (partial), Let It Be Me (partial), I Can't Stop Loving You, Walk A Mile In My Shoes/In The Ghetto, Sweet Caroline, Polk Salad Annie, Introductions, Celebrity introductions, Suspicious Minds, Can't Help Falling In Love

February 22, 1970—Dinner Show—Complete
All Shook Up, I Got A Woman, Long Tall Sally, Dialogue, Don't Cry Daddy, Hound Dog, Love Me Tender, Kentucky Rain, Let It Be Me, I Can't Stop Loving You, Walk A Mile In My Shoes/In The Ghetto, C.C. Rider, Sweet Caroline, Polk Salad Annie, Introductions, Suspicious Minds, Can't Help Falling In Love

February 22, 1970—Midnight Show—Complete
All Shook Up, I Got A Woman, Long Tall Sally, Elvis introduces Vernon Presley, Don't Cry Daddy, Hound Dog, Love Me Tender, Kentucky Rain, Let It Be Me, I Can't Stop Loving You, Walk A Mile In My Shoes/In The Ghetto, C.C. Rider, Sweet Caroline, Polk Salad Annie, Introductions, Celebrity introductions Gary Lockwood, John Phillips, Jim Webb, Johnny Rivers, Kenny Rogers, Suspicious Minds, Can't Help Falling In Love

February 23, 1970—Dinner Show—Complete
All Shook Up, I Got A Woman, Long Tall Sally, Dialogue, Don't Cry Daddy, Monologue Life Story, Celebrity introduction Dean Martin, Everybody Loves Somebody Sometime (partial), Hound Dog, Love Me Tender (Elvis kisses Priscilla), Kentucky Rain, Let It Be Me, I Can't Stop Loving You, C.C. Rider, True Love Travels On A Gravel Road, Sweet Caroline, Polk Salad Annie, Introductions, Kentucky Rain, Suspicious Minds, Can't Help Falling In Love

February 23, 1970—Closing Show Midnight—Complete
All Shook Up, I Got A Woman, Long Tall Sally, Don't Cry Daddy, Hound Dog, Love Me Tender, Kentucky Rain, Let It Be Me, I Can't Stop Loving You, C.C. Rider, Sweet Caroline, Polk Salad Annie, Introductions, Blueberry Hill/Lawdy Miss Clawdy (Elvis plays piano), Heartbreak Hotel, One Night (Elvis plays electric guitar), It's Now Or Never, Suspicious Minds, Introductions, Celebrity introductions Colonel Parker, Bill Porter, Felton Jarvis, Can't Help Falling In Love

Songs Sung by Elvis During This Engagement
All Shook Up, Blueberry Hill (partial), Blueberry Hill/Lawdy Miss Clawdy, (Elvis plays piano), Can't Help Falling In Love, C.C. Rider, Don't Cry Daddy, Everybody Loves Somebody Sometime (partial), Heartbreak Hotel, Hound Dog, I Can't Stop Loving You, I Got A Woman, I Got A Woman/Amen, In The Ghetto, It's Now Or Never, Kentucky Rain, Kentucky Rain (funny version), Kentucky Rain (partial), Let It Be Me, Let It Be Me (partial), Long Tall Sally, Love Me, Love Me Tender, My Heavenly Father (partial), One Night (Elvis plays electric guitar), Polk Salad Annie, Proud Mary, Release Me, Suspicious Minds, Sweet Caroline, Teddy Bear/Don't Be Cruel, That's All Right, True Love Travels On A Gravel Road, True Love Travels On A Gravel Road (with false start), Walk A Mile In My Shoes, Walk A Mile In My Shoes (false start), Walk A Mile In My Shoes/In The Ghetto, The Wonder Of You

The following songs are rumored to have been sung at this engagement but are not verifiable.

More. Old Shep, Runaway, Sweet Inspiration, Teddy Bear, When The Swallows Come Back To Capistrano (partial)

VEGAS SEASON 3 1970, International Hotel
Monday, August 10, 1970 through Tuesday, September 8, 1970–On September 8 Elvis added a 3:00 a.m. show to accommodate the overflow crowd—58 shows—Total attendance 127,600

Jumpsuits Worn During This Engagement—White Chain Suit with white macramé belt, White Chain Suit with red Ladder leather belt, White Chain Suit with brown macramé belt, White Concho Suit white macramé concho belt, Beaded Fringe Suit with blue macramé belt, Beaded Fringe Suit with turquoise macramé belt, Beaded Fringe Suit with white macramé belt, Beaded Fringe Suit with dark green macramé belt, White Ladder Suit with red leather trim, I Got Lucky Suit with brown macramé belt, I Got Lucky Suit with red macramé belt, I Got Lucky Suit with white long fringe belt, White Tie Suit with white tie belt, Long Fringe Suit (please note that many experts have stated that this suit was worn once during this engagement), White Concho Suit with dark blue macramé belt.

Show Member—Musicians: Lead Guitar—James Burton, Rhythm Guitar—John Wilkinson, Acoustic Guitar and Backup Vocals—Charlie Hodge, Bass—Jerry Scheff, Piano—Glen D. Hardin, Drums—Ronnie Tutt, Backup Singers: Sweet Inspirations: Ann Williams, Myrna Smith, Sylvia Shemwell, Estelle Brown, The Imperials: Jake Hess, Jim Murray, Gary McSpadden, Armond Morales, High Voice Singers—Millie Kirkham and Kathy Westmoreland, Comedian—Sammy Shore, Orchestra —Joe Guercio

August 10, 1970—Opening Night—10:15 P.M.—Complete
That's All Right, Mystery Train/Tiger Man, Dialogue, I Can't Stop Loving You, Love Me Tender, The Next Step Is Love, Words, I Just Can't Help Believin', Something, Sweet Caroline, You've Lost That Lovin' Feeling, You Don't Have To Say You Love Me, Polk Salad Annie, Introductions, I've Lost You, Dialogue, Bridge Over Troubled Water, Patch It Up, Can't Help Falling In Love

August 11, 1970—Dinner Show—Complete
That's All Right, I Got A Woman, Hound Dog, Dialogue, Heartbreak Hotel, Dialogue, Love Me Tender, I've Lost You, Dialogue, I Just Can't Help Believin', Something, I Can't Stop Loving You, Sweet Caroline, You've Lost That Lovin' Feeling, Introductions, Bridge Over Troubled Water, Suspicious Minds, Can't Help Falling In Love

August 11, 1970—Midnight Show—Complete
That's All Right, I Got A Woman, Hound Dog, Love Me Tender, There Goes My Everything, Just Pretend, I Just Can't Help Believin', Something, Men With Broken Hearts (Poem), Walk A Mile In My Shoes, You've Lost That Lovin' Feeling, Polk Salad Annie, One Night, Don't Be Cruel, Love Me, Heartbreak Hotel, Introductions, Bridge Over Troubled Water, Suspicious Minds, Can't Help Falling In Love

August 12, 1970—Dinner Show—Complete
That's All Right, I Got A Woman, Hound Dog, Heartbreak Hotel, Dialogue, Love Me Tender, I've Lost You, I Just Can't Help Believin', Patch It Up, Dialogue, Twenty Days And Twenty Nights, You've Lost That Lovin' Feeling, Polk Salad Annie, Introductions, Blue Suede Shoes, You Don't Have To Say You Love Me, Bridge Over Troubled Water, Suspicious Minds, Can't Help Falling In Love

August 12, 1970—Midnight Show—Complete
That's All Right, Mystery Train/Tiger Man, Dialogue, Hound Dog, Dialogue, Love Me Tender, Just Pretend, Walk A Mile In My Shoes, There Goes My Everything, Words, Sweet Caroline, You've Lost That Lovin' Feeling, Polk Salad Annie, Introductions, Heartbreak Hotel, One Night, Blue Suede Shoes, All Shook Up, Little Sister/Get Back, I Was The One, Love Me, Are You Lonesome Tonight, Bridge Over Troubled Water, Suspicious Minds, Can't Help Falling In Love

August 13, 1970—Dinner Show—Complete
That's All Right, I Got A Woman, Hound Dog, Dialogue, Love Me Tender, Don't Cry Daddy, In The Ghetto, I Just Can't Help Believin', Stranger In The Crowd, Make The World Go Away, Sweet Caroline, You've Lost That Lovin' Feeling, Polk Salad Annie, Introductions, Celebrity Introduction Art Carney, The Wonder Of You, Heartbreak Hotel, Blue Suede Shoes, One Night, All Shook Up, Bridge Over Troubled Water, Suspicious Minds, Can't Help Falling In Love

August 13, 1970—Midnight Show—Complete
That's All Right, Mystery Train/Tiger Man, Hound Dog, Love Me Tender, Just Pretend, Walk A Mile In My Shoes, There Goes My Everything, Words, Sweet Caroline, You've Lost That Lovin' Feeling, Polk Salad Annie, Heartbreak Hotel, One Night, Blue Suede Shoes, All Shook Up, Little Sister/Get Back, I Was The One, Love Me, Are You Lonesome Tonight, Bridge Over Troubled Water, Suspicious Minds, Can't Help Falling In Love

August 14, 1970—Dinner Show—Complete
That's All Right/Amen/I Got A Woman, You Don't Know Me, Mystery Train/Tiger Man, Folsom Prison Blues/I Walk The Line, Love Me Tender, Johnny B. Goode, Whole Lotta Shakin' Goin' On, Blueberry Hill, The Wonder Of You, You've Lost That Lovin' Feeling, Polk Salad Annie, Introductions, Oh Happy Day, Surfin' Bird, Blue Suede Shoes, One Night, Hound Dog, Bridge Over Troubled Water, Suspicious Minds, Can't Help Falling In Love

August 14, 1970—Midnight Show—Complete
That's All Right, Amen/I Got A Woman/You Don't Know Me/I Got A Woman, Mystery Train/Tiger Man, Folsom Prison Blues/I Walk The Line, Dialogue, Love Me Tender, Johnny B. Goode, Whole Lotta Shakin' Goin' On/Blueberry Hill, The Wonder Of You, You've Lost That Lovin' Feeling, Polk Salad Annie, Introductions, Oh Happy Day, All Shook Up, Blue Suede Shoes, One Night, Hound Dog (partial), Bridge Over Troubled Water, Suspicious Minds, Can't Help Falling In Love

August 15, 1970—Dinner Show—Not Available

August 15, 1970—Midnight Show—Incomplete
That's All Right, I Got A Woman

August 16-17 1970—Not Available

August 18, 1970—Dinner Show—Not Available

August 18, 1970—Midnight Show—Complete
Tiger Man, I Got A Woman/Amen, Dialogue, You Don't Have To Say You Love Me, You've Lost That Lovin' Feeling, Polk Salad Annie, The Wonder Of You, Heartbreak Hotel (3 false starts), One Night (partial), Blue Suede Shoes, Along Came Jones (partial), Hound Dog, Bridge Over Troubled Water, Suspicious Minds, Can't Help Falling In Love

August 19, 1970—Dinner Show—Complete
That's All Right, I Got A Woman, Tiger Man, Dialogue, Love Me Tender, I've Lost You, I Just Can't Help Believin', You've Lost That Lovin' Feeling, Polk Salad Annie, Introductions, Johnny B. Goode, Introductions, The Wonder Of You, Heartbreak Hotel, One Night, All Shook Up, Blue Suede Shoes, Hound Dog, Bridge Over Troubled Water, Suspicious Minds, Can't Help Falling In Love

August 19, 1970—Midnight—Complete
That's All Right, I Got A Woman, Tiger Man, Dialogue, Love Me, I've Lost You, I Just Can't Help

Believin', You've Lost That Lovin' Feeling, Polk Salad Annie, Dialogue, Introductions, Johnny B. Goode, Introductions, The Wonder Of You, Heartbreak Hotel, One Night, All Shook Up, Blue Suede Shoes, Along Came Jones (partial), Hound Dog, Bridge Over Troubled Water, Suspicious Minds, Can't Help Falling In Love

August 20, 1970—Dinner Show—Complete
That's All Right, I Got A Woman/Amen/I Got A Woman, Tiger Man, Dialogue, Love Me Tender, I've Lost You, I Just Can't Help Believin', You've Lost That Lovin' Feeling, Polk Salad Annie, Introductions, Sweet Inspiration, Johnny B. Goode, Celebrity introductions Ruth Boyd & The Rinky Dinks, The Wonder Of You, Heartbreak Hotel, Memphis Tennessee (partial), One Night, Blue Suede Shoes, Hound Dog, Bridge Over Troubled Water, Suspicious Minds, Can't Help Falling In Love

August 20, 1970—Midnight Show—Complete
That's All Right, I Got A Woman/Ave Maria, Tiger Man, Love Me Tender, I've Lost You, Sweet Caroline, You've Lost That Lovin' Feeling, Polk Salad Annie, Introductions, Sweet Inspiration, Johnny B. Goode, The Wonder Of You, Heartbreak Hotel, Blue Suede Shoes, Hound Dog, More (partial), Bridge Over Troubled Water, Suspicious Minds (laughing version), Can't Help Falling In Love

August 21, 1970—Dinner Show—Complete
That's All Right, I Got A Woman (slow ending), Tiger Man, Dialogue, Love Me Tender, I Just Can't Help Believin', Sweet Caroline, You've Lost That Lovin' Feeling, Polk Salad Annie, Introductions, Johnny B. Goode, Happy Birthday to James Burton, Celebrity introduction Neil Diamond, Holly Holy (partial), Elvis' grandmother Minnie Mae Presley, The Wonder Of You, Heartbreak Hotel, One Night, Blue Suede Shoes/Whole Lotta Shakin' Goin' On, Hound Dog, Bridge Over Troubled Water, Suspicious Minds, Can't Help Falling In Love

August 21, 1970—Midnight Show—Complete
That's All Right, I Got A Woman/Ave Maria/I Got A Woman, Tiger Man, Dialogue, Love Me Tender (false start), I've Lost You, Crying Time (false start), I Just Can't Help Believin', You've Lost That Lovin' Feeling (false start), Polk Salad Annie, Introductions, Johnny B. Goode, Introductions, Celebrity introductions Henry Silva, Jack E. Leonard, Rusty Warren (not present), The Wonder Of You, Along Came Jones (partial), Heartbreak Hotel (2 false starts), One Night, All Shook Up (2 false starts only), Blue Suede Shoes/Whole Lotta Shakin' Goin' On/Blue Suede Shoes, Hound Dog, Bridge Over Troubled Water, Suspicious Minds, Can't Help Falling In Love

August 22, 1970—Dinner Show—Not Available

August 22, 1970—Midnight Show—Complete
That's All Right, I Got A Woman, Tiger Man, Love Me Tender, I've Lost You, Sweet Caroline, You've Lost That Lovin' Feeling, Polk Salad Annie, Sweet Inspiration, Introductions, Johnny B. Goode, The Wonder Of You, Heartbreak Hotel, Blue Suede Shoes, Hound Dog, Bridge Over Troubled Water, Suspicious Minds, Can't Help Falling In Love

August 23, 1970 –Dinner Show—Complete
That's All Right, I Got A Woman/Ave Maria, Tiger Man, Love Me Tender, I've Lost You, I Just Can't Help Believin', You've Lost That Lovin' Feeling, Polk Salad Annie, Introductions, Johnny B. Goode, The Wonder Of You, Heartbreak Hotel, One Night, All Shook Up/Blue Suede Shoes/ Whole Lotta Shakin' Goin' On, Hound Dog, Bridge Over Troubled Water, Suspicious Minds, Dialogue, Release Me, Can't Help Falling In Love

August 23, 1970—Midnight Show—Complete
That's All Right, I Got A Woman/Ave Maria, Tiger Man, Love Me Tender, I've Lost You, I Just Can't Help Believin', You've Lost That Lovin' Feeling, Polk Salad Annie, Introductions, Johnny B. Goode, Celebrity introductions—Introduces a congressman and local Vegas disc jockeys, The Wonder Of You, Heartbreak Hotel, One Night, All Shook Up/Blue Suede Shoes/Whole Lotta Shakin' Goin' On, Hound Dog, Bridge Over Troubled Water, Suspicious Minds, Release Me, Can't Help Falling In Love

August 24, 1970—Dinner Show—Complete
That's All Right, I Got A Woman/Ave Maria, I Just Can't Help Believin', You've Lost That Lovin' Feeling, Polk Salad Annie, Introductions, Johnny B. Goode, The Wonder Of You, One Night, All Shook Up, Blue Suede Shoes, Hound Dog, Bridge Over Troubled Water, Suspicious Minds, Can't Help Falling In Love

August 24, 1970—Midnight Show—Complete
That's All Right, I Got A Woman/Ave Maria, Spanish Eyes (partial), Tiger Man, I Just Can't Help Believin', You've Lost That Lovin' Feeling, Polk Salad Annie, Introductions, Johnny B. Goode, Celebrity introduction Darlene Love, When The Snow Is On The Roses, Celebrity introduction Ed Ames, The Wonder Of You, Heartbreak Hotel, One Night, All Shook Up (false start only), Blue Suede Shoes/Whole Lotta Shakin' Goin' On/Blue Suede Shoes, Hound Dog, Bridge Over Troubled Water, Suspicious Minds, Release Me, Can't Help Falling In Love

August 25–31, 1970—Not Available

September 1, 1970—Dinner Show—Complete
That's All Right, I Got A Woman/Ave Maria, Tiger Man, Love Me Tender, I've Lost You, I Just Can't Help Believin', Polk Salad Annie, Sweet Inspiration, Introductions, Johnny B. Goode, The Wonder Of You, Heartbreak Hotel, Memphis Tennessee (partial), One Night, Blue Suede Shoes, Hound Dog, Bridge Over Troubled Water, Can't Help Falling In Love

September 1, 1970—Midnight Show—Complete
That's All Right, I Got A Woman/Amen, Folsum Prison Blues (partial), Dialogue, Love Me Tender, San Antonio Rose (partial), I've Lost You, I Just Can't Help Believin', You've Lost That Lovin' Feeling, Polk Salad Annie, Introductions, Johnny B. Goode, The Wonder Of You, Heartbreak Hotel, One Night, All Shook Up, Blue Suede Shoes/Whole Lotta Shakin' Goin' On/Blue Suede Shoes, Hound Dog, Bridge Over Troubled Water, Introductions, Can't Help Falling In Love

September 2– 3, 1970—Not Available

September 4, 1970—Dinner Show—Complete
That's All Right, I Got A Woman, I Walk The Line (partial), Dialogue, Love Me Tender, I've Lost You, You've Lost That Lovin' Feeling, Polk Salad Annie, Introductions, Johnny B. Goode, Introductions, The Wonder Of You, One Night, Blue Suede Shoes, Hound Dog, Bridge Over Troubled Water, Can't Help Falling In Love

September 4, 1970—Midnight Show—Incomplete
That's All Right, I Got A Woman/Amen, I Walk The Line (partial), Dialogue, Love Me Tender (false start), I've Lost You, I Just Can't Help Believin', You've Lost That Lovin' Feeling, Polk Salad Annie (with impersonations), Crying Time, Introductions, Johnny B. Goode, Introductions, Celebrity introductions Trini Lopez, Paul Anka, My Way (partial), The Wonder Of You, Dialogue, Heartbreak Hotel (false start only), One Night, Blue Suede Shoes

September 5, 1970—Dinner Show—Incomplete
That's All Right, I Got A Woman/Amen, I Walk The Line (partial), Love Me Tender, I've Lost You, I Just Can't Help Believin', You've Lost That Lovin' Feeling

September 5, 1970—Midnight Show—Complete
That's All Right, I Got A Woman/Amen, I Walk The Line (partial), Dialogue, Love Me Tender, I've Lost You, I Just Can't Help Believin', You've Lost That Lovin' Feeling, Polk Salad Annie, Introductions, Johnny B. Goode, Introductions, Elvis impersonates Bob Dylan, Celebrity Introductions, The Wonder Of You, Heartbreak Hotel, All Shook Up (2 false starts only), Blue Suede Shoes, Hound Dog (partial), Bridge Over Troubled Water, Can't Help Falling In Love

September 6, 1970—Dinner Show—Complete
That's All Right, I Got A Woman/Amen, I Walk The Line, Dialogue, I've Lost You, I Just Can't Help Believin', You've Lost That Lovin' Feeling, Polk Salad Annie/Release Me/Polk Salad Annie, Introductions, Johnny B. Goode, Dialogue, Celebrity Introductions, The Wonder Of You, Dialogue, Heartbreak Hotel, Blue Suede Shoes/ Whole Lotta Shakin' Goin' On, Here In My Lonely Room (partial), Hound Dog, Bridge Over Troubled Water, Suspicious Minds, Can't Help Falling In Love

September 6, 1970—Midnight Show—Complete
That's All Right, I Got A Woman/Amen, I Walk The Line (partial), I've Lost You, I Just Can't Help Believin', You've Lost That Lovin' Feeling, Polk Salad Annie, Introductions, Johnny B. Goode, Heartbreak Hotel (partial), Blue Suede Shoes/Whole Lotta Shakin' Goin' On, Hound Dog, Bridge Over Troubled Water, Can't Help Falling In Love

September 7, 1970—Dinner Show—Complete
That's All Right, I Got A Woman, Dialogue, I Walk The Line (partial), I've Lost You, I Just Can't Help Believin', You've Lost That Lovin' Feeling, Polk Salad Annie, Introductions, Heartbreak Hotel, Blue Suede Shoes, All Shook Up, Hound Dog, Bridge Over Troubled Water, Can't Help Falling In Love.

September 7, 1970—Midnight Show—Complete
That's All Right, I Got A Woman/Amen, I Walk The Line (partial), Dialogue, I've Lost You, I Just Can't Help Believin', You've Lost That Lovin' Feeling, Polk Salad Annie, Release Me (partial), Introductions, Blowin' In The Wind (partial), Blue Suede Shoes/Whole Lotta Shakin' Goin' On, All Shook Up, Hound Dog, Bridge Over Troubled Water, Can't Help Falling In Love

September 8, 1970—Closing Show 3:00 a.m. Only Show—Complete
That's All Right, I Walk The Line (partial), Dialogue, I've Lost You, I Just Can't Help Believin', You've Lost That Lovin' Feeling, Polk Salad Annie, Introductions, Blue Suede Shoes, All Shook Up, Hound Dog, Bridge Over Troubled Water, Can't Help Falling In Love

Songs Sung by Elvis During Engagement
All Shook Up, All Shook Up (false start only), All Shook Up (2 false starts only), All Shook Up/Blue Suede Shoes/Whole Lotta Shakin' Goin' On, Along Came Jones (partial), Amen/I Got A Woman/You Don't Know Me/I Got A Woman, Are You Lonesome Tonight, Blowin' In The Wind (partial), Blueberry Hill, Blue Suede Shoes, Blue Suede Shoes/Whole Lotta Shakin' Goin On, Blue Suede Shoes/Whole Lotta Shakin' Goin' On/Blue Suede Shoes, Bridge Over Troubled Water, Can't Help Falling In Love, Crying Time, Crying Time (false start), Don't Be Cruel, Don't Cry Daddy, Folsom Prison Blues (partial), Folsom Prison Blues/I Walk The Line, Happy Birthday to James Burton, Heartbreak Hotel, Heartbreak Hotel (partial), Heartbreak Hotel (false start only), Heartbreak Hotel (2 false starts), Heartbreak Hotel (3 false starts), Here In My Lonely Room (partial), Holly Holy (partial), Hound Dog, Hound Dog (partial), I Can't Stop Loving You, I Got A Woman, I Got A Woman (slow ending), I Got A Woman/Amen, I Got A Woman/ Amen/I Got A Woman, I Got A Woman/Ave Maria, I Got A Woman/Ave Maria (partial), I Got A Woman/ Ave Maria/I Got A Woman, I Just Can't Help Believin', In The Ghetto, I've Lost You, I Walk The Line (partial), I Was The One, Johnny B. Goode, Just Pretend, Little Sister/Get Back, Love Me, Love Me Tender, Love Me Tender (false start), Make The World Go Away, Memphis Tennessee (partial), Men With Broken Hearts (Poem), More (partial), Mystery Train/Tiger Man, My Way (partial), Oh Happy Day, One Night, Polk Salad Annie, Polk Salad Annie/Release Me/Polk Salad Annie, Release Me, Release Me (partial), Release Me/Can't Help Falling In Love, San Antonio Rose (partial), Something, Spanish Eyes (partial), Stranger In The Crowd, Surfin' Bird, Suspicious Minds, Suspicious Minds (laughing version), Sweet Caroline, Sweet Inspiration, That's All Right, That's All Right/Amen/I Got A Woman, That's All Right/I Got A Woman/Amen, There Goes My Everything, Tiger Man, Walk A Mile In My Shoes, When The Snow Is On The Roses, Whole Lotta Shakin' Goin' On, Whole Lotta Shakin' Goin' On/Blueberry Hill, The Wonder Of You, Words, You Don't Know Me, You've Lost That Lovin' Feeling, You've Lost That Lovin' Feeling (false start)

The following songs are rumored to have been sung at this engagement are not verifiable.

The Next Step Is Love, Patch It Up, Twenty Days And Twenty Nights, Mary In The Morning, Santa Claus Is Back In Town, The Next Step Is Love

VEGAS SEASON 4 1971, Hilton Hotel

Tuesday, January 26, 1971 through February. 23, 1971—57 shows—Total attendance 125,400

Jumpsuits Worn During This Engagement—Cisco Kid Suit black and green with gold World Champion Attendance belt, Cisco Kid Suit white and black with gold World Championship Attendance belt, Cisco Kid Suit black and red with gold World Championship Attendance belt, White Concho Suit with white macramé belt, Cisco Kid Suit black and blue with studded Lion Head belt, Beaded Fringe Suit with turquoise macramé belt, Elvis Now Suit with white macramé belt with blue turquoise conchos, White Tie Suit with beaded white macramé belt, White Tie Suit with beaded brown macramé belt, I Got Lucky Suit with beaded white macramé belt, I Got Lucky Suit with beaded brown macramé belt, I Got Lucky Suit with beaded red macramé belt, various two-piece Vest Suits

Show Members—Musicians: Lead Guitar—James Burton, Rhythm Guitar—John Wilkinson, Acoustic Guitar and Backup Vocals—Charlie Hodge, Bass—Jerry Scheff, Piano—Glen D. Hardin, Drums—Ronnie Tutt, Backup Singers: Sweet Inspirations: Ann Williams, Myrna Smith, Sylvia Shemwell, Estelle Brown, The Imperials: Jake Hess, Jim Murray, Gary McSpadden, Armond Morales, High Voice Singer—Kathy Westmoreland, Comedian—Sammy Shore, Orchestra—Joe Guercio

January 26, 1971—Opening Night 10:15 p.m. —Complete
That's All Right, I Got A Woman, Mystery Train/Tiger Man, Love Me Tender, Can't Help Falling In Love (this is one of the few times Elvis sang this song as part of the show and not his closing number), Make The World Go Away, Sweet Caroline, You've Lost That Lovin' Feeling, Polk Salad Annie, How Great Thou Art, Introductions, Johnny B. Goode, The Wonder Of You, Something, Heartbreak Hotel, Blue Suede Shoes,

One Night, Hound Dog, Introductions, Suspicious Minds, The Impossible Dream, (one of the very rare times Elvis closed his show with anything other than Can't Help Falling In Love)

January 27, 1971—Dinner Show—Not Available

January 27, 1971—Midnight Show—Complete
That's All Right, You Don't Have To Say You Love Me, Love Me Tender, There Goes My Everything, Sweet Caroline, You've Lost That Lovin' Feeling, Polk Salad Annie, Only Believe, How Great Thou Art, Introductions, Johnny B. Goode, The Wonder Of You, Something, Make The World Go Away, Love Me, One Night, Blue Suede Shoes, Hound Dog, Mystery Train/Tiger Man, Love Me Tender, Can't Help Falling In Love

January 28, 1971—Dinner Show—Complete

That's All Right, You Don't Have To Say You Love Me, Love Me Tender, Sweet Caroline, You've Lost That Lovin' Feeling, Polk Salad Annie, Introductions, Johnny B. Goode, Introductions, Something, Release Me, Blue Suede Shoes, Hound Dog, It's Now Or Never, Suspicious Minds, Dialogue, The Impossible Dream (one of the very rare times Elvis closed his show with anything other than Can't Help Falling In Love)

January 28, 1971—Midnight Show—Complete
That's All Right, I Got A Woman, Love Me Tender, You Don't Have To Say You Love Me, Sweet Caroline, You've Lost That Lovin' Feeling, Polk Salad Annie, Introductions, Johnny B. Goode, Introductions, Something, Introductions, The Wonder Of You, Heartbreak Hotel, Blue Suede Shoes, Hound Dog, One Night, Teddy Bear, Suspicious Minds, Impossible Dream (one of the very rare times Elvis closed his show with anything other than Can't Help Falling In Love)

January 29, 1971—Dinner Show—Complete
That's All Right, I Got A Woman, Love Me Tender, You Don't Have To Say You Love Me, Sweet Caroline, You've Lost That Lovin' Feeling, Polk Salad Annie, Introductions, Johnny B. Goode, Introductions, Something, Heartbreak Hotel, Blue Suede Shoes, Teddy Bear, Hound Dog, Snowbird, The Impossible Dream (one of the very rare times Elvis closed his show with anything other than Can't Help Falling In Love)

January 29, 1971—Midnight Show—Complete
That All Right, I Got A Woman, Love Me Tender, You Don't Have To Say You Love Me, Sweet Caroline, You've Lost That Lovin' Feeling, Polk Salad Annie, Introductions, Johnny B. Goode, Introductions, Something, Heartbreak Hotel, Blue Suede Shoes, Teddy Bear/Don't Be Cruel, Hound Dog, Snowbird, The Impossible Dream (one of the very rare times Elvis closed his show with anything other than Can't Help Falling In Love

January 30, 1971—Dinner Show—Complete
That's All Right, I Got A Woman, Love Me Tender, There Goes My Everything, You Don't Have To Say You Love Me, You've Lost That Lovin' Feeling, Polk Salad Annie, Introductions, *2001* intro (one of the rare times that Elvis' opening was used during the show), Something, Dialogue, How Great Thou Art, Dialogue, Blue Suede Shoes, Little Sister/Get Back, Hound Dog, Introductions, Suspicious Minds, The Impossible Dream (one of the very rare times Elvis closed his show with anything other than Can't Help Falling In Love)

January 30, 1971—Midnight Show—Complete
That's All Right, I Got A Woman, Love Me Tender, There Goes My Everything, You Don't Have To Say You Love Me, You've Lost That Lovin' Feeling, Polk Salad Annie, Introductions, Something, Dialogue, How Great Thou Art, Blue Suede Shoes, Little Sister/Get Back, Hound Dog, Suspicious Minds, The Impossible Dream (one of the very rare times Elvis closed his show with anything other than Can't Help Falling In Love)

January 31–February 8, 1971—Not Available

February 9, 1971—Dinner Show—Incomplete
By The Time I Get To Phoenix (partial)

February 9, 1971—Midnight Show—
Not Available

February 10—12, 1971—Not Available

February 13, 1971—Dinner Show—Incomplete
By The Time I Get To Phoenix (partial)

February 13, 1971—Midnight Show—Complete
That's All Right, I Got A Woman, Can't Help Falling In Love (this is one of the few times Elvis sang this song as part of the show and not his closing number), Sweet Caroline, You've Lost That Lovin' Feeling, Polk Salad Annie, Introductions, Johnny B. Goode, Something, Introductions, How Great Thou Art, Mystery Train/Tiger Man, Love Me, Don't Be Cruel, Heartbreak Hotel, Blue Suede Shoes, Little Sister/Get Back, Hound Dog, Introductions, Suspicious Minds, The Impossible Dream, (one of the rare times Elvis closed his show with anything other than Can't Help Falling In Love)

February 14–February 17 Dinner Show—
Not Available

February 17, 1971—Midnight Show—Complete
That's All Right, I Got A Woman, Jailhouse Rock, Love Me, Mystery Train/Tiger Man, Polk Salad Annie, Sweet Caroline, You've Lost That Lovin' Feeling, Something, Introductions, Johnny B. Goode, How Great Thou Art, Don't Be Cruel, Heartbreak Hotel, Blue Suede Shoes, Little Sister/Get Back, It's Now Or Never, Hound Dog, The Impossible Dream, (one of the very rare times Elvis closed his show with anything other than Can't Help Falling In Love

February 18, 1971—Not Available

February 19, 1971—Dinner Show—Complete
That's All Right, I Got A Woman, Dialogue, Can't Help Falling In Love (this is one of the few times Elvis sang this song as part of the show and not his closing number), Sweet Caroline, You've Lost That Lovin' Feeling, Polk Salad Annie, Dialogue, Johnny B. Goode, Dialogue, Something, How Great Thou Art, Mystery Train/Tiger Man, Love Me, Don't Be Cruel, Bridge Over Troubled Water, Blue Suede Shoes, Heartbreak Hotel, Little Sister/Get Back, It's Now Or Never, Hound Dog, Suspicious Minds, Introductions, Lawdy Miss Clawdy, Help Me Make It Through The Night, There Goes My Everything, Just Pretend, Old Shep (partial), In The Ghetto, *2001* intro (one of the rare times that Elvis' opening was used during the show), Snowbird, The Impossible Dream (one of the rare times Elvis closed his show with anything other than Can't Help Falling In Love)

February 19, 1971—Midnight Show—Complete
That's All Right, I Got A Woman/By The Time I Get To Phoenix, Love Me Tender, Loving You (partial), Jailhouse Rock, Can't Help Falling In Love (this is one of the few times Elvis sang this song as part of the show and not his closing number), Sweet Caroline, You've Lost That Lovin' Feeling, Polk Salad Annie, Introductions, Johnny B. Goode, Something, How Great Thou Art, Mystery Train/Tiger Man, Love Me, Don't Be Cruel, Bridge Over Troubled Water, Blue Suede Shoes, Heartbreak Hotel, Little Sister/Get Back, It's Now Or Never, Hound Dog, Suspicious Minds, Introductions, Lawdy Miss Clawdy, Help

Me Make It Through The Night, There Goes My Everything, Just Pretend, I Was The One (partial), Old Shep (partial), In The Ghetto, *2001* intro (one of the rare times that Elvis' opening was used during the show), Snowbird, The Impossible Dream (one of the very rare times Elvis closed his show with anything other than Can't Help Falling In Love)

February 20, 1971—Dinner Show—Complete
That's All Right, Proud Mary, Love Me Tender, Sweet Caroline, Polk Salad Annie, Johnny B. Goode, It's Impossible, Love Me, Blue Suede Shoes/Whole Lotta Shakin' Goin' On, Heartbreak Hotel, Teddy Bear/Don't Be Cruel, Hound Dog, Little Sister/Get Back, Lawdy Miss Clawdy, Introductions, I'm Leavin', Help Me Make It Through The Night, Mystery Train/Tiger Man, Can't Help Falling In Love

February 20, 1971—Midnight Show—Complete
That's All Right, I Got A Woman/By The Time I Get To Phoenix, Love Me, Mystery Train/Tiger Man, Sweet Caroline, You've Lost That Lovin' Feeling, Polk Salad Annie, Something, Johnny B. Goode, How Great Thou Art, Don't Be Cruel, Heartbreak Hotel, Blue Suede Shoes, Little Sister/Get Back, It's Now Or Never, Hound Dog, Introductions, The Impossible Dream (one of the rare times Elvis closed his show with anything other than Can't Help Falling In Love)

February 21, 1971—Dinner Show—Complete
That's All Right, I Got A Woman/Amen, Mystery Train/Tiger Man, Sweet Caroline, Dialogue, You've Lost That Lovin' Feeling, Polk Salad Annie, Introductions, Something, Johnny B. Goode, How Great Thou Art, Don't Be Cruel, Heartbreak Hotel/Blue Suede Shoes, Little Sister/Get Back, It's Now Or Never, Hound Dog, Introductions, The Impossible Dream (one of the rare times Elvis closed his show with anything other than Can't Help Falling In Love)

February 21, 1971—Midnight Show—Complete
That's All Right, I Got A Woman, Jailhouse Rock/Love Me, Mystery Train/Tiger Man, Dialogue, Sweet Caroline, You've Lost That Lovin' Feeling, Polk Salad Annie, Introductions, Something, Johnny B. Goode, Don't Be Cruel/Heartbreak Hotel/Blue Suede Shoes, Little Sister/Get Back, It's Now Or Never, Hound Dog, The Impossible Dream (one of the rare times Elvis closed his show with anything other than Can't Help Falling In Love)

February 22, 1971—Dinner Show—Complete
That's All Right, I Got A Woman, Dialogue, Love Me, Mystery Train/Tiger Man, Sweet Caroline, You've Lost That Lovin' Feeling, Polk Salad Annie, Love Me Tender, Johnny B. Goode, Something, Introductions, Bridge Over Troubled Water, Don't Be Cruel, Heartbreak Hotel, Lawdy Miss Clawdy, How Great Thou Art, Blue Suede Shoes, Little Sister/Get Back, It's Now Or Never, Hound Dog, Suspicious Minds, Karate dialogue and demonstration, Snowbird, There Goes My Everything (partial), My Babe, Just Pretend, *2001* intro (one of the rare times that Elvis' opening was used during the show), The Impossible Dream (one of the very rare times Elvis closed his show with anything other than Can't Help Falling In Love)

February 22, 1971—Midnight Show—Complete
That's All Right, I Got A Woman/By The Time I Get To Phoenix, Love Me Tender/Jailhouse Rock (partial), Love Me, Mystery Train/Tiger Man, Sweet Caroline, You've Lost That Lovin' Feeling, Polk Salad Annie, Love Me Tender, Johnny B. Goode, Something, Bridge Over Troubled Water, Don't Be Cruel, Heartbreak Hotel, Lawdy Miss Clawdy, How Great Thou Art, Blue Suede Shoes, Little Sister/Get Back, It's Now Or Never, Hound Dog, Suspicious Minds, Introductions, Snowbird, There Goes My Everything, My Babe, Just Pretend, *2001* intro (one of the rare times that Elvis' opening was used during the show), Celebrity introductions Bobby Goldsboro, Donny Osmond, The Impossible Dream (one of the rare times Elvis closed his show with anything other than Can't Help Falling In Love)

February 23, 1971—Dinner Show—Complete
That's All Right, I Got A Woman/By The Time I Get To Phoenix, Love Me Tender (false start), Love Me, Mystery Train/Tiger Man, Sweet Caroline, You've Lost That Lovin' Feeling, Polk Salad Annie, Something, Johnny B. Goode, How Great Thou Art, Don't Be Cruel/Lawdy Miss Clawdy, Heartbreak Hotel, Blue Suede Shoes, Bridge Over Troubled Water, Little Sister/Get Back, Hound Dog, Suspicious Minds, Don't Be Cruel/Lawdy Miss Clawdy, How Great Thou Art, Blue Suede Shoes, Little Sister/Get Back, It's Now Or Never, Hound Dog, Suspicious Minds, The Impossible Dream (one of the very rare times Elvis closed his show with anything other than Can't Help Falling In Love)

February 23, 1971—Closing Show—Complete
That's All Right, I Got A Woman/By The Time I Get To Phoenix, Love Me, Mystery Train/Tiger Man, Sweet Caroline, You've Lost That Lovin' Feeling, Polk Salad Annie, Something, Introductions, Johnny B. Goode, How Great Thou Art, Don't Be Cruel, Heartbreak Hotel, Blue Suede Shoes, Bridge Over Troubled Water, Little Sister/Get Back, Hound Dog, Suspicious Minds (karate dialogue and demonstration by Elvis), Introductions, Help Me Make It Through The Night, Celebrity introductions Vic Damone, Juliet Prowse, Nancy Sinatra, Phyllis McGuire, Lamar Fike, Felton Jarvis, Bill Porter, Colonel Parker, Vernon Presley, Elvis thanks the audience for coming. saying "The economy of the country is down, but you came out anyway." The Impossible Dream (one of the rare times Elvis closed his show with anything other than Can't Help Falling In Love)

Songs Sung by Elvis During This Engagement
2001 intro (one of the rare times that Elvis' opening was used during the show), Blue Suede Shoes, Bridge Over Troubled Water, By The Time I Get To Phoenix (partial),Can't Help Falling In Love, Can't Help Falling In Love (this is one of the few times Elvis sang this song as part of the show and not his closing number), Don't Be Cruel, Don't Be Cruel/Heartbreak Hotel/Blue Suede Shoes, Don't Be Cruel/Lawdy Miss Clawdy, Heartbreak Hotel, Heartbreak Hotel (partial), Heartbreak Hotel/Blue Suede Shoes, Help Me Make It Through The Night, Hound Dog, How Great Thou Art, I Got A Woman, I Got A Woman/Amen, I Got A Woman/By The Time I Get To Phoenix, The Impossible Dream, In The Ghetto, It's Now Or Never, I Was The One (partial), Jailhouse Rock, Jailhouse Rock (partial), Jailhouse Rock/Love Me, Johnny B. Goode, Just Pretend, Lawdy Miss Clawdy, Little Sister/Get Back, Love Me, Love Me Tender, Love Me Tender (false start), Loving You (partial), Make The World Go Away, My Babe, Mystery Train/Tiger Man, Old Shep (partial), One Night, Only Believe, Polk Salad Annie, Release Me, Snowbird, Something, Suspicious Minds, Sweet Caroline, Teddy Bear, Teddy Bear/ Don't Be Cruel, That's All Right, There Goes My Everything, There Goes My Everything (partial), The Wonder Of You, You Don't Have To Say You Love Me, You've Lost That Lovin' Feeling

The following songs are rumored to have been sung at this engagement but are not verifiable.

I've Got A Woman/Ave Maria, It's Only Make Believe, All Shook Up

VEGAS SEASON 5 1971, Hilton Hotel
Monday, August 9, 1971 through Monday, September 6, 1971—57 shows—Total attendance 125,400

Jumpsuits Worn During This Engagement—Cisco Kid Suit black and green with gold World Champion Attendance belt, Cisco Kid Suit white and black with gold World Championship Attendance belt, Cisco Kid Suit black and red with gold World Championship Attendance belt, Cisco Kid Suit black and blue with studded Lion Head belt. Elvis Now Suit with white macramé belt with blue turquoise conchos, White Tie Suit with beaded white macramé belt, White Tie Suit with beaded brown macramé belt

Show Members—Musicians: Lead Guitar—James Burton, Rhythm Guitar—John Wilkinson, Acoustic Guitar and Backup Vocals—Charlie Hodge, Bass—Jerry Scheff, Piano—Glen D. Hardin, Drums—Ronnie Tutt, Backup Singers: Sweet Inspirations: Ann Williams, Myrna Smith, Sylvia Shemwell, Estelle Brown, The Imperials: Jake Hess, Jim Murray, Gary McSpadden, Armond Morales, High Voice Singer—Kathy Westmoreland, Comedian—Bob Melvin, Orchestra —Joe Guercio

August 9, 1971—Opening Show 10:15 p.m. —Complete
That's All Right, Proud Mary, Love Me Tender, You Don't Have To Say You Love Me, You've Lost That Lovin' Feeling, Polk Salad Annie, Dialogue, Johnny B. Goode, It's Impossible, Love Me, Blue Suede Shoes/Whole Lotta Shakin' Goin' On, Heartbreak Hotel, Teddy Bear/Don't Be Cruel, Hound Dog, Suspicious Minds, Elvis karate dialogue and demonstration, Introductions, I'm Leavin', Lawdy Miss Clawdy, I Can't Stop Loving You, Can't Help Falling In Love

August 10, 1971—Dinner Show—Complete
That's All Right, Proud Marry, Jailhouse Rock, You Don't Have To Say You Love Me, You've Lost That Lovin' Feeling, Polk Salad Annie, It's Over, Love Me, Blue Suede Shoes, Heartbreak Hotel, Teddy Bear/Don't Be Cruel, Love Me Tender, Hound Dog (false start), Suspicious Minds, Elvis karate dialogue and demonstration, Celebrity introductions: Mike Stone and Charlie Pride, Kaw Liga (partial), I'm Leavin', Lawdy Miss Clawdy, Bridge Over Troubled Water (reprise), Can't Help Falling In Love

August 10, 1971—Midnight Show—Complete
That's All Right, Proud Mary, Jailhouse Rock/Amen, Love Me Tender, You Don't Have To Say You Love Me, You've Lost That Lovin' Feeling, Polk Salad Annie, Johnny B. Goode, It's Over, Love Me, Blue Suede Shoes/Whole Lotta Shakin' Goin' On/Blue Suede Shoes, Heartbreak Hotel, Teddy Bear/Don't Be Cruel, Dialogue, Hound Dog, Suspicious Minds, Elvis karate dialogue and demonstration, I'm Leavin', Bridge Over Troubled Water, Can't Help Falling In Love

August 11, 1971—Dinner Show—Complete
That's All Right, Proud Mary, You Don't Have To Say You Love Me, Sweet Caroline, Polk Salad Annie, Johnny B. Goode, It's Impossible, Love Me, Blue Suede Shoes/Whole Lotta Shakin' Goin' On, Heartbreak Hotel, Teddy Bear/Don't Be Cruel, Hound Dog, Memphis Tennessee, Trying To Get To You, Suspicious Minds, Introductions, I'm Leavin', Lawdy Miss Clawdy, The Impossible Dream, Bridge Over Troubled Water, Can't Help Falling In Love

August 11, 1971—Midnight Show—Incomplete
That's All Right, Proud Mary, You Don't Have To Say You Love Me, Sweet Caroline, Polk Salad Annie, Johnny B. Goode, It's Impossible, Love Me, Blue Suede Shoes, Heartbreak Hotel, Teddy Bear/Don't Be Cruel, Hound Dog, Memphis Tennessee, Trying To Get To You, Suspicious Minds, Introductions, I'm Leavin', Lawdy Miss Clawdy, The Impossible Dream

August 12, 1971—Dinner Show—Complete
That's All Right, Proud Mary, Jailhouse Rock, You Don't Have To Say You Love Me, You've Lost That Lovin' Feeling, Polk Salad Annie, Johnny B. Goode, It's Over, Love Me, Blue Suede Shoes/Whole Lotta Shakin' Goin' On/Blue Suede Shoes, Heartbreak Hotel, Teddy Bear/Don't Be Cruel, Celebrity introduction Richard Egan, Love Me Tender, I Don't Wanna Sing These Songs/Hound Dog, Suspicious Minds, Elvis karate dialogue and demonstration, Introductions, I'm Leavin', Lawdy Miss Clawdy, Bridge Over Troubled Water, Can't Help Falling In Love

August 12, 1971—Midnight Show—Complete
That's All Right, Proud Mary, Jailhouse Rock, You Don't Have To Say You Love Me, You've Lost That Lovin' Feeling, Polk Salad Annie, Johnny B. Goode, It's Over, Love Me, Blue Suede Shoes/Whole Lotta Shakin' Goin' On, Heartbreak Hotel, Teddy Bear/Don't Be Cruel, Love Me Tender, I Don't Wanna Sing That Song/Hound Dog, Suspicious Minds, I'm Leavin', Lawdy Miss Clawdy, Bridge Over Troubled Water (reprise), Can't Help Falling In Love

August 13, 1971—Not Available

August 14, 1971—Dinner Show—Complete
That's All Right, Proud Mary, You Don't Have To Say You Love Me, You've Lost That Lovin' Feeling, Polk Salad Annie, Johnny B. Goode, It's Impossible, Love Me, Blue Suede Shoes/Whole Lotta Shakin' Goin' On/Blue Suede Shoes, Heartbreak Hotel, Teddy Bear/Don't Be Cruel, Rip It Up (partial), Hound Dog, I Need Your Lovin' Every Day (partial), Suspicious Minds, Introductions, I'm Leavin', Lawdy Miss Clawdy, Bridge Over Troubled Water, Can't Help Falling In Love

August 14, 1971—Midnight Show—Complete
That's All Right, Proud Mary, You Don't Have To Say You Love Me, You've Lost That Lovin' Feeling, Polk Salad Annie, Johnny B. Goode, Blue Suede Shoes/Whole Lotta Shain' Goin' On, Heartbreak Hotel, Teddy Bear/Don't Be Cruel, Rip It Up (partial), Hound Dog, I Need Your Lovin' Everyday (partial), Suspicious Minds, Introductions, I'm Leavin', Lawdy Miss Clawdy, Bridge Over Trouble Water (reprise), Can't Help Falling In Love

August 15, 1971—Not Available

August 16, 1971—Dinner Show—Complete
That's All Right, Proud Mary, Love Me Tender, Sweet Caroline, Polk Salad Annie, Johnny B. Goode, It's Impossible, Love Me, Blue Suede Shoes/Whole Lotta Shakin' Goin' On/Blue Suede Shoes, Teddy Bear/Don't Be Cruel, Dialogue, Hound Dog, Suspicious Minds, Elvis karate dialogue and demonstration, I'm Leavin', Lawdy Miss Clawdy, Help Me Make It Through The Night, Mystery Train/Tiger Man, Can't Help Falling In Love

August 16, 1971—Midnight Show—Complete
That's All Right, Proud Mary, Love Me Tender (false start), Sweet Caroline, Polk Salad Annie, Dialogue, Johnny B. Goode, It's Impossible, Love Me, Blue Suede Shoes/Whole Lotta Shakin' Goin' On/Blue Suede Shoes, Teddy Bear/Don't Be Cruel, Dialogue, Hound Dog, Suspicious Minds, Introductions, I'm Leavin', Lawdy Miss Clawdy, Help Me Make It Through The Night, Mystery Train/Tiger Man, Can't Help Falling In Love

August 17, 1971—Dinner Show—Complete
That's All Right, Proud Mary, Love Me Tender, Sweet Caroline, Polk Salad Annie, Dialogue, Johnny B. Goode, It's Impossible, Love Me, Blue Suede Shoes/Whole Lotta Shakin' Goin' On/Blue Suede Shoes, Heartbreak Hotel, Teddy Bear/Don't Be Cruel, Hound Dog (false start), Suspicious Minds, Introductions, I'm Leavin', Lawdy Miss Clawdy, It's Over, Little Sister/Get Back, Can't Help Falling In Love

August 17, 1971—Midnight Show—Complete
That's All Right, Proud Mary, I Got A Woman/ Amen, Sweet Caroline, Polk Salad Annie, Johnny B. Goode, It's Impossible, Love Me, Blue Suede Shoes/Whole Lotta Shakin' Goin' On/Blue Suede Shoes, Heartbreak Hotel, Teddy Bear/Don't Be Cruel, I'm Not In The Mood To Sing That Song/ Hound Dog (blues version partial), Dialogue, Hound Dog, Love Me Tender, Suspicious Minds, Elvis karate dialogue and demonstration, Celebrity introduction Tom Jones, I Need Your Lovin' Everyday (partial), I'm Leavin', Lawdy Miss Clawdy, Mystery Train/Tiger Man, Can't Help Falling In Love

August 18, 1971—Dinner Show—Complete
That's All Right, Proud Mary, Love Me Tender, Sweet Caroline, Polk Salad Annie, Johnny B. Goode, It's Impossible, Love Me, Blue Suede Shoes, Heartbreak Hotel, Teddy Bear/Don't Be Cruel, Hound Dog, Suspicious Minds, Introductions, I'm Leavin', Lawdy Miss Clawdy, Can't Help Falling In Love

August 18, 1971—Midnight Show—Complete
That's All Right, Proud Mary, Love Me Tender, Sweet Caroline, Polk Salad Annie, Johnny B. Goode, It's Impossible, Love Me, Blue Suede Shoes/Whole Lotta Shakin' Goin' On, Heartbreak Hotel, Teddy Bear/Don't Be Cruel, Dialogue, Hound Dog, Suspicious Minds, Elvis karate dialogue and demonstration, Elvis introduces Japanese fans, I'm Leavin', Lawdy Miss Clawdy, Can't Help Falling In Love

August 19, 1971—Dinner Show—Complete
That's All Right, Proud Mary, I Got A Woman/ Amen, Love Me Tender (false start), Sweet Caroline, Polk Salad Annie, Dialogue, Johnny B. Goode, It's Impossible, Love Me, Blue Suede Shoes/Whole Lotta Shakin' Goin' On/Blue Suede Shoes, Heartbreak Hotel, Teddy Bear/Don't Be Cruel, Hound Dog, Suspicious Minds, Introductions, I'm Leavin', Lawdy Miss Clawdy, Dialogue, Can't Help Falling In Love

August 19, 1971—Midnight Show—Complete
That's All Right, Proud Mary, You Don't Have To Say You Love Me, You've Lost That Lovin' Feeling, Polk Salad Annie, Johnny B. Goode, It's Impossible, Love Me, Blue Suede Shoes/Whole Lotta Shakin' Goin' On, Heartbreak Hotel, Teddy Bear/Don't Be Cruel, Hound Dog, Suspicious Minds, Introductions, I'm Leavin', Lawdy Miss Clawdy, I Can't Stop Loving You, Can't Help Falling In Love

August 20, 1971—Dinner Show—Complete
That's All Right, Proud Mary, Love Me Tender, Sweet Caroline, Polk Salad Annie, Introductions, Johnny B. Goode, It's Impossible (false start), Love Me, Blue Suede Shoes/Whole Lotta Shakin' Goin' On/Blue Suede Shoes, Heartbreak Hotel, Teddy Bear/Don't Be Cruel, So High (partial), Hound Dog, Little Sister/Get Back, Lawdy Miss Clawdy, Introductions, I'm Leavin', Help Me Make It Through The Night, Mystery Train/Tiger Man, Can't Help Falling In Love

**August 20, 1971—Midnight Show—
Not Available**

August 21, 1971—Dinner Show—Complete
That's All Right, I Got A Woman/Amen, Proud Mary, Sweet Caroline, Polk Salad Annie, Johnny B. Goode, It's Impossible, Love Me, Blue Suede Shoes/Whole Lotta Shakin' Goin' On, Heartbreak Hotel, Teddy Bear/Don't Be Cruel, Dialogue, Hound Dog, Love Me Tender, Introductions, I'm Leavin', Suspicious Minds, Elvis karate dialogue and demonstration, Introductions, Lawdy Miss Clawdy, Can't Help Falling In Love

August 21, 1971—Midnight Show—Complete
That's All Right, Proud Mary, I Got A Woman/ Amen, Polk Salad Annie, Johnny B. Goode, Love Me, Blue Suede Shoes/Whole Lotta Shakin' Goin' On, Heartbreak Hotel, Teddy Bear/Don't Be Cruel, I Don't Want To Sing That Song Hound Dog, It's Impossible, Love Me Tender, Little Sister/Get Back, Mystery Train/Tiger Man, Introductions, I'm Leavin', Suspicious Minds, Lawdy Miss Clawdy, Bridge Over Troubled Water, Can't Help Falling In Love

August 22, 1971—Dinner Show—Complete
That's All Right, Proud Mary, I've Got A Woman/ Amen, Sweet Caroline, Polk Salad Annie, Johnny B. Goode, It's Impossible, Love Me, Blue Suede Shoes/Whole Lotta Shakin' Goin' On/Blue Suede Shoes, Heartbreak Hotel, Teddy Bear/Don't Be Cruel, Dialogue, Hound Dog, Love Me Tender, Introductions, I'm Leavin', Suspicious Minds, Elvis karate dialogue and demonstration, Introductions, Lawdy Miss Clawdy, Can't Help Falling In Love

August 22, 1971—Midnight Show—Complete
That's All Right, Proud Mary, I Got A Woman/Amen, Sweet Caroline, Polk Salad Annie, Johnny B. Goode, It's Impossible, Love Me, Blue Suede Shoes, Heartbreak Hotel, Teddy Bear/Don't Be Cruel, Hound Dog, Love Me Tender, I'm Leavin', Suspicious Minds, Karate dialogue, Introductions, Lawdy Miss Clawdy, Can't Help Falling In Love

August 23, 1971—Dinner Show—Complete
That's All Right, Proud Mary, I Got A Woman/ Amen, Sweet Caroline, Polk Salad Annie, Johnny B. Goode, It's Impossible, Love Me, Blue Suede Shoes/Whole Lotta Shakin' Goin' On/Blue Suede Shoes, Heartbreak Hotel, Teddy Bear/Don't Be Cruel, Hound Dog, Love Me Tender, Suspicious Minds, Introductions, I'm Leavin', Lawdy Miss Clawdy, Can't Help Falling In Love

August 23, 1971—Midnight Show—Complete
That's All Right, I Got A Woman, Proud Mary, Sweet Caroline, Polk Salad Annie, Dialogue, Johnny B. Goode, It's Impossible, Love Me, Blue Suede Shoes/Whole Lotta Shakin' Goin' On/Blue Suede Shoes, Heartbreak Hotel, Teddy Bear/Don't Be Cruel, Dialogue, Hound Dog, Love Me Tender, Bridge Over Troubled Water, Introductions, I'm Leavin', Suspicious Minds, Elvis karate dialogue and demonstration, Introductions, Celebrity introduction Bill Medley, Lawdy Miss Clawdy, Can't Help Falling In Love

August 24, 1971—Dinner Show—Complete
That's All Right, Proud Mary, Sweet Caroline, Polk Salad Annie, Johnny B. Goode, It's Impossible, Love Me, Blue Suede Shoes/Whole Lotta Shakin' Goin' On/Blue Suede Shoes, Heartbreak Hotel, Teddy Bear/Don't Be Cruel, Dialogue, Hound Dog, Love Me Tender, I'm Leavin', Suspicious Minds, Elvis karate dialogue and demonstration, Mystery Train/Tiger Man, Can't Help Falling In Love

August 24, 1971—Midnight Show—Complete
That's All Right, I Got A Woman/Amen, Proud Mary, Sweet Caroline, Polk Salad Annie, Johnny B. Goode, Love Me, Blue Suede Shoes/Whole Lotta Shakin' Goin' On, Blue Suede Shoes, Heartbreak Hotel, Teddy Bear/Don't Be Cruel, Dialogue, Hound Dog, Suspicious Minds, Introductions, I'm Leavin', Lawdy Miss Clawdy, All Shook Up, Can't Help Falling In Love

August 25, 1971—Dinner Show—Complete
That's All Right, Proud Mary, I Walk The Line (partial), Love Me Tender, Sweet Caroline, Polk Salad Annie, Johnny B. Goode, Love Me, Blue Suede Shoes/Whole Lotta Shakin' Goin' On/Blue Suede Shoes, Heartbreak Hotel, Teddy Bear/ Don't Be Cruel, Dialogue, Hound Dog, Suspicious Minds, Elvis karate dialogue and demon-

stration, Introductions, Celebrity introduction Brenda Lee, I'm Leavin', Lawdy Miss Clawdy, Can't Help Falling In Love

August 25, 1971—Midnight Show—Complete
That's All Right, Proud Mary, Love Me Tender/Sweet Caroline, Polk Salad Annie, Dialogue, Johnny B. Goode, Love Me, Blue Suede Shoes/A Whole Lotta Shakin' Goin' On/Blue Suede Shoes, Heartbreak Hotel, Teddy Bear, Don't Be Cruel, Hound Dog, Introductions, I'm Leavin', Lawdy Miss Clawdy, Can't Help Falling In Love.

August 26, 1971—Dinner Show—Not Available

August 26, 1971—Midnight Show—Complete
That's All Right, I Got A Woman, Proud Mary, Sweet Caroline, Polk Salad Annie, Dialogue, Johnny B. Goode, It's Impossible, Love Me, Blue Suede Shoes/Whole Lotta Shakin' Goin' On/Blue Suede Shoes, Heartbreak Hotel, Teddy Bear/Don't Be Cruel, Dialogue, Hound Dog, Suspicious Minds, Elvis karate dialogue and demonstration, Introductions, I'm Leavin', Lawdy Miss Clawdy, Can't Help Falling In Love

August 27, 1971—Dinner Show—Not Available

August 27, 1971—Midnight Show—Complete
That's All Right, I Got A Woman, Proud Mary, Sweet Caroline, Polk Salad Annie, Dialogue, Johnny B. Goode, It's Impossible, Love Me, Blue Suede Shoes/Whole Lotta Shakin' Goin' On/Blue Suede Shoes, Heartbreak Hotel, Teddy Bear/Don't Be Cruel, Dialogue, Hound Dog, Love Me Tender, Introductions, I'm Leavin', Bridge Over Troubled Water (reprise), Can't Help Falling In Love

August 28, 1971—Dinner Show—Complete
That's All Right, I Got A Woman, Proud Mary, Sweet Caroline, Polk Salad Annie, Dialogue, Johnny B. Goode, It's Impossible, Love Me, Blue Suede Shoes/Whole Lotta Shakin' Goin' On/Blue Suede Shoes, Heartbreak Hotel, Dialogue, Hound Dog, Teddy Bear/Don't Be Cruel, Suspicious Minds, Elvis karate dialogue and demonstration, Introductions, Celebrity introduction Ed Parker, I'm Leavin', Bridge Over Troubled Water, Can't Help Falling In Love

**August 28, 1971—Midnight Show—
Not Available**

August 29, 1971—Not Available

August 30, 1971—Dinner Show—Complete
That's All Right, I Got A Woman/Amen, Proud Mary, Sweet Caroline, Polk Salad Annie, Johnny B. Goode, It's Impossible, Love Me, Blue Suede Shoes/Whole Lotta Shakin' Goin' On, Heartbreak Hotel, Teddy Bear/Don't Be Cruel, Hound Dog, Dialogue, Love Me Tender, Introductions, I'm Leavin', Bridge Over Troubled Water, Can't Help Falling In Love

August 30, 1971—Midnight Show—Complete
That's All Right, I Got A Woman/Amen, Proud Mary, Sweet Caroline, Polk Salad Annie, Introductions, Johnny B. Goode, It's Impossible, Love Me, Blue Suede Shoes/Whole Lotta Shakin' Goin' On/Blue Suede Shoes, Heartbreak Hotel, Teddy Bear/Don't Be Cruel, It's Over, Dialogue, Hound Dog (false start), Hound Dog (reprise), Suspicious Minds, Elvis karate dialogue and demonstration, Celebrity introduction Johnny Rivers, Dialogue, I'm Leavin', Bridge Over Troubled Water (reprise), Can't Help Falling in Love

August 31, 1971—Dinner Show—Complete
That's All Right, I Got A Woman/Amen, Proud Mary, Sweet Caroline, Polk Salad Annie, Johnny B. Goode, It's Impossible, Love Me, Blue Suede Shoes/Whole Lotta Shakin' Goin' On/Blue Suede Shoes, Heartbreak Hotel, Teddy Bear/Don't Be Cruel, Dialogue, Hound Dog, Love Me Tender, Suspicious Minds, Elvis karate dialogue and demonstration, Introductions, I'm Leavin', Bridge Over Troubled Water (reprise), Can't Help Falling In Love

August 31, 1971—Midnight Show—Complete
That's All Right, I Got A Woman/Amen, Proud Mary, Sweet Caroline, Polk Salad Annie, Johnny B. Goode, It's Impossible, Love Me, Blue Suede Shoes/ Whole Lotta Shakin' Goin' On, Heartbreak Hotel, Teddy Bear/Don't Be Cruel, It's Over, Dialogue, Hound Dog, Suspicious Minds, Elvis karate dialogue and demonstration, Celebrity introduction Jerry Lee Lewis, I'm Leavin', Lawdy Miss Clawdy, Can't Help Falling In Love (partial), Bridge Over Troubled Water (One of the rare times Elvis closed the show with anything other than Can't Help Falling In Love)

September 1, 1971—Not Available

September 2, 1971—Dinner Show—Complete
That's All Right, I Got A Woman/Amen, Proud Mary, Sweet Caroline, Polk Salad Annie, Dialogue, Johnny B. Goode, It's Impossible, Love Me, Blue Suede Shoes/Whole Lotta Shakin' Goin' On/Blue Suede Shoes, Heartbreak Hotel, Teddy Bear/Don't Be Cruel, Dialogue, Hound Dog, Suspicious Minds, Elvis karate dialogue and demonstration, Introductions, I'm Leavin', Lawdy Miss Clawdy, Can't Help Falling In Love

**September 2, 1971—Midnight Show—
Not Available**

September 3, 1971—Dinner Show—Complete
That's All Right, I Got A Woman/Ave Maria, His Latest Flame (partial), Tiger Man, Dialogue, I've Lost You, Treat Me Nice (partial), Wooden Heart (partial), I Just Can't Help Believin', Polk Salad Annie, Sweet Inspiration, The Wonder Of You, Heartbreak Hotel, Memphis Tennessee, One Night, Blue Suede Shoes, Hound Dog, Bridge Over Troubled Water, Can't Help Falling In Love

**September 3, 1971—Midnight Show—
Complete**
That's All Right, I Got A Woman/Amen, Proud Mary, Sweet Caroline, Polk Salad Annie, I John (partial), Johnny B. Goode, It's Impossible, Love Me, Blue Suede Shoes/Whole Lotta Shakin' Goin' On/Blue Suede Shoes, Heartbreak Hotel, Teddy Bear/Don't Be Cruel, Hound Dog, Love Me Tender, Introductions, His Latest Flame (partial), Little Sister/Get Back, Jailhouse Rock, Wooden Heart sung in German), One Night, Introductions, I'm Leavin', Lawdy Miss Clawdy, Can't Help Falling In Love

September 4, 1971—Dinner Show—Complete
That's All Right, Proud Mary, Jailhouse Rock, You Don't Have To Say You Love Me, You've Lost That Lovin' Feeling, Polk Salad Annie, Johnny B. Goode, It's Over, Love Me, Blue Suede Shoes/ Whole Lotta Shakin' Goin' On/Blue Suede Shoes, Heartbreak Hotel, Teddy Bear/Don't Be Cruel, Love Me Tender, I Don't Want To Sing That Song/Hound Dog, Suspicious Minds, Introductions, I'm Leavin', Lawdy Miss Clawdy, Bridge Over Troubled Water, Can't Help Falling In Love

**September 4, 1971—Midnight Show—
Complete**
That's All Right, I Got A Woman/Amen, Proud Mary, Sweet Caroline, Polk Salad Annie/I John, Johnny B. Goode, It's Impossible, Love Me, Blue Suede Shoes/Whole Lotta Shakin' Goin' On/Blue Suede Shoes, Heartbreak Hotel, Teddy Bear/Don't Be Cruel, Dialogue, Hound Dog, Suspicious Minds, Elvis karate dialogue and demonstration, I'm Leavin', Lawdy Miss Clawdy, Bridge Over Troubled Water, Can't Help Falling In Love

September 5, 1971—Dinner Show—Complete
That's All Right, I Got A Woman/Amen, Proud Mary, Sweet Caroline, Polk Salad Annie, Johnny B. Goode, It's Impossible, Love Me, Blue Suede Shoes/Whole Lotta Shakin' Goin' On/Blue Suede Shoes, Heartbreak Hotel, Teddy Bear/Don't Be Cruel, Dialogue, Hound Dog, Love Me Tender, Suspicious Minds, Elvis karate dialogue and demonstration, Introductions, I'm Leavin', Lawdy Miss Clawdy, Can't Help Falling In Love

September 5, 1971—Midnight Show—Complete
That's All Right, I Got A Woman/Amen, Proud Mary, Sweet Caroline, Polk Salad Annie, Johnny B. Goode, It's Impossible, Love Me, Blue Suede Shoes/Whole Lotta Shakin' Goin' On/Blue Suede Shoes, Heartbreak Hotel, Teddy Bear/Don't Be Cruel, Dialogue, Hound Dog, Ave Maria/Love Me Tender, Love Me Tender, Suspicious Minds, Elvis karate dialogue and demonstration, Introductions, I'm Leavin', Lawdy Miss Clawdy, Can't Help Falling In Love

September 6, 1971—Dinner Show—Complete
That's All Right, I Got A Woman/Amen, Proud Mary, Sweet Caroline, Polk Salad Annie, Dialogue, Johnny B. Goode, It's Impossible, Love Me, Blue Suede Shoes/Whole Lotta Shakin' Goin' On/Blue Suede Shoes, Heartbreak Hotel, Teddy Bear/Don't Be Cruel, Dialogue, Hound Dog (slow version), Hound Dog (fast version), Love Me Tender, Suspicious Minds, Introductions, Celebrity introduction Raquel Welch, I'm Leavin', Bridge Over Troubled Water (One of the rare times Elvis closed the show with anything other than Can't Help Falling In Love)

September 6, 1971—Closing Show—Complete
That's All Right, I Got A Woman/Amen, Proud Mary, Sweet Caroline, Polk Salad Annie, Love Me Tender, Johnny B. Goode, It's Impossible, Love Me, Blue Suede Shoes/Whole Lotta Shakin' Goin' On, Heartbreak Hotel, Teddy Bear/Don't Be Cruel, Are You Lonesome Tonight, Dialogue, Hound Dog, Suspicious Minds, Elvis karate dialogue and demonstration, Introductions, Celebrity introduction Charlie Pride, Livin' Alone (partial), Elvis introduces Vernon Presley and Priscilla Presley, The Easy Part's Over (partial), Elvis introduces Bob Melvin, I'm Leavin', Lawdy Miss Clawdy (reprise), Can't Help Falling In Love

Songs Sung by Elvis During This Engagement
All Shook Up, Are You Lonesome Tonight, Ave Maria (partial), Blue Suede Shoes, Blue Suede Shoes/Whole Lotta Shakin' Goin' On, Blue Suede Shoes/Whole Lotta Shakin' Goin' On/Blue Suede Shoes, Bridge Over Troubled Water (note: Elvis closed with this song at the dinner show on August 31 and September 6), Bridge Over Trouble Water (reprise), Can't Help Falling In Love, Can't Help Falling In Love (partial), The Easy Part's Over (partial), Heartbreak Hotel, Help Me Make It Through The Night, His Latest Flame, His Latest Flame (partial), Hound Dog, Hound Dog (Blues version partial), Hound Dog (slow version), Hound Dog (fast version), Hound Dog (false start), Hound Dog (reprise), I Can't Stop Loving You, I Don't Wanna Sing This Song/Hound Dog, I Don't Wanna Sing This Song/Hound Dog, I Got A Woman, I Got a Woman/Amen, I Got A Woman/Ave Maria, I John (partial), I Just Can't Help Believin', I'm Leavin', I'm Not In The Mood To Sing That Song (partial), I Need Your Lovin' Everyday (partial), It's Impossible, It's Impossible (false start), It's Over, I've Lost You, I Walk The Line (partial), Jailhouse Rock, Jailhouse Rock/Amen, Johnny B. Goode, Kaw-Liga (partial), Lawdy Miss Clawdy, Lawdy Miss Clawdy (reprise), Little Sister/Get Back, Livin' Alone (partial), Love Me, Love Me Tender, Love Me Tender (false start), Love Me Tender/Sweet Caroline, Memphis Tennessee, Mystery Train/Tiger Man, One Night, Polk Salad Annie, Polk Salad Annie/I John, Proud Mary, Rip It Up (partial), So High (partial), Suspicious Minds, Sweet Caroline, Sweet Inspiration, Teddy Bear/Don't Be Cruel, That's All Right, Tiger Man, Treat Me Nice (partial), Trying To Get To You, The Wonder of You, Wooden Heart, Wooden Heart (German), Wooden Heart (partial), You Don't Have To Say You Love Me, You've Lost That Lovin' Feeling

The following song is rumored to have been sung at this engagement but is not verifiable.

He Touched Me (partial)

VEGAS SEASON 6 1972, Hilton Hotel
Wednesday, January 26, 1972 through Tuesday, February 23 1972—57 shows—Total attendance—125,400

Jumpsuits Worn At This Engagement—Red Burning Love Suit with white lined cape, White Lion Head Suit with red lined cape, Black Lion Head Suit with green lined cape, Black Matador Suit with red lined cape, White Comet Suit with gold lined cape, White Comet Suit with blue lined cape, White Diamond Suit with gold lined cape, Black Spectrum Suit with red lined cape, White Spectrum Suit with black lined cape, Blue Nail Suit with white lined cape, White Star Suit with blue lined cape (first jumpsuit with cape), Blue Owl Suit with silver lined cape

Show Members—Musicians: Lead Guitar—James Burton, Rhythm Guitar—John Wilkinson, Acoustic Guitar and Backup Vocals—Charlie Hodge, Bass—Jerry Scheff, Piano—Glen D. Hardin, Drums—Ronnie Tutt, Backup Singers: Sweet Inspirations: Myrna Smith, Sylvia Shemwell, Estelle Brown, J.D. Sumner & The Stamps Quartet: J.D. Sumner, Donnie Sumner, Bill Baize, Ed Enoch, Richard Sterban, High Voice Singer - Kathy Westmoreland, Comedian—Jackie Kahane, Orchestra —Joe Guercio

January 26, 1972—Opening Night 10:15 P.M.—Complete
C.C. Rider, Proud Mary, Never Been To Spain, You Gave Me A Mountain, Until It's Time For You To Go, Polk Salad Annie, Love Me, Little Sister/Get Back, All Shook Up, Teddy Bear/Don't Be Cruel, One Night, Hound Dog, Big Hunk O' Love, Bridge Over Troubled Water, Lawdy Miss Clawdy, American Trilogy, Introductions, I'll Remember You, Suspicious Minds, Can't Help Falling In Love

January 27, 1972—Not Available

January 28, 1972—Not Available

January 29, 1972—Dinner Show—Not Available

January 29, 1972—Midnight Show—Complete
C.C. Rider, Proud Mary, Never Been To Spain, You Gave Me A Mountain, Until It's Time For You To Go, Polk Salad Annie, Love Me, Little Sister/Get Back, All Shook Up, One Night, Don't Be Cruel, Hound Dog, Big Hunk O' Love, Bridge Over Troubled Water, Lawdy Miss Clawdy, American Trilogy, Introductions, Suspicious Minds, Can't Help Falling In Love

January 30, 1972 Through February 5, 1972—Not Available

February 6, 1972—Dinner Show—Complete
C.C. Rider, Proud Mary, Never Been To Spain, You Gave Me A Mountain, Until It's Time For You To Go, Polk Salad Annie, Love Me, Little Sister/Get Back, All Shook Up, Teddy Bear/Don't Be Cruel, One Night, Hound Dog, Big Hunk O' Love, Bridge Over Troubled Water, Suspicious Minds, Introductions, Celebrity introduction Jim Nabors, American Trilogy, Can't Help Falling In Love

February 6, 1972—Midnight Show—Complete
C.C. Rider, Proud Mary, Never Been To Spain, You Gave Me A Mountain, Until It's Time For You To Go, Polk Salad Annie, Love Me, Little Sister/Get Back, All Shook Up, Teddy Bear/Don't Be Cruel, One Night, Hound Dog, Big Hunk O' Love, Bridge Over Troubled Water, Suspicious Minds, Introductions, American Trilogy, Can't Help Falling In Love

February 7, 1972—Dinner Show—Complete
C.C. Rider, Proud Mary, Never Been To Spain, You Gave Me A Mountain, Until It's Time For You To Go, Polk Salad Annie, Love Me, All Shook Up, Teddy Bear/Don't Be Cruel, Hound Dog, Big Hunk O' Love, Bridge Over Troubled Water, Suspicious Minds, Introductions, American Trilogy, Can't Help Falling In Love

February 7, 1972—Midnight Show—Not Available

February 8, 1972—Dinner Show—Not Available

February 8, 1972—Midnight Show—Complete
C.C. Rider, Proud Mary, Never Been To Spain, You Gave Me A Mountain, Until It's Time For You To Go, Polk Salad Annie, Love Me, Little Sister/Get Back, All Shook Up, Teddy Bear/Don't Be Cruel, Hound Dog, Big Hunk O' Love, Help Me Make It Through The Night, I'm Leaving It Up To You, Bridge Over Troubled Water, Suspicious Minds, Introductions, American Trilogy, Can't Help Falling In Love

February 9, 1972—Not Available

February 10, 1972—Dinner Show—Not Available

February 10, 1972—Midnight Show—Complete
C.C. Rider, Proud Mary, Never Been To Spain, You Gave Me A Mountain, Until It's Time For You To Go, Polk Salad Annie, Love Me, Little Sister/Get Back, All Shook Up, Teddy Bear/Don't Be Cruel, Hound Dog, Big Hunk O' Love, Help Me Make It Through The Night, I'm Leaving It Up To You, Bridge Over Troubled Water, Suspicious Minds, Introductions, American Trilogy, Can't Help Falling In Love

**February 11, 1972—Dinner Show—
Not Available**

February 11, 1972—Midnight Show—Complete
C.C. Rider, Proud Mary, Never Been To Spain, You Gave Me A Mountain, Until It's Time For You To Go, Polk Salad Annie, Love Me, Little Sister/Get Back, All Shook Up/Teddy Bear/Don't Be Cruel, Hound Dog, Big Hunk O' Love, Help Me Make It Through The Night, Bridge Over Troubled Water, Suspicious Minds, Introductions, American Trilogy, Can't Help Falling In Love

February 12, 1972 –February 13, 1972—Not Available

February 14, 1972—Dinner Show—Incomplete
C.C. Rider, Proud Mary, Never Been To Spain, Love Me, Teddy Bear/Don't Be Cruel, Little Sister/Get Back, Hound Dog, Big Hunk O' Love, American Trilogy, You Gave Me A Mountain, Can't Help Falling In Love

February 14, 1972—Midnight Show—Complete
C.C. Rider, Proud Mary, Never Been To Spain, You Gave Me A Mountain, Until It's Time For You To Go, Polk Salad, Love Me, Little Sister/Get Back, All Shook Up, Teddy Bear/Don't Be Cruel, Hound Dog, Big Hunk O' Love, Help Me Make It Through The Night, Bridge Over Troubled Water, Suspicious Minds, Introductions, American Trilogy, Can't Help Falling In Love

February 15, 1972—Dinner Show—Incomplete
C.C. Rider, Proud Mary, Never Been To Spain, Love Me, Teddy Bear/Don't Be Cruel, Little Sister/Get Back, Hound Dog, Big Hunk O' Love, American Trilogy, You Gave Me A Mountain, Can't Help Falling In Love

February 15, 1972—Midnight Show—Complete
C.C. Rider, Proud Mary, Never Been To Spain, You Gave Me A Mountain, Until It's Time For You To Go, Polk Salad Annie, Love Me, All Shook Up, Teddy Bear/Don't Be Cruel, Hound Dog, Big Hunk O' Love, Bridge Over Troubled Water, Suspicious Minds, Introductions, American Trilogy, Can't Help Falling In Love

February 16, 1972—Dinner Show—Complete
C.C. Rider, Proud Mary, Never Been To Spain, You Gave Me A Mountain, Until It's Time For You To Go, Polk Salad Annie, Love Me, All Shook Up, Teddy Bear/Don't Be Cruel, Hound Dog, Big Hunk O' Love, Bridge Over Troubled Water, Suspicious Minds, Introductions, American Trilogy, Can't Help Falling In Love

February 16, 1972—Midnight Show—Complete
C.C. Rider, Proud Mary, Never Been To Spain, You Gave Me A Mountain, Until It's Time For You To Go, Polk Salad Annie, Love Me, All Shook Up, Teddy Bear/Don't Be Cruel, Hound Dog, Big Hunk O' Love, It's Impossible, The Impossible Dream, Bridge Over Troubled Water, Suspicious Minds, Introductions, American Trilogy, Can't Help Falling In Love

February 17, 1972—Dinner Show—Complete
C.C. Rider, Proud Mary, Never Been To Spain, You Gave Me A Mountain, Until It's Time For You To Go, Polk Salad Annie, Love Me, All Shook Up, Teddy Bear/Don't Be Cruel, Hound Dog, Big Hunk O' Love, Bridge Over Troubled Water, Suspicious Minds, Introductions, Celebrity introduction Johnny Tillotson, American Trilogy, Can't Help Falling In Love

February 17, 1972—Midnight Show—Complete
C.C. Rider, Proud Mary, Never Been To Spain, Love Me, Teddy Bear/Don't Be Cruel, Until It's Time For You To Go, Polk Salad Annie, All Shook Up, Little Sister/Get Back, Hound Dog, It's Over, Big Hunk O' Love, American Trilogy, You Gave Me A Mountain, Suspicious Minds, Can't Help Falling Love

February 18, 1972—Not Available

February 19, 1972—Dinner Show—Complete
C.C. Rider, Proud Mary, Never Been To Spain, You Gave Me A Mountain, Until It's Time For You To Go, Polk Salad Annie, Love Me, All Shook Up, Teddy Bear/Don't Be Cruel, Hound Dog, Big Hunk O' Love, Bridge Over Troubled Water, Suspicious Minds, Introductions, Celebrity introduction Robert W. Morgan, American Trilogy, Can't Help Falling In Love

February 19, 1972—Midnight Show—Complete
C.C. Rider, Proud Mary, Never Been To Spain, You Gave Me A Mountain, Until It's Time For You To Go, Polk Salad Annie, Love Me, All Shook Up, Teddy Bear/Don't Be Cruel, Hound Dog, Big Hunk O' Love, Bridge Over Troubled Water, Suspicious Minds, Introductions, Celebrity introduction Chill Wills, American Trilogy, Can't Help Falling In Love

February 20, 1972—Not Available

February 21, 1972—Dinner Show—Complete
C.C. Rider, Proud Mary, Never Been To Spain, You Gave Me A Mountain, Until It's Time For You To Go, Polk Salad Annie, Love Me, All Shook Up, Teddy Bear/Don't Be Cruel, Hound Dog, Big Hunk O' Love, Bridge Over Troubled Water, Suspicious Minds, Introductions, American Trilogy, Can't Help Falling In Love

February 21, 1972—Midnight Show—Complete
C.C. Rider, Proud Mary, Never Been To Spain, You Gave Me A Mountain, Until It's Time For You To Go, Polk Salad Annie, Love Me, All Shook Up, Teddy Bear/Don't Be Cruel, Hound Dog, Big Hunk O' Love, Help Me Make It Through The Night, Bridge Over Troubled Water, Suspicious Minds, Introductions, American Trilogy, Can't Help Falling In Love

February 22, 1972—Dinner Show—Complete
C.C. Rider, Proud Mary, Carry Me Back To Old Virginny (partial), Never Been To Spain, You Gave Me A Mountain (false start), Until It's Time For You To Go, Polk Salad Annie, Love Me, All Shook Up, Teddy Bear/Don't Be Cruel, Hound Dog, Big Hunk O' Love, Hawaiian Wedding Song (partial), Bridge Over Troubled Water, Suspicious Minds, Introductions, Celebrity introduction Michael Caine, American Trilogy, Can't Help Falling In Love

February 22, 1972—Midnight Show—Complete
C.C. Rider, Proud Mary, Never Been To Spain, You Gave Me A Mountain, Until It's Time For You To Go, Polk Salad Annie, Love Me, All Shook Up, Blue Hawaii (partial), Teddy Bear/Don't Be Cruel, Hound Dog, Big Hunk O' Love, Help Me Make It Through The Night, Bridge Over Troubled Water, Suspicious Minds, Introductions, American Trilogy, Can't Help Falling In Love

February 23, 1972—Dinner Show—Complete
C.C. Rider, Proud Mary, Never Been To Spain, You Gave Me A Mountain, Until It's Time For You To Go, Polk Salad Annie, Love Me, All Shook Up, Teddy Bear/Don't Be Cruel, Hound Dog, Big Hunk O' Love, Help Me Make It Through The Night, Suspicious Minds, Introductions, American Trilogy, Can't Help Falling In Love

February 23, 1972—Closing Night—Complete
C.C. Rider, Proud Mary, Never Been To Spain, You Gave Me A Mountain, Until It's Time For You To Go, Polk Salad Annie, Love Me, All Shook Up, Teddy Bear/Don't Be Cruel, Hound Dog, Big Hunk O' Love, Help Me Make It Through The Night, Bridge Over Troubled Water, Suspicious Minds, Introductions, Celebrity introductions Vernon Presley, Colonel Parker, Priscilla Presley, American Trilogy, Can't Help Falling In Love

Songs Sung by Elvis During Engagement
All Shook Up, All Shook Up/Teddy Bear/Don't Be Cruel, American Trilogy, Big Hunk O' Love, Blue Hawaii (partial), Bridge Over Troubled Water, Can't Help Falling In Love, Carry Me Back To Old Virginny (partial), C.C. Rider, Don't Be Cruel, Hawaiian Wedding Song (partial), Help Me Make It Through The Night, Hound Dog, I'll Remember You, I'm Leaving It Up To You, The Impossible Dream, It's Impossible, It's Over, Lawdy Miss Clawdy, Little Sister/Get Back, Love Me, Never Been To Spain, One Night, Polk Salad Annie, Proud Mary, Suspicious Minds, Teddy Bear/Don't Be Cruel, Until It's Time For You To Go, You Gave Me A Mountain, You Gave Me A Mountain (false start)

The following songs are rumored to have been sung at this engagement but are not verifiable.

Blue Suede Shoes/Whole Lotta Shakin' Goin' On, Chain Gang (partial), I Can't Stop Loving You, Return To Sender, That's All Right, The First Time Ever I Saw Your Face, Young & Beautiful, Heartbreak Hotel

VEGAS SEASON 7 1972, Hilton Hotel
Friday, August 4, 1972 through Monday, September 4, 1972—64 shows—Total attendance—140,800

Jumpsuits Worn at This Engagement—Dude Suits (various two-piece suits in both white and light-blue) with various lined capes in black, paisley, blue, white and silver, Blue Tiffany Suit with silver lined cape, Blue Apollo Suit with gold lined cape, White Diamond Suit with yellow lined cape, Black Diamond Suit with gold lined cape, White Square Lion Head Suit with red lined cape, Black Matador Suit with red lined cape, BlackWay Down Suit with red lined cape, Black and Red two-piece Spanish Amigo Suit, Blue Swirl Suit with silver lined cape. Note: Elvis also wore some sleeveless vest-type outfits on rare occasion.

Show Members—Musicians: Lead Guitar—James Burton, Rhythm Guitar—John Wilkinson, Acoustic Guitar and Backup Vocals—Charlie Hodge, Bass—Jerry Scheff, Piano—Glen D. Hardin, Drums—Ronnie Tutt, Backup Singers: Sweet Inspirations: Myrna Smith, Sylvia Shemwell, Estelle Brown, J.D. Sumner & The Stamps Quartet: J.D. Sumner, Donnie Sumner, Bill Baize, Ed Enoch, Richard Sterban, High Voice Singer -Kathy Westmoreland, Comedian—Jackie Kahane, Orchestra —Joe Guercio

August 4, 1972—Opening Show 10:15 p.m.—Complete
C.C. Rider, Big Hunk O' Love, Never Been To Spain, You've lost That Lovin' Feeling, Love Me Tender, Mystery Train/Tiger Man, What Now My Love, Love Me, Little Sister/Get Back, Blue Suede Shoes, One Night, You Don't Have To Say You Love Me, Hound Dog, My Way, Introductions, My Babe, Celebrity introductions Sammy Davis Jr., Paul Anka, Telly Savalas ,and Richard Harris, Can't Help Falling In Love

August 5, 1972—Dinner Show—Complete
C.C. Rider, Proud Mary, Never Been To Spain, You've Lost That Lovin' Feeling, Polk Salad Annie, What Now My Love, Fever, Carry Me Back To Old Virginny (partial), Love Me, Little Sister/Get Back, Big Hunk O' Love, The Wonder Of You, Hound Dog, Blue Suede Shoes, My Way, Suspicious Minds, Introductions, American Trilogy, Can't Help Falling In Love

August 5, 1972—Midnight Show—Complete
C.C. Rider, Proud Mary, Never Been To Spain, You've Lost That Lovin' Feeling, Polk Salad Annie, What Now My Love, Fever, Love Me, Little Sister (partial), Hound Dog (partial), Jailhouse Rock, Heartbreak Hotel, Big Hunk O' Love, For The Good Times, My Way, Suspicious Minds, Introductions, Johnny B. Goode, Introductions, American Trilogy, Can't Help Falling In Love

August 6, 1972—Dinner Show—Complete
C.C. Rider, Proud Mary, Never Been To Spain, You've Lost That Lovin' Feeling, Polk Salad Annie, Love Me, Blue Suede Shoes, Teddy Bear/Don't Be Cruel, Little Sister/Get Back, Hound Dog, Big Hunk O' Love, My Way, Suspicious Minds, Introductions, What Now My Love, American Trilogy, Can't Help Falling In Love

August 6, 1972—Midnight Show—Complete
C.C. Rider, Proud Mary, Until It's Time For You To Go, You Don't Have To Say You Love Me, You've Lost That Lovin' Feeling, Polk Salad Annie, What Now My Love, Fever, Blue Suede Shoes, Heartbreak Hotel, Little Sister/Get Back, Suspicious Minds, Introductions, My Way, Introductions, American Trilogy, Can't Help Falling In Love

August 7, 1972—Dinner Show—Complete
C.C. Rider, Big Hunk O' Love, Never Been To Spain, You've Lost That Lovin' Feeling, Love Me Tender, Mystery Train/Tiger Man, What Now My Love, Love Me, Little Sister/Get Back, Blue Suede Shoes, The Wonder Of You, One Night, You Don't Have To Say You Love Me, Hound Dog, My Way, Introductions, My Babe, American Trilogy, Can't Help Falling In Love

August 7, 1972—Midnight Show—Complete
C.C. Rider, Proud Mary, Until It's Time For You To Go, You Don't Have To Say You Love Me, You've Lost That Lovin' Feeling, Polk Salad Annie, What Now My Love, Fever, Love Me, Blue Suede Shoes, One Night, Little Sister/Get Back, Heartbreak Hotel, Hound Dog, Steamroller Blues (first live performance), Suspicious Minds, Introductions, My Way, Big Hunk O' Love, I Can't Stop Loving You, Can't Help Falling In Love

August 8, 1972—Dinner Show—Complete
C.C. Rider, Proud Mary, Until It's Time For You To Go, You Don't Have To Say You Love Me, You've Lost That Lovin' Feeling, Polk Salad Annie, What Now My Love, Fever, Love Me, Blue Suede Shoes, One Night, Little Sister/Get Back, Hound Dog, Love Me Tender, Suspicious Minds, Introductions, Big Hunk O' Love, Can't Help Falling In Love

August 8, 1972—Midnight Show—Complete
C.C. Rider, Proud Mary, Until It's Time For You To Go (reprise), You Don't Have To Say You Love Me, You've Lost That Lovin' Feeling, Polk Salad Annie, Dialogue, What Now My Love, Fever, Love Me, Blue Suede Shoes, One Night, Little Sister/Get Back, Heartbreak Hotel, Hound Dog, Love Me Tender, Suspicious Minds, Introductions, Celebrity introduction Bill Medley, My Way, Big Hunk O' Love, Can't Help Falling In Love

August 9, 1972—Dinner Show—Complete
C.C. Rider, Proud Mary, Never Been To Spain, You've Lost That Lovin' Feeling, Polk Salad Annie, Love Me, Blue Suede Shoes, Teddy Bear/Don't Be Cruel, Little Sister/Get Back, Hound Dog, Big Hunk O' Love, My Way, Suspicious Minds, Introductions, What Now My Love, American Trilogy, Can't Help Falling In Love

August 9, 1972—Midnight Show—Complete
C.C. Rider, Proud Mary, Until It's Time For You To Go, You Don't Have To Say You Love Me, You've Lost That Lovin' Feeling, Polk Salad Annie, What Now My Love, Fever, Love Me, Blue Suede Shoes, One Night, Little Sister/Get Back, Heartbreak Hotel, Hound Dog, Introductions, For The Good Times, Suspicious Minds, Introductions, My Way, Big Hunk O' Love, American Trilogy, Can't Help Falling In Love

August 10, 1972—Dinner Show—Complete
C.C. Rider, I Got A Woman/Amen, Proud Mary, Until It's Time For You To Go, You've Lost That Lovin' Feeling, Polk Salad Annie, What Now My Love, You Don't Have To Say You Love Me, Love Me, Blue Suede Shoes, One Night, Little Sister/Get Back, Heartbreak Hotel, All Shook Up, Teddy Bear/Don't Be Cruel, Hound Dog, For The Good Times, Suspicious Minds, Introductions, My Way, American Trilogy, Can't Help Falling In Love

August 10, 1972—Midnight Show—Complete
C.C. Rider, I Got A Woman/Amen, Proud Mary, Until It's Time For You To Go, You've Lost That Lovin' Feeling, Polk Salad Annie, What Now My Love, You Don't Have To Say You Love Me, Love Me, Blue Suede Shoes, Heartbreak Hotel, All Shook Up, Teddy Bear/Don't Be Cruel, Hound Dog, For The Good Times, Suspicious Minds, Introductions, My Way, American Trilogy, Can't Help Falling In Love

August 11, 1972—Dinner Show—Complete
C.C. Rider, I Got A Woman, Until It's Time For You To Go, You Don't Have To Say You Love Me, You've Lost That Lovin' Feeling, Polk Salad Annie, What Now My Love, Fever, Love Me, Blue Suede Shoes, One Night, All Shook Up, Teddy Bear/Don't Be Cruel, Heartbreak Hotel, Hound Dog, Love Me Tender, Suspicious Minds, Introductions, My Way, American Trilogy, Can't Help Falling In Love.

August 11, 1972—Midnight Show—Complete
C.C. Rider, I Got A Woman, Proud Mary, Until It's Time For You To Go, You've Lost That Lovin' Feeling, Polk Salad Annie, What Now My Love, Fever, Love Me, All Shook Up, Teddy Bear/Don't Be Cruel, Heartbreak Hotel, Blue Suede Shoes, Little Sister/Get Back, Hound Dog, It's Over, Suspicious Minds, Introductions, My Way, Big Hunk O' Love, American Trilogy, Can't Help Falling In Love

August 12, 1972—Dinner Show—Complete
C.C. Rider, Proud Mary, Until It's Time For You To Go, You Don't Have To Say You Love Me, You've Lost That Lovin' Feeling, Polk Salad Annie, What Now My Love, Fever, Love Me, Blue Suede Shoes, One Night, All Shook Up, Teddy Bear/Don't Be Cruel, Heartbreak Hotel, Hound Dog, Love Me Tender, Suspicious Minds, Introductions, Celebrity introduction Telly Savalas, My Way, American Trilogy, Can't Help Falling In Love

August 12, 1972—Midnight Show—Complete
C.C. Rider, I Got A Woman/Amen, Proud Mary, Never Been To Spain, Until It's Time For You To Go, You've Lost That Lovin' Feeling, Polk Salad Annie, What Now My Love, Fever, Love Me, Blue Suede Shoes, One Night, All Shook Up, Teddy Bear/Don't Be Cruel, Heartbreak Hotel, Hound Dog, For The Good Times, Suspicious Minds, Introductions, My Way, American Trilogy, Big Hunk O' Love, Tiger Man (partial), Can't Help Falling In Love

August 13, 1972—Dinner Show—Complete
C. C. Rider, I Got A Woman/Amen, Proud Mary, Until It's Time For You To Go, You've Lost That Lovin' Feeling, Polk Salad Annie, Dialogue, What Now My Love (false start), Fever, Love Me, Blue Suede Shoes, One Night (partial), All Shook Up, Heartbreak Hotel, Teddy Bear/Don't Be Cruel, Hound Dog, Ave Maria (partial), For The Good Times, Suspicious Minds, Introductions, My Way, American Trilogy, Big Hunk O' Love, Can't Help Falling In Love

August 13, 1972—Midnight Show—Complete
C.C. Rider, I Got A Woman/Amen, Proud Mary, Until It's Time For You To Go, You've Lost That Lovin' Feeling, Polk Salad Annie, What Now My Love, Fever, Love Me, Blue Suede Shoes, One Night, All Shook Up, Teddy Bear/Don't Be Cruel, Ave Maria, Hound Dog, For The Good Times, Suspicious Minds, Introductions, My Way, American Trilogy, Big Hunk O' Love, Can't Help Falling In Love

August 14, 1972—Not Available

August 15, 1972—Dinner Show—Complete
C.C. Rider, Johnny B. Goode, Proud Mary, Until It's Time For You To Go, You Don't Have To Say You Love Me, You've Lost That Lovin' Feeling, Polk Salad Annie, What Now My Love, Fever, Love Me, Blue Suede Shoes, Love Me Tender, Little Sister/Get Back, Hound Dog, I'll Remember You, Suspicious Minds, Introductions, My Way, Big Hunk O' Love, American Trilogy, Tiger Man, Can't Help Falling In Love

August 15, 1972—Midnight Show—Complete
C. C. Rider, Johnny B. Goode, Until It's Time For You To Go, You Don't Have To Say You Love Me, Polk Salad Annie, Dialogue, What Now My Love, Fever, Love Me, Blue Suede Shoes, Heartbreak Hotel, All Shook Up, Love Me Tender, Teddy Bear/Don't Be Cruel, Little Sister/Get Back, Hound Dog, I'll Remember You, Walk That Lonesome Road (J. D. Sumner & The Stamps Quartet), Suspicious Minds, Introductions, For The Good Times, Big Hunk O' Love, You Gave Me A Mountain, Can't Help Falling In Love

August 16, 1972—Dinner Show—Complete
C.C. Rider, Johnny B. Goode, Proud Mary, Until It's Time For You To Go, You've Lost That Lovin' Feeling, Polk Salad Annie, What Now My Love, Love Me, Blue Suede Shoes, Heartbreak Hotel, All Shook Up, Little Sister/Get Back, Love Me Tender, Hound Dog, I'll Remember You, Suspicious Minds (partial), Introductions, My Way, Big Hunk O' Love, American Trilogy, Can't Help Falling In Love

August 16, 1972—Midnight Show—Complete
C.C. Rider, Johnny B. Goode, Proud Mary, Until It's Time For You To Go, You Don't Have To Say You Love Me, You've Lost That Lovin' Feeling, Polk Salad Annie, What Now My Love, Fever, Love Me, Blue Suede Shoes, All Shook Up, Love Me Tender, Little Sister/Get Back, Hound Dog, I'll Remember You, Suspicious Minds, Introductions, My Way, Big Hunk O' Love, American Trilogy, Can't Help Falling In Love

August 17, 1972—Dinner Show—Complete
C.C. Rider, Johnny B. Goode, Until It's Time For You To Go, You Don't Have To Say You Love Me, You've Lost That Lovin' Feeling, Polk Salad Annie, What Now My Love, Fever, Love Me, Blue Suede Shoes, One Night, All Shook Up, Heartbreak Hotel, Little Sister/Get Back, Hound Dog, Suspicious Minds, Introductions, My Way, Big Hunk O' Love, Can't Help Falling In Love

August 17, 1972—Midnight Show—Complete
C.C. Rider, Johnny B. Goode, Proud Mary, Until It's Time For You To Go, You Don't Have To Say You Love Me, You've Lost That Lovin' Feeling, Polk Salad Annie, What Now My Love, Fever, Love Me, Blue Suede Shoes, Heartbreak Hotel, All Shook Up, Hound Dog, I'll Remember You, Little Sister/Get Back, Love Me Tender, Suspicious Minds, Introductions, For The Good Times, Big Hunk O' Love, American Trilogy, Tiger Man, Can't Help Falling In Love.

August 18, 1972—Dinner Show—Complete
C.C. Rider, Johnny B. Goode, Until It's Time For You To Go, You Don't Have To Say You Love Me, You've Lost That Lovin' Feeling, Polk Salad Annie, Dialogue. What Now My Love, Fever, Love Me, Blue Suede Shoes, One Night, All Shook Up, Little Sister/Get Back, Heartbreak Hotel, Hound Dog, Love Me Tender, Burning Love (partial), Suspicious Minds, Introductions, Ave Maria (partial), My Way, I'll Remember You, Big Hunk O' Love, How Great Thou Art, Can't Help Falling In Love

August 18, 1972—Midnight Show—Complete
C.C. Rider, Johnny B. Goode, Never Been To Spain, Until It's Time For You To Go, You Don't Have To Say You Love Me, You Gave Me A Mountain, You've Lost That Lovin' Feeling, Polk Salad Annie, What Now My Love, Fever, Love Me, Blue Suede Shoes, Heartbreak Hotel, All Shook Up, Hound Dog, I'll Remember You, Suspicious Minds, Introductions, My Way, Big Hunk O' Love, American Trilogy, Can't Help Falling In Love

August 19, 1972—Dinner Show—Complete
C.C. Rider, Johnny B. Goode, Never Been To Spain, Until It's Time For You To Go, You Don't Have To Say You Love Me, You Gave Me A Mountain, You've Lost That Lovin' Feeling, Polk Salad Annie, What Now My Love, Fever, Love Me, Blue Suede Shoes, Heartbreak Hotel, All Shook Up, Hound Dog, I'll Remember You, Suspicious Minds, Introductions, My Way, Big Hunk O' Love, American Trilogy, Can't Help Falling In Love

August 19, 1972—Midnight Show—Complete
C.C. Rider, Johnny B. Goode, Never Been To Spain, Until It's Time For You To Go, You Don't Have To Say You Love Me, You Gave Me A Mountain, You've Lost That Lovin' Feeling, Polk Salad Annie, What Now My Love, Fever, Love Me, Blue Suede Shoes, Heartbreak Hotel, All Shook Up, Hound Dog, I'll Remember You, Suspicious Minds, Introductions, My Way, Big Hunk O' Love, American Trilogy, Can't Help Falling In Love

August 20, 1972—Dinner Show—Complete
C.C. Rider, Johnny B. Goode, Until It's Time For You To Go, You Don't Have To Say You Love Me, You've Lost That Lovin' Feeling, Polk Salad Annie, What Now My Love, Fever, Love Me, Blue Suede Shoes, One Night, All Shook Up, Hound Dog, I'll Remember You, Suspicious Minds, Introductions, My Way, Big Hunk O' Love, American Trilogy, Can't Help Falling In Love

August 20, 1972—Midnight Show—Complete
C.C. Rider, Johnny B. Goode, Proud Mary, Until It's Time For You To Go, You Don't Have To Say You Love Me, You've Lost That Lovin' Feeling, Polk Salad Annie, What Now My Love, Fever, Love Me, Blue Suede Shoes, Heartbreak Hotel, All Shook Up, Hound Dog, I'll Remember You, Little Sister/Get Back, Love Me Tender, Suspicious Minds, Introductions, For The Good Times, Big Hunk O' Love, American Trilogy, Cant' Help Falling In Love

August 21, 1972—Dinner Show—Complete
CC Rider, Proud Mary, Never Been To Spain, You Gave Me A Mountain, Until It's Time For You To Go, Polk Salad Annie, Love Me, All Shook Up, Teddy Bear/Don't Be Cruel, Hound Dog, Big Hunk O' Love, Help Me Make It Through The Night, Bridge Over Troubled Water, Suspicious Minds, Introductions, American Trilogy, Can't Help Falling In

August 21, 1972—Midnight Show—Complete
C.C. Rider (partial), Johnny B. Goode, Proud Mary, Until It's Time For You To Go, You Don't Have To Say You Love Me, You've Lost That Lovin' Feeling, Polk Salad Annie, What Now My Love, Fever, Love Me, Blue Suede Shoes, Heartbreak Hotel, All Shook Up, Little Sister/Get Back, Hound Dog, I'll Remember You, Suspicious Minds, Introductions, My Way, Big Hunk O' Love, Love Me Tender, Mystery Train/Tiger Man, Can't Help Falling In Love

August 22, 1972—Dinner Show—Not Available

August 22, 1972—Midnight Show—Complete
C.C. Rider, Johnny B. Goode, Proud Mary, Until It's Time For You To Go, You Don't Have To Say You Love Me, You've Lost That Lovin' Feeling, Polk Salad Annie, What Now My Love, Fever, Love Me, Heartbreak Hotel (partial), All Shook Up, Little Sister/Get Back, Love Me Tender, Hound Dog, I'll Remember You, Suspicious Minds, Introductions, Celebrity introductions: Tom Jones, Big Hunk O' Love, Mystery Train/Tiger Man, Can't Help Falling In Love

August 23, 1972—Dinner Show—Not Available

August 23, 1972—Midnight Show—Complete
C.C. Rider, Johnny B. Goode, Proud Mary, Until It's Time For You To Go, You Don't Have To Say You Love Me, You Gave Me A Mountain, You've Lost The Lovin' Feeling, Polk Salad Annie, Dialogue, What Now My Love, Fever, Love Me, Blue Suede Shoes, Heartbreak Hotel, All Shook Up, Little Sister/Get Back, Love Me Tender, Hound Dog, I'll Remember You, Suspicious Minds, Introductions, My Way, Big Hunk O' Love, For The Good Times, Can't Help Falling In Love

August 24, 1972—Dinner Show- Complete
C.C. Rider, Johnny B. Goode, Proud Mary, Until It's Time For You To Go, You Don't Have To Say You Love Me, You Gave Me A Mountain, You've Lost That Lovin' Feeling, Polk Salad Annie, What Now My Love, Fever, Love Me, Blue Suede

Shoes, Heartbreak Hotel, All Shook Up, Little Sister/Get Back, Teddy Bear/Don't Be Cruel, Hound Dog, Love Me Tender, Suspicious Minds, Introductions, My Way, Big Hunk O' Love, American Trilogy, Can't Help Falling In Love

August 24, 1972—Midnight Show—Complete
C.C. Rider, Johnny B. Goode, Proud Mary, Until It's Time For You To Go, You Don't Have To Say You Love Me, You Gave Me A Mountain, You've Lost That Lovin' Feeling, Polk Salad Annie, What Now My Love, Fever, Love Me, Blue Suede Shoes, Heartbreak Hotel, All Shook Up, Little Sister/Get Back, Love Me Tender, Walk That Lonesome Road (J.D. Sumner & The Stamps Quartet), American Trilogy, Can't Help Falling In Love

August 25, 1972—Dinner Show—Complete
C.C. Rider, Johnny B. Goode, Proud Mary, Until It's Time For You To Go, You Don't Have To Say You Love Me, You Gave Me A Mountain, You've Lost That Lovin' Feeling, Polk Salad Annie, What Now My Love, Fever, Love Me, Blue Suede Shoes, Heartbreak Hotel, All Shook Up, Little Sister/Get Back, Love Me Tender, Walk That Lonesome Road (J. D. Sumner & The Stamps Quartet), Suspicious Minds, Introductions, My Way, Big Hunk O' Love, American Trilogy, Can't Help Falling in Love

August 25, 1972—Midnight Show—Complete
C.C. Rider, Johnny B. Goode, Until It's Time For You To Go, You Don't Have To Say You Love Me, You Gave Me A Mountain, What Now My Love, Fever, Little Sister/Get Back, Hound Dog, I'll Remember You, Walk That Lonesome Road (J. D. Sumner & The Stamps Quartet), For The Good Times, Big Hunk O' Love, I Can't Stop Loving You, Mystery Train/Tiger Man, Can't Help Falling In Love

August 26, 1972—Dinner Show—Complete
C.C. Rider, Johnny B. Goode, Until It's Time For You To Go, You Don't Have To Say You Love Me, Love Me Tender, You've Lost That Lovin' Feeling, Polk Salad Annie, What Now My Love, Fever, Love Me, Blue Suede Shoes, Heartbreak Hotel, All Shook Up, Little Sister/Get Back, Hound Dog, I'll Remember You, Walk That Lonesome Road (J. D. Sumner & The Stamps Quartet), Suspicious Minds, Introductions, My Way, Big Hunk O' Love, You Gave Me A Mountain, Mystery Train/Tiger Man, Can't Help Falling In Love

August 26, 1972—Midnight Show—Complete
C.C. Rider, Johnny B. Goode, Until It's Time For You To Go, You Don't Have To Say You Love Me, You've Lost That Lovin' Feeling, Polk Salad Annie, What Now My Love, Fever, Love Me, Blue Suede Shoes, Heartbreak Hotel, All Shook Up, Little Sister/Get Back, Love Me Tender, Hound Dog, I'll Remember You, Walk That Lonesome Road (J. D. Sumner & The Stamps Quartet), Suspicious Minds, Introductions, For The Good Times, Big Hunk O' Love, I Can't Stop Loving You, Mystery Train/Tiger Man, Can't Help Falling In Love

August 27, 1972—Dinner Show—Complete
C.C. Rider, Johnny B. Goode, Until It's Time For You To Go, You Don't Have To Say You Love Me, Love Me Tender, You've Lost That Lovin' Feeling, Polk Salad Annie, What Now My Love, Fever, Love Me, Heartbreak Hotel, All Shook Up, Little Sister/Get Back, Hound Dog, I'll Remember You, Walk That Lonesome Road (J. D. Sumner & The Stamps Quartet), Suspicious Minds, Introductions, My Way, Big Hunk O' Love, You Gave Me A Mountain, Mystery Train/Tiger Man, Can't Help Falling In Love

August 27, 1972—Midnight Show—Complete
C.C. Rider, Johnny B. Goode, Until It's Time For You To Go, You Don't Have To Say You Love Me, You've Lost That Lovin' Feeling, Polk Salad Annie, What Now My Love, Fever, Love Me, Blue Suede Shoes, Heartbreak Hotel, Little Sister/Get Back, Love Me Tender, Hound Dog, I'll Remember You, Walk That Lonesome Road (J. D. Sumner & The Stamps Quartet), Suspicious Minds, Introductions, For The Good Times, Big Hunk O' Love, I Can't Stop Loving You, Mystery Train/Tiger Man, Can't Help Falling In Love

August 28, 1972—Dinner Show—Not Available

August 28, 1972—Midnight Show—Complete
C.C. Rider, Johnny B. Goode, Until It's Time For You To Go, You Don't Have To Say You Love Me, You've Lost That' Lovin' Feeling, Polk Salad Annie, Dialogue, What Now My Love, Fever, Love Me, Blue Suede Shoes, Heartbreak Hotel, All Shook Up, Love Me Tender, Hound Dog (false start), I'll Remember You, Walk That Lonesome Road (J. D. Sumner & The Stamps Quartet), Suspicious Minds, Introductions, My Way, Big Hunk O' Love, You Gave Me A Mountain, Mystery Train/Tiger Man, Can't Help Falling In Love

August 29–August 31, 1972—Not Available

September 1, 1972—Dinner Show—Complete
C.C. Rider, Johnny B. Goode, Until It's Time For You To Go, You Don't Have To Say You Love Me, You've Lost That Lovin' Feeling, Polk Salad Annie, Dialogue, What Now My Love (2 false starts), Fever, Dialogue, Love Me, Blue Suede Shoes, Heartbreak Hotel, All Shook Up, Love Me Tender, Hound Dog (false start), I'll Remember You, Walk That Lonesome Road (J.D. Sumner & The Stamps Quartet), Suspicious Minds, Introductions, For The Good Times, Big Hunk O' Love, You Gave Me A Mountain, Mystery Train/Tiger Man, Can't Help Falling In Love

September, 1, 1972—Midnight Show—Complete
C.C. Rider, Johnny B. Goode, Until It's Time For You To Go, You Don't Have To Say You Love Me, You've Lost That Lovin' Feeling, Polk Salad Annie, Introductions, What Now My Love, Fever, Guadalajara (partial), Love Me, Blue Suede Shoes, Heartbreak Hotel, Love Me Tender, Monologue Life Story, Hound Dog, I'll Remember You, Walk That Lonesome Road (J.D. Sumner &The Stamps Quartet), Suspicious Minds, Introductions, My Way, Big Hunk O' Love, You Gave Me A Mountain, Mystery Train/Tiger Man, Can't Help Falling In Love

September 2, 1972—Dinner Show—Complete
C.C. Rider, Johnny B. Goode, Until It's Time For You To Go, You Don't Have To Say You Love Me, Polk Salad Annie, What Now My Love, Fever, Love Me, Blue Suede Shoes, Heartbreak Hotel, All Shook Up, Love Me Tender, Hound Dog, I'll Remember You, Walk That Lonesome Road (J.D. Sumner & The Stamps Quartet), Suspicious Minds, Introductions, For The Good Times, Big Hunk O' Love, You Gave Me A Mountain, Mystery Train/Tiger Man, Can't Help Falling In Love

September 2, 1972—Midnight Show—Complete
C.C. Rider, Johnny B. Goode, Until It's Time For You To Go, You Don't Have To Say You Love Me, Polk Salad Annie, Dialogue, What Now My Love, Fever, Love Me, Blue Suede Shoes, Heartbreak Hotel, Love Me Tender, Hound Dog, I'll Remember You, Suspicious Minds, Introductions, Celebrity introduction David Brinkley, My Way, Mystery Train/Tiger Man, Can't Help Falling in Love

September 3, 1972—3 a.m. Show—Complete
C.C. Rider, Johnny B. Goode, Until It's Time For You To Go, You Don't Have To Say You Love Me, Polk Salad Annie, What Now My Love, Fever, Love Me, Blue Suede Shoes, Heartbreak Hotel, All Shook Up, Love Me Tender, Walk That Lonesome Road (J. D. Sumner & The Stamps Quartet), Suspicious Minds, Introductions, Celebrity introductions William Campbell, Shirley MacLaine,

Marty Allen, Tom Jones, Gunther Williams, Pat Hingle, The 5th Dimension, My Way, Big Hunk O' Love, You Gave Me A Mountain, Mystery Train/Tiger Man, Can't Help Falling In Love

September 3, 1972—Dinner Show—Complete
C.C. Rider, Johnny B. Goode, Until It's Time For You To Go, You Don't Have To Say You Love Me, Polk Salad Annie, What Now My Love, Fever, Love Me Tender, Blue Suede Shoes, All Shook Up, Heartbreak Hotel, Love Me Tender, Teddy Bear, Little Sister/Get Back, Hound Dog, I'll Remember You, Walk That Lonesome Road (J. D. Sumner & The Stamps Quartet), Suspicious Minds, Introductions, Elvis introduces the British fan club, For The Good Times, Big Hunk O' Love, You Gave Me A Mountain, Can't Help Falling In Love

September 3, 1972—Midnight Show—Complete
C.C. Rider, Johnny B. Goode, Until It's Time For You To Go, You Don't Have To Say You Love Me, Polk Salad Annie, What Now My Love, Fever, Love Me, Blue Suede Shoes, Heartbreak Hotel, All Shook Up, Love Me Tender, Hound Dog, I'll Remember You, Walk That Lonesome Road (J. D. Sumner & The Stamps Quartet), Suspicious Minds, Introductions, Celebrity introduction Shirley Bassey, My Way, Big Hunk O' Love, You Gave Me A Mountain, Mystery Train/Tiger Man, Can't Help Falling In Love

September 4, 1972—Dinner Show—Complete
C.C. Rider, Johnny B. Goode, Until It's Time For You To Go, You Don't Have To Say You Love Me, Polk Salad Annie, Dialogue, What Now My Love, Fever, Love Me, Blue Suede Shoes, Heartbreak Hotel, All Shook Up, Love Me Tender, Teddy Bear/Don't Be Cruel, Little Sister/Get Back, Hound Dog, I'll Remember You, Walk That Lonesome Road (J. D. Sumner & The Stamps Quartet), Suspicious Minds, Introductions, Elvis introduces the British fan club, For The Good Times, Big Hunk O' Love, You Gave Me A Mountain, Can't Help Falling In Love

September 4, 1972—Closing Show—Complete
C.C. Rider, Johnny B. Goode, Until It's Time For You To Go, You Don't Have To Say You Love Me, Polk Salad Annie, What Now My Love, Fever, Love Me, Blue Suede Shoes, Heartbreak Hotel, All Shook Up, Hound Dog, I'll Remember You, Walk That Lonesome Road (J. D. Sumner & The Stamps Quartet), Suspicious Minds, Introductions, Celebrity introductions Bobby Darin and Colonel Parker, My Way, Big Hunk O' Love, You Gave Me A Mountain, Mystery Train/Tiger Man, Can't Help Falling In Love

Songs Sung by Elvis During Engagement
All Shook Up, American Trilogy, Ave Maria, Ave Maria (partial), Big Hunk O' Love, Blue Suede Shoes, Bridge Over Troubled Water, Burning Love (partial), Can't Help Falling In Love, Carry Me Back To Old Virginny (partial), C.C. Rider, C.C. Rider (partial), Fever, For The Good Times, Guadalajara (partial), Heartbreak Hotel, Heartbreak Hotel (partial), Help Me Make It Through The Night, Hound Dog, Hound Dog (false start), Hound Dog (partial), How Great Thou Art, I Can't Stop Loving You, I Got A Woman, I Got A Woman/Amen, I'll Remember You, It's Over, Jailhouse Rock, Johnny B. Goode, Little Sister (partial), Little Sister/Get Back, Love Me, Love Me Tender, My Babe, Mystery Train/Tiger Man, My Way, Never Been To Spain, One Night, One Night (partial), Polk Salad Annie, Proud Mary, Steamroller Blues, Suspicious Minds, Suspicious Minds (partial), Teddy Bear/ Don't Be Cruel, Tiger Man, Tiger Man (partial), Until It's Time For You To Go, Until It's Time For You To Go (reprise), Walk That Lonesome Road (J. D. Sumner & The Stamps Quartet), What Now My Love, What Now My Love (false start), What Now My Love (2 false starts), The Wonder Of You, You Don't Have To Say You Love Me, You Gave Me A Mountain, You've Lost That Lovin' Feeling

The following songs are rumored to have been sung at this engagement but are not verifiable.

Little Sister/Hound Dog, Little Sister, G.I. Blues (partial), Release Me, Trouble

VEGAS SEASON 8 1973, Hilton Hotel

Friday, January 26, 1973 through Tuesday, February 23, 1973—51 shows—Elvis canceled six additional shows due to illness: January 31 dinner and midnight shows, February 1 midnight show, February 13 midnight show, February 14 midnight show, February 15 midnight show—Total attendance—112,200

Jumpsuits Worn at This Engagement—Aloha From Hawaii Suit with blue lined cape, Black Spanish Flower Suit with green lined cape, Elvis Today Suit with yellow lined cape, Orange Target Suit with orange lined cape, White Jewel Of Nile Suit with blue lined cape, American Eagle Suit with blue lined cape, Stone Eagle Suit with cape, Orange Jewel Suit with orange lined cape, Orange Cosmo Suit with orange lined cape, Stud Suit with blue lined cape. Thunderbird Suit with blue lined cape.

Show Members—Musicians: Lead Guitar—James Burton, Rhythm Guitar—John Wilkinson, Acoustic Guitar and Backup Vocals—Charlie Hodge, Bass—Jerry Scheff, Piano—Glen D. Hardin, Drums—Ronnie Tutt, Backup Singers: Sweet Inspirations: Myrna Smith, Sylvia Shemwell, Estelle Brown, J. D. Sumner & The Stamps Quartet: J. D. Sumner, Donnie Sumner, Bill Baize, Ed Enoch, Richard Sterban, High Voice Singer -Kathy Westmoreland, Comedian—Jackie Kahane, Orchestra—Joe Guercio

January 26, 1973—Opening Night—10:15 P.M.—Complete
C.C. Rider, Burning Love, Something, Introductions, You Gave Me A Mountain, Steamroller Blues, Sweet Caroline, My Way, Love Me, Blue Suede Shoes, Johnny B. Goode, Lawdy Miss Clawdy, Fever, Hound Dog, I Can't Stop Loving You, I'm So Lonesome I Could Cry, What Now My Love, Suspicious Minds, Introductions, Celebrity introductions Redd Fox, I'll Remember You, Long Tall Sally/Whole Lotta Shakin' Goin' On, American Trilogy, Big Hunk O' Love, Walk That Lonesome Road (J.D. Sumner & The Stamps Quartet), Can't Help Falling In Love

January 27, 1973—Dinner Show—Complete
C.C. Rider, Long Tall Sally/Whole Lotta Shakin' Goin' On, Until It's Time For You To Go, You Don't Have To Say You Love Me, Steamroller Blues, You Gave Me A Mountain, Fever, Love Me, Blue Suede Shoes, Love Me Tender, Johnny B. Goode, Hound Dog, What Now My Love, Suspicious Minds, Introductions, I'll Remember You, I Can't Stop Loving You, American Trilogy, Burning Love, Can't Help Falling In Love

January 27, 1973—Midnight Show—Complete
C.C. Rider, I Got A Woman/Amen, Love Me, Let Me Be There, You've Lost That Lovin' Feeling, Sweet Caroline, Love Me Tender, Long Tall Sally/Whole Lotta Shakin' Goin' On/ Flip Flop And Fly/Your Mama Don't Dance/Jailhouse Rock/Hound Dog, Fever, Polk Salad Annie, Killing Me Softly (Voice), Spanish Eyes duet with Sherrill Nielsen, Suspicious Minds, Introductions, Celebrity introductions Lorne Greene, George Burns, Jack Lord, Mike Connors, I Can't Stop Loving You, American Trilogy, Big Hunk O' Love, Can't Help Falling In Love

January 28, 1973—Dinner Show—Complete
C.C. Rider, I Got A Woman/Amen, Until It's Time For You To Go, You Don't Have To Say You Love Me, Steamroller Blues, You Gave Me A Mountain, Fever, Love Me, All Shook Up, Blue Suede Shoes, Love Me Tender, Johnny B. Goode, Hound Dog, What Now My Love, Suspicious Minds, Introductions, I'll Remember You, I Can't Stop Loving You, American Trilogy, Burning Love, Can't Help Falling In Love

January 28, 1973—Midnight Show—Complete
C.C. Rider, I Got A Woman, Until It's Time For You To Go, You Don't Have To Say You Love Me, Steamroller Blues, You Gave Me A Mountain, Fever, Love Me, All Shook Up, Love Me Tender, Johnny B. Goode, Hound Dog, What Now My Love, Suspicious Minds, Introductions, I'll Remember You, I Can't Stop Loving You, American Trilogy, Can't Help Falling In Love

January 29, 1973—Dinner Show—Complete
C.C. Rider, I Got A Woman/Amen, Until It's Time For You To Go, Sweet Caroline, Steamroller Blues, You Gave Me A Mountain, Fever, Love Me, Blue Suede Shoes, Love Me Tender, Johnny B. Goode, Hound Dog, What Now My Love, Suspicious Minds, Introductions, I Can't Stop Loving You, American Trilogy, Can't Help Falling In Love

January 29, 1973—Midnight Show—Complete
C.C. Rider, I Got A Woman/Amen, Until It's Time For You To Go, You Don't Have To Say You Love Me, Steamroller Blues, You Gave Me A Mountain, Fever, Love Me, Blue Suede Shoes, Love Me Tender, Johnny B. Goode, Hound Dog, What Now My Love, Suspicious Minds, Introductions, I'll Remember You, I Can't Stop Loving You, American Trilogy, Burning Love, Can't Help Falling In Love

January 30, 1973—Dinner Show—Complete
C.C. Rider, I Got A Woman/Amen, Until It's Time For You To Go, You Don't Have To Say You Love Me, Steamroller Blues, You Gave Me A Mountain, Fever, Love Me, All Shook Up, Blue Suede Shoes, Love Me Tender, Johnny B. Goode, Hound Dog, What Now My Love, Suspicious Minds, Introductions, I'll Remember You, I Can't Stop Loving You, American Trilogy, Burning Love, Can't Help Falling In Love

January 30, 1973—Midnight Show—Complete
C.C. Rider, Long Tall Sally/Whole Lotta Shakin' Goin' On, Until It's Time For You To Go, You Don't Have To Say You Love Me, Steamroller Blues, You Gave Me A Mountain, Fever, Love Me, Blue Suede Shoes, Love Me Tender, Johnny B. Goode, Hound Dog, What Now My Love, Suspicious Minds, Introductions, I'll Remember You, I Can't Stop Loving You, American Trilogy, Burning Love, Can't Help Falling In Love

January 31, 1973—Dinner Show—Cancelled due to illness

January 31, 1973—Midnight Show—Cancelled due to illness

February 1, 1973—Dinner Show—Not Available

February 1, 1973—Midnight Show—Cancelled due to illness

February 2, 1973—Dinner Show—Not Available

February 2, 1973—Midnight Show—Complete
C.C. Rider, I Got A Woman/Amen, Until It's Time For You To Go, Sweet Caroline, Steamroller Blues, You Gave Me A Mountain, Fever, Love Me, Blue Suede Shoes, Love Me Tender, Johnny B. Goode, Hound Dog, What Now My Love, Suspicious Minds, Introductions, I Can't Stop Loving You, American Trilogy, Can't Help Falling in Love

February 3, 1973—Dinner Show—Complete
C.C. Rider, I Got A Woman/Amen, Until It's Time For You To Go, You Don't Have To Say You Love Me, Steamroller Blues, You Gave Me A Mountain, Fever, Love Me, Blue Suede Shoes, Love Me Tender, Johnny B. Goode, Hound Dog, What Now My Love, Suspicious Minds, Introductions, I'll Remember You, I Can't Stop Loving You, American Trilogy, Can't Help Falling In Love

February 3, 1973—Midnight Show—Complete
C.C. Rider, I Got A Woman, Until It's Time For You To Go, You Don't Have To Say You Love Me, Steamroller Blues, You Gave Me A Mountain, Fever, Love Me, Blue Suede Shoes, Love Me Tender, Johnny B. Goode, Hound Dog, What Now My Love, Suspicious Minds, Introductions, I Can't Stop Loving You, American Trilogy, Can't Help Falling In Love

February 4, 1973—Not Available

February 5, 1973—Dinner Show—Complete
C.C. Rider, I Got A Woman/Amen, Until It's Time For You To Go, You Don't Have To Say You Love Me, Steamroller Blues, You Gave Me A Mountain, Fever, Love Me, Blue Suede Shoes, Love Me Tender, Johnny B. Goode, Hound Dog, What Now My Love, Suspicious Minds, Introductions, I'll Remember You, I Can't Stop Loving You, American Trilogy, Can't Help Falling In Love

February 5, 1973—Midnight Show—Complete
C.C. Rider, I Got A Woman/Amen, Until It's Time For You To Go, You Don't Have To Say You Love Me, Steamroller Blues, You Gave Me A Mountain, Fever, Love Me, Blue Suede Shoes, Love Me Tender, Johnny B. Goode, Hound Dog, What Now My Love (false start), How Great Thou Art, Suspicious Minds, Introductions, I Can't Stop Loving You, American Trilogy, Can't Help Falling In Love

February 6, 1973—Dinner Show—Not Available

February 6, 1973—Midnight Show—May Have Been Canceled

February 7, 1973—Dinner Show—Not Available

February 7, 1973—Midnight Show—May Have Been Canceled

February 8, 1973—Not Available

February 9, 1973—Dinner Show
C.C. Rider, I Got A Woman/Amen, Love Me Tender, You Don't Have To Say You Love Me, Steamroller Blues, You Gave Me A Mountain, Fever, Love Me, Blue Suede Shoes, Heartbreak Hotel, Johnny B. Goode, Hound Dog, What Now My Love, Suspicious Minds, Introductions, I'll Remember You (reprise), I Can't Stop Loving You, American Trilogy, Can't Help Falling In Love.

February 9. 1973—Midnight Show—Not Available

February 10, 1973—Dinner Show—Complete
C.C. Rider, I Got A Woman/Amen, Love Me Tender, You Don't Have To Say You Love Me, Steamroller Blues, You Gave Me A Mountain, Fever, Love Me, Blue Suede Shoes, Heartbreak Hotel, Johnny B. Goode, Hound Dog, What Now My Love, Suspicious Minds, Karate Dialogue, Introductions, Celebrity Introduction—Jack Lord, I'll Remember You, I Can't Stop Loving You, American Trilogy, Can't Help Falling In Love

February 10, 1973—Midnight Show—Complete
C.C. Rider, I Got A Woman/Amen, Love Me Tender, You Don't Have To Say You Love Me, Steamroller Blues, You Gave Me A Mountain, Fever, Love Me, Blue Suede Shoes, Heartbreak Hotel,

Johnny B. Goode, Hound Dog, What Now My Love, Suspicious Minds, Introductions, Celebrity introductions Jack Lord, Jerry Quarry, I Can't Stop Loving You, American Trilogy, Can't Help Falling In Love

February 11, 1973—Dinner Show—Complete
C.C. Rider, I Got A Woman/Amen, Love Me Tender, You Don't Have To Say You Love Me, Steamroller Blues, You Gave Me A Mountain, Fever, Love Me, Blue Suede Shoes, Heartbreak Hotel, Johnny B. Goode, Hound Dog, How Great Thou Art, What Now My Love, Suspicious Minds, Introductions, I Can't Stop Loving You, American Trilogy, Can't Help Falling In Love

February 11, 1973—Midnight Show—Complete
C.C. Rider, I Got A Woman/Amen, Love Me Tender, You Don't Have To Say You Love Me, Steamroller Blues, You Gave Me A Mountain, Fever, Love Me, Blue Suede Shoes, Johnny B. Goode, Hound Dog, How Great Thou Art, Suspicious Minds, Introductions, Celebrity introduction Jack Lord, I Can't Stop Loving You, American Trilogy, Can't Help Falling In Love

February 12, 1973—Dinner Show—Complete
C.C. Rider, I Got A Woman/Amen, Love Me Tender, You Don't Have To Say You Love Me, Steamroller Blues, You Gave Me A Mountain, Fever, Love Me, Blue Suede Shoes, Heartbreak Hotel, Johnny B. Goode, Hound Dog, What Now My Love, Suspicious Minds, Introductions, I'll Remember You, I Can't Stop Loving You, Can't Help Falling In Love

February 12, 1973—Midnight Show—Complete
C.C. Rider, I Got A Woman/Amen, Love Me Tender, You Don't Have To Say You Love Me, Steamroller Blues, You Gave Me A Mountain, Fever, Love Me, Blue Suede Shoes, Heartbreak Hotel, Johnny B. Goode, Hound Dog, What Now My Love, Suspicious Minds, Introductions, I'll Remember You, I Can't Stop Loving You, American Trilogy, Can't Help Falling In Love

February 13, 1973—Dinner Show—
Not Available

February 13, 1973—Midnight Show Canceled Due to Illness

February 14, 1973—Dinner Show—Complete
C.C. Rider, I Got A Woman/Amen, Love Me Tender, You Don't Have To Say You Love Me, Steamroller Blues, You Gave Me A Mountain, Fever, Love Me, Blue Suede Shoes, Heartbreak Hotel, Johnny B. Goode, Hound Dog, What Now My Love, Suspicious Minds, Introductions, I Can't Stop Loving You, American Trilogy, Can't Help Falling In Love

February 14, 1973—Midnight Show—Canceled due to illness

February 15, 1973—Dinner Show—Complete
C.C. Rider, I Got A Woman/Amen, Love Me Tender, You Don't Have To Say You Love Me, Steamroller Blues, You Gave Me A Mountain, Fever, *Elvis who is suffering from the flu walks off stage in the middle of Fever and does not return for 20 minutes, J. D. Sumner & The Stamps Quartet are forced into action and sing the following songs: Walk That Lonesome Road, Sweet Sweet Spirit, When It's My Time (solo by Bill Baize), How Great Thou Art, I Should Have Been Crucified, Elvis reappears and sings Can't Help Falling In Love. Elvis decides to continue the show and sings:* Faded Love, I'm So Lonesome I Could Cry, Polk Salad Annie, American Trilogy, Can't Help Falling In Love

February 15, 1973—Midnight Show—Canceled due to illness

February 16, 1973—Dinner Show—Complete
C.C. Rider, I Got A Woman/Amen, Love Me Tender, You Don't Have To Say You Love Me, Steamroller Blues, You Gave Me A Mountain, Fever, Love Me, Blue Suede Shoes, Hound Dog, What Now My Love, Johnny B. Goode, Suspicious Minds, Introductions, Celebrity Introductions: Johnny Tillotson, I Can't Stop Loving You, American Trilogy, Can't Help Falling In Love

February 16, 1973—Midnight Show—
Not Available

February 17, 1973—Dinner Show—Incomplete
C.C. Rider, I Got A Woman/Amen, Love Me Tender, You Don't Have To Say You Love Me, Steamroller Blues, You Gave Me A Mountain, Fever, I Can't Stop Loving You, American Trilogy, Can't Help Falling In Love

February 17, 1973—Midnight Show—
Incomplete
C.C. Rider, I Got A Woman/Amen, Love Me Tender, You Don't Have To Say You Love Me, Steamroller Blues, You Gave Me A Mountain, Fever, I Can't Stop Loving You, American Trilogy, Can't Help Falling In Love

February 18, 1973—Dinner Show—Incomplete
Love Me Tender, Steamroller Blues, Love Me Tender, You Don't Have To Say You Love Me, Fever, Love Me, Johnny B. Goode, What Now My Love, How Great Thou Art, Suspicious Minds, Introductions, I Can't Stop Loving You, American Trilogy, Can't Help Falling In Love

February 18, 1973—Midnight Show—Complete
C.C. Rider, I Got A Woman/Amen, Big Boss Man (partial), Love Me Tender, You Don't Have To Say You Love Me, Steamroller Blues, You Gave Me A Mountain (reprise), Fever, Love Me, Blue Suede Shoes, Johnny B. Goode, Hound Dog, What Now My Love, Suspicious Minds, *A group of men jump on stage and attempt to get to Elvis. Elvis' bodyguards, along with Elvis, proceed to win the altercation. At its conclusion Elvis shouts into the mic, "I'll whoop his ass" along with some other angry comments. The men, who had been drinking, later claimed to be Elvis fans that only wanted to shake his hand. Elvis then proceeds with the show,* I Can't Stop Loving You, American Trilogy, Can't Help Falling In Love

February 19, 1973—Dinner Show—Complete
C.C. Rider, I Got A Woman/Amen, Love Me Tender, You Don't Have To Say You Love Me, Steamroller Blues, You Gave Me A Mountain, Fever, Love Me, Blue Suede Shoes, I'm Leavin', Hound Dog, What Now My Love, Suspicious Minds, Karate dialogue, Introductions, Celebrity Introduction: Paul Simon, I Can't Stop Loving You, American Trilogy, Can't Help Falling In Love

February 19, 1973—Midnight Show—
Not Available

February 20, 1973—Dinner Show—Complete
C.C. Rider, I Got A Woman/Amen, Love Me Tender, You Don't Have To Say You Love Me, Steamroller Blues, You Gave Me A Mountain, Fever, Love Me, Blue Suede Shoes, I'm Leavin', Hound Dog, What Now My Love (reprise), Suspicious Minds, Introductions, I'll Remember You, I Can't Stop Loving You, American Trilogy, Can't Help Falling In Love

February 20, 1973—Midnight Show—Complete
C.C. Rider, I Got A Woman/Amen, Love Me Tender, You Don't Have To Say You Love Me, Steamroller Blues, You Gave Me A Mountain, Fever, Love Me, Blue Suede Shoes, I'm Leavin', Hound Dog, What Now My Love, Suspicious Minds, karate dialogue, Introductions, Alfie (partial), I'll Remember You, I Can't Stop Loving You, American Trilogy, Can't Help Falling In Love

February 21, 1973—Dinner Show—Complete
C.C. Rider, I Got A Woman/Amen, Love Me Tender, You Don't Have To Say You Love Me, Steamroller Blues, You Gave Me A Mountain, Fever, Love Me, Blue Suede Shoes, I'm Leavin', Hound Dog, What Now My Love, Suspicious Minds, karate dialogue, Introductions, I'll Remember You, I Can't Stop Loving You, American Trilogy, Can't Help Falling In Love

February 21, 1973—Midnight Show—Complete
C.C. Rider, I Got A Woman/Amen, Love Me Tender, You Don't Have To Say You Love Me, Steamroller Blues, Fever, Love Me, Blue Suede Shoes, I'm Leavin', Hound Dog, What Now My Love, Suspicious Minds, karate dialogue, Introductions, Celebrity introduction: Marty Allen, I'll Remember You, I Can't Stop Loving You, American Trilogy, Can't Help Falling In Love

February 22, 1973—Dinner Show—Complete
C.C. Rider, I Got A Woman/Amen, You Don't Have To Say You Love Me, Steamroller Blues, You Gave Me A Mountain, Fever, Love Me, Blue Suede Shoes, I'm Leavin', Hound Dog, What Now My Love, Suspicious Minds, karate dialogue, Introductions, I'll Remember You, I Can't Stop Loving You, American Trilogy, Can't Help Falling In Love

February 22, 1973—Midnight Show—Complete
C.C. Rider, I Got A Woman/Amen, Love Me Tender, You Don't Have To Say You Love Me, Steamroller Blues, You Gave Me A Mountain, Fever, Love Me, I'm Leavin', Hound Dog, What Now My Love, Suspicious Minds, Introductions, I'll Remember You, I Can't Stop Loving You, American Trilogy, Can't Help Falling In Love

February 23, 1973—Dinner Show—Complete
C.C. Rider, I Got A Woman/Amen, Love Me Tender, You Don't Have To Say You Love Me, Steamroller Blues, You Gave Me A Mountain, Fever, Love Me, Blue Suede Shoes, I'm Leavin', Hound Dog, What Now My Love, Suspicious Minds, karate dialogue, Introductions, I'll Remember You, I Can't Stop Loving You, American Trilogy, Can't Help Falling In Love

February 23, 1973—Closing Show—Complete
C.C. Rider, I Got A Woman/Amen, Love Me Tender, You Don't Have To Say You Love Me, Steamroller Blues, You Gave Me A Mountain, Fever, Love Me, Blue Suede Shoes, Hound Dog, What Now My Love (reprise), Suspicious Minds, Introductions, Celebrity introductions Pierre Hadidge, Bill Porter, Ed Parker, Buzz Aldrin, Mama Cass Elliot, Dane Clark, Ernest Borgnine, George Hamilton, Ann-Margret, I'll Remember You, I Can't Stop Loving You, American Trilogy, Can't Help Falling In Love

Songs Sung By Elvis During Engagement
Alfie (partial), All Shook Up, American Trilogy, Big Boss Man (partial), Big Hunk O' Love, Blue Suede Shoes, Burning Love, Can't Help Falling In Love, C.C. Rider, Faded Love, Fever, Heartbreak Hotel, Hound Dog, How Great Thou Art, How Great Thou Art (J. D. Sumner & The Stamps Quartet), I Can't Stop Loving You, I Got A Woman, I Got A Woman/Amen, I'll Remember You, I'll Remember You (reprise), I'm Leavin', I'm So Lonesome I Could Cry, I Should Have Been Crucified (J. D. Sumner & The Stamps Quartet), Johnny B. Goode, Killing Me Softly (Voice), Lawdy Miss Clawdy, Long Tall Sally/Whole Lotta Shakin' Goin' On, Long Tall Sally/Whole Lotta Shakin' Goin' On/Flip Flop And Fly/Your Mama Don't Dance/Jailhouse Rock/Hound Dog, Love Me, Love Me Tender, My Way, Polk Salad Annie, Something, Spanish Eyes duet with Sherrill Nielsen, Steamroller Blues, Suspicious Minds, Sweet Caroline, Sweet Sweet Spirit (J. D. Sumner & The Stamps Quartet), Until It's Time For You To Go, Walk That Lonesome Road (J. D. Sumner & The Stamps Quartet), What Now My Love, What Now My Love (false start), What Now My Love (reprise), When It's My Time (J. D. Sumner & The Stamps Quartet—solo by Bill Baize), You Don't Have To Say You Love Me, You Gave Me A Mountain, You Gave Me A Mountain (reprise)

The following songs are rumored to have been sung at this engagement but are not verifiable.

Auld Lang Syne (partial), What Now My Love (dramatic spoken version)

VEGAS SEASON 9 1973, Hilton Hotel
Monday, August 6, 1973 through Monday, September 3, 1973—58 shows—Total attendance—129,000

Jumpsuits Worn at This Engagement—Blue Target Suit with blue lined cape, White Snowflake Suit with gold lined cape, White Nail Suit with gold lined cape, Elvis Today Suit with yellow lined cape, Raised On Rock Suit with red lined cape, Memphis Suit with blue lined cape, Light-blue Flower Suit with blue lined cape, Red Flower Suit with red lined cape, Black Spanish Conquistador Suit with blue lined cape

Show Members—Musicians: Lead Guitar—James Burton, Rhythm Guitar—John Wilkinson, Acoustic Guitar and Backup Vocals—Charlie Hodge, Bass—Emory Gordy, Piano—Glen D. Hardin, Drums—Ronnie Tutt, Backup Singers: Sweet Inspirations: Myrna Smith, Sylvia Shemwell, Estelle Brown, J. D. Sumner & The Stamps Quartet: J. D. Sumner, Donnie Sumner, Bill Baize, Ed Enoch, Richard Sterban, High Voice Singer—Kathy Westmoreland, Comedian—Jackie Kahane, Orchestra—Joe Guercio

August 6, 1973—Opening Show—Complete
C.C. Rider, Trouble, Raised On Rock, Love Me, Steamroller Blues, What Now My Love, Blue Suede Shoes, Memphis Tennessee, Long Tall Sally/Whole Lotto Shaken' Going' On/Your Mama Don't Dance/Flip Flop And Fly/Jailhouse Rock/Whole Lotto Shaken' Going' On, Love Me Tender, Hound Dog, Fever, My Boy, Suspicious Minds, Introductions, Celebrity Introductions: Petula Clark, Guy Mitchell, Phyllis McGuire, Liza Minnelli, I Can't Stop Loving You, American Trilogy, Bridge Over Troubled Water, How Great Thou Art, Big Hunk O' Love, Help Me Make It Through The Night, Can't Help Falling In Love

August 7, 1973—Dinner Show—Complete
C.C. Rider, I Got A Woman/Amen, Love Me, Steamroller Blues, You Gave Me A Mountain, Trouble, Blue Suede Shoes, Long Tall Sally/Whole Lotto Shaken' Going' On/Your Mama Don't Dance/Flip, Flop And Fly/Jailhouse Rock/Whole Lotto Shaken' Going' On, Love Me Tender, Hound Dog, Fever, What Now My Love, Suspicious Minds, Introductions, I Can't Stop Loving You, American Trilogy, Big Hunk O' Love, Can't Help Falling In Love

August 7, 1973—Midnight Show—Complete
C.C. Rider, I Got A Woman/Amen, Love Me, Steamroller Blues, You Gave Me A Mountain, Trouble, Blue Suede Shoes, Long Tall Sally/Whole Lotto Shaken' Going' On/Your Mama Don't Dance/Flip, Flop And Fly/Jailhouse Rock, Hound Dog, Love Me Tender, Fever, Bridge Over Troubled Water, Suspicious Minds, Introductions, My Boy, I Can't Stop Loving You, American Trilogy, Release Me, Mystery Train/Tiger Man, Funny How Time Slips Away, Faded Love, Can't Help Falling In Love

August 8, 1973—Dinner Show—Complete
C.C. Rider, I Got A Woman/Amen, Love Me, Steamroller Blues, You Gave Me A Mountain, Trouble, Blue Suede Shoes, Long Tall Sally/

Whole Lotto Shaken' Going' On/Your Mama Don't Dance/Flip Flop And Fly/Jailhouse Rock/ Whole Lotto Shaken' Going' On, Love Me Tender, Hound Dog, Fever, Teddy Bear/Don't Be Cruel, What Now My Love, Suspicious Minds, Introductions, My Boy, I Can't Stop Loving You, American Trilogy, How Great Thou Art, Release Me, Can't Help Falling In Love

August 8, 1973—Midnight Show—Complete
C.C. Rider, I Got A Woman/Amen, Love Me, Steamroller Blues, You Gave Me A Mountain, Trouble, Blue Suede Shoes, Long Tall Sally/ Whole Lotta Shakin' Goin' On/Your Mama Don't Dance/Flip Flop And Fly/Jailhouse Rock/Whole Lotta Shakin' Goin' On, Love Me Tender, Hound Dog, Fever, What Now My Love, Bridge Over Troubled Water, Suspicious Minds, Introductions, My Boy, I Can't Stop Loving You, American Trilogy, Big Hunk O' Love, Release Me, Make The World Go Away, Can't Help Falling In Love

August 9, 1973—Dinner Show—Complete
C.C. Rider, I Got A Woman/Amen, Love Me, Steamroller Blues, You Gave Me A Mountain, Trouble, Blue Suede Shoes, Long Tall Sally/ Whole Lotta Shakin' Goin' On/Your Mama Don't Dance/Flip Flop And Fly/Jailhouse Rock/Whole Lotta Shakin' Goin' On, Love Me Tender, Hound Dog, Fever, What Now My Love, Suspicious Minds, Introductions, Celebrity Introductions: James Darren, I Can't Stop Loving You, American Trilogy, Big Hunk O' Love, Can't Help Falling In Love

August 9, 1973—Midnight Show—Complete
C.C. Rider, I Got A Woman/Amen, Love Me, Steamroller Blues, You Gave Me A Mountain, Trouble, Long Tall Sally/Whole Lotta Shakin' Goin' On/Your Mama Don't Dance/ Flip Flop And Fly/Jailhouse Rock, Love Me Tender, Hound Dog, Fever, What Now My Love, Suspicious Minds, Introductions, My Boy, I Can't Stop Loving You, American Trilogy, Release Me, Mystery Train/Tiger Man, Can't Help Falling In Love

August 10, 1973—Dinner Show—Complete
C.C. Rider, I Got A Woman/Amen, Love Me, Steamroller Blues, You Gave Me A Mountain, Trouble, Blue Suede Shoes, Long Tall Sally/ Whole Lotta Shakin' Goin' On/Your Mama Don't Dance/Flip Flop And Fly/Jailhouse Rock/Whole Lotta Shakin' Goin' On, Love Me Tender, Hound Dog, Fever, What Now My Love, Suspicious Minds, Introductions, My Boy, I Can't Stop Loving You, American Trilogy, Mystery Train/Tiger Man, Release Me, Teddy Bear/Don't Be Cruel, Can't Help Falling In Love

August 10, 1973—Midnight Show—Complete
CC Rider, I Got A Woman/Amen, Love Me, Steamroller Blues, You Gave Me A Mountain, Trouble, Blue Suede Shoes, Long Tall Sally/Whole Lotta Shakin' Goin' On/Your Mama Don't Dance/Flip Flop And Fly/Jailhouse Rock/Whole Lotta Shakin' Goin' On, Love Me Tender, Hound Dog, Fever, Bridge Over Troubled Water, Suspicious Minds, Introductions, My Boy, I Can't Stop Loving You, American Trilogy, Release Me, Mystery Train/Tiger Man, Can't Help Falling In Love

August 11, 1973—Dinner Show—Complete
C.C. Rider, I Got A Woman/Amen, Dialogue, Love Me, Steamroller Blues, You Gave Me A Mountain, Trouble, Blue Suede Shoes, Long Tall Sally/Whole Lotta Shakin' Goin' On/Your Mama Don't Dance/Flip Flop And Fly/Jailhouse Rock/Whole Lotta Shakin' Goin' On, Love Me Tender, Hound Dog, Fever, What Now My Love, Suspicious Minds, Introductions, My Boy, I Can't Stop Loving You, American Trilogy, Dialogue, It's Over, Release Me, Big Hunk O' Love, My Way, Can't Help Falling In Love

August 11, 1973—Midnight Show—Complete
C.C. Rider, I Got A Woman/Amen, Love Me, Steamroller Blues, You Gave Me A Mountain, Trouble, Blue Suede Shoes, Long Tall Sally/Your Mama Don't Dance/Flip, Flop And Fly/Jailhouse Rock/ Whole Lotta Shakin' Goin' On/Hound Dog, Love Me Tender, Fever, Bridge Over Troubled Water, Suspicious Minds, Introductions, My Boy, I can't Stop Loving You, The First Time Ever I Saw Your Face, Mystery Train/Tiger Man, Tiger Man (slow version), American Trilogy, Release Me, Can't Help Falling In Love

August 12, 1973—Dinner Show—Complete
C.C. Rider, I Got A Woman/Amen, Love Me, Steamroller Blues, You Gave Me A Mountain, Trouble, Blue Suede Shoes, Long Tall Sally/Whole Lotta Shakin' Goin' On/Your Mama Don't Dance/Flip Flop And Fly/Jailhouse Rock/Hound Dog, Love Me Tender, Fever, Bridge Over Troubled Water, Guadalajara (partial), Suspicious Minds, Introductions, My Boy, I Can't Stop Loving You, American Trilogy, Mystery Train/Tiger Man, Release Me, Help Me Make It Through The Night, Heartbreak Hotel, What Now My Love, Can't Help Falling In Love

August 12, 1973—Midnight Show—Complete
C.C. Rider, I Got A Woman/Amen, Love Me, Steamroller Blues, You Gave Me A Mountain, Trouble, Blue Suede Shoes, Long Tall Sally/ Whole Lotta Shakin' Goin' On/Your Mama Don't Dance/Flip Flop And Fly/Whole Lotta Shakin' Goin' On, Love Me Tender, Fever, Bridge Over Troubled Water, It's Crying Time, Suspicious Minds, My Boy, I Can't Stop Loving You, American Trilogy, Mystery Train/Tiger Man, Release Me, Help Me Make It Through The Night, Heartbreak Hotel, What Now My Love, Can't Help Falling In Love

August 13, 1973—Not Available

August 14, 1973—Dinner Show—Complete
C.C. Rider, I Got A Woman/Amazing Grace/Amen, Love Me, You Gave Me A Mountain, Trouble, Blue Suede Shoes, Long Tall Sally/Whole Lotta Shakin' Goin' On/Shake Rattle And Roll/Your Mama Don't Dance/Flip Flop And Fly/Jailhouse Rock/Whole Lotta Shakin' Goin' On, Hound Dog, Love Me Tender, Fever, Bridge Over Troubled Water, Suspicious Minds, Introductions, My Boy, I Can't Stop Loving You, American Trilogy, Release Me, How Great Thou Art, Can't Help Falling In Love

August 14, 1973—Midnight Show —Complete
C.C. Rider, I Got A Woman/Amen, Love Me, Steamroller Blues, You Gave Me A Mountain, Trouble, Blue Suede Shoes, Long Tall Sally/Whole Lotta Shakin' Goin' On/Your Mama Don't Dance/Flip Flop And Fly/Jailhouse Rock/Whole Lotta Shakin' Goin' On, Love Me Tender, Hound Dog, Fever, Bridge Over Troubled Water, Suspicious Minds, Introductions, My Boy, I Can't Stop Loving You, American Trilogy, Mystery Train/Tiger Man, Release Me, Can't Help Falling In Love

August 15, 1973—Dinner Show—Complete
C.C. Rider, I Got A Woman/Amen, Love Me, Steamroller Blues, You Gave Me A Mountain, Trouble, Blue Suede Shoes, Long Tall Sally/ Whole Lotta Shakin' Goin' On/Your Mama Don't Dance/Flip Flop And Fly/Jailhouse Rock/Whole Lotta Shakin' Goin' On, Love Me Tender, Hound Dog, Fever, What Now My Love, Suspicious Minds, Introductions, My Boy, I Can't Stop Loving You, American Trilogy, Release Me, Mystery Train/Tiger Man, Can't Help Falling In Love

August 15, 1973—Midnight Show—Complete
C.C. Rider, I Got A Woman/Amen, Love Me,

Hawaiian Wedding Song, You Gave Me A Mountain, Trouble, Blue Suede Shoes, Long Tall Sally/Your Mama Don't Dance/Flip Flop And Fly/Jailhouse Rock/Hound Dog, Love Me Tender, Fever, Bridge Over Troubled Water, Suspicious Minds, My Boy, I Can't Stop Loving You, American Trilogy, Release Me, Mystery Train/Tiger Man, Help Me Make It Through The Night, Something, How Great Thou Art, Can't Help Falling In Love

August 16 1973—Dinner Show—Complete
C.C. Rider, I Got A Woman/Amen, Love Me, You Gave Me A Mountain, Trouble, Blue Suede Shoes, Long Tall Sally/Your Mama Don't Dance/Flip Flop And Fly/Jailhouse Rock/Hound Dog, Love Me Tender, Fever, What Now My Love, Suspicious Minds, My Boy, I Can't Stop Loving You, American Trilogy, Release Me, Help Me Make It Through The Night, Mystery Train/Tiger Man, How Great Thou Art, Can't Help Falling In Love

August 16, 1973—Midnight Show—Complete
C.C. Rider, I Got A Woman/Amen, Love Me, You Gave Me A Mountain, Trouble, Blue Suede Shoes, Long Tall Sally/Your Mama Don't Dance/Flip Flop And Fly/Jailhouse Rock/Hound Dog, Love Me Tender, Fever, Bridge Over Troubled Water, Suspicious Minds, My Boy, I Can't Stop Loving You, American Trilogy, Mystery Train/Tiger Man, Can't Help Falling In Love

August 17, 1973—Dinner Show—Complete
C.C. Rider, I Got A Woman/Amen, Love Me, You Gave Me A Mountain, Trouble, Blue Suede Shoes, Long Tall Sally/Your Mama Don't Dance/ Flip Flop and Fly/Jailhouse Rock, Hound Dog, Love Me Tender, Fever, Bridge Over Troubled Water, Suspicious Minds, My Boy, I Can't Stop Loving You, American Trilogy, Big Hunk O' Love, Teddy Bear/Don't Be Cruel, Can't Help Falling In Love

August 17, 1973—Midnight Show—Complete
C.C. Rider, I Got A Woman/Amen, Love Me, Steamroller Blues, You Gave Me A Mountain, Trouble, Blue Suede Shoes, Long Tall Sally/Your Mama Don't Dance/Flip Flop And Fly/Jailhouse Rock, Hound Dog, Love Me Tender, Fever, Bridge Over Troubled Water, Suspicious Minds, What Now My Love, Release Me, Something, Mystery Train/Tiger Man, How Great Thou Art, Help Me Make It Through The Night, Can't Help Falling In Love

August 18, 1973—Dinner Show—Complete
C.C. Rider, I Got A Woman/Amen, Love Me, You Gave Me A Mountain, Trouble, Blue Suede Shoes, Long Tall Sally/Your Mama Don't Dance/Flip Flop And Fly/Jailhouse Rock, Hound Dog, Love Me Tender, Fever, What Now My Love, Suspicious Minds, Introductions, My Boy, I Can't Stop Loving You, American Trilogy, Mystery Train/Tiger Man, Help Me Make It Through The Night, Can't Help Falling In Love

August 18, 1973—Midnight Show—Complete
C.C. Rider, I Got A Woman/Amen, Love Me, Steamroller Blues, You Gave Me A Mountain, Trouble, Blue Suede Shoes, Long Tall Sally/Whole Lotta Shakin' Goin' On/Your Mama Don't Dance/Flip Flop And Fly/Jailhouse Rock/Hound Dog, Love Me Tender, Fever, Bridge Over Troubled Water, Suspicious Minds, Introductions, My Boy, Release Me, American Trilogy, How Great Thou Art, Help Me Make It Through The Night, Can't Help Falling In Love

August 19, 1973—Dinner Show—Complete
C.C. Rider, I Got A Woman/Amen, Love Me, You Gave Me A Mountain, Trouble, Blue Suede Shoes, Long Tall Sally/Whole Lotta Shakin' Goin' On/Your Mama Don't Dance/Flip Flop And Fly/Jailhouse Rock/Hound Dog, Love Me Tender, Fever, What Now My Love, Suspicious Minds, Introductions, My Boy, Release Me, American Trilogy, Mystery Train/Tiger Man, Can't Help Falling In Love

August 19, 1973—Midnight Show—Complete
C.C. Rider, I Got A Woman/Amen, Love Me, You Gave Me A Mountain, Love Me Tender, Blue Suede Shoes, Long Tall Sally/Whole Lotta Shakin' Goin' On/Your Mama Don't Dance/Flip, Flop And Fly/Whole Lotta Shakin' Goin' On, Fever, What Now My Love, Suspicious Minds, Introductions, Help Me Make It Through The Night, American Trilogy, Big Hunk O' Love, How Great Thou Art, Can't Help Falling In Love

August 20, 1973—Dinner Show—Complete
C.C. Rider, I Got A Woman/Amen, Love Me, Steamroller Blues, You Gave Me A Mountain, Trouble, Blue Suede Shoes, Long Tall Sally/Your Mama Don't Dance/Flip Flop & Fly/Jailhouse Rock, Hound Dog, Love Me Tender, Fever, What Now My Love, Suspicious Minds, My Boy, I Can't Stop Loving You, American Trilogy, Mystery Train/Tiger Man, Can't Help Falling In Love

August 20, 1973—Midnight Show—Complete
C.C. Rider, I Got A Woman/Amen, Love Me, Steamroller Blues, You Gave Me A Mountain, Trouble, Blue Suede Shoes, Long Tall Sally/Whole Lotta Shakin' Goin' On/Your Mama Don't Dance/Flip Flop And Fly/Jailhouse Rock/ Hound Dog, Love Me Tender, Fever, What Now My Love, Suspicious Minds, Introductions, My Boy, Release Me, American Trilogy, Mystery Train/Tiger Man, Help Me Make It Through The Night, How Great Thou Art, Can't Help Falling In Love

August 21, 1973—Dinner Show—Complete
C.C. Rider, I Got A Woman/Amen, Love Me, Steamroller Blues, You Gave Me A Mountain, Trouble, Blue Suede Shoes, Long Tall Sally/Whole Lotta Shakin' Goin' On/Your Mama Don't Dance, Flip Flop And Fly/Jailhouse Rock/Whole Lotta Shakin' Goin' On, Love Me Tender, Hound Dog, Fever, What Now My Love, Suspicious Minds, Introductions, I Can't Stop Loving You, American Trilogy, Big Hunk O' Love, Can't Help Falling In Love

August 21, 1973—Midnight Show—Complete
C.C. Rider, I Got A Woman/Amen, Love Me, You Gave Me A Mountain, Blue Suede Shoes, Long Tall Sally/Your Mama Don't Dance/Flip Flop And Fly/Jailhouse Rock, Hound Dog, Love Me Tender, Fever, What Now My Love, Suspicious Minds, My Boy, Release Me, American Trilogy, Big Hunk O' Love, Help Me Make It Through The Night, Can't Help Falling In Love

August 22, 1973—Dinner Show—Complete
C.C. Rider, I Got A Woman/Amen, Love Me, You Gave Me A Mountain, Blue Suede Shoes, Long Tall Sally/Your Mama Don't Dance/Flip Flop And Fly/Jailhouse Rock, Hound Dog, Love Me Tender, Fever, What Now My Love, Suspicious Minds, My Boy, Release Me, American Trilogy, Teddy Bear/Don't Be Cruel, Can't Help Falling In Love

August 22, 1973—Midnight Show—Complete
C.C. Rider, I Got A Woman/Amen, Love Me, Steamroller Blues, You Gave Me A Mountain, Blue Suede Shoes, Long Tall Sally/Your Mama Don't Dance/Flip Flop and Fly/Jailhouse Rock, Hound Dog, Love Me Tender, Fever, What Now My Love, Suspicious Minds, My Boy, Release Me, American Trilogy, Big Hunk O' Love, Can't Help Falling In Love

August 23, 1973—Dinner Show—Complete
C.C. Rider, I Got A Woman/Amen, Love Me, You Gave Me A Mountain, Blue Suede Shoes, Long Tall Sally/Your Mama Don't Dance/Flip Flop And Fly/Jailhouse Rock, Hound Dog, Love Me Tender, Fever, How Great Thou Art, Suspicious Minds,

My Boy, Release Me, Something, American Trilogy, Big Hunk O' Love, Can't Help Falling In Love

August 23, 1973—Midnight Show—Complete
C.C. Rider, I Got A Woman/Amen, Love Me, Steamroller Blues, You Gave Me A Mountain, Blue Suede Shoes, Long Tall Sally/Whole Lotta Shakin' Goin' On/Your Mama Don't Dance/Flip Flop And Fly/Jailhouse Rock/Hound Dog, Love Me Tender, Fever, What Now My Love, Suspicious Minds, Introductions, The First Time Ever I Saw Your Face, American Trilogy, Release Me, Mystery Train/Tiger Man, Can't Help Falling In Love

August 24, 1973—Not Available

August 25, 1973—Dinner Show—Complete
C.C. Rider, I Got A Woman/Amen, Love Me, Steamroller Blues, You Gave Me A Mountain, Blue Suede Shoes, Long Tall Sally/Whole Lotta Shakin' Goin' On/Your Mama Don't Dance/Flip Flop And Fly/Jailhouse Rock/Hound Dog, Love Me Tender, Fever, Bridge Over Troubled Water, Suspicious Minds, Introductions and introduces Lisa Marie, Release Me, Teddy Bear/Don't Be Cruel, American Trilogy, Big Hunk O' Love, Heartbreak Hotel (false start) The First Time Ever I Saw Your Face (Elvis dedicates this song to Lisa Marie), Can't Help Falling In Love

August 25, 1973—Midnight Show—Complete
C.C. Rider, I Got A Woman/Amen, Love Me, Steamroller Blues, You Gave Me A Mountain, Blue Suede Shoes, Long Tall Sally/Whole Lotta Shakin' Goin' On/Your Mama Don't Dance/Flip, Flop And Fly/Jailhouse Rock/Hound Dog, Love Me Tender, Fever, What Now My Love, Elvis leaves the stage, Suspicious Minds, Introductions, My Boy, I Can't Stop Loving You, American Trilogy, Release Me, It's A Matter Of Time, Elvis dedicates the next song to Dee and Vernon Presley, The First Time Ever I Saw Your Face, Bridge Over Troubled Water, Can't Help Falling In Love

August 26, 1973—Dinner Show—Complete
C.C. Rider/I Got A Woman/Amen, Love Me, Steamroller Blues, You Gave Me A Mountain, Blue Suede Shoes, Long Tall Sally/Whole Lotta Shakin' Goin' On/Your Mama Don't Dance/Flip Flop And Fly/Jailhouse Rock/Hound Dog, Love Me Tender, Fever, Bridge Over Troubled Water, Suspicious Minds, Introductions, Elvis introduces Lisa Marie, Teddy Bear/Don't Be Cruel, I Can't Stop Loving You, American Trilogy, Big Hunk O' Love, The First Time Ever I Saw Your Face, Can't Help Falling In Love

August 26, 1973—Midnight Show—Complete
C.C. Rider, I Got A Woman/Amen, Love Me, Steamroller Blues, You Gave Me A Mountain, Blue Suede Shoes, Long Tall Sally/Whole Lotta Shakin' Goin' On/Your Mama Don't Dance/Flip, Flop And Fly/Jailhouse Rock/Hound Dog, Love Me Tender, Fever, What Now My Love, Suspicious Minds, Introductions, Release Me, American Trilogy, Elvis introduces Lisa Marie, Teddy Bear/Don't Be Cruel, The First Time Ever I Saw Your Face, Johnny B. Goode, How Great Thou Art (reprise), Can't Help Falling In Love

August 27, 1973—Dinner Show—Complete
C.C. Rider, I Got A Woman/Amen, Dialogue, Love Me, Steamroller Blues, You Gave Me A Mountain, Blue Suede Shoes, Long Tall Sally/Whole Lotta Shakin' Goin' On/Your Mama Don't Dance/Flip Flop And Fly/Jailhouse Rock/Hound Dog, Love Me Tender, Fever, Dialogue, Bridge Over Troubled Water, Suspicious Minds, Introductions, Elvis introduces Lisa Marie, Release Me, I Can't Stop Loving You, Big Hunk O' Love, The First Time Ever I Saw Your Face, Can't Help Falling In Love

August 27, 1973—Midnight Show—Complete
C.C. Rider, I Got A Woman/Amen, Love Me, Steamroller Blues, You Gave Me A Mountain, Blue Suede Shoes, Long Tall Sally/Whole Lotta Shakin' Goin' On/Your Mama Don't Dance/Flip Flop And Fly/Jailhouse Rock/Hound Dog, Love Me Tender, Fever, Bridge Over Troubled Water, Suspicious Minds, Introductions, Release Me, I Can't Stop Loving You, Teddy Bear/Don't Be Cruel, Dialogue, American Trilogy, Johnny B. Goode, The First Time Ever I Saw Your Face, How Great Thou Art, Can't Help Falling In Love

August 28, 1973—Dinner Show—Complete
C.C. Rider, I Got A Woman/Amen, Love Me, Love Me Tender, Dialogue, You Gave Me A Mountain, Blue Suede Shoes, Long Tall Sally/Whole Lotta Shakin' Goin' On/Your Mama Don't Dance/Flip Flop And Fly/Jailhouse Rock/Hound Dog, Fever, What Now My Love, Suspicious Minds, Introductions, Release Me, Johnny B. Goode, Dialogue, Elvis introduces Lisa Marie, My Boy, I Can't Stop Loving You, Dialogue, American Trilogy, The First Time Ever I Saw Your Face, Dialogue, Heartbreak Hotel (false start), Teddy Bear/Don't Be Cruel, How Great Thou Art, Can't Help Falling In Love

August 28, 1973—Midnight Show—Complete
C.C. Rider, I Got A Woman/Amen, Love Me, Steamroller Blues, You Gave Me A Mountain, Trouble, Blue Suede Shoes, Long Tall Sally/Whole Lotta Shakin' Goin' On/Your Mama Don't Dance/Flip, Flop And Fly/Jailhouse Rock/Hound Dog, Love Me Tender, Fever, Bridge Over Troubled Water, Suspicious Minds, Introductions, My Boy/Take These Chains From My Heart/My Boy, Release Me/My Boy/What A Friend We Have In Jesus/My Boy, I Can't Stop Loving You, American Trilogy, Heartbreak Hotel, Mystery Train/Tiger Man, Johnny B. Goode, The First Time Ever I Saw Your Face, How Great Thou Art, Can't Help Falling In Love

August 29, 1973—Dinner Show—Complete
C.C. Rider, I Got A Woman/Amen, Love Me, Steamroller Blues, You Gave Me A Mountain, Blue Suede Shoes, Long Tall Sally/Whole Lotta Shakin' Goin' On/Your Mama Don't Dance/Flip Flop And Fly/Jailhouse Rock/Hound Dog, Love Me Tender, Fever, What Now My Love (false start), Suspicious Minds, Introductions, My Boy, I Can't Stop Loving You, American Trilogy, Big Hunk O' Love, The First Time Ever I Saw Your Face (false start), Can't Help Falling In Love

August 29, 1973—Midnight Show—Complete
C.C. Rider, I Got A Woman/Amen, Love Me, Steamroller Blues, You Gave Me A Mountain, Trouble, Blue Suede Shoes, Long Tall Sally/Whole Lotta Shakin' Goin' On/Your Mama Don't Dance/Flip Flop And Fly/Jailhouse Rock/ Hound Dog, Love Me Tender, Fever, Bridge Over Troubled Water (reprise), Suspicious Minds, Introductions, My Boy, I Can't Stop Loving You, American Trilogy, Introductions Vernon Presley, Lisa Marie, Felton Jarvis, The First Time Ever I Saw Your Face, How Great Thou Art, Can't Help Falling In Love

August 30, 1973—Dinner Show—Complete
C.C. Rider, I Got A Woman/Amen, Love Me, Steamroller Blues, You Gave Me A Mountain, Trouble, Long Tall Sally/Whole Lotta Shakin' Goin' On/Your Mama Don't Dance/Flip Flop And Fly/Hound Dog, Love Me Tender, Fever, Bridge Over Troubled Water, Suspicious Minds, Introductions, Release Me, American Trilogy, The First Time Ever I Saw Your Face, Heartbreak Hotel, Johnny B. Goode, How Great Thou Art, Can't Help Falling In Love

August 30, 1973—Midnight Show—Complete
C.C. Rider, I Got A Woman/Amen, Love Me, Steamroller Blues, You Gave Me A Mountain, Trouble, Long Tall Sally/Whole Lotta Shakin' Goin'

On/Your Mama Don't Dance/Flip Flop And Fly/Hound Dog, Love Me Tender, Fever, Bridge Over Troubled Water (reprise), Suspicious Minds, Introductions, My Boy, I Can't Stop Loving You, American Trilogy, Johnny B. Goode, Lady Of Spain (partial), The First Time Ever I Saw Your Face, How Great Thou Art (reprise), Can't Help Falling In Love

August 31, 1973—Dinner Show—Complete
C.C. Rider, I Got A Woman/Amen, Love Me, Steamroller Blues, You Gave Me A Mountain, Trouble, Long Tall Sally/Whole Lotta Shakin' Goin' On/Your Mama Don't Dance/Flip Flop And Fly/Hound Dog, Love Me Tender, Fever, Bridge Over Troubled Water (reprise), Suspicious Minds, Introductions, Celebrity introduction Charles Bronson, My Boy, I Can't Stop Loving You, American Trilogy, Big Hunk O' Love, The First Time Ever I Saw Your Face, How Great Thou Art, Can't Help Falling In Love.

August 31, 1973—Midnight Show—Complete
C.C. Rider, I Got A Woman/Amen, Love Me, Release Me, Fever, You Gave Me A Mountain, Long Tall Sally/Whole Lotta Shakin' Goin' On/Your Mama Don't Dance/Flip Flop And Fly/Hound Dog, Teddy Bear/Don't Be Cruel, Bridge Over Troubled Water, Suspicious Minds, Introductions, Love Me Tender, How Great Thou Art, Heartbreak Hotel, The First Time Ever I Saw Your Face, Mystery Train/Tiger Man, American Trilogy, Funny How Time Slips Away, Johnny B. Goode, Dialogue, Can't Help Falling In Love

September 1, 1973—Dinner Show—Complete
C.C. Rider, I Got A Woman/Amen, Love Me, Steamroller Blues, You Gave Me A Mountain, Trouble, Long Tall Sally/Whole Lotta Shakin' Goin' On/Your Mama Don't Dance/Flip Flop And Fly/Hound Dog, Love Me Tender, Fever, Bridge Over Troubled Water, Suspicious Minds, Introductions, My Boy, I Can't Stop Loving You, American Trilogy, Dialogue, Elvis introduces Vernon Presley, The First Time Ever I Saw Your Face, How Great Thou Art, Can't Help Falling In Love

September 1, 1973—Midnight Show—Complete
C.C. Rider, Love Me, I Got A Woman/Amen, Steamroller Blues, You Gave Me A Mountain, Trouble, Long Tall Sally/Whole Lotta Shakin' Goin' On/Your Mama Don't Dance/Flip Flop And Fly/Hound Dog, Love Me Tender, Fever, Bridge Over Troubled Water, Suspicious Minds, Introductions, Release Me, American Trilogy, The First Time Ever I Saw Your Face, How Great Thou Art, Can't Help Falling In Love

September 2, 1973—3:00 A.M. Show—Complete
C.C. Rider, I Got A Woman/Amen, Love Me, Steamroller Blues, You Gave Me A Mountain, Trouble, Blue Suede Shoes, Long Tall Sally/Whole Lotta Shakin' Goin' On/Your Mama Don't Dance/Flip Flop And Fly/Jailhouse Rock, Love Me Tender, Hound Dog, Fever, What Now My Love, Suspicious Minds, Introductions, Release Me, American Trilogy, Mystery Train/Tiger Man, The First Time Ever I Saw Your Face, How Great Thou Art, Can't Help Falling In Love

September 2, 1973—Dinner Show—Complete
C.C. Rider, I Got A Woman/Amen, Love Me, Steamroller Blues, You Gave Me A Mountain, Trouble, Long Tall Sally/Whole Lotta Shakin' Goin' On/Your Mama Don't Dance/Flip Flop And Fly/Jailhouse Rock, Hound Dog, Love Me Tender, Fever, Bridge Over Troubled Water, Suspicious Minds, Introductions, Celebrity introduction Gloria Loring, My Boy, I Can't Stop Loving You, Teddy Bear/Don't Be Cruel, American Trilogy, The First Time Ever I Saw Your Face, How Great Thou Art, Can't Help Falling In Love

September 2, 1973—Midnight Show—Complete
C.C. Rider, I Got A Woman/Amen, Love Me, Steamroller Blues, You Gave Me A Mountain, Trouble, Long Tall Sally/Whole Lotta Shakin' Goin' On/Your Mama Don't Dance/Flip, Flop And Fly/Hound Dog, Love Me Tender, Fever, Bridge Over Troubled Water (reprise), Suspicious Minds, Introductions, My Boy, I Can't Stop Loving You, American Trilogy, The First Time Ever I Saw Your Face, Mystery Train/Tiger Man, How Great Thou Art, Big Hunk O' Love, Release Me, What Now My Love, Can't Help Falling In Love

September 3, 1973—Dinner Show—Complete
C.C. Rider, I Got A Woman/Amen, Love Me, Steamroller Blues, You Gave Me A Mountain, Guadalajara (partial), Trouble, Long Tall Sally/Whole Lotta Shakin' Goin' On/Your Mama Don't Dance/Flip Flop And Fly/Hound Dog, Love Me Tender, Fever, Bridge Over Troubled Water, Suspicious Minds, Introductions, Farther Along (partial), Release Me, American Trilogy, Mystery Train/Tiger Man, Jailhouse Rock (partial), Teddy Bear/Don't Be Cruel, It's Now Or Never, How Great Thou Art, The First Time Ever I Saw Your Face, Miracle Of The Rosary (partial), Polk Salad Annie, Can't Help Falling In Love

September 3, 1973—Closing Show 10:15 p.m. —Complete
C.C. Rider, I Got A Woman/Amen, Dialogue, Love Me, Steamroller Blues, You Gave Me A Mountain, Trouble, Long Tall Sally/Whole Lotta Shakin' Goin' On/Your Mama Don't Dance/Flip Flop And Fly/Hound Dog, Fever, Dialogue, Love Me Tender, What Now My Love, Elvis sings Bridge Over Troubled Water to the music of Suspicious Minds, Bridge Over Troubled Water, Suspicious Minds, Introductions, My Boy, I Can't Stop Loving You, American Trilogy, Big Hunk O' Love, The First Time Ever I Saw Your Face, Dialogue, Mystery Train/Tiger Man, How Great Thou Art, Help Me Make It Through The Night, Softly As I Leave You, Can't Help Falling In Love

Songs Sung by Elvis During Engagement
American Trilogy, Big Hunk O' Love, Blue Suede Shoes, Bridge Over Troubled Water, Bridge Over Troubled Water (reprise), Bridge Over Troubled Water (to the music of Suspicious Minds), Can't Help Falling In Love, C.C. Rider, Faded Love, Farther Along (partial), Fever, The First Time Ever I Saw Your Face, The First Time Ever I Saw Your Face (false start), Funny How Time Slips Away, Guadalajara (partial), Hawaiian Wedding Song, Heartbreak Hotel, Heartbreak Hotel (false start), Help Me Make It Through The Night, Hound Dog, How Great Thou Art, How Great Thou Art (reprise), I Can't Stop Loving You, I Got A Woman/Amazing Grace/Amen, I Got A Woman/Amen, It's A Matter Of Time, It's Crying Time, It's Over, Jailhouse Rock (partial), Johnny B. Goode, Lady Of Spain (partial), Long Tall Sally/Whole Lotta Shakin' Goin' On/Shake Rattle And Roll/Your Mama Don't Dance/Flip Flop And Fly/Jailhouse Rock/Whole Lotta Shakin' Goin' On, Long Tall Sally/Whole Lotta Shakin' Goin' On/Your Mama Don't Dance/Flip Flop And Fly/Hound Dog, Long Tall Sally/Whole Lotta Shakin' Goin' On/Your Mama Don't Dance/ Flip Flop And Fly/Jailhouse Rock, Long Tall Sally/Whole Lotta Shakin' Goin' On/Your Mama Don't Dance/Flip Flop And Fly/Jailhouse Rock/Hound Dog, Long Tall Sally/Whole Lotta Shakin' Goin' On/Your Mama Don't Dance/Flip Flop And Fly/Jailhouse Rock/Whole Lotta Shakin' Goin On, Long Tall Sally/Whole Lotta Shakin' Goin' On/Your Mama Don't Dance/Flip Flop And Fly/Whole Lotta Shakin' Goin' On, Long Tall Sally/Your Mama Don't' Dance/Flip Flop And Fly/Jailhouse Rock, Long Tall Sally/Your Mama Don't Dance/Flip Flop And Fly/Jailhouse Rock/Hound Dog, Love Me, Love Me Tender, Make The World Go Away, Memphis Tennessee, Miracle Of The Rosary (partial), My Boy, My Boy/Take These Chains From My Heart/My Boy, Mystery Train/ Tiger Man, My Way, Polk Salad Annie,

Raised On Rock, Release Me, Release Me/My Boy/What A Friend We Have In Jesus/My Boy, Softly As I Leave You, Something, Steamroller Blues, Suspicious Minds, Teddy Bear/Don't Be Cruel, Tiger Man (slow version), Trouble, What Now My Love, What Now My Love (false start), You Gave Me A Mountain

The following songs are rumored to have been sung at this engagement but are not verifiable.

Hound Dog/Fever, I Just Can't Help Believin', Lawdy Miss Clawdy, When My Blue Moon Turns To Gold again (partial)

VEGAS SEASON 10 1974, Hilton Hotel

Saturday, January 26, 1974 Through Saturday February 9, 1974—29 Shows—Total attendance—63,800

Jumpsuits Worn at This Engagement—Blue Target Suit, Rainbow Suit, Black Vine Suit, White with turquoise Phoenix Suit, Jewel Suit, Orange Target Suit, White Nail Suit, King Suit, Tiger Suit, White Stone Eagle suit, Orange Starburst suit

Show Members—Musicians: Lead Guitar—James Burton, Rhythm Guitar—John Wilkinson, Acoustic Guitar and Backup Vocals—Charlie Hodge, Bass—Duke Bardwell, Piano—Glen D. Hardin, Drums—Ronnie Tutt, Backup Singers: Sweet Inspirations: Myrna Smith, Sylvia Shemwell, Estelle Brown, J.D. Sumner & The Stamps Quartet: J.D. Sumner, Bill Baize, Ed Enoch, Dave Rowland, Voice: Sherrill Nielsen, Tim Baty, Donnie Sumner, High Voice Singer—Kathy Westmoreland, Comedian—Jackie Kahane, Orchestra —Joe Guercio

January 26, 1974—Opening Show 8:15 p.m.—Complete
C.C. Rider, I Got A Woman/Amen, Love Me, Let Me Be There, You've Lost The Lovin' Feeling, Sweet Caroline, Love Me Tender, Long Tall Sally/Whole Lotta Shakin' Goin' On/Your Mama Don't Dance/Flip Flop And Fly/Jailhouse Rock/Hound Dog, Fever, Polk Salad Annie, Elvis introduces the group Voice who then perform Killing Me Softly,
Spanish Eyes duet with Sherrill Nielsen, Suspicious Minds, Introductions, Celebrity introductions Glen Campbell, I Can't Stop Loving You, Help Me, American Trilogy, Big Hunk O' Love, Can't Help Falling In Love

January 27, 1974—Dinner Show—Complete
C.C. Rider, I Got A Woman/Amen, My Baby Left Me, You've Lost That Lovin' Feeling, Sweet Caroline, Love Me Tender, Long Tall Sally/Whole Lotta Shakin' Goin' On/Your Mama Don't Dance/Shake Rattle And Roll/Jailhouse Rock/Hound Dog, Fever, Polk Salad Annie, Killing Me Softly (Voice), Spanish Eyes duet with Sherrill Nielson, Suspicious Minds, Introductions, I Can't Stop Loving You, Help Me, American Trilogy, Let Me Be There, Can't Help Falling In Love

January 27, 1974—Midnight Show—Complete
CC Rider, I Got A Woman/Amen, Love Me, Let Me Be There, You've Lost That Lovin' Feeling, Sweet Caroline, Love Me Tender, Long Tall Sally/Whole Lotta Shakin' Goin' On/Your Mama Don't Dance/Flip Flop And Fly/Jailhouse Rock/Hound Dog, Fever, Polk Salad Annie, Killing Me Softly (Voice), Spanish Eyes duet with Sherrill Nielson, Suspicious Minds, Introductions, Celebrity introductions Marty Allen, Charlie Rich, The Most Beautiful Girl In The World (partial), I Can't Stop Loving You, Help Me, American Trilogy, Let Me Be There, Can't Help Falling In Love

January 28, 1974—Dinner Show—Complete
C.C. Rider, I Got A Woman/Amen, Love Me, My Baby Left Me, You've Lost That Lovin' Feeling, Sweet Caroline, Love Me Tender, Tryin' To Get To You, Long Tall Sally/Whole Lotta Shakin' Goin' On/Your Mama Don't Dance/Flip Flop And Fly/Jailhouse Rock/Hound Dog, Fever, Polk Salad Annie, Killing Me Softly (Voice), Spanish Eyes duet with Sherrill Nielson, Why Me Lord (J. D. Sumner & The Stamps Quartet with Elvis singing harmony), Suspicious Minds, Introductions, I Can't Stop Loving You, Help Me, American Trilogy, Let Me Be There (reprise), Can't Help Falling In Love

January 28, 1974—Midnight Show—Complete
C.C. Rider, I Got A Woman/Amen, Love Me, My Baby Left Me, Tryin' To Get To You, You've Lost That Lovin' Feeling, Sweet Caroline, Love Me Tender, Long Tall Sally/Whole Lotta Shakin' Goin' On/Your Mama Don't Dance/Flip Flop And Fly/Jailhouse Rock/Hound Dog, Fever, Polk Salad Annie, Killing Me Softly (Voice), Spanish Eyes duet with Sherrill Nielson, Suspicious Minds, Introductions, I Can't Stop Loving You, Help Me, American Trilogy, Let Me Be There, Can't Help Falling In Love

January 29, 1974—Dinner Show—Complete
C.C. Rider, I Got A Woman/Amen, Love Me, My Baby Left Me, Tryin' To Get To You, You've Lost That Lovin' Feeling, Sweet Caroline, Love Me Tender, Long Tall Sally/Whole Lotta Shakin' Goin' On/Your Mama Don't Dance/Flip Flop & Fly/Jailhouse Rock/Hound Dog, Fever, Polk Salad Annie, Killing Me Softly (Voice), Spanish Eyes duet with Sherrill Nielson, Suspicious Minds, Introductions, I Can't Stop Loving You, Help Me, American Trilogy, Let Me Be There (reprise), Can't Help Falling In Love

January 29, 1974—Midnight Show—Complete
C.C. Rider, I Got A Woman/Amen, Love Me, My Baby Left Me, Tryin' To Get To You, You've Lost That Lovin' Feeling, Love Me Tender, Long Tall Sally/Whole Shakin' Goin' On/Your Mama Don't Dance/Flip Flop And Fly/Jailhouse Rock/Hound Dog, Fever, Polk Salad Annie, Spanish Eyes due with Sherrill Nielson, Suspicious Minds, Introductions, I Can't Stop Loving You, Help Me, American Trilogy, Let Me Be There, Can't Help Falling In Love

January 30, 1974—Dinner Show—Complete
C.C. Rider, I Got A Woman/Amen, Love Me, Tryin' To Get To You, You've Lost That Lovin' Feeling, Love Me Tender, Long Tall Sally/Whole Lotta Shakin' Goin' On/Your Mama Don't Dance/Flip Flop And Fly/Jailhouse Rock/Hound Dog, Fever, Polk Salad Annie, Spanish Eyes duet with Sherrill Nielson, Killing Me Softly (Voice), Why Me Lord (J.D. Sumner & The Stamps Quartet with Elvis singing harmony), Suspicious Minds, Introductions, I Can't Stop Loving You, Help Me, American Trilogy, Let Me Be There, Can't Help Falling In Love

January 30, 1974—Midnight Show—Complete
C.C. Rider, I Got A Woman/Amen, Love Me, Tryin' To Get To You, You've Lost That Lovin' Feeling, Love Me Tender, Blue Suede Shoes, Hound Dog, Fever, Polk Salad Annie, Killing Me Softly (Voice), Spanish Eyes duet with Sherrill Nielson, Suspicious Minds, Introductions, I Can't Stop Loving You, Help Me, American Trilogy, Let Me Be There, Can't Help Falling In Love

January 31, 1974—Dinner Show—Complete
C.C. Rider, I Got A Woman/Amen, Love Me, Tryin' To Get To You, Sweet Caroline, Love Me Tender, Long Tall Sally/Whole Lotta Shakin' Goin' On/Jailhouse Rock, Fever, Polk Salad Annie, Killing Me Softly (Voice), Spanish Eyes duet with Sherrill Nielson, Why Me Lord (J. D. Sumner & The Stamps Quartet with Elvis singing harmony), Suspicious Minds, Introductions, I

Can't Stop Loving You, Help Me, American Trilogy, Let Me Be There, Can't Help Falling In Love

January 31, 1974—Midnight Show—Complete
C.C. Rider, I Got A Woman/Amen, Love Me, Tryin' To Get To You, Sweet Caroline, Love Me Tender, Long Tall Sally/Whole Lotta Shakin' Goin' On/Your Mama Don't Dance/Flip Flop And Fly/Jailhouse Rock/Hound Dog, Fever, Polk Salad Annie, Killing Me Softly (Voice), Introductions, Spanish Eyes duet with Sherrill Nielson, Suspicious Minds, Introductions, Blueberry Hill/I Can't Stop Loving You, Help Me, American Trilogy, Let Me Be There, Can't Help Falling In Love

February 1, 1974—Dinner Show—Complete
C.C. Rider, I Got A Woman/Amen, Love Me, Tryin' To Get To You, Sweet Caroline, Love Me Tender, Long Tall Sally/Whole Lotta Shakin' Goin' On/Your Mama Don't Dance/Flip Flop And Fly/Jailhouse Rock/Hound Dog, Fever, Polk Salad Annie, Dialogue, Killing Me Softly (Voice), Spanish Eyes duet with Sherrill Nielson, Why Me Lord (J. D. Sumner & The Stamps Quartet with Elvis singing harmony), Suspicious Minds, Introductions, I Can't Stop Loving You, Help Me, American Trilogy, Dialogue, Let Me Be There (reprise), Can't Help Falling In Love

February 1, 1974—Midnight Show—Complete
C.C. Rider, I Got A Woman/Amen, Love Me, Tryin' To Get To You, Sweet Caroline, Love Me Tender, Long Tall Sally/Whole Lotta Shakin' Goin' On/Your Mama Don't Dance/Flip Flop And Fly/Jailhouse Rock/Hound Dog, Fever, Polk Salad Annie, Killing Me Softly (Voice), Spanish Eyes duet with Sherrill Nielson, Why Me Lord (J. D. Sumner & The Stamps Quartet with Elvis singing harmony), Suspicious Minds, Introductions, I Can't Stop Loving You, Help Me, American Trilogy, Let Me Be There, The First Time Ever I Saw Your Face, Can't Help Falling In Love

February 2, 1974—Dinner Show—Complete
C.C. Rider, I Got A Woman/Amen, Love Me, Tryin' To Get To You, Sweet Caroline, Love Me Tender, Johnny B. Goode, Hound Dog, Fever, Polk Salad Annie, Dialogue, Killing Me Softly (Voice), Spanish Eye duet with Sherrill Nielson, Why Me Lord (J. D. Sumner & The Stamps Quartet with Elvis singing harmony), Suspicious Minds, Introductions, Celebrity Introductions: Johnny Ray, I Can't Stop Loving You, Help Me, American Trilogy, Let Me Be There, Can't Help Falling In Love

February 2, 1974—Midnight Show—Complete
C.C. Rider, I Got A Woman/Amen, Love Me, Tryin' To Get To You, Sweet Caroline, Love Me Tender, Johnny B. Goode, Hound Dog, Fever, Polk Salad Annie, Killing Me Softly (Voice), Spanish Eyes duet with Sherrill Nielson, Why Me Lord (J. D. Sumner & The Stamps Quartet with Elvis singing harmony), Suspicious Minds, Introductions, I Can't Stop Loving You, Help Me, American Trilogy, Let Me Be There (reprise), Can't Help Falling In Love

February 3, 1974—Dinner Show—Complete
C.C. Rider, I Got A Woman/Amen, Love Me, Tryin' To Get To You, Sweet Caroline, Love Me Tender, Johnny B. Goode, Hound Dog, Fever, Polk Salad Annie, Killing Me Softly (Voice), Spanish Eyes duet with Sherrill Nielson, Why Me Lord (J. D. Sumner & The Stamps Quartet with Elvis singing harmony), Suspicious Minds, Introductions, I Can't Stop Loving You, Help Me, American Trilogy, Let Me Be There, Can't Help Falling In Love

February 3, 1974—Midnight Show—Complete
C.C. Rider, I Got A Woman/Amen, Love Me, Tryin' To Get To You, Sweet Caroline, Love Me Tender, Johnny B. Goode, Hound Dog, Fever, Polk Salad Annie, Killing Me Softly (Voice), Spanish Eyes duet with Sherrill Nielson, Why Me Lord (J. D. Sumner & The Stamps Quartet with Elvis singing harmony), Suspicious Minds, Introductions, I Can't Stop Loving You, Help Me, American Trilogy, Let Me Be There, The First Time Ever I Saw Your Face, Can't Help Falling In Love

February 4, 1974—Dinner Show—Complete
C.C. Rider, I Got A Woman/Amen, Love Me, Tryin' To Get To You, Sweet Caroline, Love Me Tender, Johnny B. Goode, Hound Dog, Fever, Polk Salad Annie, Killing Me Softly (Voice), Spanish Eyes duet with Sherrill Nielson, Why Me Lord (J. D. Sumner & The Stamps Quartet with Elvis singing harmony), Suspicious Minds, Introductions, I Can't Stop Loving You, Help Me, American Trilogy, Let Me Be There, Can't Help Falling In Love

February 4, 1974—Midnight Show—Complete
C.C. Rider, I Got A Woman/Amen, Love Me, Tryin' To Get To You, Sweet Caroline, Love Me Tender, Johnny B. Goode, Hound Dog, Fever, Polk Salad Annie, Killing Me Softly (Voice), Spanish Eyes duet with Sherrill Nielson, Why Me Lord (J. D. Sumner & The Stamps Quartet with Elvis singing harmony), Suspicious Minds, Introductions, I Can't Stop Loving You, Help Me, American Trilogy, Let Me Be There (reprise), Can't Help Falling In Love

February 5, 1974—Dinner Show—Complete
C.C. Rider, I Got A Woman/Amen, Love Me, Tryin' To Get To You, Sweet Caroline, Love Me Tender, Johnny B. Goode, Hound Dog, Fever, Polk Salad Annie, Killing Me Softly (Voice), Spanish Eyes duet with Sherrill Nielson, Why Me Lord (J. D. Sumner & The Stamps Quartet with Elvis singing harmony), Suspicious Minds, Introductions, I Can't Stop Loving You, Help Me, American Trilogy, Let Me Be There (reprise), Can't Help Falling In Love

February 5, 1974—Midnight Show—Complete
C.C. Rider, I Got A Woman/Amen, Love Me, Tryin' To Get To You, Sweet Caroline, Love Me Tender, Johnny B. Goode, Hound Dog, Fever, Polk Salad Annie, Killing Me Softly (Voice), Spanish Eyes duet with Sherrill Nielson, Why Me Lord (J. D. Sumner & The Stamps Quartet with Elvis singing harmony), Suspicious Minds (false start), Introductions, Release Me, Help Me, American Trilogy, Let Me Be There (reprise), Can't Help Falling In Love

February 6, 1974—Dinner Show—Complete
C.C. Rider, I Got A Woman/Amen, Love Me, Tryin' To Get To You, Sweet Caroline, Love Me Tender, Johnny B. Goode, Hound Dog, Fever, Polk Salad Annie, Killing Me Softly (Voice), Spanish Eyes duet with Sherrill Nielson, Why Me Lord (J. D. Sumner & The Stamps Quartet with Elvis singing harmony), Suspicious Minds, Introductions, Release Me, Help Me, American Trilogy, Let Me Be There, Can't Help Falling In Love

February 6, 1974—Midnight Show—Complete
C.C. Rider, I Got A Woman/Amen, Love Me, Tryin' To Get To You, Love Me Tender, Sweet Caroline, Johnny B. Goode, Hound Dog, Fever, Polk Salad Annie, Killing Me Softly (Voice), Spanish Eyes duet with Sherrill Nielson, Why Me Lord (J. D. Sumner & The Stamps Quartet with Elvis singing harmony), Suspicious Minds, Introductions, Celebrity introductions The Checkmates and Nancy Sinatra, Blueberry Hill/I Can't Stop Loving You, Help Me, American Trilogy, Let Me Be There, Can't Help Falling In Love

February 7, 1974—Dinner Show—Complete
C.C. Rider, I Got A Woman/Amen, Love Me, Tryin' To Get To You, Sweet Caroline, Love Me Tender, Johnny B. Goode, Hound Dog, Fever, Polk Salad Annie, Killing Me Softly (Voice), Spanish Eyes duet

with Sherrill Nielson, Why Me Lord (J. D. Sumner & The Stamps Quartet with Elvis singing harmony), Suspicious Minds, Introductions, I Can't Stop Loving You, Help Me, American Trilogy, Let Me Be There, Can't Help Falling In Love

February 7, 1974—Midnight Show—Complete
C.C. Rider, I Got A Woman/Amen, Dialogue, Love Me, Tryin' To Get To You, Sweet Caroline, Love Me Tender, Johnny B. Goode, Hound Dog, Fever, Polk Salad Annie, Killing Me Softly (Voice), Spanish Eyes duet with Sherrill Nielson, Suspicious Minds, Introductions, I Can't Stop Loving You, Blueberry Hill (partial), Help Me, American Trilogy, Let Me Be There, Can't Help Falling In Love

February 8, 1974—Dinner Show—Complete
C.C. Rider, I Got A Woman/Amen, Love Me, Tryin' To Get To You, Sweet Caroline, Love Me Tender, Johnny B. Goode, Hound Dog, Fever, Polk Salad Annie, Killing Me Softly (Voice), Spanish Eyes duet with Sherrill Nielson, Why Me Lord (J. D. Sumner & The Stamps Quartet with Elvis singing harmony), Suspicious Minds, Introductions, I Can't Stop Loving You (false start), Help Me, American Trilogy, Let Me Be There (reprise), The First Time Ever I Saw Your Face, Can't Help Falling In Love

February 8, 1974—Midnight Show—Complete
C.C. Rider, I Got A Woman/Amen, Love Me, Tryin' To Get To You, Sweet Caroline, Love Me Tender, Johnny B. Goode, Hound Dog (reprise), Fever, Polk Salad Annie, Killing Me Softly (Voice), Spanish Eyes duet with Sherrill Nielson, Why Me Lord (J. D. Sumner & The Stamps Quartet with Elvis singing harmony), Suspicious Minds (false start), Introductions, Celebrity introductions: Michael Caine, I Can't Stop Loving You, Blueberry Hill/I Can't Stop Loving You, Help Me, American Trilogy, Let Me Be There (reprise), Can't Help Falling In Love

February 9, 1974—Dinner Show—Complete
C.C. Rider, When My Blue Moon Turns To Gold Again (partial), I Got A Woman/Amen, Marguerita (partial), Love Me, Tryin' To Get To You, Sweet Caroline, Love Me Tender, Fever, Johnny B. Goode, Hound Dog, Polk Salad Annie, Killing Me Softly (Voice), Spanish Eyes duets with Sherrill Nielson, Why Me Lord (J. D. Sumner & The Stamps Quartet with Elvis singing harmony), Suspicious Minds, Introductions, I Can't Stop Loving You, Help Me, American Trilogy, Let Me Be There (reprise), Can't Help Falling In Love

February 9, 1974—Closing Night—Complete
C.C. Rider, I Got A Woman/Amen, Love Me, Tryin' To Get To You, Sweet Caroline, Love Me Tender, Johnny B. Goode, Hound Dog, Fever, Polk Salad Annie, Killing Me Softly (Voice), Spanish Eyes duet with Sherrill Nielson, Why Me Lord (J. D. Sumner & The Stamps Quartet with Elvis singing harmony), Suspicious Minds, Introductions, Celebrity introductions Bill Cosby, Mark Lindsay, Rich Little, Blueberry Hill/ I Can't Stop Loving You, Help Me, American Trilogy, Let Me Be There, Can't Help Falling In Love

Songs Sung by Elvis During Engagement
American Trilogy, Big Hunk O' Love, Blueberry Hill (partial), Blueberry Hill/I Can't Stop Loving You, Blue Suede Shoes, Can't Help Falling In Love, C.C. Rider, Fever, The First Time Ever I Saw Your Face, Help Me, Hound Dog, Hound Dog (reprise), I Can't Stop Loving You, I Can't Stop Loving You (false start), I Got A Woman/ Amen, Johnny B. Goode, Killing Me Softly (Voice), Let Me Be There, Let Me Be There (reprise), Long Tall Sally/Whole Lotta Shakin' Goin' On/Jailhouse Rock, Long Tall Sally/Whole Lotta Shakin' Goin' On/Your Mama Don't Dance/ Flip Flop And Fly/Jailhouse Rock/Hound Dog, Long Tall Sally/Whole Lotta Shakin' Goin' On/ Your Mama Don't Dance/Shake Rattle And Roll/Jailhouse Rock/Hound Dog, Love Me, Love Me Tender, Marguerita (partial), The Most Beautiful Girl In The World (partial), My Baby Left Me, Polk Salad Annie, Release Me, Spanish Eyes duet with Sherrill Nielsen, Suspicious Minds, Suspicious Minds (false start), Sweet Caroline, Tryin' To Get To You, When My Blue Moon Turns To Gold Again (partial), Why Me Lord (J. D. Sumner & The Stamps Quartet with Elvis singing harmony), You've Lost The Lovin' Feeling

The following songs are rumored to have been sung at this engagement but are not verifiable.

The Lord's Prayer (partial), Long Tall Sally/Whole Lotta Shakin' Goin' On/Your Mama Don't Dance/Shake Rattle & Roll/Jailhouse Rock

VEGAS SEASON 11 1974, Hilton Hotel

Monday, August 19, 1974 through Monday, September 2, 1974—27 shows—Elvis canceled two additional shows due to illness—August 26 dinner and midnight shows—Total attendance—59,400

Jumpsuits Worn at This Engagement—Peacock Suit, Embroidered Eagle Suit, Rainbow Suit, Aztec Indian Suit, White with red Phoenix Suit, White with turquoise Phoenix Suit, North Beach Leather various two-piece suits some featuring paintings, some featuring studs, some plain with fancy stitching (these suits had no official name but in recent times fans have referred to the various North Beach suits as The Matador Suit, The Western Suit, The Rhinestone Suit and the Mermaid Suit)

Show Members—Musicians: Lead Guitar—James Burton, Rhythm Guitar—John Wilkinson, Acoustic Guitar and Backup Vocals—Charlie Hodge, Bass—Duke Bardwell, Piano—Glen D. Hardin, Drums—Ronnie Tutt, Backup Singers: Sweet Inspirations: Myrna Smith, Sylvia Shemwell, Estelle Brown, J.D. Sumner & The Stamps Quartet: J. D. Sumner, Bill Baize, Ed Enoch, Ed Hill, Voice: Sherrill Nielsen, Tim Baty, Donnie Sumner, High Voice Singer—Kathy Westmoreland, Comedian—Jackie Kahane, Orchestra—Joe Guercio

August 19, 1974—Opening Night 8:15 P.M.—Complete
Big Boss Man, Proud Mary, Down In The Alley, Good Time Charlie's Got The Blues, Never Been To Spain, It's Midnight, If You Talk In Your Sleep, I'm Leavin', Let Me Be There (reprise), Softly As I Leave You, If You Love Me Let Me Know, Love Me Tender, Polk Salad Annie, Introductions and Linda Thompson, Promised Land, Celebrity introduction Telly Savalas, My Baby Left Me, Bridge Over Troubled Water, Fever, Hound Dog, Can't Help Falling In Love

August 20, 1974—Dinner Show—Complete
C.C. Rider, I Got A Woman/Amen, Love Me, If You Love Me Let Me Know, It's Midnight, Proud Mary, Tryin' To Get To You, Big Boss Man, Fever, Promised Land, Love Me Tender, All Shook Up, I'm Leavin', Softly As I Leave You, Hound Dog, You Gave Me A Mountain, Polk Salad Annie, Introductions and Linda Thompson, If You Talk In Your Sleep, Why Me Lord (J. D. Sumner & The Stamps Quartet with Elvis singing harmony), Teddy Bear/Don't Be Cruel, Hawaiian Wedding Song, Let Me Be There, Can't Help Falling In Love

August 20, 1974—Midnight Show—Complete
C.C. Rider, I Got A Woman/Amen, Love Me, If You Love Me Let Me Know, It's Midnight, Proud Mary, Tryin' To Get To You, Big Boss Man, Fever, Promised Land, Love Me Tender, All Shook Up, I'm Leavin', Softly As I Leave You, Hound Dog,

You Gave Me A Mountain, Polk Salad Annie, Introductions and Linda Thompson, If You Talk In Your Sleep, Why Me Lord (J. D. Sumner & The Stamps Quartet with Elvis singing harmony), Teddy Bear/Don't Be Cruel, Hawaiian Wedding Song, Let Me Be There, Can't Help Falling In Love

August 21, 1974—Dinner Show—Complete
C.C. Rider, I Got A Woman/Amen, Love Me, If You Love Me Let Me Know, It's Midnight, Big Boss Man, Fever, Tryin' To Get To You, Love Me Tender, All Shook Up, I'm Leavin', Softly As I Leave You, Hound Dog, You Gave Me A Mountain, Polk Salad Annie, Introductions and Linda Thompson, Celebrity introductions: Jackie Wilson, Higher And Higher (partial), If You Talk In Your Sleep, Why Me Lord (J. D. Sumner & The Stamps Quartet with Elvis singing harmony), Teddy Bear/Don't Be Cruel, Heartbreak Hotel, Bridge Over Troubled Water, Hawaiian Wedding Song, Let Me Be There, Can't Help Falling In Love

August 21, 1974—Midnight Show—Complete
C.C. Rider, I Got A Woman/Amen/I Got A Woman, Love Me, If You Love Me Let Me Know, It's Midnight, Big Boss Man, Fever, Love Me Tender, All Shook Up, I'm Leavin', Softly As I Leave You, Hound Dog, You Gave Me A Mountain, Polk Salad Annie, Introductions, Dialogue, Take These Chains From My Heart (partial), If You Talk In Your Sleep, Why Me Lord (J. D. Sumner & The Stamps Quartet with Elvis singing harmony), Teddy Bear/Don't Be Cruel, Hawaiian Wedding Song, The First Time Ever I Saw Your Face (partial), Let Me Be There, Can't Help Falling In Love

August 22, 1974—Dinner Show—Complete
C.C. Rider, I Got A Woman/Amen, Love Me, If You Love Me Let Me Know, It's Midnight, Big Boss Man, Fever, Love Me Tender, All Shook Up, I'm Leavin', Softly As I Leave You, Hound Dog, You Gave Me A Mountain, Polk Salad Annie, Introductions, If You Talk In Your Sleep, Why Me Lord (J. D. Sumner & The Stamps Quartet with Elvis singing harmony), Teddy Bear/Don't Be Cruel, Heartbreak Hotel, Hawaiian Wedding Song, Let Me Be There, Can't Help Falling In Love

August 22, 1974—Midnight Show—Complete
C.C. Rider, I Got A Woman/Amen, Love Me, If You Love Me Let Me Know, It's Midnight, Big Boss Man, Fever, Love Me Tender, All Shook Up, I'm Leavin', Softly As I Leave You, Hound Dog, You Gave Me A Mountain, Dialogue, Celebrity introduction John O'Grady, Suspicious Minds, Introductions, If You Talk In Your Sleep, Why Me Lord (J. D. Sumner & The Stamps Quartet with Elvis singing harmony), Teddy Bear/Don't Be Cruel, Help Me, The First Time Ever I Saw Your Face, Let Me Be There, Can't Help Falling In Love

August 23, 1974—Dinner Show—Complete
C.C. Rider, I Got A Woman/Amen, Love Me, If You Love Me Let Me Know, It's Midnight, Big Boss Man, Fever, Love Me Tender, All Shook Up, The Wonder Of You, I'm Leavin', Softly As I Leave You, Hound Dog, You Gave Me A Mountain (reprise), Polk Salad Annie, Introductions, If You Talk In Your Sleep, Why Me Lord (J. D. Sumner & The Stamps Quartet with Elvis singing harmony), Teddy Bear/Don't Be Cruel, Hawaiian Wedding Song, Let Me Be There, Can't Help Falling In Love

August 23, 1974—Midnight Show—Complete
C.C. Rider, I Got A Woman/Amen/I Got A Woman, Dialogue: Elvis tells funky angel story, Love Me, If You Love Me Let Me Know, It's Midnight, Big Boss Man, All Shook Up, The Wonder Of You, I'm Leavin', Softly As I Leave You, Hound Dog, You Gave Me A Mountain, Polk Salad Annie, Introductions, If You Talk In Your Sleep, Teddy Bear/Don't Be Cruel, Elvis sings Happy Birthday to Kathy Westmoreland, Hawaiian Wedding Song duet with Kathy Westmoreland, Let Me Be There, Dialogue: Elvis talks about his ring, Can't Help Falling In Love

August 24, 1974—Dinner Show—Complete
C.C. Rider, Dialogue, I Got A Woman/Amen, Love Me, If You Love Me Let Me Know, It's Midnight, Big Boss Man, Fever, Love Me Tender, All Shook Up, The Wonder Of You, Happy Birthday to Mario (Hilton employee), I'm Leavin', Softly As I Leave You, Hound Dog, You Gave Me A Mountain, Polk Salad Annie, Introductions, If You Talk In Your Sleep, Why Me Lord, Teddy Bear/Don't Be Cruel, Hawaiian Wedding Song, O Sole Mio/It's Now Or Never, Let Me Be There (reprise), Can't Help Falling In Love

August 24, 1974—Midnight Show—Complete
C.C. Rider, I Got A Woman/Amen, Love Me (kidding, sings Love My Daughter), If You Love Me Let Me Know, It's Midnight, Big Boss Man, Fever, Love Me Tender, All Shook Up, The Wonder Of You, I'm Leavin', Softly As I Leave You, Spanish Eyes duet with Sherrill Nielson, Hound Dog, You Gave Me A Mountain, Polk Salad Annie, Introductions, If You Talk In Your Sleep, Why Me Lord (J. D. Sumner & The Stamps Quartet with Elvis singing harmony), Teddy Bear/Don't Be Cruel, Hawaiian Wedding Song, Bridge Over Troubled Water, Let Me Be There, Can't Help Falling In Love

August 25, 1974—Dinner Show—Complete
C.C. Rider, I Got A Woman/Amen, Dialogue, Love Me, If You Love Me Let Me Know, It's Midnight, Big Boss Man, Fever, Love Me Tender, All Shook Up, Dialogue, The Wonder Of You, I'm Leavin', Dialogue, Softly As I Leave You, Dialogue, Hound Dog, You Gave Me A Mountain, Polk Salad Annie, Dialogue, Introductions, If You Talk In Your Sleep, Why Me Lord (J. D. Sumner & The Stamps Quartet with Elvis singing harmony), Dialogue, Teddy Bear/Don't Be Cruel, Let Me Be There, Can't Help Falling In Love

August 25, 1974—Midnight Show—Complete
C.C. Rider, I Got A Woman/Amen, Love Me, If You Love Me Let Me Know, It's Midnight, Big Boss Man, Fever, Love Me Tender, All Shook Up, The Wonder Of You, I'm Leavin', Softly As I Leave You, Hound Dog, You Gave Me A Mountain, Polk Salad Annie, Introductions, Guadalajara (partial), Celebrity introduction Sammy Davis Jr., If You Talk In Your Sleep, Why Me Lord (J. D. Sumner & The Stamps Quartet with Elvis singing harmony), Teddy Bear/Don't Be Cruel, It's Now Or Never, Hawaiian Wedding Song, Let Me Be There (reprise), Sweet Caroline, Dialogue, Can't Help Falling In Love

August 26, 1974—Dinner Show—Canceled Due to Illness

August 26, 1974—Midnight Show—Canceled Due to Illness

August 27, 1974—Dinner Show—Complete
C.C. Rider, I Got A Woman/Amen, Dialogue, Love Me (false start), If You Love Me Let Me Know, It's Midnight, Big Boss Man, Fever, Love Me Tender, All Shook Up, I'm Leavin', Softly As I Leave You, Dialogue, Hound Dog, You Gave Me A Mountain, Polk Salad Annie, Introductions, If You Talk In Your Sleep, Why Me Lord (J. D. Sumner & The Stamps Quartet with Elvis singing harmony), Dialogue, Teddy Bear/Don't Be Cruel, It's Now Or Never, Hawaiian Wedding Song, Let Me Be There, Dialogue, Can't Help Falling In Love

August 27, 1974—Midnight Show—Complete
C.C. Rider, I Got A Woman/Amen, Love Me (false start), If You Love Me Let Me Know, It's Midnight, Big Boss Man, Fever, Love Me Tender, All Shook Up, The Wonder Of You, Softly As I Leave You, Hound Dog, You Gave Me A Mountain, American Trilogy, Introductions, We Shall Overcome (partial), If You Talk In Your Sleep, Celebrity introductions Red West and Kang Rhee, Why Me Lord (J. D. Sumner & The Stamps Quartet with Elvis singing harmony), Dialogue, Teddy Bear/Don't Be Cruel, Hawaiian Wedding Song, Let Me Be There, Dialogue, It's Now Or Never, Can't Help Falling In Love

August 28, 1974—Dinner Show—Complete
C.C. Rider, I Got A Woman/Amen, Love Me, If You Love Me Let Me Know, It's Midnight, Big Boss Man, Fever, Love Me Tender, All Shook Up, I'm Leavin', Softly As I Leave You, Hound Dog, American Trilogy, Introductions, If You Talk In Your Sleep, My Boy, How Great Thou Art, Let Me Be There, Hawaiian Wedding Song, Can't Help Falling In Love

August 28, 1974—Midnight Show—Complete
C.C. Rider, I Got A Woman/Amen, Love Me, If You Love Me Let Me Know, It's Midnight, Big Boss Man, Fever, Love Me Tender, All Shook Up, I'm Leavin', Softly As I Leave You, Hound Dog, American Trilogy, Introductions, Celebrity introduction Tom Jones, If You Talk In Your Sleep, Karate Dialogue, Why Me Lord (J. D. Sumner & The Stamps Quartet with Elvis singing harmony), Teddy Bear/Don't Be Cruel, How Great Thou Art, Let Me Be There, Hawaiian Wedding Song, Can't Help Falling In Love

August 29, 1974—Dinner Show—Complete
C.C. Rider, I Got A Woman/Amen, Dialogue, Love Me, If You Love Me Let Me Know, It's Midnight, Big Boss Man, Fever, Love Me Tender, All Shook Up, The Wonder Of You, Softly As I Leave You, Hound Dog, American Trilogy, Introductions, If You Talk In Your Sleep, Dialogue, Why Me Lord (J. D. Sumner & The Stamps Quartet with Elvis singing harmony), Teddy Bear/Don't Be Cruel, How Great Thou Art, Let Me Be There, Dialogue, Early Morning Rain, Hawaiian Wedding Song, Dialogue, Can't Help Falling In Love

August 29, 1974—Midnight Show—Complete
C.C. Rider, I Got A Woman/Amen, Love Me, If You Love Me Let Me Know, It's Midnight, Big Boss Man, Fever, Love Me Tender, All Shook Up, Until It's Time For You To Go, Softly As I Leave You, Hound Dog, American Trilogy, Suspicious Minds, Introductions, Celebrity Introductions Sheila Ryan and Vernon Presley, If You Talk In Your Sleep, Karate dialogue introducing Kang Rhee, Why Me Lord (J. D. Sumner & The Stamps Quartet with Elvis singing harmony), Teddy Bear/Don't Be Cruel, How Great Thou Art, Let Me Be There, It's Now Or Never, Hawaiian Wedding Song, Drug dialogue (Note: Elvis would expand on this subject throughout the remainder of this engagement climaxing closing night), Can't Help Falling In Love

August 30, 1974—Dinner Show—Complete
C.C. Rider, I Got A Woman/Amen, Love Me, If You Love Me Let Me Know, It's Midnight, Big Boss Man, Fever, All Shook Up/Softly As I Leave You, Dialogue, Hound Dog, American Trilogy, Introductions, If You Talk In Your Sleep, Dialogue, Until It's Time For You To Go, How Great Thou Art, Let Me Be There, Hawaiian Wedding Song, Can't Help Falling In Love

August 30, 1974—Midnight Show—Complete
C.C. Rider, Dialogue, I Got A Woman/Amen, Dialogue, Love Me, If You Love Me Let Me Know, It's Midnight, Big Boss Man, Fever, All Shook Up, Dialogue, Softly As I Leave You, Hound Dog, Introductions, Hound Dog, American Trilogy, Dialogue, Celebrity introduction Dean Nichopoulos, Suspicious Minds, Karate demonstration, If You Talk In Your Sleep, Karate dialogue with introduction of Kang Rhee, Help Me, Let Me Be There (reprise), Dialogue, Introduction of Lisa Marie, How Great Thou Art (reprise), Dialogue, Hawaiian Wedding Song, Dialogue, You Gave Me A Mountain, Can't Help Falling In Love

August 31, 1974—Dinner Show—Complete
C.C. Rider, I Got A Woman/Amen, Love Me, If You Love Me Let Me Know, It's Midnight, Big Boss Man, Fever, All Shook Up, Softly As I Leave You, Hound Dog, American Trilogy, Teddy Bear/Don't Be Cruel, Introductions, If You Talk In Your Sleep, Dialogue, Until It's Time For You To Go, Let Me Be There, Hawaiian Wedding Song, Heartbreak Hotel, How Great Thou Art, Can't Help Falling In Love

August 31, 1974—Midnight Show—Complete
C.C. Rider, I Got A Woman/Amen/I Got A Woman, Dialogue, Love Me, Elvis shows gift for Lisa Marie, If You Love Me Let Me Know, Dialogue), It's Midnight, Big Boss Man, Fever, All Shook Up, Dialogue: Elvis talks about being sick and missing shows, Softly As I Leave You, Hound Dog, American Trilogy, Bridge Over Troubled Water, Introductions, Karate dialogue, If You Talk In Your Sleep, Karate dialogue, Why Me Lord (J. D. Sumner & The Stamps Quartet with Elvis singing harmony), Let Me Be There (reprise), Dialogue, Hawaiian Wedding Song, How Great Thou Art, Can't Help Falling In Love

September 1, 1974—Dinner Show—Complete
C.C. Rider, I Got A Woman/Amen, Dialogue: Elvis talks about his G.I. Blues film, Love Me, If You Love Me Let Me Know, It's Midnight, Big Boss Man, Fever, I'm Leavin', Softly As I Leave You, Hound Dog, Polk Salad Annie, Introductions, If You Talk In Your Sleep, Karate dialogue, Help Me, Why Me Lord (J. D. Sumner & The Stamps Quartet with Elvis singing harmony), Let Me Be There, Bridge Over Troubled Water, Hawaiian Wedding Song, Can't Help Falling In Love

September 1, 1974—Midnight Show—Complete
C.C. Rider, I Got A Woman/Amen, Dialogue, Until It's Time For You To Go, If You Love Me Let Me Know, It's Midnight, Big Boss Man, Fever, I'm Leavin', Softly As I Leave You, American Trilogy, It's Now Or Never, Introductions, Celebrity introductions Ed Parker, David Stanley and Sonny West, If You Talk In Your Sleep, Why Me Lord (J. D. Sumner & The Stamps Quartet with Elvis singing harmony), Let Me Be There, Bridge Over Troubled Water, Hawaiian Wedding Song, Can't Help Falling In Love

September 2, 1974—Dinner Show—Complete
C.C. Rider, I Got A Woman/Amen, Until It's Time For You To Go, If You Love Me Let Me Know, It's Midnight, Big Boss Man, Fever, The Wonder Of You, Softly As I Leave You, Hound Dog, You Gave Me A Mountain, It's Now Or Never, Introductions, The Lord's Prayer (partial), Dialogue, If You Talk In Your Sleep. Why Me Lord (J. D. Sumner & The Stamps Quartet with Elvis singing harmony), How Great Thou Art, Let Me Be There, Hawaiian Wedding Song, Can't Help Falling in Love

September 2, 1974—Closing Show—Complete
C.C. Rider, I Got A Woman/Amen, Karate dialogue, Until It's Time For You To Go, If You Love Me Let Me Know, It's Midnight, Big Boss Man, You Gave Me A Mountain, Priscilla dialogue, Softly As I Leave You, Hound Dog, American Trilogy, It's Now Or Never, Introductions, I Couldn't Live Without You (Voice), Bringing It Back

(Voice—Elvis sings bass), Aubrey (Voice—Elvis recites the lyrics), Introductions, Celebrity introductions Vikki Carr and Bill Cosby, It's Now Or Never, Let Me Be There, If You Talk In Your Sleep, Infamous drug dialogue, Hawaiian Wedding Song, Jewelry dialogue, Can't Help Falling In Love

Songs Sung By Elvis During Engagement
All Shook Up, All Shook Up/Softly As I Leave You, American Trilogy, Aubrey (Voice—Elvis recites the lyrics), Big Boss Man, Bridge Over Troubled Water, Bringing It Back (Voice—Elvis sings bass), Can't Help Falling In Love, C.C. Rider, Down In The Alley, Early Morning Rain, Fever, The First Time Ever I Saw Your Face, The First Time Ever I Saw Your Face (partial), Good Time Charlie's Got The Blues, Guadalajara (partial), Happy Birthday to Kathy Westmoreland, Happy Birthday to Mario (Hilton employee), Hawaiian Wedding Song, Hawaiian Wedding Song (duet with Kathy Westmoreland), Heartbreak Hotel, Help Me, Higher And Higher (partial), Hound Dog, How Great Thou Art, How Great Thou Art (reprise), I Couldn't Live Without You (Voice), If You Love Me Let Me Know, If You Talk In Your Sleep, I Got A Woman, I Got A Woman/Amen, I Got A Woman/Amen/I Got A Woman, I'm Leavin', It's Now Or Never, It's Midnight, Let Me Be There, Let Me Be There (reprise), The Lord's Prayer (partial), Love Me, Love Me (false start), Love Me (kidding, sings Love My Daughter), Love Me Tender, My Baby Left Me, Never Been To Spain, O Sole Mio/It's Now Or Never, Polk Salad Annie, Promised Land, Proud Mary, Softly As I Leave You, Spanish Eyes duet with Sherrill Nielson, Suspicious Minds, Sweet Caroline, Take These Chains From My Heart (partial), Teddy Bear/ Don't Be Cruel, Tryin' To Get To You, Until It's Time For You To Go, We Shall Overcome (partial), Why Me Lord, Why Me Lord (J. D. Sumner & The Stamps Quartet with Elvis singing harmony), The Wonder Of You, You Gave Me A Mountain, You Gave Me A Mountain (reprise)

The following songs are rumored to have been sung at this engagement but are not verifiable.

My Boy, What Now My Love, For Once In My Life (partial)

VEGAS SEASON 12 197, Hilton Hotel
Tuesday, March 18, 1975 through Tuesday, April 1, 1975—29 shows—Total attendance—63,800

Jumpsuits Worn at This Engagement—Cloth Western Fringe Suit (worn Opening Night invitation show), White and black two-piece Penguin Suit, White two-piece suit with blue trim, Dark-blue two-piece suit with silver and blue scalloped trim, Black two-piece suit with red, white, and gold diamond trim, Navy-blue two-piece suit with red and gold leaf trim, White V-Neck Nail Suit

Show Members—Musicians: Lead Guitar—James Burton, Rhythm Guitar—John Wilkinson, Acoustic Guitar and Backup Vocals—Charlie Hodge, Bass—Duke Bardwell, Piano—Glen D. Hardin, Electric Piano—David Briggs, Drums—Ronnie Tutt, Backup Singers: Sweet Inspirations: Myrna Smith, Sylvia Shemwell, Estelle Brown, J. D. Sumner & The Stamps Quartet: J. D. Sumner, Bill Baize, Ed Enoch, Ed Hill, Voice: Sherrill Nielsen, Tim Baty, Donnie Sumner, High Voice Singer—Kathy Westmoreland, Comedian—Jackie Kahane, Orchestra—Joe Guercio

March 18, 1975—Opening Night 8:15 p.m.—Complete
C.C. Rider, I Got A Woman/Amen, And I Love You So, Let Me Be There, It's Midnight, Big Boss Man, Green Green Grass Of Home, Burning Love, Love Me, Fairytale, Introductions, My Boy, I'll Remember You, Promised Land, Until It's Time For You To Go, When It's My Time (J.D. Sumner & The Stamps Quartet), Can't Help Falling In Love

March 19, 1975—Dinner Show—Complete
C. C. Rider, I Got A Woman/Amen, Love Me, If You Love Me Let Me Know, And I Love You So, Big Boss Man, It's Midnight, Burning Love, Fairytale, Introductions, School Days, My Boy, Help Me, Let Me Be There, Until It's Time For You To Go, The Lord's Prayer (partial), Heartbreak Hotel, Hound Dog, Bridge Over Troubled Water, Can't Help Falling In Love

March 19, 1975—Midnight—Complete
C.C. Rider, I Got A Woman/Amen, Love Me, Let Me Be There, And I Love You So, Big Boss Man, It's Midnight, Burning Love, Green Green Grass Of Home, Fairytale, My Boy, I'll Remember You, Hound Dog, It's Now Or Never, If You Love Me Let Me Know, Don't Be Cruel, American Trilogy, Can't Help Falling In Love

March 20, 1975—Dinner Show—Complete
C.C. Rider, I Got A Woman/Amen, Love Me, If You Love Me Let Me Know, And I Love You So, Big Boss Man, It's Midnight, Promised Land, Fairytale, Introductions, My Boy, I'll Remember You, Let Me Be There, Teddy Bear/Don't Be Cruel, Loving You, Love Me Tender, Can't Help Falling In Love

March 20, 1975—Midnight Show—Complete
C.C. Rider, I Got A Woman/Amen, Love Me, If You Love Me Let Me Know, And I Love You So, Big Boss Man, It's Midnight, Promised Land, Green Green Grass Of Home, Fairytale, Introductions, What'd I Say, My Boy, I'll Remember You, Let Me Be There, Teddy Bear/Don't Be Cruel, Hound Dog, I'll Be There (partial), You're The Reason I'm Living, Can't Help Falling In Love

March 21, 1975—Dinner Show—Complete
C.C. Rider, When My Blue Moon Turns To Gold Again (partial), I Got A Woman/Amen, Dialogue, Love Me, Burning Love, It's Midnight, And I Love You So, Big Boss Man, Love Me Tender, Hound Dog (2 false starts), Introductions, My Boy, If You Love Me Let Me Know, I'll Remember You, Let Me Be There (reprise), American Trilogy, Can't Help Falling In Love

March 21, 1975—Midnight Show—Complete
C.C. Rider, Dialogue, I Got A Woman/Amen, Dialogue, Love Me, If You Love Me Let Me know, And I Love You So, Big Boss Man, It's Midnight, Promised Land, Fairytale, Introductions, My Boy, Dialogue, I'll Remember You, Teddy Bear/Don't Be Cruel, Heartbreak Hotel, Hound Dog, Bridge Over Troubled Water, Let Me Be There (reprise), Can't Help Falling In Love

March 22, 1975—Dinner Show—Complete
C.C. Rider, Dialogue, I Got A Woman/Amen, Dialogue, Love Me, If You Love Me Let Me Know, And I Love You So, Big Boss Man, It's Midnight, Burning Love, Fairytale, Introductions, My Boy, I'll Remember You, Let Me Be There, Teddy Bear/Don't Be Cruel, Hound Dog, Hawaiian Wedding Song, Can't Help Falling In Love

March 22, 1975—Midnight Show—Complete
C. C. Rider, I Got A Woman/Amen, Roses Are Red My Love (partial), Love Me, If You Love Me Let Me Know, And I Love You So, Big Boss Man, It's Midnight, Promised Land, Green Green Grass Of Home, Fairytale, Introductions, What'd I Say (partial), My Boy, I'll Remember You, Let Me Be There (reprise), Teddy Bear/Don't Be Cruel, Hound Dog (reprise), I'll Be There (partial), You're The Reason I'm Living, Can't Help Falling In Love

March 23, 1975—Dinner Show—Complete
C.C. Rider, I Got A Woman/Amen, I Can Help

(partial), Love Me, If You Love Me Let Me Know, And I Love You So, Big Boss Man, It's Midnight, Dialogue, Promised Land, Fairytale, Introductions, What'd I Say (partial), School Days, My Boy, I'll Remember You, Let Me Be There, Heartbreak Hotel, Hound Dog, Can't Help Falling In Love

March 23, 1975—Midnight Show—Incomplete
C.C. Rider, I Got A Woman/Amen, Love Me, If You Love Me Let Me Know, It's Midnight, Promised Land, Fairytale, Teddy Bear/Don't Be Cruel, Love Me Tender, Introductions, What'd I Say (partial), I'll Remember You, Let Me Be There

March 24, 1975 —Not Available

March 25, 1975—Dinner Show—Complete
C.C. Rider, I Got A Woman/Amen, I Can Help (partial), Love Me, If You Love Me Let Me Know, And I Love You So, Big Boss Man, It's Midnight, Dialogue, Promised Land, Fairytale, Introductions, What'd I Say (partial) School Days, My Boy, I'll Remember You, Let Me Be There, Heartbreak Hotel, Hound Dog, Can't Help Falling In Love

March 25, 1975—Midnight Show—Complete
C.C. Rider, I Got A Woman/Amen, Dialogue, I Can Help (partial), Love Me, If You Love Me Let Me Know, And I Love You So, Big Boss Man, It's Midnight, Promised Land, Fairytale, Introductions, What'd I Say (partial), School Days, My Boy, I'll Remember You, Let Me Be There, Why Me Lord (J.D. Sumner & The Stamps Quartet), My Heavenly Father (Kathy Westmoreland), Hound Dog, Can't Help Falling In Love

March 26, 1975—Dinner Show—Complete
C.C. Rider, I Got A Woman/Amen, Love Me, If You Love Me Let Me Know, And I Love You So, Big Boss Man, It's Midnight, Promised Land, Fairytale, Introductions, School Days, My Boy, I'll Remember You, Heartbreak Hotel, Hound Dog, Can't Help Falling In Love

March 26, 1975—Midnight Show—Complete
C.C. Rider, I Got A Woman/Amen, Dialogue, Love Me, If You Love Me Let Me Know, And I Love You So, Big Boss Man, It's Midnight (false start), Promised Land, Fairytale (false start), Jambalaya (partial), Introductions, What'd I Say (partial), School Days, My Boy, I'll Remember You, Let Me Be There, Teddy Bear/Don't Be Cruel, Until It's Time For You To Go, Burning Love, Steamroller Blues, Can't Help Falling In Love

March 27, 1975—Dinner Show—Complete
C.C. Rider, I Got A Woman/Amen, Love Me, If You Love Me Let Me Know, And I Love You So, Big Boss Man, It's Midnight, Promised Land, Fairytale, Introductions, Celebrity introduction Lee Majors, My Boy, I'll Remember You (partial), Help Me, Let Me Be There, American Trilogy, Can't Help Falling In Love

March 27, 1975—Midnight Show—Complete
C.C. Rider, I Got A Woman/Amen, Dialogue, Love Me, If You Love Me Let Me Know, And I Love You So, Big Boss Man, Dialogue, It's Midnight, Burning Love, Fairytale, Introductions, What'd I Say, School Days, Celebrity introductions Darlene Love and Roy Orbison, My Boy, Help Me, Let Me Be There, Until It's Time For You To Go, The Lord's Prayer (partial), Heartbreak Hotel, Hound Dog, Bridge Over Troubled Water, Can't Help Falling In Love

March 28, 1975—Dinner Show—Complete
C.C. Rider, I Got A Woman/Amen, Love Me, And I Love You So, If You Love Me Let Me Know, Big Boss Man, It's Midnight, Help Me (false start), I'm Leavin', Introductions, What'd I Say (partial), School Days, Celebrity introduction Tanya Tucker, My Boy, I'll Remember You, Let Me Be There (reprise), Heartbreak Hotel, Teddy Bear/Don't Be Cruel, Dialogue, Can't Help Falling In Love

March 28, 1975—Midnight Show—Complete
C.C. Rider, I Got A Woman/Amen, Love Me, If You Love Me Let Me Know, And I Love You So, Big Boss Man, It's Midnight, Promised Land, Burning Love, Introductions, Celebrity introductions Trish Georges and Barbra Streisand, My Boy, I'll Remember You, My Heavenly Father (Kathy Westmoreland), Let Me Be There (reprise), Hound Dog, American Trilogy, Can't Help Falling In Love

March 29, 1975—Dinner Show—Complete
C.C. Rider, I Got A Woman/Amen, Love Me, If You Love Me Let Me Know, And I Love You So, Big Boss Man, It's Midnight, Burning Love, That's Amore (partial), Introductions, What'd I Say (partial), School Days, My Boy (2 false starts), I'll Remember You, When It's My Time (J. D. Sumner & The Stamps Quartet), Let Me Be There (reprise), Hawaiian Wedding Song duet with Kathy Westmoreland, Hound Dog, Can't Help Falling In Love

March 29, 1975—Midnight Show—Complete
C.C. Rider, Rip It Up (partial), I Got A Woman/Amen, Dialogue, Love Me, Dialogue, If You Love Me Let Me Know, And I Love You So, Dialogue, Big Boss Man (false start), It's Midnight, Burning Love, Good Rockin' Tonight (partial), Introductions, School Days, I Can Help (partial), My Boy, I'll Remember You, Dialogue, My Heavenly Father (Kathy Westmoreland), Let Me Be There, The First Time Ever I Saw Your Face, Tiger Man, Can't Help Falling In Love

March 30, 1975—Dinner Show—Complete
C.C. Rider, I Got A Woman/Amen, Love Me, If You Love Me Let Me Know, And I Love You So, Big Boss Man, Love Me Tender, It's Midnight, Promised Land, Burning Love, Introductions, What'd I Say partial), Lawdy Miss Clawdy, School Days, Let Me Be There, How Great Thou Art, Hound Dog, The First Time Ever I Saw Your Face, American Trilogy, Can't Help Falling In Love

March 30, 1975—Midnight Show—Complete
C.C. Rider, I Got A Woman/Amen, Dialogue, Love Me, Dialogue, If You Love Me Let Me Know, And I Love You So, Big Boss Man, It's Midnight, Burning Love, Introductions, What'd I Say (partial), School Days, My Boy, I'll Remember You (false start), Let Me Be There, For The Good Times (partial), Funny How Time Slips Away, Hound Dog, Sweet Caroline, Dialogue, Softly As I Leave You, Little Darlin', Can't Help Falling In Love

March 31, 1975—Dinner Show—Complete
C.C. Rider, I Got A Woman/Amen, Dialogue, Love Me, If You Love Me Let Me Know, And I Love You So, Big Boss Man, It's Midnight, Burning Love, Introductions, What'd I Say (partial), School Days, My Boy, I'll Remember You, Let Me Be There, My Heavenly Father (Kathy Westmoreland), Dialogue, Hound Dog, Can't Help Falling In Love

March 31, 1975—Midnight Show—Complete
C.C. Rider, I Got A Woman/Amen, Dialogue, Love Me, If You Love Me Let Me Know, And I Love You So (false start), Big Boss Man (partial), You Don't Have To Say You Love Me, The Wonder Of You, Burning Love, Introductions, What'd I Say (partial), School Days, Fairytale, I'll Remember You, Let Me Be There (reprise), Hound Dog, Dialogue, Bridge Over Troubled Water, Little Darlin' (2 false starts), Celebrity introduction Liberace, Hawaiian Wedding Song, Can't Help Falling In Love

April 1, 1975—Dinner Show—Complete
C.C. Rider, Dialogue, I Got A Woman/Amen, Dialogue, Love Me, If You Love Me Let Me Know, And I Love You So, Big Boss Man, The Wonder Of You, Burning Love, Introductions, What'd I Say (partial), School Days, Celebrity introduction Roy Clark, The Great Pretender (partial), Celebrity introductions: Baron & Conrad Hilton, My Boy, I'll Remember You, Let Me Be There, Celebrity introductions: Hugh O'Brian, How Great Thou Art, Hound Dog, Fairytale, Can't Help Falling In Love

April 1, 1975—Closing Show—Complete
C. C. Rider, Dialogue, I Got A Woman/Amen, Dialogue, Love Me, If You Love Me Let Me Know, And I Love You So, Big Boss Man, It's Midnight, Burning Love, Introductions, What'd I Say (partial), School Days, Elvis introduces Colonel Parker, Jingle Bells (instrumental), You Do Something To Me (partial), You Don't Have To Say You Love Me, The Wonder Of You, Let Me Be There, American Trilogy (funny version), Help Me Make It Through The Night (false start), Mickey Mouse March (partial), Little Darlin', Teddy Bear/ Don't Be Cruel, Steamroller Blues, Can't Help Falling In Love

Songs Sung by Elvis During Engagement
American Trilogy, American Trilogy (funny version), And I Love You So, And I Love You So (false start), Big Boss Man, Big Boss Man (false start), Big Boss Man (partial), Bridge Over Troubled Water, Burning Love, C.C. Rider, Can't Help Falling In Love, Don't Be Cruel, Fairytale, Fairytale (false start), For The Good Times (partial), Funny How Times Slips Away, Good Rockin' Tonight (partial), Green Green Grass Of Home, Hawaiian Wedding Song, Hawaiian Wedding Song duet with Kathy Westmoreland, Heartbreak Hotel, Help Me, Help Me (false start), Help Me Make It Through The Night (false start), Hound Dog, Hound Dog (reprise), Hound Dog (2 false starts). How Great Thou Art, I Can Help (partial), If You Love Me Let Me Know, I Got A Woman/Amen, I'll Be There (partial), I'll Remember You, I'll Remember You (false start), I'll Remember You (partial), I'm Leavin', It's Midnight, It's Midnight (false start), It's Now Or Never, Jambalaya (partial), Jingle Bells (instrumental), Lawdy Miss Clawdy, Let Me Be There, Let Me Be There (reprise), Little Darlin', Little Darlin' (2 false starts), Love Me, Love Me Tender, Mickey Mouse March (partial), My Boy, My Boy (2 false starts), My Heavenly Father (Kathy Westmoreland), Promised Land, Rip It Up (partial), Roses Are Red My Love (partial), School Days, Softly As I Leave You, Steamroller Blues, Sweet Caroline, That's Amore (partial), Teddy Bear/ Don't Be Cruel, The First Time Ever I Saw Your Face, The Great Pretender (partial), The Wonder Of You, Tiger Man, The Lord's Prayer (partial), Until It's Time For You To Go, What'd I Say (partial), When It's My Time (J. D. Sumner & The Stamps Quartet), When My Blue Moon Turns To Gold Again (partial), You Don't Have To Say You Love Me, You Do Something To Me (partial), You're The Reason I'm Living

The following songs are rumored to have been sung at this engagement but are not verifiable.

That's All Right, Loving You (partial)

VEGAS SEASON 13 1975, Hilton Hotel

Monday, August 18, 1975 through Monday, September 1, 1975—5 shows—Total attendance—11,000. This engagement was cut short by Elvis' illness after only 3 nights. All remaining shows, August 21–September 1 were canceled.

Jumpsuits Worn at This Engagement—White with black Phoenix Suit, Gypsy Star Suit, Saber Tooth Tiger Suit

Show Members—Musicians: Lead Guitar—James Burton, Rhythm Guitar—John Wilkinson, Acoustic Guitar and Backup Vocals—Charlie Hodge, Bass—Jerry Scheff, Piano—Glen D. Hardin, Drums—Ronnie Tutt, Backup Singers: Sweet Inspirations: Myrna Smith, Sylvia Shemwell, Estelle Brown, J. D. Sumner & The Stamps Quartet: J. D. Sumner, Bill Baize, Ed Enoch, Ed Hill, Larry Strickland, Voice: Sherrill Nielsen, Tim Baty, Donnie Sumner, High Voice Singer—Kathy Westmoreland, Comedian—Jackie Kahane, Orchestra—Joe Guercio

August 18, 1975—Opening Night—Complete
C.C. Rider, I Got A Woman/Amen/I Got A Woman, Dialogue, Love Me, If You Love Me Let Me Know, Dialogue, Blue Suede Shoes, Suspicious Minds, My Boy, Heartbreak Hotel, Polk Salad Annie, Dialogue, Introductions, Johnny B. Goode, School Days, The Wonder Of You, T-R-O-U-B-L-E, Why Me Lord (J.D. Sumner & The Stamps Quartet with Elvis singing harmony), How Great Thou Art, Can't Help Falling In Love

August 19, 1975—Cocktail Show—Complete
C.C. Rider, I Got A Woman/Amen/I Got A Woman, Dialogue, Blue Suede Shoes, If You Love Me Let Me Know, It's Now Or Never, My Boy, Love Me, Loving You, Suspicious Minds, I'm Left You're Right She's Gone (partial), Introductions, Johnny B. Goode, School Days, Celebrity introduction Neil Sedaka, T-R-O-U-B-L-E, Why Me Lord (J. D. Sumner & The Stamps Quartet and Elvis), How Great Thou Art, Let Me Be There, Crying In The Chapel, Can't Help Falling In Love

August 19, 1975—Midnight Show—Complete
C.C. Rider, Elvis explains the bathroom story, Blue Suede Shoes, Young And Beautiful, Are You Lonesome Tonight, If You Love Let Me Know, Softly As I Leave You (duet with Sherrill Nielsen), It's Now Or Never, Polk Salad Annie, Introductions, Johnny B. Goode, School Days, Dialogue, T-R-O-U-B-L-E, Why Me Lord (J. D. Sumner & The Stamps Quartet with Elvis singing harmony), Love Me Tender, All Shook Up, Love Me, Hound Dog (reprise), My Boy, Can't Help Falling In Love

August 20, 1975—Cocktail Show—Complete
C.C. Rider, I Got A Woman/Amen/I Got A Woman, Hound Dog, It's Now Or Never, And I Love You So, Blue Suede Shoes, Green Green Grass Of Home, Fairytale, Softly As I Leave You (duet with Sherrill Nielson), Introductions, Johnny B. Goode, School Days, T-R-O-U-B-L-E, Why Me Lord (J. D. Sumner & The Stamps Quartet with Elvis singing harmony), Are You Sincere (partial), Until It's Time For You To Go, Burning Love, Can't Help Falling In Love

August 20, 1975—Closing Show—Complete
Note: The remainder of this engagement was canceled.
That's All Right/C.C. Rider/That's All Right, I Got A Woman/Amen/I Got A Woman, Fever, If You Love Me Let Me Know, Until It's Time For You To Go, Softly As I Leave You, Burning Love, Introductions, Happy Birthday To James Burton, School Days, T-R-O-U-B-L-E, It's Now Or Never, Why Me Lord (J. D. Sumner & The Stamps Quartet with Elvis singing harmony), Let Me Be There, Can't Help Falling In Love

Songs Sung by Elvis During Engagement
All Shook Up, And I Love You So, Are You Lonesome Tonight, Are You Sincere (partial), Blue Suede Shoes, Burning Love, Can't Help Falling In Love, C.C. Rider, Crying In The Chapel, Fairytale, Fever, Green Green Grass Of Home, Happy Birthday to James Burton, Heartbreak Hotel, Hound Dog, Hound Dog (reprise), How Great Thou Art, If You Love Me Let Me Know, I

Got A Woman/Amen/I Got A Woman, I'm Right You're Left She's Gone (partial), It's Now Or Never, Johnny B. Goode, Let Me Be There, Love Me, Love Me Tender, Loving You, My Boy, Polk Salad Annie, School Days, Softly As I Leave You, Softly As I Leave You (duet with Sherrill Nielsen), Suspicious Minds, That's All Right/C.C. Rider/ That's All Right, T-R-O-U-B-L-E, Why Me Lord (J. D. Sumner & The Stamps Quartet with Elvis singing harmony), The Wonder Of You, Until It's Time For You To Go, Young And Beautiful

VEGAS SEASON 14 1975, Hilton Hotel

Tuesday, December 2, 1975 through Monday, December 15, 1975—16 shows—Total attendance—35,200

Jumpsuits Worn at This Engagement—White Bicentennial Suit (Elvis had this suit plus the Blue Bicentennial Suit custom-made featuring the Presidential Seal on the belt buckle for America's upcoming Bicentennial. He debuted the White Bicentennial at this engagement), Navy-blue with silver Phoenix Suit, Memphis Indian Suit, White with black Phoenix Suit, Saber Tooth Tiger Suit, Aztec Indian Suit, V-Neck Suit with blue trim, White Silver and Blue Studded Tear Drop Suit
Elvis performed sixteen shows at this engagement. He performed a cocktail show on weeknights and Sundays and a cocktail and midnight show on Saturdays.

Show Members—Musicians: Lead Guitar—James Burton, Rhythm Guitar—John Wilkinson, Acoustic Guitar and Backup Vocals—Charlie Hodge, Bass—Jerry Scheff, Piano—Glen D. Hardin, Drums—Ronnie Tutt (On December 7 Jerome 'Stump' Monroe substituted on drums), Backup Singers: Sweet Inspirations: Myrna Smith, Sylvia Shemwell, Estelle Brown, J.D. Sumner & The Stamps Quartet: J. D. Sumner, Bill Baize, Ed Enoch, Ed Hill, Larry Strickland, Backup Vocalist—Sherrill Nielsen, High Voice Singer—Kathy Westmoreland, Comedian—Jackie Kahane, Orchestra—Joe Guercio

December 2, 1975—Opening Night—Complete
C.C. Rider, I Got A Woman/Amen, Dialogue, Love Me, Fairytale, Big Boss Man, It's Midnight, Early Morning Rain, And I Love You So, Tryin' To Get To You, All Shook Up, Teddy Bear/Don't Be Cruel, Hound Dog, You've Lost That Lovin' Feeling, Dialogue, Blue Christmas, Dialogue, Celebrity introduction Liberace, Blue Christmas, Polk Salad Annie, My Boy, How Great Thou Art, Mystery Train/Tiger Man, Softly As I Leave You, America The Beautiful, Can't Help Falling In Love

December 3, 1975—Cocktail Show—Complete
C.C. Rider, I Got A Woman/Amen, Love Me, Fairytale, Big Boss Man, And I Love You So, Dialogue, Tryin' To Get To You, All Shook Up, Teddy Bear/Don't Be Cruel, Blue Christmas, Polk Salad Annie, Introductions, Johnny B. Goode, School Days, My Boy, Just Pretend, How Great Thou Art (reprise), Burning Love, Softly As I Leave You, Mystery Train/Tiger Man, America The Beautiful, Can't Help Falling In Love

December 4, 1975—Cocktail Show—Complete
C.C. Rider, I Got A Woman/Amen, Dialogue, Love Me, Fairytale, And I Love You So, Tryin' To Get To You, Blue Suede Shoes, It's Now Or Never, Polk Salad Annie, Introductions, Celebrity introduction Julie Newmar, Just Pretend, Bridge Over Troubled Water, Burning Love, Softly As I Leave You, Dialogue, America The Beautiful, Mystery Train/Tiger Man, Little Darlin', Can't Help Falling In Love

December 5, 1975—Cocktail Show—Complete
C.C. Rider, I Got A Woman/Amen, Love Me, Fairytale, And I Love You So, Tryin' To Get To You, All Shook Up, Teddy Bear/Don't Be Cruel, Blue Suede Shoes, Just Pretend, Polk Salad Annie, Elvis introduces Priscilla, Lisa Marie and Vernon Presley, Johnny B. Goode, School Days, It's Now Or Never, How Great Thou Art, One Night, Softly As I Leave You, America The Beautiful, Mystery Train/Tiger Man, Dialogue, Can't Help Falling In Love

December 6, 1975—Cocktail Show—Complete
C.C. Rider, I Got A Woman/Amen, Happy Birthday Lisa/Happy Birthday David, Love Me, Fairytale, And I Love You So, Tryin' To Get To You, All Shook Up, Teddy Bear/Don't Be Cruel, Hound Dog, Sweet Caroline, Polk Salad Annie, Introductions, Johnny B. Goode, School Days, Celebrity introductions Marie Parker (The Colonel's wife), Lisa Marie and Vernon Presley, Just Pretend, How Great Thou Art, Burning Love, Softly As I Leave You, America The Beautiful, Can't Help Falling In Love

December 6, 1975—Midnight Show—Complete
C.C. Rider, I Got A Woman/Amen, Love Me, Fairytale, And I Love You So, Tryin' To Get To You, All Shook Up, Teddy Bear/Don't Be Cruel, Hound Dog, Sweet Caroline, Polk Salad Annie, Introductions, Johnny B. Goode, Introductions, School Days, Elvis introduces Colonel Parker's wife (Marie), Priscilla, Lisa Marie and Vernon Presley, Just Pretend, How Great Thou Art, Burning Love, Softly As I Leave You, America The Beautiful, Can't Help Falling In Love

December 7, 1975—Cocktail Show—Complete
C.C. Rider, I Got A Woman/Amen, Dialogue, Elvis introduces Jerome "Stump" Monroe (drummer for the Sweet Inspirations filling in for Ronnie Tutt), Love Me, Hound Dog, Fairytale, And I Love You So, Tryin' To Get To You, All Shook Up, Teddy Bear/Don't Be Cruel, One Night, Polk Salad Annie, Introductions, Johnny B. Goode, School Days, I'll Remember You, How Great Thou Art (reprise), Early Morning Rain, It's Now Or Never, Softly As I Leave You (duet with Sherrill Nielsen), America The Beautiful, Can't Help Falling In Love

December 8, 1975—Cocktail Show—Complete
C.C. Rider, I Got A Woman/Amen, Love Me, Fairytale, And I Love You So, Tryin' To Get To You, All Shook Up, Teddy Bear/Don't Be Cruel, Until It's Time For You To Go, You Gave Me A Mountain, Polk Salad Annie, Introductions, School Days, Just Pretend, It's Now Or Never, One Night, How Great Thou Art (reprise), Softly As I Leave You, America The Beautiful, Mystery Train/Tiger Man, Dialogue, Fever, Can't Help Falling In Love

December 9, 1975—Cocktail Show—Complete
C.C. Rider, I Got A Woman/Amen, Love Me, Fairytale, And I Love You So, Tryin' To Get To You, All Shook Up, Teddy Bear/Don't Be Cruel, Love Me Tender, Polk Salad Annie, Introductions, Johnny B. Goode, School Days, Just Pretend, How Great Thou Art (reprise), Burning Love, Softly As I Leave You, America The Beautiful, It's Now Or Never (reprise), One Night, Mystery Train/Tiger Man, Dialogue, Can't Help Falling In Love

December 10, 1975—Cocktail Show—Complete
C.C. Rider, Can't Help Falling In Love (partial), When My Blue Moon Turns To Gold Again (partial), I Got A Woman/Amen, Love Me, Fairytale, And I Love You So, Tryin' To Get To You, All Shook Up, Teddy Bear/Don't Be Cruel, You Gave Me A Mountain, Polk Salad Annie, Introductions, Johnny B. Goode, School Days, Just Pretend (false start), How Great Thou Art, Softly As I Leave You (duet with Sherrill Nielsen) America The Beautiful, Mystery Train/Tiger Man, My

Way (duet with Sherrill Nielsen false start), Blue Christmas, Can't Help Falling In Love

December 11, 1975—Cocktail Show—Complete
C.C. Rider, I Got A Woman/Amen, Love Me, Dialogue, Fairytale, Dialogue, And I Love You So, Tryin' To Get To You, All Shook Up, Teddy Bear/Don't Be Cruel, Hound Dog, Happy Birthday, Until It's Time For You To Go, Polk Salad Annie, Introductions, Johnny B. Goode, School Days, Just Pretend, How Great Thou Art, Burning Love, Softly As I Leave You, America The Beautiful, It's Now Or Never, Can't Help Falling In Love

December 12, 1975—Cocktail Show—Complete
C.C. Rider, I Got A Woman/Amen, Love Me, Tryin' To Get To You, And I Love You So, All Shook Up, Teddy Bear/Don't Be Cruel, One Night, You Gave Me A Mountain (false start), Polk Salad Annie, Guadalajara (partial), Introductions, Johnny B. Goode, School Days, Elvis introduces Lisa Marie and Vernon Presley, Just Pretend, How Great Thou Art, Softly As I Leave You, America The Beautiful, Mystery Train/Tiger Man, Little Sister, O Sole Mio (Sherrill Nielsen), It's Now Or Never, Can't Help Falling In Love

December 13, 1975—Cocktail Show—Complete
C.C. Rider, I Got A Woman/Amen, Love Me, Help Me Make It Through The Night, Tryin' To Get To You, And I Love You So, All Shook Up, Teddy Bear/Don't Be Cruel, Wooden Heart, You Gave Me A Mountain, Polk Salad Annie, Introductions, Johnny B. Goode, School Days, How Great Thou Art, Softly As I Leave You, America The Beautiful, Mystery Train/Tiger Man, Blue Christmas, Can't Help Falling In Love

December 13, 1975—Midnight Show—Complete
C.C. Rider, I Got A Woman/Amen, Love Me, Tryin' To Get To You, And I Love You So, All Shook Up/Teddy Bear/Don't Be Cruel, You Gave Me A Mountain, Help Me Make It Through The Night, Polk Salad Annie, Introductions, Johnny B. Goode, School Days, Just Pretend, How Great Thou Art, Burning Love, Hound Dog, Welcome To My World, Softly As I Leave You, America The Beautiful, It's Now Or Never/O Sole Mio (duet with Sherrill Nielsen), Little Darlin', Little Sister, Can't Help Falling In Love

December 14, 1975—Cocktail Show—Complete
C.C. Rider, I Got A Woman/Amen, Love Me, Tryin' To Get To You, And I Love You So, All Shook Up, Teddy Bear/Don't Be Cruel, Hound Dog, Until It's Time For You To Go, You Gave Me A Mountain, Polk Salad Annie, Introductions, Sweet Sweet Spirit (J. D. Sumner & The Stamps Quartet), Johnny B. Goode, Happy Birthday to Charlie Hodge, School Days, Just Pretend, How Great Thou Art (reprise), Burning Love, Softly As I Leave You, America The Beautiful, Little Sister, Heartbreak Hotel, Elvis introduces Lisa Marie and Vernon Presley, O Solo Mio (Sherrill Nielsen), It's Now Or Never, Can't Help Falling In Love

December 15, 1975—Closing Show—Complete
C.C. Rider, I Got A Woman/Amen, Love Me, Tryin' To Get To You, And I Love You So, All Shook Up, Teddy Bear/Don't Be Cruel, Hound Dog, Dialogue, I'm Leavin', You Gave Me A Mountain, Polk Salad Annie, Introductions, Elvis introduces Bill Porter,Felton Jarvis and Vernon Presley, What'd I Say, School Days, Just Pretend, How Great Thou Art, Softly As I Leave You, America The Beautiful, Burning Love (partial), Sweet Sweet Spirit (J.D. Sumner & the Stamps Quartet), Little Sister, One Night, Until It's Time For You To Go, Dialogue, The First Time Ever I Saw Your Face, Mystery Train/Tiger Man, It's Now Or Never/O Solo Mio (duet with Sherrill Nielsen), Dialogue, Can't Help Falling In Love

Songs Sung By Elvis During Engagement
All Shook Up, All Shook Up/Teddy Bear/Don't Be Cruel, America The Beautiful, And I Love You So, Big Boss Man, Blue Christmas, Blue Suede Shoes, Bridge Over Troubled Water, Burning Love, Burning Love (partial), C.C. Rider, Can't Help Falling In Love, Can't Help Falling In Love (partial), Early Morning Rain, Fairytale, Fever, The First Time Ever I Saw Your Face, Guadalajara (partial), Happy Birthday, Happy Birthday to Charlie Hodge, Happy Birthday Lisa/Happy Birthday David, Heartbreak Hotel, Help Me Make It Through The Night, Hound Dog, How Great Thou Art, How Great Thou Art (reprise), I Got A Woman/Amen, I'll Remember You, I'm Leavin', It's Midnight, It's Now Or Never, It's Now Or Never (reprise), It's Now Or Never/O Sole Mio (due with Sherrill Nielsen), Johnny B. Goode, Just Pretend, Just Pretend (false start), Little Darlin', Little Sister, Love Me, Love Me Tender, My Boy, Mystery Train/Tiger Man, My Way duet with Sherrill Nielsen with false start, One Night, O Solo Mio (Sherrill Nielsen), Polk Salad Annie, School Days, Softly As I Leave You, Softly As I Leave You duet with Sherrill Nielsen, Sweet Caroline, Sweet Sweet Spirit (J. D. Sumner & The Stamps Quartet), Teddy Bear/Don't Be Cruel, Tryin' To Get To You, Until It's Time For You To Go, Welcome To My World, What'd I Say, When My Blue Moon Turns To Gold Again (partial), Wooden Heart, You Gave Me A Mountain, You Gave Me A Mountain (false start), You've Lost That Lovin' Feeling

VEGAS SEASON 15 1976, Hilton Hotel
Thursday, December 2, 1976 through Sunday, December 12, 1976—15 shows—Total attendance—33,000

Jumpsuits Worn at This Engagement—King Of Spades Suit, Memphis Indian Suit, Rainbow Suit, White with red Phoenix Suit, Navy-blue with silver Phoenix Suit, White with black Phoenix Suit, Blue Bicentennial Suit, White Bicentennial Suit, Sundial Suit, Saber Tooth Tiger Suit, Aztec Indian Suit, Flame Suit

Elvis performed fifteen shows at this engagement. He performed a cocktail show weeknights and Sundays and a cocktail and midnight show on Fridays and Saturdays.

Show Members—Musicians: Lead Guitar—James Burton, Rhythm Guitar—John Wilkinson, Acoustic Guitar and Backup Vocals—Charlie Hodge, Bass—Jerry Scheff, Piano—Tony Brown, Electric Piano—David Briggs, Drums—Ronnie Tutt, Backup Singers: Sweet Inspirations: Myrna Smith, Sylvia Shemwell, Estelle Brown, J.D. Sumner & The Stamps Quartet: J.D. Sumner, Buck Buckles, Ed Enoch, Ed Hill, Larry Strickland, Backup Vocalist—Sherrill Nielsen, High Voice Singer—Kathy Westmoreland, Comedian—Jackie Kahane, Orchestra—Joe Guercio

December 2, 1976—Opening Night—Complete
C.C. Rider, I Got A Woman/Amen, Dialogue, Love Me, If You Love Me Let Me Know, You Gave Me A Mountain, Jailhouse Rock, It's Now Or Never, Are You Sincere (partial), All Shook Up, Teddy Bear/Don't Be Cruel, Dialogue, And I Love You So, I Just Can't Help Believin', Fever, Softly As I Leave You, Polk Salad Annie, Introductions, Early Morning Rain, What'd I Say, Johnny B. Goode, Love Letters, School Days, Celebrity introductions Priscilla Presley, Lisa Marie, Ginger Alden, Vikki Carr and Glen Campbell, Hurt (reprise), Hound Dog (false start), Hawaiian Wedding Song(false start), Dialogue, Blue Christmas, That's All Right, Bridge Over Troubled Water, Introduction of Vernon Presley, Can't Help Falling In Love

December 3, 1976—Cocktail Show—Complete
C.C. Rider, I Got A Woman/Amen, Love Me

(false start), If You Love Me Let Me Know, You Gave Me A Mountain, It's Now Or Never, One Night, All Shook Up, Teddy Bear/Don't Be Cruel, And I Love You So, Fever, Polk Salad Annie, Introductions, Early Morning Rain, What'd I Say, Love Letters, School Days, Hurt, Hound Dog, Blue Christmas, Can't Help Falling In Love

December 3, 1976—Midnight Show—Complete
C.C. Rider, I Got A Woman/Amen, Love Me, If You Love Me Let Me Know, You Gave Me A Mountain, Jailhouse Rock, It's Now Or Never, Bridge Over Troubled Water, Tryin' To Get To You, Blue Suede Shoes, And I Love You So, Softly As I Leave You, America The Beautiful, Introductions, Early Morning Rain, What'd I Say, Johnny B. Goode, Love Letters (false start), School Days, Hurt, Hound Dog, How Great Thou Art (false start), Can't Help Falling In Love

December 4, 1976—Cocktail Show—Complete
C.C. Rider, I Got A Woman/Amen, Dialogue, Love Me, If You Love Me Let Me Know, You Gave Me A Mountain, Jailhouse Rock, It's Now Or Never, Tryin' To Get To You, Blue Suede Shoes, Fever, America The Beautiful, Bridge Over Troubled Water, What Now My Love (spoken version), Introductions, Early Morning Rain, What'd I Say, Love Letters, School Days, Celebrity introductions Engelbert Humperdinck, Roy Orbison, Elvis introduces Priscilla, Lisa Marie, and Vernon Presley, It's Over (partial), Hurt, Hound Dog, How Great Thou Art, Can't Help Falling In Love

December 4, 1976—Midnight Show—Complete
C.C. Rider, I Got A Woman/Amen, Love Me, Fairytale, You Gave Me A Mountain (spoken version), Jailhouse Rock, It's Now Or Never, Lawdy Miss Clawdy, Tryin' To Get To You, Blue Suede Shoes, Fever, Softly As I Leave You, Polk Salad Annie, Introductions, Rip It Up (partial), Early Morning Rain, What'd I Say, Love Letters, School Days, Hurt, Hawaiian Wedding Song, Hound Dog, Danny Boy (Sherrill Nielsen), Walk With Me (Sherrill Nielsen), Can't Help Falling In Love

December 5, 1976—Cocktail Show—Complete
The audience got a surprise when Charlie Hodge, not Elvis, appeared onstage and told them that Elvis was running late. He apologized and asked them to be patient. Elvis appeared on stage some 10–15 minutes later and after the first song explained that he had sprained his ankle getting out of the shower. He would perform the entire show sitting on a stool.

C.C. Rider, I Got A Woman/Amen, Dialogue, Blue Christmas, That's All Right, Dialogue, Are You Lonesome Tonight (laughing version), Dialogue, Sweet Caroline, You Gave Me A Mountain, Jailhouse Rock, O Solo Mio/It's Now Or Never (duet with Sherrill Nielsen), Dialogue, Tryin' To Get To You, Fever, America The Beautiful, Introductions, Early Morning Rain, What'd I Say, Johnny B. Goode, Introductions, Love Letters, School Days, Hurt, Hound Dog, Elvis introduces Lisa Marie and Vernon Presley, How Great Thou Art, Can't Help Falling In Love

December 6, 1976—Cocktail Show—Complete
C.C. Rider, I Got A Woman/Amen, Tip Toe Through Tulips (partial), Blue Christmas, That's All Right, Are You Lonesome Tonight, Jingle Bells (instrumental), Love Me, You Gave Me A Mountain, Jailhouse Rock, O Sole Mio/It's Now Or Never (duet with Sherrill Nielsen), And I Love You So, Blue Suede Shoes, Fever, Polk Salad Annie, Introductions, Early Morning Rain, What'd I Say, Johnny B. Goode, Love Letters, School Days, Help Me Make It Through The Night, Danny Boy (Sherrill Nielsen), Walk With Me (Sherrill Nielsen), My Heavenly Father (Kathy Westmoreland), Can't Help Falling In Love

December 7, 1976—Cocktail Show—Complete
C.C. Rider, I Got A Woman/Amen, Love Me, If You Love Me Let Me Know, You Gave Me A Mountain, O Solo Mio/It's Now Or Never (duet with Sherrill Nielsen), Blue Christmas, That's All Right, Are You Lonesome Tonight, Softly As I Leave You, Fever, All Shook Up/Teddy Bear/Don't Be Cruel, Introductions, Early Morning Rain (false start), What'd I Say, Love Letters, School Days, Hurt, Hound Dog, Hawaiian Wedding Song, You Better Run (Elvis and J. D. Sumner & The Stamps Quartet), Rock My Soul (Elvis and J. D. Sumner & The Stamps Quartet), Can't Help Falling In Love

December 8, 1976—Cocktail Show—Complete
C.C. Rider, I Got A Woman/Amen, Love Me, If You Love Me Let Me Know, You Gave Me A Mountain, Jailhouse Rock, O Solo Mio/It's Now Or Never (duet with Sherrill Nielsen), Blue Christmas, That's All Right, Are You Lonesome Tonight (laughing version), Softly As I Leave You, Blue Suede Shoes, Heartbreak Hotel, Bridge Over Troubled Water, Introductions, Early Morning Rain, What'd I Say, Love Letters, Hurt, Mystery Train/Tiger Man, How Great Thou Art, Can't Help Falling In Love

December 9, 1976—Cocktail Show—Complete
C.C. Rider, I Got A Woman/Amen, Love Me, Fairytale, You Gave Me A Mountain, Jailhouse Rock, O Solo Mio/It's Now Or Never (duet with Sherrill Nielsen), My Way, Blue Christmas, That's All Right, Are You Lonesome Tonight, Softly As I Leave You (duet with Sherrill Nielsen), Hound Dog, Help Me, America The Beautiful, Introductions, Early Morning Rain, What'd I Say, Love Letters, School Days, Hurt, Hawaiian Wedding Song, Can't Help Falling In Love

December 10, 1976—Cocktail Show—Complete
C.C. Rider, I Got A Woman/Amen, Love Me, All Shook Up/Teddy Bear/Don't Be Cruel, You Gave Me A Mountain, Jailhouse Rock, O Solo Mio/It's Now Or Never (duet with Sherrill Nielsen), Blue Christmas, That's All Right/Softly As I Leave You, Are You Lonesome Tonight, Steamroller Blues, Introductions, Early Morning Rain, What'd I Say, Love Letters, Introductions, School Days, Hurt, Hawaiian Wedding Song, Can't Help Falling In Love

December 10, 1976—Midnight Show—Complete
C.C. Rider, I Got A Woman/Amen, Love Me, If You Love Me Let Me Know, You Gave Me A Mountain, Sweet Sweet Spirit (J. D. Sumner & The Stamps Quartet), Why Me Lord (J. D. Sumner & The Stamps Quartet with Elvis singing harmony), Jailhouse Rock, O Solo Mio/It's Now Or Never (duet with Sherrill Nielsen), Polk Salad Annie, Introductions, Early Morning Rain, What'd I Say, Johnny B. Goode, Love Letters, School Days, Hurt, Dialogue, Danny Boy (Sherrill Nielsen), Walk With Me (Sherrill Nielsen), Hawaiian Wedding Song, Can't Help Falling In Love

December 11, 1976—Cocktail Show—Complete
C.C. Rider, I Got A Woman/Amen, Love Me, You Gave Me A Mountain, Rip It Up (partial), O Solo Mio/It's Now Or Never (duet with Sherrill Nielsen), Blue Suede Shoes, Help Me (false start), Dialogue, Elvis introduces Priscilla Presley and her parents Ann and Paul. He then dedicates the next song to them, My Way, Introductions, Early Morning Rain, What'd I Say, Happy Birthday to Tony Brown, Love Letters, School Days, Hurt, Dialogue, Hawaiian Wedding Song, Can't Help Falling In Love

December 11, 1976—Midnight Show—Complete
C.C. Rider, I Got A Woman/Amen, Love Me, Tryin' To Get To You, O Solo Mio/It's Now Or Never (duet with Sherrill Nielsen), Jailhouse

Rock, Until Then (partial), Blue Christmas, Softly As I Leave You, Are You Lonesome Tonight, Introduction of Lisa Marie and Priscilla Presley, My Way, Introductions, Early Morning Rain, What'd I Say, Johnny B. Goode, Love Letters, School Days, Celebrity introductions Kay Stevens and Lola Falana, Hurt, My Heavenly Father (Kathy Westmoreland), Danny Boy (Sherrill Nielsen), Walk With Me (Sherrill Nielsen), Reconsider Baby (false start), Can't Help Falling In Love

December 12, 1976—Closing Show—Complete
C.C. Rider, I Got A Woman/Amen, Love Me, My Way (false start), Fairytale, You Gave Me A Mountain, Dialogue, Jailhouse Rock, Little Sister, O Solo Mio/It's Now Or Never (duet with Sherrill Nielsen), Tryin' To Get To You, Happy Birthday to Charlie Hodge, Blue Suede Shoes, Elvis talks about his black diamond ring, Blue Christmas, Softly As I Leave You, Are You Lonesome Tonight, That's All Right, Bridge Over Troubled Water, Introductions, Early Morning Rain, What'd I Say, Johnny B. Goode, Love Letters, School Days, Hurt, Such A Night, Sweet Caroline, Can't Help Falling In Love

Songs Sung by Elvis During Engagement
All Shook Up, All Shook Up/Teddy Bear/Don't Be Cruel, America The Beautiful, And I Love You So, Are You Lonesome Tonight, Are You Lonesome Tonight (laughing version), Are You Sincere (partial), Blue Christmas, Blue Suede Shoes, Bridge Over Troubled Water, Can't Help Falling In Love, C.C. Rider, Danny Boy (Sherrill Nielsen), Early Morning Rain, Early Morning Rain (false start), Fairytale, Fever, Happy Birthday to Tony Brown, Happy Birthday to Charlie Hodge, Hawaiian Wedding Song, Hawaiian Wedding Song (false start), Heartbreak Hotel, Help Me, Help Me (false start), Hound Dog, Hound Dog (false start), How Great Thou Art, How Great Thou Art (false start), Hurt, Hurt (reprise), If You Love Me Let Me Know, I Got A Woman/Amen, I Just Can't Help Believin', It's Now Or Never, It's Over (partial), Jailhouse Rock, Jingle Bells (instrumental), Johnny B. Goode, Lawdy Miss Clawdy, Little Sister, Love Letters, Love Letters (false start), Love Me, Love Me (false start), My Heavenly Father (Kathy Westmoreland), Mystery Train/Tiger Man, My Way, My Way (false start), One Night, O Sole Mio/It's Now Or Never (duet with Sherrill Nielsen), Polk Salad Annie, Reconsider Baby (false start), Rip It Up (partial), Rock My Soul (Elvis and J. D. Sumner & The Stamps Quartet), School Days, Softly As I Leave You, Softly As I Leave You (duet with Sherrill Nielsen), Steamroller Blues, Such A Night, Sweet Caroline, Sweet Sweet Spirit (J. D. Sumner & The Stamps Quartet), Teddy Bear/Don't Be Cruel, That's All Right, That's All Right/Softly As I Leave You, Tip Toe Through The Tulips (partial), Tryin' To Get To You, Until Then (partial), Walk With Me (Sherrill Nielsen), What'd I Say, What Now My Love (spoken version), Why Me Lord (J. D. Sumner & The Stamps Quartet with Elvis singing harmony), You Better Run (Elvis and J. D. Sumner & The Stamps Quartet), You Gave Me A Mountain, You Gave Me A Mountain (spoken version)

Acknowledgments

"MEMORIES PRESSED between the pages of my mind" as Elvis sang during his 1968 NBC Presents Elvis TV special is more than appropriate for the message of this book. During the ten years of extensive research and the last two years of actually writing and compiling this work, I've had the opportunity to relive my many Las Vegas experiences with Elvis and the Colonel.

As has been the case since my first book, *Elvis in Hollywood*, to my latest, *Elvis in Vegas*, I have been able to experience a lifetime of Elvis, the Colonel, and the most wonderful people in the world, Elvis' fans. I'd like to take this opportunity to thank all of you loyal readers and friends for the opportunity to share my memories with you. In closing I'd like to say:

Viva Las Vegas! Viva Colonel Parker!
Viva Elvis Presley!

It goes without saying that a work such as this required years of research and the help of many. My sincere thanks to all who provided help during the creative process. In some cases it was as simple as answering a single question and in others it was opening their entire archives. To the photographers who shared a single image, or many, I couldn't have done it without you. To my first editor, Aaron Schlechter, and to my current editor, Stephanie Gorton, thanks for your patience and for giving me complete artistic freedom, and my appreciation to Peter Mayer and everyone at The Overlook Press.

A Special Thank You to:

Muhammad Ali, Ed Bonja, Nancy Kozikowski, James V. Roy (www.scottymoore.net), Ann-Margret, Jim Hannaford, Bruce Maltz, Mike Eder (whose contributions for Elvis song lists were extraordinary and appreciated), Bud Glass (a constant source of help and information), Joseph Kereta (www.elvisnow.com), Nicholas LeMay, Ann-Marie "Buttons" McClain, Joseph A. Tunzi (www.jatpublishing.com), Terry Mike Jeffery, Bob Heis, Robin Rosaaen, Paul Larsen, Sandy Pichon, Marie Fletcher, Priscilla Presley, John Humphrey-Seether, Marty Pasetta, Keith Russell, Paul Dowling (www.worldwideelvis.com), Bob Kline, Peter Haan, Joyce Bova, Betty Buscaglia, Gerald Buscaglia, Ginger Alden, Sean Shaver, Stephen Merves, Mark Brownstein, Esq., Linda Thompson, Sheila Ryan, Cathi Avenell, and Tony King

Select Bibliography

Bova, Joyce. *Don't Ask Forever*. New York: Kensington Books, 1994.

Burk, Bill E. *Elvis: A 30-Year Chronicle*. Brainerd, MN: Kampmann-Co. Inc., 1985.

Esposito, Joe with Elena Oumano. *Good-Rockin' Tonight*. New York: Simon & Schuster, 1994.

Fortas, Alan. *Elvis: From Memphis to Hollywood*. Ann Arbor, MI: Popular Culture, Ink, 1992.

Guralnick, Peter. *Careless Love: The Unmaking of Elvis Presley*. New York: Little, Brown and Company, 1999.

Guralnick, Peter and Ernst Jorgensen. *Elvis Day by Day*. New York: Ballantine Books, 1999.

Hopkins, Jerry. *Elvis: A Biography*. New York: Simon & Schuster, 1971.

Margret, Ann, with Todd Gold. *Ann-Margret: My Story*. New York: G.P. Putnam & Sons, 1994.

O'Grady, John, with Nolan Davis. *O'Grady: The Life and Times of Hollywood's No. 1 Private Eye*. Los Angeles: J. P. Tarcher, 1974.

Presley Beaulieu, Priscilla with Sandra Harmon. *Elvis and Me*. New York: G. P. Putnam & Sons, 1985.

Schilling, Jerry with Chuck Crisafulli. *Me and a Guy Named Elvis*. New York: Gotham Books, 2006.

Shaver, Sean. *The Elvis Book Vol. II*. USA: Timur Publishing, 1987.

———. *The Elvis Book Vol. III*. USA: Timur Publishing, 1987.

Shaver, Sean, and Hal Noland. *The Life of Elvis Presley*. USA: Timur Publishing, 1979.

Tunzi, A. Joseph. *Aloha Via Satellite*. Chicago: JAT Publishing, 1998.

———. *Elvis '69*. Chicago: JAT Publishing, 2004.

———. *Elvis '73 Hawaiian Spirit*. Chicago: JAT Publishing, 1992.

———. *Elvis Sessions III*. Chicago: JAT Publishing, 2004.

———. *Tiger Man: Elvis '68*. Chicago: JAT Publishing, 1997.

Victor, Adam. *The Elvis Encyclopedia*. New York and London: Overlook Duckworth, Peter Mayer Publishers, Inc., 2008.

West, Sonny, with Marshall Terrill. *Elvis: Still Taking Care of Business*. Chicago: Triumph Books, 2007.